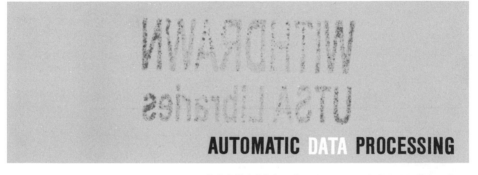

AUTOMATIC DATA PROCESSING

PRINCIPLES AND PROCEDURES

PRENTICE-HALL INC., ENGLEWOOD CLIFFS, NEW JERSEY

SECOND EDITION

AUTOMATIC DATA PROCESSING

PRINCIPLES AND PROCEDURES

ELIAS M. AWAD

GRADUATE SCHOOL OF BUSINESS, DE PAUL UNIVERSITY,

CHICAGO, ILLINOIS AND

DATA PROCESSING MANAGEMENT ASSOCIATION

13-055160-0

Library of Congress Catalog Card No.: 74-113042

Printed in the United States of America

Current printing (last digit):
10 9 8 7 6 5 4 3 2

PRENTICE-HALL INTERNATIONAL, INC., London
PRENTICE-HALL OF AUSTRALIA, PTY., LTD., Sydney
PRENTICE-HALL OF CANADA, LTD., Toronto
PRENTICE-HALL OF INDIA PRIVATE LTD., New Delhi
PRENTICE-HALL OF JAPAN, INC., Tokyo

PREFACE

Being acutely aware of the accelerated rate of change in the electronic data processing field, the authors have prepared this new edition to reflect the most recent new
developments. As was true of its predecessor, this revision strives for lucidity, makes
abundant use of illustrations, and offers a comprehensive view of the field.

MAJOR FEATURES OF THE REVISION

1. A chapter outline at the beginning of each chapter;
2. A glossary of terms, plus questions and exercises, at the end of each chapter (problems,
   case situations, and selected readings are available in a new workbook, "Problems and
   Selected Readings in Automatic Data Processing");
3. A thorough revision and updating of Chapter 13 and 14 on input/output devices stressing third generation hardware, data communication techniques, and terminal equipment.

4. Three new chapters (Chapters 20-22) on FORTRAN, COBOL, and PL/1 containing sufficient material to enable the reader to write a basic program in each language;

5. A new chapter (Chapter 24) on the techniques of data processing documentation designed to help the reader understand key aspects in user-oriented documentation of various files.

6. A thorough revision of Chapter 11, *Coded Data Representation,* on the basis of hexadecimal and octal data representation and with brief reference to EBCDIC and ASCII. (Chapter 12 dealing with arithmetic follows a similar orientation.)

7. A summary of the punched card area which can be passed over (by those who wish to do so) without loss of continuity.

8. In Chapter 18, a discussion of current flow charting symbols and procedures which constitute the bulk of the chapter—and in Chapter 19, a similarly detailed discussion of decision tables.

9. A new chapter (Chapter 15) which includes an overview of IBM's system/3.

10. In Chapter 6, a discussion of the new 96-column card.

This book is designed for use in a beginning one- or two-term course in data processing, but is equally serviceable to all beginners. Prior background in mathematics or exposure to computer equipment and techniques is not required, nor is the purchase or rental of special equipment necessary in using this edition. However, field trips to data processing centers—or films showing aspects of the computer systems in operation—are always helpful.

The authors are indebted to many individuals and organizations who directly or indirectly contributed to the preparation of the text. Our thanks to Mrs. Marjorie Homan for typing the edited version of the manuscript; to Miss Marion L'Amoreaux, director of the Reading Laboratory, Rochester Institute of Technology, for her expert editorial effort; to John Guerrieri, Assistant Education Director, DPMA, for a major contribution to the initial draft of the manuscript and for sharing in the burden of proofreading; to Donald J. MacPherson, Education Director, DPMA, for securing required technical matter from computer organizations and for his support in the revision's preparation; and to R. Calvin Elliott, Executive Director, DPMA, for his many accommodations.

We also thank the computer manufacturers for permission to reproduce photographs of their equipment and for use of technical data to support our exposition.

We are especially indebted to members of the Prentice-Hall staff. Chief among these are Fred Easter, Assistant Vice President, for his continued encouragement and counsel and for his provocative and creative ideas for the new wordbook; to Jim Bacci, Production Editor, for his guidance of the book through the production phases; and to Lee Opas, staff artist, who designed this edition.

ELIAS M. AWAD
and THE DATA PROCESSING MANAGEMENT ASSOCIATION

CONTENTS

Contents   ix

chapter twelve

chapter thirteen

chapter fourteen

chapter fifteen

PART 5

APPENDICES

AUTOMATIC DATA PROCESSING

PRINCIPLES AND PROCEDURES

PART 1

HISTORICAL
DEVELOPMENT
OF
DATA PROCESSING

chapter one

THE DEVELOPMENT OF AIDS TO MANPOWER

AUTOMATION

COMPUTERS

Record Keeping

Payroll

Inventory Accounting

Production Scheduling

Customer Billing

Simulation

Management Information System

Computer Aided Design

Information Storage and Retrieval

Computer Assisted Instruction

Medicine

Electronic Guidance and Control

Process Control System

Manned Space Flights

3

THE RAPID PACE at which technological advances are made today makes it difficult to recognize that man's development toward progressively higher standards of living has been relatively slow and sometimes painful. It took man countless years to learn just how to use animals for transporting goods. Although the discovery of the wheel was revolutionary, it was many years before man applied his discovery to wagons and bicycles. Decades elapsed between his discovery of the use of steam as a source of power and its eventual use in propelling machinery.

As man discovered new ways to harness the forces of nature to aid him in his work, his ingenuity for devising adaptations of these basic discoveries also increased. Thus the step from the first airplane flight to the development of the jet airplane is shorter than the one from "foot power" to "animal power." Once the principles behind jet flight were understood and applied, the transition to manned space flights was imminent. In fact, man has become so ingenious and imaginative in his inventive powers that it sometimes seems as if "miracles" can be performed overnight. This is especially evident in the field of automation—the use of mechanical devices to perform routine tasks with minimum human assistance.

AUTOMATION

Since the dawn of the Industrial Revolution, automation and automatic techniques have been used to mass produce goods at minimal costs. In the field of men's clothing, for instance, tailor-made suits are far from common today because in preparing ready-made garments, a clothing manufacturer can cut twenty-five to thirty pieces of fabric simultaneously for a given size. In assembly-line fashion, the suits are sewn by many stitchers. In this way many suits are completed in the same amount of time it requires to tailor-make one suit. Although some men (especially those whose proportions are not standard) consider a tailor-made suit better fitted, most men find the ready-made garments satisfactory. Moreover, the cost of ready-made suits is reduced as much as 60 percent.

Numeralization has even been applied to areas involving individual identity. The United States Internal Revenue Service, for instance, has been using electronic computers to verify and otherwise process the millions of tax forms submitted annually. Each taxpayer is assigned a number which identifies him with every tax return he files. The use of numbers, rather than names, greatly speeds up the data processing required to process the forms, because numbers are a simpler means for sorting than alphabetic characters.

Generally, the application of automated devices and techniques is based on the need of industrial organizations to produce goods and/or process information more accurately and efficiently than can be done by men alone, thus releasing human resources to engage in nonroutine, creative endeavors. Since traditional manual methods were slow and relatively costly, mechanical means were introduced to better handle the steady inflow of various types of data. An eventual increase in the productive capacity of many firms led to an equivalent increase in sales and greater demand for new products and services. Even small business firms expanded and their clerical and managerial functions multiplied, generating the so-called paperwork explosion.

The problem of finding some way to process boring, routine paperwork more efficiently than by human labor or mechanical means taxed man's mind for many years. The growth of markets and customer demands brought with it an increase in business forms, which, in turn, created new problems of record keeping. The challenge of paperwork led to almost daily improvements in our methods of coping with large volumes of routine paper handling and mathematical figuring and prompted the birth of the electronic computer. Since it appeared on the business scene, automation, as a whole, has undergone tremendous advances in usage and technology. Today, it is firmly intertwined with most facets of everyday activity.

COMPUTERS

The amazing and wonderful "world of computers" is a breakthrough in computation and represents a great step in devising better methods to aid man in performing routine and repetitive tasks more efficiently. The principles of uniformity, standardization and numeralization are the keys to successful performance. Imagination, creativeness and clever innovation are used to build into the machines the "inhuman" qualities surrounding standardization of performance. This is necessary if the machine, especially the computer, is to be useful in accomplishing the work for which it is designed.

When computers were introduced, the outcry that the computer would drive masses of people into unemployment haunted many white collar workers. Today, a knowledge of the computer's impact does not substantiate what the "prophets of doom" had predicted. On the contrary, while many clerical jobs were indeed found to be too costly to maintain, or were deemphasized because of the computer, people's growing dependence on it has created an entirely new job market in computer technology estimated to exceed one-half million positions.

It can be inferred, then, that electronic "dehumanization" plays a pleasantly constructive role in wide areas of business as well as in the areas of education, government and science. It has taken over the drudgery of routine work by processing data more accurately and quickly than man can possibly do it. In order to better illustrate its impact on our efficiency-oriented society, several typical uses, in terms of areas of application, are cited in the remainder of this chapter. Computer applications range from utilizing the computer's routing speed to process voluminous data, to thorough analysis and/or simulation of complex decision strategies.

Record Keeping

Business organizations spend large sums of money for maintaining and updating various records. Although computers were not initially developed for that particular purpose, they have been heavily committed to processing record keeping applications, such as payroll, inventory accounting, production scheduling and customer billing.[1]

[1] In the summer of 1969, a computerized bookkeeping package was developed to eliminate most of the manual work involved in maintaining ledgers and accounting system. GLAD (General Ledger Account Distribution), developed by EDP Central, Inc., does everything the bookkeeper previously had to do manually and handles such common routines as posting and drafting trial balance. The program requires a knowledge of bookkeeping but not of programming.

Payroll. Payroll involves a series of computations of each employee's gross pay, various deductions and net pay, resulting in the preparation of the "take home" pay. Related to this routine is periodic analysis of payroll for determining the allocation and distribution of the cost among various departments or among certain projects that the firm is undertaking.

Inventory Accounting. Inventory accounting handles the receipts and the disbursement of inventory items on hand as well as their cost. A computer system is used to store the previous balance, to account for incoming and outgoing items, and update the records almost flawlessly. The complexity of the system is determined by both the size of the organization and the level of activity of the particular account. In addition to the basic routine of updating the record, the system can also be programmed to compute safety stock demands, optimal order size, and to detect any unnecessary items in stock.

Production Scheduling. A manufacturing organization makes regular decisions for scheduling production of its goods. To do so means to compute the number of men needed, the required amount of raw or semifinished units and the loading requirements of each machine. The larger the production commitment of the organization, the more complex is the computation of the details of its production scheduling. A computer is used here to develop a production schedule that would minimize cost and provide the best allocation of the available resources, human and material.

Customer Billing. Many institutions (retailing, financial, industrial, government) regularly maintain the status of their customer accounts. Although the process involves only basic arithmetic operations, it often involves the performance of such operations thousands of times each day. In credit operations, for example, retail stores face the demanding task of posting, updating and billing each customer account for merchandise sold on account. Banks keep track of each depositor's account, updating it as more deposits and/or withdrawals are made. An industrial enterprise handles record keeping chores involving accounts payable and accounts receivable. State and federal bureaus record details regarding receipts and expenditures of public funds. The Internal Revenue Service compares taxes received with taxes withheld from employees' earnings. The arithmetic of checking these details is applied to millions of tax returns—the cost of this application would be prohibitive without the computer. Once manipulated by the computer, the information (usually on tape) can be used to service many areas. One such service is the availability of this information to state tax officials looking for people who might have filed federal but not state returns. Since 1935, the Internal Revenue Service has been authorized to provide state tax authorities with the contents of federal tax returns.[2]

---

[2] To date, over thirty-five states subscribe to this service. In 1968, the state of Oklahoma, for example, collected close to $4 million in additional taxes. Although federal statutes inflict penalties of $1,000 and one year in jail for unauthorized disclosure, the problem is still one of concern over the possible inevitable leakage of such information into the wrong hands.

Simulation

The term *simulation* refers to the symbolic representation of the essence of a system for learning about or testing a unique idea before its operational application on a full scale basis. The tales of Greek mythology provide a lucid illustration regarding simulation's long and varied history. Daedalus and his son Icarus decided one day to escape from Crete. To accomplish this scheme, Daedalus fashioned a pair of wings out of feathers and wax for his son (simulating those of a bird). With the wings, Icarus launched himself from a cliff and soared through the air. However, engrossed by the rapture of flight, Icarus flew too close to the sun, melting the wax in his wings, and he plunged into the sea.

Prior to the development of the computer, most simulations were based on the approach used by Daedalus and Icarus. They were concrete, physical representations of the original on a smaller scale, such as a pilot manufacturing plant, constructed to determine the feasibility of a full facility of the same type. Invariably, such concrete simulations required large expenditures of money, time and energy. However, the development of the computer's calculative power propelled simulation out of the realm of the concrete into that of the abstract. Today, simulation is most often accomplished through the use of mathematical models which, in total, define all the relevant parts of a given project. By manipulating the variables in the model and solving the expressions with the computer, significant savings in time, cost and effort are achieved.

In business, executives play various decision oriented games through the computer, by simulating conditions on which certain key decisions must be made. Errors made at this stage are less costly than those made in a live, on-going business situation. Conscious of the need for efficiency in operations, business concerns have been resorting to computer simulation in many areas. For example, in optimizing distribution costs, mathematical techniques and operations research are used to determine an optimum method of distribution in terms of cost savings and efficiency. Advanced mathematical techniques and linear programming are used to develop models of the most economical means of physical movement of goods from the factory to the warehouse or from specific warehouses to various destinations. The system also considers the effect of truckload or partial truckload shipments, the best shipment route to take, and whether or not a given warehouse can be eliminated (or added) without disrupting the existing distribution network.

The airlines, for example, often use simulation. To date, over one million dollars have been invested in flight simulators for pilot training. These simulators contain the cockpit (with a display of a runway and the airport seen through the window) and the controls. A computer makes the controls react as they would in a real airplane.

Simulation helps airlines decide whether or not to purchase a new plane or to plan new routes. A major international airline, for instance, has already acquainted its staff with its new Boeing 747 jets—prior to actual delivery. Before purchasing the planes, the airline evaluated cost factors as well as the new plane's overall performance within the flight pattern of its existing planes.

Such approach requires the use of a computer which is fed with key specifications (for example, aircraft weight and fuel consumption), various direct operating costs of maintenance and overhaul, out-of-pocket costs, depreciation and other expenses that are likely to be incurred throughout the life span of the aircraft.

In simulating a flight of the new aircraft, the distance of the simulated flight, the weight at capacity passenger load, fuel requirements, and the probability of winds at a designated altitude are fed into the computer. The theoretical hours of flight actually take seconds in the computer flight operation and cover taxiing, takeoff, climbing, cruising and landing. The final printout includes the direct operating cost per mile and the cost per available seat mile.

Management Information System

As computers continue to demonstrate their utility in the business environment, management looks expectantly to the future. Advances in computer technology, such as multiprogramming, multiprocessing, real-time and time-sharing capability, and practical mass storage devices, have increased management expectations as to what can be done with computers.

One particular application which is receiving widespread attention is the Management Information System (MIS)—an all-inclusive system designed to provide instant information that management needs for effective and efficient operation of the business. In its pure form, the MIS is not yet feasible; not because of lack of technical capability, but because of the inherent nature of the business organization.

Data base, a major component of MIS, is a single file containing all the information used by a business organization in a format applicable to any user's needs, immediately available when needed. This process poses great difficulty, since the job of assembling all pertinent information used by a given organization in a single location involves detailed analysis of that organization.

Attempts are currently underway to design and implement Management Information Systems. MIS invariably requires large, high-speed computers with mass auxiliary storage devices and real-time input/output capability. These conditions would limit the application of MIS to organizations with the capability of acquiring such sophisticated equipment, and which have the necessary talent for successful development.

Computer Aided Design

Engineering design, typically, involves the development of several feasible designs, covering a range of variables, and the selection of the design that best satisfies cost and performance criteria. The computer has been used to great advantage in performing the often tedious calculation of mathematical expressions for a wide range of incremental variables, allowing the engineer a greater measure of choice among feasible designs. More recently, the advent of improved graphic input/output units allows the engineer to view completed designs in three dimensions on cathode ray tubes, rotate them for perspective views, and alter them on-line with the use of "light pens." When the design is completed, it can be reproduced in blueprint form by high-speed plotters, devices which draw the designs on paper under computer control.

Information Storage and Retrieval

The masses of information generated daily in business operations suggest an urgent need for efficient and rapid means of classifying, storing and retrieving information of various types. The development of larger and faster computers, low-cost mass information storage devices, and efficient input-output display terminals, such as the cathode ray tube display stations, have had a profound impact on the information storage and retrieval effort.

Under development are new techniques of classification and indexing which will permit selected information to be arranged in the mass storage devices with more accuracy and in a format more amenable to interaction with the users. With the development of more sophisticated input/output display terminals and time-sharing systems, the interaction between man and the machine is now more feasible and vital for the proper responsiveness of the retrieval system.

Computer Assisted Instruction. The use of electronic computers in education contributed to the development of new and revolutionary areas of research. Computer assisted instruction (CAI) and computer managed instruction (CMI) are receiving widespread attention from various sectors in education. CAI is a concept that applies computers and specialized input/output display terminals directly to individualized student instruction. The student faces the display terminal as he begins his lesson. A typical lesson presents a short tutorial section, followed by questions on the material covered. The answers given (entered on the display terminal) determine the next step in the instruction process. The computer grades the answers and, if they are correct, presents the next, higher level of material to the student. On the other hand, if the answers given are incorrect, the computer presents a remedial section designed to review the ideas of the original section in greater depth and clarity. This scene may be multiplied hundreds of times for a single computer with the use of time-sharing facilities. CMI is a concept that leaves the actual instruction under the instructor's control; this means that the computer is used here as a tool to evaluate the progress of a student at each step in the learning process and plot a new course of study based on that progress.

Medicine. Great advances have been made in the use of computers to assist physicians in the diagnosis, testing and evaluation of various human ailments. For example, using a color electro-optical scanner (developed by Oleh Tretiak, of MIT, in May 1969), Professor Murray Eden, of the MIT Research Laboratory of Electronics, demonstrated the feasibility of computerized technique to locate white blood cells and sort the blood cells into five types with 90-95 percent accuracy and faster than the time-consuming manual process which costs millions of dollars each year.

Recently, an attempt was made by a medical doctor to computerize an entire poison control center. In the interest of saving vital time and getting a little sleep for himself, Dr. Vernon Green, of Children's Mercy Hospital, Kansas City, Missouri, developed a system ingested with the names of about 300 drugs and 1,000 household products. When an emergency case of poison arrives in the hospital, the nurse (linked directly to the computer located elsewhere) simply keys in the suspected brand of poison and, within one minute, the computer prints out information relevant to the particular poison. However, it still remains for the physician to evaluate the seriousness of the patient's illness.

Electronic Guidance and Control

Computers have been programmed to serve as automatic navigating and control robots in manufacturing process control, manned space flights, and missile and submarine guidance. In the latter areas, a computer's primary operation is to calculate continuously the effect of changes in variables, such as distance and position, and to produce an updated strategy for keeping a submarine or a missile on its proper course.

Process Control System. Petroleum and chemical industries operate production processes which require continuous monitoring of output and adjustment of component functions to maintain production within predetermined constraints. The computer has been successfully employed as the key subsystem of closed-loop process control systems. Once it is fed the numerical measurements of critical variables, it compares the variable data against predefined criteria, determines the necessary type of adjustments to the production process, and makes the required modifications to the process to insure quality output. With the entire production process under the control of the computer, the organization can be certain of detecting and correcting any "out-of-limit" conditions which might interfere with the attainment of pronounced goals. (See Fig. 1-1.)

FIG. 1-1 Schematic diagram of a computer oriented process control

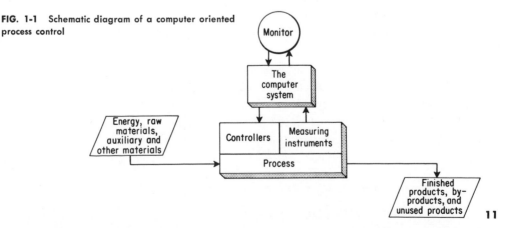

Manned Space Flights. It has been said that the initial mathematical calculations for the space effort would have required hundreds of man-years of manual effort. In fact, it is beyond the capability of even the most proficient mathematician to perform the split second calculations necessary to maintain the course of a spacecraft traveling at 25,000 miles per hour.

Christopher C. Kraft, Jr., Director of Flight Operations NASA Manned Spacecraft Center, remarked,

> If I had to single out the piece of equipment that, more than any other, has allowed us to go from earth-orbit Mercury flights to Apollo lunar trips in just over seven years, it would be the high-speed computer.

The role of the computer in manned space flight, then, is obvious. Since its inception, thousands of technically oriented organizations, research centers and scientists have pooled their resources and talent to explore outer space and to put a man on the surface of the moon. A *Computerworld* editorial summed up the computer's role in manned space flight:

> The role of the computer in manned space flights has quite properly been overshadowed by the daring of the astronauts who bet their lives on these electronic marvels.

> But it is also time to reflect on the fact that these incredible journeys would be impossible without electronic computers. In less than 25 years, computers have become man's scout, guide, protector, helpmate, and backup memory.

> In honoring the men who go to the moon and the depths of the sea, we should also honor those men whose vision and research led to the development of man's best friend, the electronic computer.[3]

Since it is impossible to include every computer use and application within the constraints of this chapter, the following additional uses are presented in condensed form and are intended as a further reminder of what computers are doing in our society.

> Electronics production lines are now computer controlled.
> Small cities will go EDP in five years.
> A stock brokerage firm uses computer for total order matching.
> Debtors may be traced via data bank.
> Computers will help analyze moon rocks.
> Payment system eliminates invoices and checks.
> Dealer's orders are speeded by auto data network.
> Seafood producer controls distribution through computer assisted scheduling.
> Punch card stock certificates may replace traditional forms.
> Computer study may answer question: Is speed major cause of accidents?

[3] *Computerworld* (July 30, 1969), p. 8.

New computerized real estate listings help companies to relocate executives.

Magnetic strips on credit cards speed handling.

Math test is computerized.

Computer helps choose compatible roommates.

No longer is a slide rule the mark of an engineer.

Data bank will track 300,000 children.

Computer assisted farms reduce enterprise costs.

Computer helps race horse owners find unique names for new entries.

Computers are used as stock swappers.

Farmers use time-sharing system to watch their profit margins.

School adopts "checkless" method of paying its 130 faculty members.

Medical school uses computer assisted instruction to keep doctors up to date.

EDP helps the job find the candidate.

Chicago's water supply is monitored by computer.

Computer/scanner aids analysis of dental X rays.

Students, ages 7-17, use computers for homework assignments.

Transplant donors are picked with computer matching.

Computerization helps firm recover from hurricane. A garment manufacturer, hit by hurricane Camille in August 1969, made normal fall deliveries due to the storage, on magnetic tape, of his garment patterns, which were reproduced in a few hours.

This text stresses "automatic" rather than "electronic" data processing principles, because in modern business mechanical techniques as well as electronic ones are used. Punched card equipment, although not as widely used as computers, is still helpful in solving many business problems in smaller firms.

The use of the term *automatic data processing*, therefore, is much broader than the term *electronic data processing*, since all of the data processing methods which will be discussed in later chapters are automatic, although not all are necessarily electronic.

The foregoing examples illustrate the potential of ADP equipment in various fields of endeavor. The gap between what is being done and what can be done does not show clear signs of closing, but it does show the tremendous challenge in developing computer technology.

Automatic data processing machines seem to accomplish routine jobs so fast that we often overlook the great number of people working behind the scenes to prepare the computers for their data processing routines. We are often tempted to believe that industry has become completely "dehumanized," but it is an observable fact that the introduction and use of machinery usually results in the employment of more people to handle a wide variety of newly created jobs. Particular jobs may become "dehumanized," but the industry as a whole usually ends up using more, rather than less, humans. Promising rewards as well as new freedom from the frustrations of doing routine, repetitive work await those who are willing to meet the challenge.

Glossary of Terms

AUTOMATION: (1) The implementation of processes by automatic means. (2) The investigation, design, development, and application of methods of rendering procedures automatic, self-moving, or self-controlling. (3) The theory, art, or technique of making a process more automatic.

COMPUTER: A calculating device which processes data represented by combination of discrete (in digital computers) or continuous (descriptive of analog computers) data.

COMPUTER ASSISTED INSTRUCTION: A concept that applies computers and specialized input/output display terminals directly to individualized student instruction.

DATA BASE: A single file containing information in a format applicable to any user's needs and available when needed.

INFORMATION RETRIEVAL: A technique of classifying and indexing useful information in mass storage devices, in a format amenable to interaction with the user(s).

MANAGEMENT INFORMATION SYSTEM: An all-inclusive system designed to provide instant information to management for effective and efficient business operation.

NUMERALIZATION: Representation of alphabetic data through the use of digits, a desired step in automatic data processing.

PAYROLL: A list of employees, showing their earnings for a stated period together with other relevant information.

SIMULATION: Symbolic representation (in terms of a model) of the essence of a system for testing an idea or a product before operationalizing its full-scale production.

STANDARDIZATION: Established specific procedural requirements for the efficient production of a large volume of goods or for automatic processing of data.

Questions for Review

1. How is automation integrated in electronic data processing? Explain.
2. What is the role of the computer in:
   a. payroll
   b. inventory accounting
   c. production scheduling
   d. customer billing
3. Elaborate a simulation of your own and indicate how the computer can be used in handling various phases of it.
4. Contrast the relationship between Management Information System and information storage and retrieval.
5. Illustrate an application of your own where computer assisted instruction can be used.
6. Discuss the role of the computer in guidance and control.
7. Explain three uses (other than the ones mentioned in the chapter) where computers are actively applied.
8. If you were asked to point out the significance of electronic computers in industrial organizations, what would be the single, most important contribution that they offer?

chapter two

THE DEVELOPMENT OF
THE "THINKING MACHINE"

THE PRE-AUTOMATED DATA PROCESSING ERA

AN ERA OF TRANSITION

THE NEED FOR AND THE COST OF KEEPING
BUSINESS RECORDS

AUTOMATIC DATA PROCESSING—ITS ROLE AND IMPACT
A New Revolution
Is the Computer a "Thinking Machine"?

DATA PROCESSING, whether manual or automatic, business or scientific, involves collecting, recording, and manipulating the necessary alphabetic and/or numeric symbols to achieve a given result. Data processing is a means to an end, not an end in itself.

Data are everywhere. In writing a term paper, for example, a student goes to the library, reads one or more reference books, records selected ideas or summarizes certain sections, adds more ideas of his own, writes from his notes, and finally, types his findings and presents them to his instructor. Likewise, a housewife first finds out what items she needs for the day, checks the amount of cash available for those items, puts the cash in her purse, goes to the supermarket, selects the needed items, pays the cashier, and drives back home with the groceries.

A businessman processes business data in a similar manner. He determines his needs and checks his budget for the available cash. He orders the needed items and pays for them after an itemized bill has been received. These operations often are done manually with a pencil and paper. Sometimes they are supplemented by an adding machine, a desk calculator, or a slide rule.

THE PRE-AUTOMATED DATA PROCESSING AREA

There always has been a need for man to "calculate." In early times, there was a need to count his family, his flock and the number of his enemies. As a farmer or a breeder, he found it necessary to keep track of the seasons, and therefore he developed a calendar. Tying knots in thongs or cutting notches in sticks helped him keep track of such data.

In the early days of banking, notches in a stick were used to keep the borrower and the banker honest. The notches represented the amount of the loan, and the stick was cut in half lengthwise through the notches. The bank kept half the stick and the borrower held the matching half. The half held by the banker was known as the "stock"; hence, the banker became known as the "stockholder." Other early calculations were recorded by making scratches in the dust.

Although notches in sticks and straight-line scratches in clay tablets were adequate for man's early needs, it later became necessary for him to create written numerals. Greek and Roman numerals served the purpose of representing numbers but were cumbersome. It was not until Hindu and Arabic numerals were invented that man had a truly workable system of written numbers.

Each number system had its own symbols, beginning with "zero" and progressing through "nine." The use of digits made it possible to use the decimal "place" system, in which the position of a given digit indicated its value (that is, ones, tens, hundreds, thousands, and so on).

The foregoing shows us that man was forced to create better calculating devices as his paperwork expanded. In Charles Dickens' story *A Christmas Carol*, Bob Cratchit is pictured sitting on a high stool working on Mr. Scrooge's books. At that period in history, this was the approved method of calculating and recording. It is quite a contrast to today's bookkeeper, who has adding machines, calculators and other devices at his disposal. The "green eye-shade" bookkeeper is almost a thing of the past.

AN ERA OF TRANSITION

During the late nineteenth and the early twentieth centuries, man progressed beyond these primitive methods of data recording and processing. He was forced to find better ways of doing things because business was expanding, demand for better products was increasing, and consequently the recording, reporting, and manipulation of data began to present a greater problem. Business went through a transition from the one-man firm, where records were negligible and the need for recording data was slight, to firms owned by many people, employing many hundreds or thousands of workers. This made it necessary to maintain an endless variety of business records involving the sale of goods, updating the receipt and disbursement of cash, and the periodical preparation of payroll. These and other functions, then, revealed a need for a gradual transition from the use of relatively inadequate tools to a more efficient utilization of an automatic data processing system.

THE NEED FOR AND THE COST OF KEEPING BUSINESS RECORDS

If we analyze the needs of a business firm for obtaining accurate and adequate information, we find several areas of business activity that must be controlled. Just as an early shepherd had to keep track of the sheep in his flock, a businessman must keep track of the things he owns. This is known as keeping an inventory. When a businessman's inventory falls below a safe minimum, he must know how many units to reorder and how long it will take to replace his stock so that he may continue to carry on his business activities without interruption.

Large or small, a business firm needs records. An automobile is equipped with an oil pressure gauge to indicate whether or not the engine is receiving proper lubrication. Without this device, it is unlikely that the driver would be aware of a lubrication failure until serious trouble developed. Likewise, a business firm needs "gauges" to determine its operating performance. These "gauges" of business are its accounting records.

Payroll must be prepared regularly. This involves the preparation of a paycheck for each employee, as well as the maintenance of information regarding his earnings and deductions for the year. The firm must have ready cash to pay creditors such as suppliers, the landlord or the mortgage holder, and the advertising agency.

All accounts receivable and accounts payable information must be recorded. City, state and federal governments require more records and reports from business firms each year. These reports and others of a similar nature must be prepared, and numerous workers often are required to get the job done.

In relation to the total number of workers in a firm, the number of clerical employees is quite high. Clerical requirements have continued to grow each year creating higher costs of doing business. A higher and higher percentage of a firm's working capital and personnel are required for recording, classifying, summarizing, and filing masses of vital business data. If it were possible to total the annual cost of creating and maintaining business records, the sum would be staggering.

At present, it is estimated that one out of every three employees is engaged in clerical work. This ratio seems high, considering the fact that it is the production and sale of goods which sustains the firm and provides the revenue. The salaries of clerical help are direct overhead, eating into business profits. To keep these costs down, business firms are always looking for better and cheaper methods of keeping their records.

Economy is not the only factor that a businessman considers, however. Speed is equally important. Timing is critical in decision making, and to aid the executive in arriving at a decision, business data must be available as soon as possible. Management may speed up the processing of business data by increasing the clerical force, of course, but this would only mean increased clerical costs.

Not only are the volume of data and the need for data increasing, but as businesses become more complex, the distance between a manager and the activity he is to control also is increasing. When the manager becomes farther removed from operations, decisions which previously could be made on the basis of personal knowledge and experience now must be based on "second-hand" information. It is important, then, that this information be accurate and on time to be of use. *Effective* management control requires the "feed-back" of information in time to affect important decisions. If information does not reach the manager when he needs it, it is of little value to him. Since the chief objective of automatic data processing is to *aid* management, the aim of manufacturers of data processing equipment is to build machines that will process information *quickly, accurately* and *economically*.

AUTOMATIC DATA PROCESSING—ITS ROLE AND IMPACT

A New Revolution

When the Industrial Revolution began, there were warnings that man would become a "useless slave" of the machines which he had created. Since machines could do the work of many men, it was argued that there soon would be no work for man to do.

The evidence of history has proved these fears groundless. Modern machines with their many uses have freed man from much of his manual labor so that he can devote his energies to more productive work. As a result, it is now possible to communicate instantly with people half a world away. Man can enjoy the music of great orchestras in the comfort of his home. He can travel from continent to continent in a few hours. With the twist of a dial, he can have comfort in his home, whether there is a blizzard or a heat wave outside. Modern man can enjoy things that the most powerful emperors of the past centuries could not.

The developments in automatic data processing are making possible a new kind of industrial revolution. The first revolution relieved man of much of his manual labor and gave him powerful tools to help him accomplish great physical feats. The new "computer" revolution gives him powerful new tools that will relieve him of much of his mental drudgery and make it possible for him to use his mind more profitably.

In the scientific field, the computer has made possible many things that could not have been accomplished otherwise. Problems that would require many man-years of human computation are solved by computers in a matter of minutes. No human being would be capable of performing the split-second calculations necessary to orbit a manned spacecraft or direct a missile to the moon.

Many problems were left unsolved for years because there were no computers to handle them. Many areas of research were ignored because it was impossible to complete projects using manual methods of computation. Automatic data processing has opened many doors previously closed to the scientist, as well as the businessman.

Every business firm has its own data processing requirements. The manner in which they are handled depends on the volume of work to be done, the elapsed time, the degree of accuracy required, the necessary speed, and the cost. Regardless of its other requirements, however, every business must pay its personnel, make reports to the government, and record the buying and selling of goods or services—all functions involving the processing of data. Information necessary for management decision making can be obtained from these and other sources of operating data through the use of automatic machines.

In automatic data processing, figures represent facts and are manipulated in various ways to create additional useful information. The original information is referred to as *input*. The result of processing *input* is called *output*. Facts (data) are manipulated (processed) to create information (output) which provides answers to specific problems. Complete, accurate, and timely information aids both the businessman and the scientist to form a sound basis for decisions.

Data can be processed in several ways. In the use of a pencil and paper, the pencil is the *device* and the paper is the *medium*. The development of machines such as the cash register, bookkeeping machine, and accounting machine has been a more advanced answer to data processing. These devices are halfway between the paper-and-pencil method and the relatively complex computer system.

A cash register, for instance, combines the functions of a cash drawer and an adding machine. With its capability to classify data, as in the case of a grocery store register which identifies items as meat, produce, grocery, etc., it also becomes a sorting machine.

Bookkeeping and accounting machines, on the other hand, combine the functions of a typewriter and a calculator, with controls which permit automating simple operations. When coupled with equipment for producing punched paper tape, these pieces of equipment can be used to prepare *input* data for computers.

Punched card machines were developed as a step toward the use of fully automatic equipment. Except for the initial preparation of the punched cards and the need to transport them from one machine to another, the entire operation of a punched-card system is automatic. That is, any or all of the necessary calculations are worked out with minimum human intervention.

Next came the electronic computer. Operations became even more automatic. While punched card data processing requires the handling of cards through various mechanical devices, the components of an electronic system are interconnected in such a way that all processing functions (including input and output) are done automatically.

Electronic data processing transfers data in the form of electrical impulses through electrical circuits, making it possible to attain much greater speeds than can be achieved by a mechanical system. Instructions for processing given data are stored in the *memory* of the computer and can be changed to suit particular needs, thereby allowing greater flexibility in the system.

To the uninitiated, a "computer" refers to a room full of mysterious "boxes" costing millions of dollars. Although there are computer systems that fit this description, computers of smaller size and lower cost are more common. Small to medium size computers play a vital part in the data processing field today and have made it economically possible for many firms to enjoy the benefits of automatic data processing.

Is the Computer a "Thinking Machine"?

Science-fiction books are filled with stories of powerful *thinking machines*. Depending on the whim of the writer, these machines can become either great benefactors or monsters that control or destroy mankind.

The behavior of computers and the tasks they perform are similar to those a human being would perform in the same situations. Because of this similarity, the computer often is referred to as an "electronic brain." While highly flattering to the machine, this comparison is far from accurate.

Computer designers face the challenge of building a computer with the size, function and storage capacity of the human brain. To do so would mean the creation of a computer the size of a grapefruit, powered by only one tenth of a watt of electricity, yet having a memory 10,000 times the size of any computer yet built.

The computer is like a highly efficient, fast and accurate robot. It must be told when to start, stop, add and subtract. It must be told precisely what to do, at what time, and in what manner. Although some "sophisticated" computers are capable of catching certain errors in the instructions given to them, data fed into a computer must be accurate and complete. If they are not clear and properly organized, the results of processing will be largely a wasted effort.

Computers can detect, but generally cannot correct, an inaccurate entry. The initials GIGO, meaning "Garbage In, Garbage Out," emphasize the fact that processing is only as accurate as the input received. Since errors in input can be compounded during processing, it is essential to take every precaution to avoid them.

Computers have been used to compose music, write poetry and play chess, but so far these activities are relatively limited and involve "thinking" in a very restrictive sense. They are still subject to human direction and control. However, these accomplishments present all kinds of new opportunities for computer scientists and users.

Automatic data processing equipment puts unique demands on the knowledge of those who use it. Without proper direction, the most sophisticated computer is nothing but a helpless complex of wires. The equipment can be no more accurate than the persons who prepare the instructions and the data for its use.

Glossary of Terms

DATA PROCESSING: Any operation or combination of operations on data.

INPUT: (1) The data to be processed. (2) The state or sequence of states occurring on a specified input channel. (3) The device or collective set of devices used for bringing data into another device. (4) A channel for impressing a state on a device or logic element. (5) The processes of transferring data from an external storage to an internal storage.

INPUT DEVICE: The mechanical unit designed to bring data to be processed into a computer; e.g., a card reader, a tape reader, or a keyboard.

OUTPUT: (1) Data that has been processed. (2) The state or sequence of states occurring on a specified output channel. (3) The device or collective set of devices used for taking data out of a device. (4) A channel for expressing a state of a device or logic element. (5) The process of transferring data from an internal storage to an external storage.

OUTPUT DEVICE: The part of a machine which translates the electrical impulses representing data processed by the machine into permanent results such as printed forms, punched cards, and magnetic writing on tape.

Questions for Review

1. For what reason(s) was man forced to create better calcualting devices? Explain.
2. List and explain briefly the factors which led many business firms to resort to automated data processing.
3. What three significant advantages can be achieved from automatic data processing? Discuss.
4. Why is a computer referred to as an "electronic brain"? What are some of its capabilities? Explain.

chapter three

HISTORY OF DATA PROCESSING

FURTHER DEVELOPMENT OF RECORD-KEEPING METHODS
Early Mechanical Calculating Devices

Napier's "Bones"
Early Calculators
Key-driven Calculating Machines
Joseph Marie Jacquard
Herman Hollerith and the Punched Card Era
James Powers

INDUSTRY DEVELOPMENTS
Developments in Automatic Data Processing

Charles P. Babbage
The Difference Engine
Babbage's Analytical Engine
The Mark I Computer
The Eniac
The Edvac
The Univac

A WORD ABOUT GENERATIONS

MAN HAS ALWAYS BEEN CHALLENGED by the computations needed to solve various kinds of problems. To most people, the task of manipulating or working out problems is boring and time-consuming. While "processing" information is not a new creation, the means by which data are processed has changed steadily in an attempt to make data processing less tedious, more accurate, and much faster.

EARLY MANUAL METHODS OF CALCULATING

The first external method of calculation was counting items on the ten fingers. When the total began to exceed ten, man began to use more sophisticated methods of counting, such as knotted ropes and notched rods. Eventually, even these advanced techniques became inadequate as man's use of mathematics and his desire for greater calculating power multiplied.

Finger Counting

Until the nineteenth century, most business calculations were performed mentally. To reduce this problem, Roman schools taught finger counting and actually devised various methods of doing such advanced operations as multiplication and division on the fingers.

The Roman student was required to learn the multiplication table only up through 5×5. To figure out the product of any numbers between 5 and 10, he used his fingers. Suppose, for example, he wished to multiply 7×9. To find the product, he would raise two fingers on one hand to represent the numbers over 5 (that is, 6 and 7) plus four fingers on the other hand to represent 6, 7, 8 and 9 (Fig. 3-1). He obtained the product as follows:

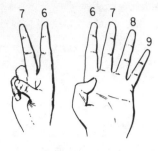

FIG. 3-1

1. Add the number of fingers raised.

   $2 + 4 = 6$ (the value of ten's position)

2. Multiply the number of fingers not raised in each hand.

   $3 \times 1 = 3$ (the value of the unit's position)

Therefore

   $7 \times 9 = 63$

Try this method using other values between 5 and 10. Also consider how impractical such a method would be today in computing thousands of customer bills a day.

The Abacus

The abacus is a manual calculating device which uses beads instead of fingers to represent decimal numbers. The beads are strung in rows, each row containing 10 beads representing the 10 fingers. The position of the row represents the decimal value of the beads in it. That is, the beads in row A have a value of one each; those in row B have a value of 10 each; those in row C, 100 each; and so on. (See Fig. 3-2.)

A	A = Unit's Position
B	B = Ten's Position
C	C = Hundred's Position
D	D = Thousand's Position
E	E = Ten Thousand's Position
F	F = Hundred Thousand's Position

FIG. 3-2 An abacus

The origin of the abacus remains obscure. Many nations claim to have invented it. It is probable that the idea was developed in several countries and later carried into other parts of the world by travelers and merchants. Its earliest home is believed to have been Babylon or Egypt. Whatever its origin, however, the abacus has withstood the test of time, since it is still being used to advantage in several parts of the world.

The practice of record keeping existed ages before the recording of formal history. Barbarians kept records by scratching them on rocks. Later, they learned to use their fingers for counting. From these crude forms of picture-writing and counting, the process of rudimentary bookkeeping began, spurred by the growth of civilization and the establishment of government. Later, it became necessary to convert recorded facts into timely, useful information.

Babylon

In Babylonia, clay tablets over four thousand years old have been discovered, proving to be records of banks and moneylending firms in operation at that time. The code of Hammurabi, ruler of Babylonia (2285–2242 B.C.), includes references to business transactions such as contracts, deeds, bonds, receipts, inventories, sales, and other similar types of accounts. It also reveals that drafts and checks were commonly used and that customs dues and ferry and high-way tolls were collected. Similarly, state records of property ownership which were used for taxation purposes have been discovered.

Egypt and Greece

In Egypt, accounts were kept on parchment or papyrus. The state's revenues and disbursements were carefully recorded. Taxes paid in kind caused the building of granaries and warehouses. Taxpayers were given receipts when their grain or livestock was delivered. These receipts were accounted for, along with the inventories of all commodities.

Ancient Greece also required a relatively strict accounting from all public officials. Upon leaving office, an official made a "public accounting" on stone and exposed it to public view. It is also known that the Greeks developed a kind of clearing house system for financial transactions.

Rome

In ancient Rome, the father of the family kept records of receipts and payments in a memorandum record. Each month, these entries were transferred to a "register," accepted as evidence in lawsuits. Roman bankers also used registers and a kind of account book for clients to show individual deposits, loans, payments, and balances. Checks were used, but evidently only by the wealthy.

Later, the state developed a new system of accounting control. The official in charge of funds (treasurer) had no authority to disburse them without a "voucher" issued by another body of officials to substantiate the payment. Further, the Romans drew up budgets for the needs of the imperial household and the army which served as a basis for levying taxes, which later were collected on a decentralized basis but with central offices handling all of the accounting and control aspects.

England

The Exchequer, established during the reign of Henry I (1100–1135), is the earliest known accounting system in England. This was based on the Domesday Book, in which were recorded all taxable estates in the country. From it, the treasurer's Great Roll was made up. Each sheriff was held responsible for collecting his portion of taxes and was required to render an account twice a year. On the first accounting, he received half of a tally stick, notched to show the amount; the other half was retained by the treasurer. On the next accounting, the sheriff's tally stick was turned in as evidence of the first payment and matched against the treasurer's half.

ITALY'S DOUBLE-ENTRY BOOKKEEPING

Double-entry bookkeeping began in Italy in the fourteenth century. In 1340 in Genoa, a double-entry ledger was used which shows a merchandise account for pepper, debited with expenses, credited with receipts, and the balance transferred to "profit and loss." A similar system was also used in Venice.

In Venice in 1494, Luca Paciolo, a monk, published a book entitled *Everything about Arithmetic, Geometry, and Proportion.* At the end of the treatise on arithmetic, Paciolo made a summary of the existing practice in bookkeeping. He stated that the purpose of bookkeeping was the furnishing of timely information with regard to assets and liabilities. The system described the use of three books: a memorial (daybook or blotter), a journal (formal debits and credits in standard currency), and a quaderno (ledger). Merchandise accounts in the ledger were kept on a single-venture basis, with balances between debits and credits closed out to the Profit and Loss account.

FURTHER DEVELOPMENT OF RECORD-KEEPING METHODS

Between the early 1400s and the 1800s, record keeping methods were developed and expanded, but little was done to *speed up* the process of recording business transactions, calculating various amounts, or producing business reports.

Early Mechanical Calculating Devices

Napier's "Bones." Arab, Hindu, and European mathematicians were the first to develop techniques of written calculations. However, most of those techniques were in the form of *tables* to aid multiplication and other arithmetic operations. The "table" approach was used in 1614 by John Napier, of Merchiston, Scotland, and culminated in the development of Napier's "bones."

Napier divided rods into nine squares. The top square holds a decimal digit (that is, 1 through 9) and represents the product of its multiplication by 1. Each of the remaining eight squares is divided diagonally and holds (top to bottom) the product of the digit in the top square by 2, 3, 4, 5, 6, 7, and 8, respectively. Once the set is completed, the product of any two numbers can be obtained by adding the values pertaining to them diagonally.

Figure 3-3 shows the rods for multiplying 1, 3, 7, and 4.

Suppose we wish to multiply 3×374. Using Napier's "bones," we first identify the multiplier (3) in the third square of the left rod. The multiplicand (374) is the remaining three rods. The product is obtained by adding diagonally the values in the third square of each of the rods of the multiplicand (from right):

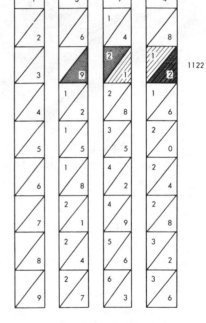

FIG. 3-3 Napier's bones

Unit's position . . . 2 (the contents of the right diagonal column).

Ten's position . . . the sum of the second diagonal column, or $1 + 1 = 2$.

Hundred's position . . . the sum of the third diagonal column, or $2 + 9 = 1$ and a carry 1. The carry is in the thousand's position, therefore the product is 1,122.

Early Calculators. The first mathematical digital calculator was invented by Blaise Pascal in 1642 (Fig. 3-4). It also is referred to as the numerical wheel calculator, because it was the world's first mechanical adding machine.

At age eighteen, Pascal wanted to help his father, who at that time was the Superintendent of Taxes. The calculator he designed registered decimal values by rotating a wheel by one to nine steps, with a carry lever to operate the next higher digit wheel whenever the first wheel reached 10 units.

At the age of 25, Gottfried Wilhelm von Leibnitz built his "stepped-wheel" calculator, which was manufactured in 1694. It was capable of performing all four arithmetic functions; however, it was not considered dependable in its operation.

Another attempt was made in 1829 by Charles Xavier Thomas, of Colmar, France. His calculator was the first to perform all four functions accurately. An idea similar to Thomas' was used in 1872 by Frank Stephen Baldwin, marking the beginning of the calculating machine industry in the United States.

FIG. 3-4   Pascal's calculator

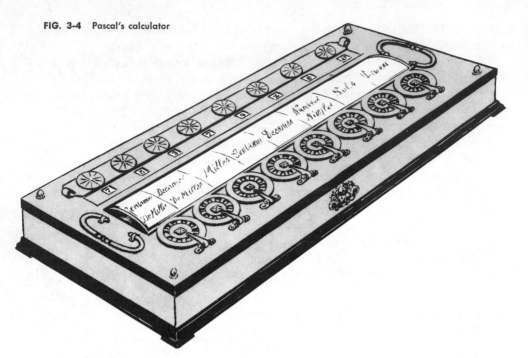

Key-Driven Calculating Machines.   The invention and development of devices and machines such as the typewriter, the letterpress, and the cash register played a big part in the advancement of data processing, particularly in the recording and reporting functions. In 1887, Dorr Eugene Felt patented his comptometer, improved versions of which are still widely used. The first practical adding and listing (printing) machines were produced by Felt in 1889 and, three years later, by W. S. Burroughs. Burroughs developed a 90-key machine with a capacity of up to nine decimal digits.

In 1914, Oscar and David Sundstrand produced a 10-key adding machine. About that time, the Monroe calculator was invented by Jay R. Monroe and Frank S. Baldwin, and although considered a nonprinting device, it went beyond simple adding machine functions in that it could multiply and divide automatically at much greater speeds.

The so-called accounting machines were not developed until after World War I. These were machines capable of printing values in a columnar arrangement, in addition to performing the functions of recording, calculating, and summarizing, which are common characteristics of most adding machines. Included in this category are billing machines which automatically extend amounts on invoices, and payroll machines that handle tax and other deductions in arriving at the net pay, while simultaneously providing copies or registers for accounting purposes.

Although electric motors provide greater speed and facility, all devices classified as adding machines, calculators, or accounting machines are considered "nonautomatic" equipment. All of them require a human worker to control and operate each step of processing.

Joseph Marie Jacquard. In 1801, an event occurred which was to have far-reaching effects on the later development of automatic equipment. It was the perfection of the first punched-card machine, built by Joseph Marie Jacquard, of France, to weave intricate designs into cloth. The outstanding feature of this machine was its ability to follow a set of instructions punched into cards. Due to the "fear of machines," Jacquard had difficulty gaining public acceptance for his machine. In the City of Lyons, he was physically attacked and his machine was destroyed. Through Napoleon's support, he rebuilt his machine and proved its usefulness in weaving. Lyons' prosperity in the mid-1800s was attributed largely to the success of Jacquard's loom.

Herman Hollerith and the Punched Card Era. The year 1880 marks the beginning of the modern punched card era. During this year, Dr. Herman Hollerith, a statistician, was engaged by the United States Census Bureau as a special agent to speed up the processing of census data.

The 1880 census took seven and a half years to complete. Manual tabulating methods were used in the survey of a population of 50 million people and proved hopelessly inadequate. It was obvious that the 1890 census could not be processed by the same means if the information was to have any real value. Furthermore, many facts of interest could not be compiled at all, or could not be handled in a manner which satisfied the Census Bureau's objectives.

Dr. Hollerith set out to mechanize the census operations. By 1887, he had completed a system using the punched card principle, although the first machine used paper strips with holes punched into them according to a code, similar to a player piano roll. The paper strip was found to be impractical, so a standard-size card was developed and the system eventually included 3 in. × 5 in. corner-cut cards, a punch, a "pin-press," electromagnetic counters, and a sorting box.

In operation, a punched card was placed into the pin-press, and a hinged box was lowered to activate a counter and open the lid of a sorting slot. Cards were deposited at a speed of 50 to 80 cards a minute. A test tabulation of 10,000 returns showed that enumeration time was three fourths and tabulating time was one eighth of that required for earlier systems. Despite an increase in the population to 63 million, the 1890 census was tabulated in two and a half years, a job which would have taken several more years to do manually.

In 1896, Dr. Hollerith organized the Tabulating Machine Company to develop his machines for commercial sale. In 1901, he introduced the basic form of a numerical punch keyboard, and other system improvements were completed before his retirement in 1914.

James Powers. In the meantime S. N. D. North, Director of the United States Census Bureau, was making plans for the 1910 census. Realizing the necessity of greater processing speed and accuracy, and in the absence of Hollerith, he engaged James Powers (a comparatively unknown statistician from New Jersey) to develop more equipment in a new mechanical laboratory subsidized by Congress.

Powers designed completely mechanical machines with many desirable features. In 1908, he produced a die-set punch capable of punching 20-column cards on a "simultaneous punching" principle. The principle involves the accumulation of information to be punched in a card; then, by depressing a key, all the information is punched simultaneously. With this technique, there is an advantage in checking to see that all data to be punched are keyed in correctly. The simultaneous punching principle has been used in the Univac keypunch. Later, Powers developed a two-deck horizontal sorter.

Powers' machines performed so well that 300 punches, related sorters, and tabulators were installed for the 1910 census. Powers became convinced that there was a commercial market for his machines. In 1911, he formed the Powers Accounting Machine Company (which was later acquired by Remington Rand Corporation).

INDUSTRY DEVELOPMENTS

About 1911, punched card machine developments began to accelerate. During that year, the Tabulating Machine Company, originally organized by Dr. Hollerith, merged with the International Time Recording Company and the Dayton Scale Company to form the Computing-Tabulating Recording Company. Three years later, in 1914, Thomas J. Watson, Sr., became its president. In 1924, the name of the company was changed to the International Business Machines Corporation.

Meanwhile, the Accounting and Tabulating Machine Corporation was organized to distribute internationally the products of Powers Accounting Machine Company. Powers' machines were successfully demonstrated in Europe, and sales agencies were established in several countries. Among these was the Accounting and Tabulating Corporation of Great Britain, Ltd., which separated from Powers in 1919. In 1922, *Samas* (Société Anonyme des Machines à Statistiques), another sales agency, was established in France. In 1929, the French and British companies consolidated, forming Powers-Samas Accounting Machines, Ltd. In 1958, the merger of Powers-Samas Accounting Machines, Ltd., and the British Tabulating Machine Company led to the organization of International Computers and Tabulators, Ltd.

In the United States, the Powers line merged in 1927 with other office supply companies to form Remington Rand Corporation, which in 1955 merged with the Sperry Corporation to form Sperry Rand Corporation. Presently, data processing equipment is marketed through the Univac Division of Sperry Rand Corporation.

Developments in Automatic Data Processing

The word *computer* had long been used to describe anything that has a "computing" ability: adding, subtracting, multiplying, or dividing. Only recently has the term come to have its current meaning.

Charles P. Babbage. It is generally agreed that the first major step in the development of computers can be attributed to Charles P. Babbage, a professor of mathematics at Trinity College, Cambridge, England.

Babbage became interested in computing extensive mathematical tables which would make the metric system easier to use. In 1812, he selected three groups of people, assigning the first group of five men to the task of defining the formulas and of describing the mathematical methods to be used. The second group was assigned to take these formulas and to compute some numerical values for them. The third group of about 100 men was to complete all necessary computations. Babbage's idea was to replace this third group ultimately with a piece of equipment he called the *Difference Engine*. Unfortunately, it never was perfected.

The Difference Engine. In 1812, Babbage thought of building the Difference Engine, a machine capable of computing mathematical tables automatically (Fig. 3-5). Ten years later, a model of the Difference Engine was

FIG. 3-5 Babbage's Difference Engine

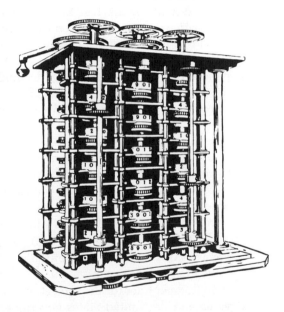

completed and received wide attention. This led to a substantial subsidy from the Royal Society and the British Government for the construction of the machine. Soon thereafter, however, Babbage became interested instead in developing a new idea involving a general purpose machine. This shift in plans left him unsupported by the Government and the original plan for the difference engine was abandoned.

Babbage's Analytical Engine. Babbage's next project was the "analytical engine," designed and partially built in 1830. This was to be the first completely automatic general purpose digital computer. According to the plan, the machine was to have an arithmetic unit designed to perform calculations based on numbers from a storage unit. Both the arithmetic and the storage units were to be governed by a control unit which would coordinate and supervise the sequence of operations.

Babbage worked on the analytical engine for the remaining years of his life but died in 1871 with the job uncompleted. Even though the analytical engine was never put into actual use, he must be given credit for having the original idea, and for recognizing the kind of problems which later occupied the efforts and talents of two generations of engineers. He is considered one of the great pioneers in the field of computation. In addition to having been a mathematician and a professor, he wrote over eighty books and papers. His son, Major General H. P. Babbage, took up his father's project and succeeded in completing part of the arithmetic unit after his father's death.

The Mark I Computer.   After Babbage died in 1871, no major advance in automatic computation was made until 1937, when Professor Howard Aiken of Harvard University became interested in combining some established principles with the punched cards pioneered by Hollerith and Powers to build an automatic calculating device. In May 1944, with the cooperation of I.B.M., an automatic-sequence-controlled calculator named the Harvard Mark I was built and formally presented to Harvard University.

Aiken's machine was built on the concept of using information from punched cards as input, making decimal calculations through electromechanical devices, and producing the results on punched cards again. The sequence of calculations was controlled through a wide-punched paper tape.

The machine was adapted to solve various kinds of problems for engineers, physicists and mathematicians, and was the first machine to do long series of arithmetic and logical problems. After the Mark I, Professor Aiken also constructed three more models, the Mark II, the Mark III, and the Mark IV.

The Mark I computer is considered to be the first successful general purpose digital computer. It is now on display at Harvard. Compared to today's computers, it is slow, but it is still in working condition.

The Eniac.   In the early 1940s, Dr. John W. Mauchly of the University of Pennsylvania became aware of the need for a high speed electronic device able to do great quantities of statistical calculations for weather data. During World War II, a contract for the project was made between the University of Pennsylvania and the United States government.

In 1945, Dr. Mauchly and J. Presper Eckert used the facilities at the Moore School of Electrical Engineering to design and build the Electronic Numerical Integrator and Calculator (ENIAC). Eniac was completely electronic in that it had no moving parts other than input/output gear. It was installed at the Aberdeen Proving Grounds in Maryland and was used until 1956, when it was removed to be placed in the Smithsonian Institution.

Mauchly and Eckert formed a company, subsequently acquired by the Sperry Rand Corporation, that played a major role in the development of the first commercial computer, the Univac.

Eniac was a large machine, containing 18,000 vacuum tubes. It had a small memory of 20 accumulators for storing data. Each accumulator was capable of carrying 10 digits. The accumulators consisted of vacuum tubes, tied together in packages of two, so that two tubes would represent one binary digit (*bit*) in computer storage. The machine was externally programmed, but had internal capacities of a multiplier, divider (which also functioned as a unit to take a square root), and three function tables. Input and output were made through punched cards.

In the mid-1940s, the best available electromechanical equipment could perform a maximum of one multiplication per second. By contrast, Eniac could process 300 multiplications per second. A job that took 300 days to complete by hand could be accomplished in a day with Eniac. The main point was not so much that the Eniac worked faster than other equipment, but that—by combining operations—jobs that had been considered impossible before could now be performed.

Also in the mid-1940s, Dr. J. von Neumann, another pioneer, issued a report to a group connected with the Moore School of Electrical Engineering at the University of Pennsylvania, in which he described the basic philosophy of computer design. This philosophy has been incorporated in today's computers. Von Neumann himself did not believe that all his theories were practical, but with today's advanced technology, almost everything he described in his theoretical paper has become reality. It is not uncommon to hear that computers were designed based on the "von Neumann concept."

The Edvac.   As a result of Dr. von Neumann's paper, the Electronic Discrete Variable Automatic Computer (EDVAC) was built. It was smaller in size, but greater in power, than its predecessors. Numbers were represented internally in powers of 2, or in what is referred to as the *binary* numbering system.

Before Edvac, all computer programs had been wired externally by hand. Coincident with its design, the notion of internal programming was born. In May 1945, Dr. von Neumann wrote the first program, an internal sorting routine consisting of the rearrangement of numbers in ascending sequences, in an attempt to prove that computers could be used in projects *other than those of a scientific* nature. The sorting routine ran a job three times faster than a card sorter.

The Univac.   The Univac (Universal Automatic Calculator), manufactured and designed by the Sperry Rand Corporation, is considered the first step toward completely automatic data processing. Previously computers had been built only for scientific and engineering data processing purposes. The Univac was popularized through television quiz shows and various other demonstrations, and is well known for having predicted the victory of President Dwight D. Eisenhower in the presidential election of 1952. It was the Univac that led the public to believe that the computer was an "electronic brain" and might become a replacement for "brains."

Although many tube-type computers are still operating satisfactorily, the advent of the transistor (commonly referred to as "solid state") has greatly improved the efficiency of computer operations. A transistor is much smaller than a vacuum tube. Solid state computers are much more compact than tube type computers; they require less rigid air conditioning, have a greater life expectancy, and are less susceptible to failure. Solid state computers are much more reliable than tube-type computers.

Computer manufacturers are constantly trying to develop computers with a longer life and of a smaller size, capable of storing more data and operating at greater speeds.

In 1943 there were no electronic computers available. Ten years later, many electronic calculators were commercially available, but the general purpose, stored-program electronic digital computer was not yet widely used. Between 1953 and 1958, hundreds of vacuum tube computers were put into operation. Most of the small size to medium size models had magnetic drum storage, while only the largest computers contained magnetic core storage. In 1959 the use of vacuum tube computers almost ceased when transistorized computers began to appear on the market. Since their appearance, thousands of transistorized computers have been delivered and installed.

Computers are generally classified as small, medium, or large scale. This classification is not necessarily an indication of their physical size (although large scale computers do require more floor space), but rather is used as a general price-scale categorization. Small scale computers range up to $100,000 each; medium scale computers between $100,000 and $750,000; and large scale computers, from $750,000 upward.

A recent industry report indicated that approximately 61,000 computer systems were installed in 1970, with a cumulative net value of over $26 billion. By contrast, 244 systems were installed in 1955 (cumulative value of $177 million); 5,400 systems in 1960; 23,000 systems in 1965; 47,000 systems in 1968; and 54,000 systems in 1969. It is estimated that over 200,000 computers will be in operation by 1975 and approximately 375,000 computers by 1980, at a cost of over $75 billion.

Many computer firms are engaged in supplying the market with computers of various sizes and speed. The following table illustrates the value of shipments made in 1968 by key American computer firms and the percentage of the total shipments each firm contributed:

Computer Firm *	Shipments in $ Millions	Percentage
International Business Machines	$5,200	72.2%
Univac	380	5.3
Honeywell	340	4.7
Control Data Corporation	305	4.2
General Electric	280	3.9
Radio Corporation of America	225	3.1
Burroughs	170	2.4
National Cash Register	170	2.4
Scientific Data Systems	75	1.0
Digital Equipment Corporation	35	0.5
Others	20	0.3
	$7,200	100.0

* SOURCE: EDP Industry Report (March 25, 1969), p. 2.

In recent years, the trend has been toward producing medium scale computer systems. The larger, more powerful systems have been used primarily for scientific and engineering purposes. Current and future trends may very likely move toward the production of small scale computers, especially since electronic data processing has made a powerful appeal to the small businessman.

A WORD ABOUT GENERATIONS

Traditionally, computer systems have been classified by "generations." *First generation* computers (e.g., the UNIVAC I) were made of vacuum tubes. The larger systems were so bulky that they required the space of two or more rooms. By contrast, *second generation* computers (e.g., IBM 1401) were built of transistors (originally developed in 1948 by Bell Laboratories) which reduced the whole computer to the size of a standard size desk. The beginning of transistorized commercial computers came in 1959. Today, we have *third generation* computers (e.g., IBM 360), which utilize solid state logic technology and have over one thousand times the speed of the first commercial computers of the early 1950s.

Conjecture regarding *fourth generation* computers began while the first third generation computers were being delivered. *Hardware* (or equipment) specialists believe that fourth generation systems are likely to be characterized either by medium scale or by large scale integration of circuitry. This means that the concept of solid state logic will be extended and combined to produce more compact computer circuits. While this viewpoint is tacitly acknowledged, it does not seem representative of the actual progression of computer development, since it is mainly concerned with increasing the speed of computation rather than changes in basic philosophy.

The *software* conception of "generations" suggests a classification of a different orientation. *First generation* computers used machine-language programming technique, while *second generation* computers marked the advent of symbolic assembly language programming languages such as Autocoder. *Third generation* computers emphasize the use of high-level programming languages such as COBOL. It can be inferred that each generation of computers represents a step in the march toward a truly user-oriented computer system. In this respect, the software orientation provides a relatively clearer chronicle of the advancement of the computer.

Glossary of Terms

ABACUS: A manual calcualting device that uses beads to represent decimal values.

EDVAC: An electronic automatic computer which represents data in a binary form.

ENIAC: A high-speed electronic computer designed and built by Mauchly and Eckert at the University of Pennsylvania.

NAPIER'S "BONES": A technique introduced by John Napier to aid multiplication through the use of data tables or rods.

SIMULTANEOUS PUNCHING PRINCIPLES: Introduced by James Powers, whereby all the required information to be punched is initially accumulated and then punched simultaneously in a card.

Questions for Review

1. What is finger counting? Show how the product of multiplying 7 x 8 is obtained.
2. What is an abacus? Explain its basic operation and origin.
3. Discuss the primitive era of manual record keeping.
4. List and describe briefly three early mechanical calculating devices.
5. How do Napier's "bones" perform multiplication?
6. Who invented the first mechanical digital calculator? Why?
7. In what way did Jacquard contribute to the development of automatic equipment? Explain.
8. Describe the main contributions of Hollerith to the development of punched-card data processing.
9. Explain the main contributions of Powers to punched card data processing. What company currently practices and develops machines based on his ideas?
10. Present a brief historical review of I.B.M. How is Hollerith connected with this firm?
11. What is the main idea behind Babbage's difference engine? Illustrate.
12. What are some of the unique characteristics of the Mark I?
13. In reviewing the steady growth of the computer industry over the past two decades, what is your assessment of its future? Why?
14. Distinguish the difference among the three generations of computers. How are fourth generation computers likely to be different from the ones used at present?
15. In view of the current state of technology in this field, do you feel there is a need for fourth generation computers? Why?

chapter four

BUSINESS AND SCIENTIFIC DATA PROCESSING

DATA PROCESSING, functionally described, is subject to an all-inclusive interpretation. Operations as simple as routine additions or as complex as processing linear programming or operations research models have been labeled as data processing. Historically, however, data processing, *per se,* became a commonly used term when the electronic computer became commercially available. The process of data handling by mechanical or electromechanical methods adopted the label "machine tabulation" and the machines used in this process were referred to as "tabulating (or tab) equipment."

Generally, data processing applications are oriented to either business or science. Due to the nature and/or requirements of business data, business applications are characterized by a large volume of input and output, requiring a relatively small amount of machine calculation or "internal" processing. Scientific applications, while they function with relatively limited input or output volume, require extensive machine calculation. With this distinction, a scientific installation is often characterized as a "large computer humming away for hours to produce one or two pages of vital output." By contrast, business applications are typical of a single computer digesting data from thousands of punched cards or many reels of magnetic tape and printing information (output) on a continuous stream of paper.

It has been estimated that at least one sixth of our total gross national product (GNP) is devoted to handling paper. Computers make a tremendous contribution by doing this work more quickly, efficiently and economically.

A businessman's judgment can be no better than his source of information. Through the use of automatic data processing, today's decisions can be based on today's conditions, not on last month's. Masses of confusing details can quickly be analyzed to produce the information needed to operate the business. Changes in business requirements, in turn, encourage a sustaining development of new data processing systems.

There are three main ways in which computers are used in business. First they are used to print the necessary information for instructing the organization how to act in accordance with certain predetermined decisions. Second, routine management decisions may be made by programming the computers to signal certain conditions and perform the necessary action, such as reordering stock when the inventory reaches a predetermined "low limit." Finally, the most important way in which computers are being used in business is in the preparation of feedback information and progress reports for management's use in controlling the whole operation.

With these factors in mind, it becomes increasingly evident that a knowledge of the principles of automatic data processing is essential to anyone who plans to enter the business world. In this chapter, the term "business" is used in a broad sense, and "business applications" are any nonscientific data processing requirements of industry and government.

BUSINESS DATA PROCESSING

Business data processing is an area including the storage and maintenance of records required in the everyday conduct of a business organization. The business may be as small as the corner soda fountain or as large and complex as General Motors. The more complex a business organization, the greater is the amount of data.

Regardless of size, the general requirements of data processing are about the same. Records must be maintained and periodically updated. Reports must be prepared and presented to the proper administrators. Materials must be ordered at the proper time. Employees must be paid the correct amount and on time.

For illustrative purposes, let us take a look at a corner soda fountain and see just what requirements the proprietor has for a data processing system. He sells ice cream and a few other refreshments. When the need arises, he employs part-time student help after school hours and on weekends. His business is considered a one-man operation and is referred to as a "proprietorship."

A small business like this would not require the use of a computer, perhaps not even an adding machine, to keep going. Despite the simplicity of a small business, however, certain records must be kept, and other details related to those records must be filed for future reference. They may be filed either in one's head, as might be the case here, or in the case of documents such as receipts and tax reports, filed in an old roll-top desk or a filing cabinet.

Suppose that the proprietor has introduced a special sale on strawberry sundaes. For what reason is a reduction in price made? Does he need to increase his sales because of his immediate need for cash, or is it done out of the goodness of his heart? Assuming that he is an experienced businessman, the introduction of a "special" on any item presumably is done to minimize costs (or losses) and to maximize profits. The store's proprietor might have looked in his back room the day before the sale and found an excess of six gallons of strawberry syrup. He knew then that if he did not sell it quickly, it might spoil and he would have to throw it out. Besides, since his stock room is limited in size, he probably felt the need to conserve space. Expected delivery of other items may have put pressure on him to find room for the new merchandise. Regardless of the exact reason for the sale, it is obvious that the proprietor must keep regular control over his salable stock. This practice is one of the main functions performed by data processing.

For his part-time helper, the owner determines the amount of time he should work, his hourly rate and his total weekly pay. This process is as simple, in some instances, as multiplying 22 hours of work by $1.50 per hour, arriving at $33.00 in weekly wages. The problem becomes more involved when we consider the fact that the proprietor is required by law to withhold federal income tax, state tax (if any), social security (FICA), and other related taxes from his helper's earnings each week. At the end of the year, he also must be prepared to report both to his helper and to the Internal Revenue Service the exact earnings of his employee and the amount(s) withheld. The procedure of determining employee earnings, and the preparation of their checks for a given period, is referred to as preparing "payroll."

This payroll problem, even when it involves only one employee, is not simple. There is the need to prepare some sort of Profit and Loss Statement, compute various taxes, pay a variety of insurance premiums, and other similar items. One may wonder how the owner ever has enough time to do anything but keep records.

The proprietor must have a system which he follows regularly. As soon as data originate, he files them away—in his head or in his desk—for future reference. After the data are processed in some way (such as filling out a tax form), the results, or reports, are filed for future reference.

Not all business firms operate in this relatively simple manner. Larger firms have established highly advanced and more efficient systems of processing data due to the fact they have more paperwork problems to be handled, the magnitude of each problem is greater, and the problems are infinitely more complex.

THE BUSINESS ORGANIZATION—ITS MAKEUP AND INFORMATION FLOW

To get a better understanding of the factors involved in processing business data, it is necessary to understand the makeup of a business organization and the way in which information flows between its various departments or divisions.

A business organization is defined as a human relationship in group activity, similar to that of a social structure. It usually consists of a group of people whose activities are varied and who are related to one another by a superior-subordinate relationship (the governing basis of business operations), referred to as the "chain of command." This superior-subordinate relationship forms the pathway of control and is one of the components of information flow. Its function is to accomplish a major goal or combination of goals, such as the manufacture of a product or the rendering of a service.

In Fig. 4-1, we diagram the functions of the proprietor of a soda fountain. These functions include buying, selling, receiving, maintaining records, hiring and preparing financial statements.

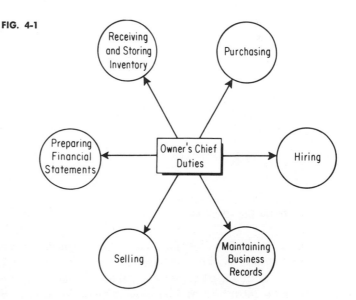

FIG. 4-1

As a small business concern expands, additional help is needed. This point is reached usually when the owner and a helper no longer can handle all the various activities effectively. The helper probably was hired originally because of sporadic increases in sales during some store hours, especially on weekends. In this case, the subordinate may be assigned to do certain chores, thus relieving his superior to do other things or to help keep up with the extra work generated as a result of the increase in business.

Figure 4-2 shows how this subordinate-superior relationship affects a reorganization of the workload.

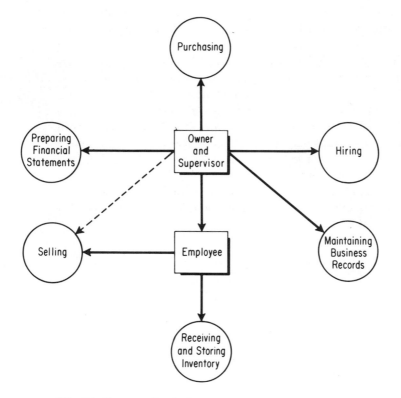

FIG. 4-2   The expanding business

A Growing Business

The owner may expand his soda fountain business by adding more tables and stools, and by ordering more merchandise. If he desires to have a unique product of his own, he may decide to make his own ice cream. When a decision to introduce and produce a new product is made, the owner quite possibly will be faced with a need for more men, materials, money, methods (techniques), and "know-how."

Figure 4-3 shows the growing business, which now includes two main departments, Sales and Production.

FIG. 4-3   The new organization chart in condensed form

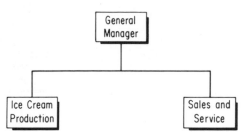

In order to begin producing ice cream, the owner will need to hire enough employees to make the desired quantity within the required specifications. Having more employees will increase the payroll problem. A bookkeeper may be hired to maintain records, file reports, prepare financial statements, and produce the payroll. Two girls may be needed as sales clerks.

Figure 4-4 is an organization chart showing these new employees, the work they do, and their relationship to the "boss" and to each other. Rectangles denote the position held. Circles stand for the duties performed.

Basic Requirements of a Business

In order to set up and operate this growing business, the owner (or perhaps, by now, he has taken in a partner) must (1) buy from other companies, called vendors, such items as machinery, equipment, paper supplies, and other goods needed to make and package the product he wishes to sell; and (2) sell, or market, his product either to the consumer or to other companies or both.

Production Planning.   Figure 4-4 shows the areas in which data are originated, collected, manipulated and later summarized in the form of financial reports for the manager. A description of how the information flows and the data it creates is helpful in understanding the stages of data processing to be described later.

In a large manufacturing firm, a decision is made involving the quantity and type of products to be made. A quota is determined, based on the actual amount sold, the quantity on hand, and the estimated sales volume for a specified period of time in the future. The sales department provides information concerning the actual quantity sold to date and also helps to forecast future sales. A production order is prepared, authorizing the manufacture of the needed quantity.

Suppose, for example, the owner estimates sales of 1,000 gallons of ice cream during the month of December. A check on the warehouse shows a stock of 800 gallons on hand. This means that a production order for 200 gallons should be executed to fill the projected sales quota of 1,000 gallons.

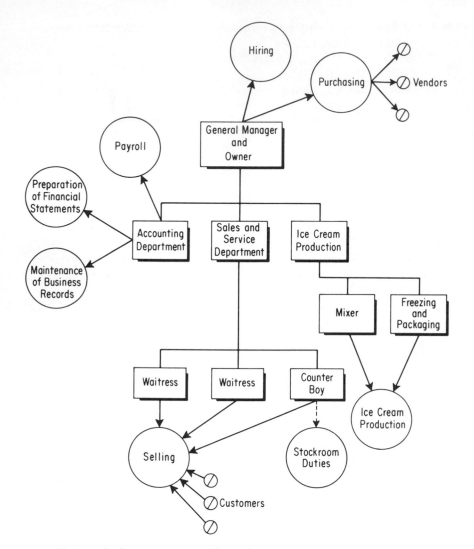

FIG. 4-4 The business structure—selling and producing

Purchasing. The stock room should hold all raw materials needed for the production of a finished unit. It must be prepared to give the production department the right quantity of each raw material at the time it is needed. Any depleted ingredient must be reordered and restocked promptly.

Suppose there are enough ingredients in the stock room to manufacture only 80 gallons of ice cream. A purchase order (Fig. 4-5) must be issued to authorize the acquisition of ingredients for an additional 120 gallons, plus enough extra ingredients to provide a satisfactory inventory backup to cover unforeseen emergencies and the start of the following month's production. If the vendor requires two weeks to receive, process, and deliver the order, the stock room must maintain enough "safety stock" to prevent a complete shutdown during that period.

The purchasing process is a common application of data processing. Purchasing involves obtaining the materials that go into the finished product and making sure that it is available on time. Before purchasing an item, several competitive brands of similar quality are sampled. After consideration of factors such as price, quality, and value is made, a purchase order for the needed quantity is mailed to the chosen vendor. A carbon copy of the order is sent also to the stock room as advance notice of the forthcoming shipment.

Figure 4-6 shows the relationship of this function to the operation of a manufacturing business (see page 48).

Receiving. When a shipment arrives from a vendor, the stock-room clerk verifies the items in the shipment, their quantity, and their specifications against a copy of the original purchase order. Next he notifies the purchasing department of its arrival and the satisfactory condition of the contents. Upon receiving an invoice from the supplier, the purchasing department approves payment and sends the invoice to the accounting department for payment.

FIG. 4-5 Purchase order—an example

No. 1607

FRANK'N MARY'S SODA FOUNTAIN
1137 Oak Avenue,
Park Ridge, Ill.

To: DELIGIANNIS, INC.,
    601 Jackson St.,
    Chicago, Ill.

Date   *Aug. 30. 1970*
Delivery   *Before Sept. 15*
Ship via   *Best way*
f.o.b.
Terms   *2/10, n/30*

Quantity	Description	Price
20 dozens	sugar cones	3.80
5 lbs.	espresso coffee	4.75
1 gallon	cognac	4.25
11 lbs.	vanilla	8.14
20 lbs.	granulated sugar	11.00
10 lbs.	almond extract	9.60
9 lbs.	pistachio nuts	9.54
3 lbs.	macadamia nuts	3.90
2 lbs.	cinnamon	3.10
4 gallons	light rum	17.20

FRANK 'N MARY

Req. No. *T 01*

By *Frank Whitehead*
authorized signature

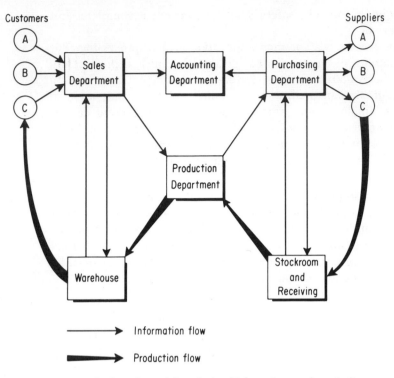

Customers

A

B

Sales Department → Accounting Department ← Purchasing Department

C

Suppliers

A

B

C

Production Department

Warehouse

Stockroom and Receiving

⟶ Information flow

⟹ Production flow

FIG. 4-6 The flow of materials and related information—a schematic diagram

An invoice (Fig. 4-7) is a detailed account of the merchandise shipped by the vendor, including the quantity, the unit price, and the total dollar value of the order, including any allowable discounts to which the purchaser is entitled.

Disbursements. Once the accounting department receives the invoice, the bookkeeper goes through the routine of writing and mailing a check (Fig. 4-8) for the amount owed, less any applicable discounts.

Discounts frequently are offered to those who order merchandise in relatively large quantities (for example, units of 100 or 1,000 case lots, etc., depending upon the product involved). The idea is that such a discount will encourage volume buying, and that the person or company which does so is entitled to a reduced unit price.

Cash discounts, on the other hand, are designed to encourage prompt payment. It is common for a vendor to allow a discount of, say 2 percent if the bill is paid within a specified period of time (for example, 10 days from the date of the invoice).

Stockkeeping. The incoming shipment of materials is sent to the stock room, where a record is marked to indicate that such items now are "on hand." Every time the production department requisitions part of the stock, this record is used to indicate the amount withdrawn and the amount remaining on hand.

DELIGIANNIS, INC.,
601 Jackson St.,
Chicago, Ill.

Invoice No. _4001_

FOR CUSTOMER'S USE ONLY

Register No.	Voucher No.
f.o.b. checked	
Terms approved	Price approved _Q.E.T._
Calculations checked _CRE_	
Satisfactory and approved	
Materials received _9/9/70_ _T Jones_	
date	signature
	Secretary title
Adjustments	
Audited _B. Clark_ Final Approval _F. Stukes_	

Customer's Order No. _1607_
and Date _8/30/70_

Requisition No. _T 10_

Contract No.

Sold To: FRANK 'N MARY'S SODA FOUNTAIN
           1137 Oak Avenue,
           Park Ridge, Ill.

Date Shipped: _Sept 8, 1970_   from _Cicero_

How shipped
& Route   _Gould & Sons, Inc._

Terms: _2/10, n/30_

Quantity	Description of Item	unit price	Amount
20 dozens	sugar cones	.19	3.80
5 lbs.	espresso coffee	.95	4.75
1 gallon	cognac	4.25	4.25
11 lbs.	vanilla	.74	8.14
20 lbs.	granulated sugar	.55	11.00
10 lbs.	almond extract	.96	9.60
9 lbs.	pistachio nuts	1.06	9.54
3 lbs.	macadmia nuts	1.30	3.90
2 lbs.	cinnamon	1.55	3.10
4 gallons	light rum	4.30	17.20

FIG. 4-7   Sales invoice—an example

49

Date	Invoice	Amount	FIRST NATIONAL BANK
9/11/70	4001	75.28	No. __1706__
			Chicago Sept. 11, 1970
			Pay to the Order of DELIGIANNIS, INC. $ __73.77__
			EXACTLY $ 73.00 and 73 CTS. ---------- dollars
			FRANK 'N MARY'S SODA FOUNTAIN
Total		75.28	*Frank Whitehead*
Discount		1.51	Authorized Signature
Net		73.77	

FIG. 4-8 Payment check

This procedure, referred to as inventory keeping, lets management know its materials situation at all times, and is helpful in assuring that production will never have to stop for lack of materials.

Periodically, a physical count of the inventory in stock is taken to verify the actual materials on hand with those shown on the records. This operation not only verifies the accuracy of the inventory records, but it also performs two other vital functions: (1) it helps to pinpoint waste, loss, or pilferage; and (2) it provides management with important information to be used for cost analyses, financial reports (inventory, after all, is an "asset"), government reports, and the like.

Production.   No sale can be made unless a product is available, both for sale and delivery. Products are made either by special order or in advance of sale. In the former case, orders first must be received from a customer and then the production department begins to manufacture the merchandise to meet the customer's requirements.

The more common type of production is the manufacture of merchandise in advance of its sale or the receipt of an order. This requires a reasonable forecast of future sales volume, and the risk is commensurate with the reliability of the data from which such a forecast is made. If the forecast was low, the company will run out of merchandise and have to pass up sales. If it was high, the company will overproduce and an excess of merchandise will have to be held in costly warehouses or be sold at reduced prices in order to prevent it from spoiling, going out of style, etc.

All finished merchandise is transferred from the production department to a warehouse, where it is stored until receipt of authorization to ship it to a specific customer.

Sales.   Basically, the ice-cream company used in our example—like any other business organization—operates with *profit* as its ultimate goal. Profit comes from sales, either of a product or a service. Thus, in most organizations, a sales department is set up. The number of salesmen depends largely on the volume of sales, the type of product, the number of customers, the demand for the product, and the geographic area to be covered.

When a customer orders a given product, the transaction may be in cash or in credit. If the order is on credit, approval of the customer's credit rating becomes necessary. A copy of the sales invoices is sent to the credit or accounting department, along with the customer's history card (if any). The history card contains a complete record of the customer's past purchases and history of payment.

Usually, customers have a credit limit, based on their ability to pay and on their reliability. If the present order exceeds the credit limit, the credit manager may either disapprove the sale or may ask the customer for an advance payment equal to the amount beyond this limit.

Assuming that an agreement is reached regarding credit terms, the credit department approves the sale, setting a number of activities into action. A copy of the invoice is sent to the warehouse, authorizing shipment of the merchandise. When the merchandise is shipped, the sales and credit departments are notified. The sale is recorded in the accounts receivable journal, where an entry is made to debit the customer's account by the amount of the purchase. Next, a statement is prepared and mailed to the customer for payment. When the bill is paid, an entry is made in the journal to reduce the customer's obligation by that amount, and a suitable entry is recorded on the customer's credit history card.

Preparation of Reports. Business reports are statements used as controls by management in conducting business activities. They provide feedback to various internal and external sources, such as owners, managers, creditors and government agencies. A report is a key function, involving various segments of the organization.

The foregoing illustration described a manufacturing and distribution cycle, which begins with planning for production and ends in the sale of a finished product. This cycle continues as long as the firm remains in *profitable* operation.

The company's earning capability usually is shown through an Income Statement (Fig. 4-9). This financial statement is constructed from data collected in the general ledger and contains all financial details pertaining to sales, cost of goods sold, operating expenses and other related information.

Note that the statement is developed by subtracting expenses from revenues. If revenues exceed expenses, the remainder is profit. If expenses exceed revenues, the difference is loss.

At present, major changes in data processing orientation dominate various organizations. Quantitative approach to decision making through the use of the computer in manipulating mathematical and statistical techniques sheds a different light on the training and background of decision makers. Executives of various levels now need to have an understanding of the makeup and interrelationship of a data processing system in order to be better able to evaluate and analyze the changes made and the requirements demanded by electronic computers.

FRANK'N MARY'S SODA FOUNTAIN
INCOME STATEMENT
FOR THE YEAR ENDED 12/31/70

Net sales		$16,000
Cost of goods sold:		
Beginning inventory (12/31/69)	$4,000	
Net purchases	2,500	
	$6,500	
Ending inventory (12/31/70)	2,600	
		3,900
Gross profit on sales		$12,100
Selling expenses	$3,000	
General expenses	3,450	
Total operating expenses		6,450
Net income before taxes		$ 5,650
Income tax		2,700
NET INCOME		$ 2,950

FIG. 4-9 Income statement—an example

At this point, we can conclude that for a firm's information system to function properly requires the joint, coordinated effort of its human, procedural and physical components which generate and feed desired information to areas such as production, purchasing, personnel, sales, distribution and accounting. Each of these areas relies on data processing systems for proper operation of its activities. (See Fig. 4-10.) Integrating these areas into a data

FIG. 4-10 Formal information system

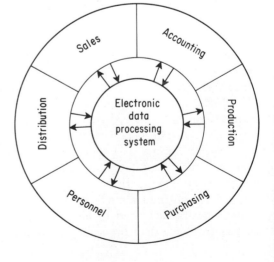

processing system is not always easy to do, but accomplishing such a goal usually reduces data processing costs and produces more meaningful reports for more effective control of the organization. This is the aim and objective of an automatic data processing system.

AUTOMATIC DATA PROCESSING IN THE SCIENTIFIC WORLD

In the past, many scientific problems were left unsolved because of the seemingly impossible task of processing a variety of complex formulas by manual methods. The present use of electronic data processing has given the scientist and engineer tools with which to handle such involved computations. Problems that would have taken a lifetime of calculations to solve in the past now are being processed by computers in a matter of minutes. Some problems with a large number of variables and restrictions could never have been handled by ordinary means; today, computers process them with comparative ease. With the new tools of automatic data processing, scientists in both basic and applied research have widened their horizons and have given new freedom to creative thought.

What Is Scientific Data Processing?

Scientific data processing consists mainly of solving mathematical problems such as engineering formulas, research and development problems, or any type of calculation that normally requires a "one-time" solution. Unlike most business problems, scientific problems are generally not repetitive.

The scientist and engineer must solve problems with many variables, dealing with probabilities, statistical equations, and so on. This presents a different kind of problem for the computer than the typical business application, which usually involves a high volume of input and output but limited arithmetic requirements. Consequently, scientific and business computers have generally been different in design, despite the fact that many so-called business computers are being used for certain scientific and engineering applications. The reverse is also true in a few cases.

Depending on the complexity of the project, the data gathering function in a scientific setting extends over a long period of time and produces a large volume of raw data for processing. This function is usually delegated to the rank-and-file subordinates, including graduate students. Once the raw data become available, they are converted (reduced) to a form appropriate for analysis. Since manual reduction is a tedious process and subject to error, automated electronic methods become instrumental in speeding up this phase.

Analysis of reduced data is a comparatively complex and sophisticated phase. The calculative power of an electronic computer is used to ease the burden of analysis, which is often unmanageable by manual or electromechanical devices. Finally, analyzed data are evaluated by the scientist(s) in charge and the results are interpreted in light of prior knowledge and experience.

Based on the foregoing, it can be observed that a scientific organization approaches a scientific problem in a unique way. Science is generally concerned with the production of new knowledge through the creative manipulation of existing knowledge. By contrast, business is primarily concerned with the production of physical goods through the utilization of other physical goods. However, although scientific data may differ from business data, the pattern of processing is quite similar. That is, a system must first be devised. Second, a problem must exist that can be represented in a form acceptable to the data processing system at hand.

As tools for the engineer, computers are one of the vital elements in the field of automation. They have been linked to metal-working tools, production mills, and processing plants. Some computers are even being used to design other computers—planning the wiring circuitry and issuing instructions to the automatic equipment which physically wires the circuits.

Through the use of a device called a *plotter,* which may be connected to a computer, charts and graphs may be produced. By the introduction of engineering specifications into such a machine, mechanical drawings can be created. Multiple drawings, representing views from changing angles, also have been used to "animate" movies of such complex things as the approach of an attacking aircraft on a "pursuit curve."

Researchers at the University of Pennsylvania in Philadelphia, working with the American Cancer Society, are using computers to simulate the growth of cancer cells, saving many years of study. Computer analyses of millions of medical records are giving the medical profession new insights into causes and possible cures of many diseases. Other uses include certain specialized applications. A patient's symptoms can be entered into the computer as source data, for example, and then the system can manipulate these data and correctly diagnose the patient's illness.

The Armed Forces require many types of problem solutions produced by a workable data processing system. After missiles are launched into orbit, for example, they are constantly checked to make sure they are following a preplanned course.

Enemy aircraft are detected and positioned by radar. Courses and speed are worked out by computer systems to enable our own fighter planes or rockets to intercept and destroy them.

These and other problems can be solved in fractions of seconds, provided the proper electronic data processing techniques are employed. But again, regardless of the system used, the steps in solving the problem are much the same as those described earlier.

Glossary of Terms

BUSINESS DATA PROCESSING: Data processing for business purposes, e.g., recording and summarizing the financial transactions of a business.

BUSINESS ORGANIZATION: A framework which ties together the activities of a business to induce integrated performance. Also, a human relationship in group activity.

CASH DISCOUNT: A fixed amount or a percentage deducted by the seller from the price of an item for inducing cash payment by the buyer.

PLOTTER: A visual display or board in which a dependent variable is graphed by an automatically controlled pen or pencil as a function of one or more variables.

PRODUCTION: Conversion of basic raw materials into a product sold by a business firm.

PROFIT AND LOSS STATEMENT: A financial statement showing the company's earning capability during a specific period of time.

PURCHASE ORDER: A requisition made by the purchasing department to a supplier for meeting the needs of a division or a department (for example, production department) of the firm.

Questions for Review

1. In what ways are computers used in business? Explain.
2. What is business data processing? What are some of its requirements?
3. Prepare a 300–400 word report about the data processing requirements of a small business in your neighborhood.
4. Discuss the primary functions of a business organization.
5. Explain briefly the information flow that takes place in a manufacturing enterprise.
6. What is purchasing? How does a purchasing department contribute to the smooth operation of the production division of a business firm?
7. Why are discounts of various types introduced? Explain.
8. What are the chief reasons for taking a physical count of inventory in stock?
9. "Persia, Incorporated," is an independent rug dealer in Chicago, Ill. His ledger accounts for the month of January, 1970 show the following data:

Sales for the month	$27,000
Cost of goods sold	11,000
Rent expense	1,200
Salaries	3,400
Office supplies	200

Based on the above account balances, prepare a profit and loss statement.

10. How is scientific data processing similar to business data processing? For what reason(s) is it used?

chapter five

THE DATA PROCESSING CYCLE

CHAPTER 4 PRESENTED the makeup of a business organization, the major departments it contains, and the flow of information between those departments. To facilitate this flow of information, many steps are necessary. They might be as easy as typing a purchase order or transferring an invoice from one department to another, or as complex as determining a detailed payroll of several thousand employees each week. The composite of these steps is commonly referred to as the data processing cycle.

Data processing may be divided into five separate but related steps. They are: (1) origination, (2) input, (3) manipulation, (4) output, and (5) storage.

ORIGINATION

It should be kept in mind that "to process" means to do something with or to "manipulate" existing information so that the result is a meaningful contribution to the goals set by the company. The existing information is generally original in nature and is either handwritten or typewritten. Original papers are commonly referred to as *source documents*. Examples of source documents are checks, time cards and sales orders.

What type of source documents did the soda fountain proprietor have, for example, and where did they originate? The proprietor received an invoice from the vendor every time merchandise was delivered. The invoice is a source document. The number of hours the clerks and employees worked constituted the source information to be used by the bookkeeper. Presumably, those hours were recorded on some sort of time card or sheet—a source document. The "checks" that were written by the waitresses, presented to the customers, and paid to the cashier contained source information regarding the day's sales. They are source documents.

In Fig. 5-1 two transactions have been completed: (1) the sale of two radios, and (2) the sale of one television set. The invoice containing these two transactions is a source document. Producing source documents, then, is the first step in a series of steps included in the data processing cycle.

INPUT

The input phase involves collecting data generated by various types of transactions. In a business organization, for example, basic data are generated when an order is placed, when a complaint is filed, when a given service is requested, or when an invoice is received. They could be in the nature of names and addresses, product description, quantities, or special instructions, making up the stage upon which the manipulation phase is later performed.

Thus, after certain source documents are originated, or have been made available, the next step is to introduce the information they contain into the data proc-

ABC Company				
Alton, Illiniois				
Cat. No.	Quan-tity	Description	Unit Cost	Total
56041	2	Radio	1500	3000
42461	1	Television	9500	9500

FIG. 5-1 Source document—a sales invoice showing two transactions

essing system. This system may be manual, mechanical, electromechanical, or electronic. Let us assume, for this illustration, that the system is manual, where people are used to process data with the aid of paper and pencil.

Input data consist of original (raw) transactions in need of processing. The device used to record the two transactions in Fig. 5-1 is called an input device. In manual data processing, a pencil is an input device, since it records the transaction and other related information. The pencil also is used as an output device, since once a computation has been completed, it records the answer.

Recording is the means by which an input device facilitates the presentation of source data for processing. Proper recording of source data involves: (1) determining what transaction needs processing. This is necessary especially in cases where the result of processing a given transaction is required for the successful processing of subsequent transactions. (2) The transaction should be checked to make sure it accurately represents the event or condition involved. Manual recording of transactions is not as accurate as machine recording. The human eye can deceive. Catalog number 56041 in Fig. 5-1 may be incorrectly recorded as 56401 or 50641. This type of error is referred to as "transposition." Extra care must be taken to assure the accuracy of recorded data.

A given transaction can be coded, or condensed, to help make further processing more efficient and convenient. For example, an employee's name may be coded by assigning him a number (for example, his social security number or telephone number). Reading a number is more convenient and more accurate than reading a name since several people may have the same name.

The result of data processing can be no more accurate than the source information, so input accuracy is paramount.

MANIPULATION

When input data are recorded and verified, they are ready to be processed. The human eye is the device used to feed input data to the brain, where mental calculations are made. The "eye" of a punched card data processing system is the reading brush, which is installed in an input device to "read" input data and transfer them into the system for manipulation or processing.

"Manipulation" involves the actual work performed on the source data before any meaningful results can be realized. To *manipulate* data means to perform any or all of the subfunctions of (1) classifying, (2) sorting, (3) calculating, (4) recording, and (5) summarizing.

Classifying

Classifying facilitates the arrangement of data in a proper form so that they can be used effectively in the preparation of reports. Assume, for example, that a stack of invoices needs to be filed.

Following the manual process, a filing clerk can do one of two things. He can take the first invoice in the stack and file it in the proper folder by locating the identifying code name, number, etc., as in Fig. 5-2, where the clerk would take the invoice bearing the name "Jones" and file it in the "Jones" folder in the file cabinet.

Locating Jones's folder involves searching the file alphabetically until Jones's file is found. This becomes time-consuming when a great number of names are involved, ranging from "Adams" to "Zona," and the entire file must be searched for each name as it appears.

A more convenient and faster approach to the filing procedure is to *classify* all invoices by pregrouping or presorting them into alphabetical order. Following this approach, the ten invoices in Fig. 5-2 would be grouped as shown in Fig. 5-3. It is easier to file each invoice by dropping it into its proper location during a single alphabetical search through the cabinet.

In a mechanized procedure, a machine called the keypunch punches holes in standard size cards to record coded data representing each invoice. The data cards then can be fed through a *sorter* which places them in the same order as the existing file, and then into a *collator* which is wired to

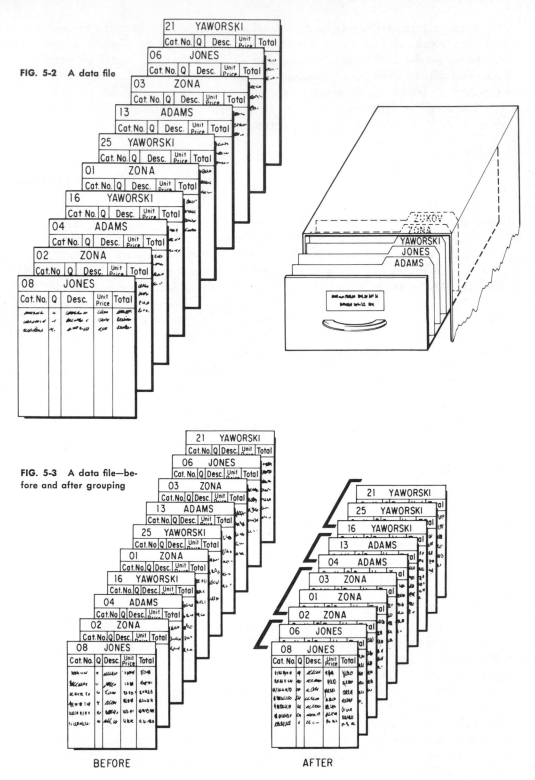

FIG. 5-2   A data file

FIG. 5-3   A data file—before and after grouping

BEFORE

AFTER

"merge" the new cards with the existing file automatically, producing the same result as that shown in Fig. 5-3.

Sorting is the process of arranging data into a predetermined alphabetic or numeric order, or of selecting particular data from a file according to some predetermined code classification.

Once the invoices in Fig. 5-3 are classified, further sorting of each group by invoice number before filing would help the filing clerk to complete his job much more quickly and efficiently (see Fig. 5-4).

FIG. 5-4 A grouped data file sorted by invoice number

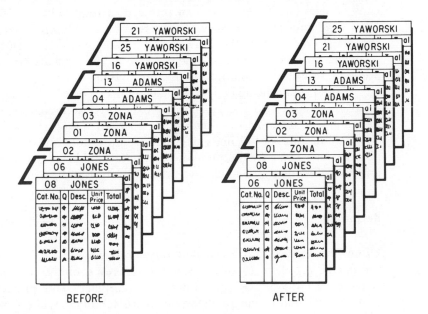

BEFORE   AFTER

After having sorted the invoices within each group by number, the clerk may simply pull out a group at a time and file the appropriate invoices accordingly.

These procedures could well be applied to many types of business. In the case of inventory work, for example, classification takes place when a stack of receipts is sorted by type, such as frozen foods, canned goods, school supplies. Once classified, each "substack" of receipts is used to verify the quantity of merchandise available in the store. Failure to classify and/or sort the receipts will cause the clerk to make a great many unnecessary visits to various parts of the store—to the freezer, where frozen foods are stored; to the back room, where canned foods are kept; and to the front of the store, where school supplies are displayed.

Even a small business can entail a great deal of time and trouble recording, classifying, and sorting data, as the previous examples illustrate. By contrast, a large business finds it an unacceptably time-consuming—and expensive—task to do the same thing, using manual methods. Most businesses, therefore, have resorted to a more efficient and sophisticated classifying and sorting technique. The more up-to-date firm already has resorted to mechanical, electro-mechanical, or electronic data processing equipment, motivated by the factors of accuracy, speed and economy.

Calculating

Calculating aids in the reconstruction of data by condensing and/or "rephrasing" certain facts leading to a desired solution. For example, to multiply five cans of soup by 10 cents per can produces a total value of 50 cents for the lot. Calculating is the most crucial phase of data manipulation, since it is in this stage that most of the work is performed toward the solution of a given problem. Calculating involves one or more of the four arithmetic functions of addition, subtraction, multiplication, and division.

Referring to the inventory problem, items received (say, 10 units of frozen goods) are added to the balance on hand, at last inventory 85 units, for a new total of 95 units—the *amount of goods available for sale.* In order to calculate the number of units sold, one would reduce the total quantity available for sale (95) by the number of units available in the freezer (say, 60); and the difference (35 units) would constitute the desired information.

Recording

Often, the answer to a given *part* of a problem is only a partial solution to the *overall* problem. In such cases, the recording of the intermediate answer is required until further processing can take place. This process is similar to that of a calculator that prints one or more subtotals, while retaining them in storage until a grand total can be reached. The subtotal is a partial answer which is recorded as a part of the report, but must be used later to produce the final result (the grand total).

Summarizing

Summarizing involves the compression of a mass of data into a concise and meaningful form. For decision making or control purposes, it is not necessary to present all the facts (for example, the entire list of items in inventory) to management if the total (say, the combined dollar value of the inventory) is all that management requires. As a manager, the storekeeper doesn't necessarily care to know that there are six gallons of strawberry syrup at the soda counter and twelve more in the back room; all he cares to know is that the total on hand equals eighteen gallons, or that the value of those eighteen gallons is so many dollars.

Summary reports are used for various purposes, some of which include income tax reporting, preparation of inventory status, profit and loss statements, and many others pertaining to the internal, as well as the external, activities of the business. It is important to remember at this point that the purpose of data processing is to provide useful management information, not to say how many calculations can be performed or how many reports can be generated.

OUTPUT

After input data have been fed into a data processing system and properly manipulated, the result is called "output." That is, the output phase (with form defined in advance) consists primarily of the preparation of business information in a form acceptable to the data processing system either for analysis or as input for a second cycle. In manual systems, this phase might be as basic as inserting a permanent record into the information flow. In automated data processing systems, the process might be one of converting a permanent record (readable by man) into a format that can be understood by a machine. An example is keypunching sales orders into order transaction cards.

Included in "output" is *communication*. Output is of little value unless it is communicated promptly and effectively. A report which indicates that a certain variety of frozen foods is out of stock is of no value until it reaches the attention of the manager who is responsible for ordering a new supply. Failure to communicate this information promptly—and to the proper person—is as wasteful as figuring out one's income tax and then failing to file the return.

The output, then, is the ultimate goal in data processing. The system must be capable of communicating quickly, completely, and accurately with the outside world (that is, with people who are related to the data processed by the system), in order to make available the results of its calculations. Only by communicating properly can corrective action be initiated.

The data processing cycle is incomplete without the concept (loop) of control. In a business organization, control depends basically upon a comparison between the attained results and the predetermined goals. When the results are compared with the goals, they either agree or they are different. If they agree, no action is taken and the operation is repeated as before. However, if a disagreement is detected, a decision is made to make the necessary changes before the operation is repeated again. This *feedback concept of control* is an essential part of data processing. That is, output is compared with a predetermined standard and a decision is made (if necessary) on a course of action and is communicated to the stage where it is to be taken.

STORAGE

Data related to or resulting from the previous four data processing steps can be *stored,* either temporarily or permanently, for future reference. It is necessary to store data, especially that pertaining to periodic reports, since they often are used over and over again in other related applications. A monthly profit and loss statement, for example, is used in compiling an annual report. A bank statement is carried over from one month to another in determining the balance-to-date. Employees' weekly wages are accumulated from payday to payday for use in annual and social security (FICA) reports.

Stored information can be raw, semiprocessed, or output data. Quite often, the output of one problem becomes the input to another. When this occurs, a cycle is created that can be repeated continuously until the major application is completely processed. In the case of inventory, any unsold canned goods at the end of the year (*ending* inventory) constitute the *beginning* inventory for the ensuing year.

There are several ways of storing information, ranging from a simple record in a ledger book (manual data storage) to the "memory" of a large-scale electronic computer (automatic data storage).

In conclusion, it must be kept in mind that within each of the areas comprising the data processing cycle are substeps related to input, manipulation and output. Some overlap can easily take place and the degree of interaction among these areas is governed by a continually changing relationship among the systems. In other words, the preparation of new data continues as previous data are processed and vice versa. While the phases can be isolated for descriptive purposes, their operations in practice, however, are constantly intertwined.

SUMMARY

The five basic functions of data processing are:

1. *Origination.* Determination of the nature, type, and origin of source documents.
2. *Input.* The introduction and feeding of source documents into a data processing system.
3. *Manipulation.* The performance of certain necessary operations on source data or input.
   (a) *Classifying.* Identification of like data according to common characteristics or types.
   (b) *Sorting.* Re-sequencing source data into some logical order or form.
   (c) *Calculating.* Reconstructing source data to create meaningful results through addition, subtraction, multiplication, or division.
   (d) *Recording.* Registering the result of calculations in a written or other suitable form.

(e) *Summarizing.* Reducing a mass of data into a meaningful and concise form.

4. *Output.* Producing and communicating the results of data manipulation in an intelligible form to the appropriate user.

5. *Storage.* Retaining a record of the output for future use or reference.

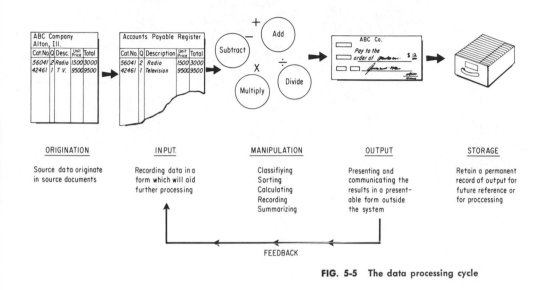

FIG. 5-5   The data processing cycle

Glossary of Terms

FEEDBACK: The part of a closed loop system which automatically brings back information about the condition under control.

MERGE: To combine two or more sets of data into one, usually in a specified sequence.

SOURCE DOCUMENT: A document from which basic data is extracted.

Questions for Review

1. What is a source document? Give examples.
2. List the five steps of data processing. Define each step briefly.
3. What is the difference between an input device and input medium? Explain by defining each and giving an example.
4. What factors are involved in the recording of source data? Explain.
5. Define the following terms:
   (a) Originating
   (b) Classifying
   (c) Calculating
   (d) Summarizing
   (e) Merging.
6. What is meant by feedback? Explain and give an example.

PUNCHED CARD
DATA PROCESSING–
A
SUMMARY

2

THE PUNCHED CARD

PART 2 OF THIS TEXT summarizes the basic steps of punched card data processing and the equipment involved.

The data processing cycle presented in Chapters 4 and 5 is similar to the data processing cycle employed in punched card processing. The chief differences are that punched card machines are mechanical (or electromechanical) rather than electronic, and that each machine performs its own independent function rather than working in union with the other machines in the system. The input medium is the punched card, and most card handling must be performed manually.

PUNCHED CARD CYCLE

The following outline introduces the punched card data processing cycle (see Fig. 6-1):

(1) Data Preparation. This involves the preparation of source documents such as time cards, checks, and invoices. These are prepared manually, either by manipulating a keyboard machine (for example, a typewriter or adding machine) or by using a pencil and paper (filling out a purchase order). A source document itself may be used as input under some circumstances.

Information from the source document is copied (recorded) on punched cards or punched paper tape. Represented by a coded system of holes, round or rectangular, the information can be read by various machines. It is then ready to be used for machine input.

(2) Data Processing. Once input cards are prepared, they are sorted, classified, and/or calculated, depending on the type of results required. Sort-

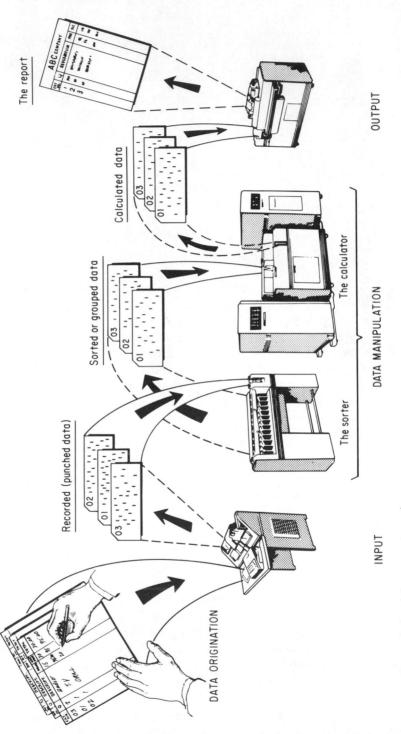

FIG. 6-1 The punched-card data processing cycle

DATA ORIGINATION

INPUT

The report

Calculated data

Sorted or grouped data

Recorded (punched data)

The calculator

The sorter

DATA MANIPULATION

OUTPUT

ABC COMPANY

ing is accomplished on a machine referred to as the *sorter*. Classifying is performed on a *collator*, and calculating is worked out on a *calculator*.

The subsequent chapters discuss these and other related machines which record, reproduce, verify, sort, merge, calculate and report facts. All use the punched card as an input medium.

WHAT IS A PUNCHED CARD?

The Hollerith card (referred to as the IBM card) is a rectangular piece of sturdy, high-quality paper that measures 7⅜ in. × 4¼ in. × .007 in. Data are stored by punching rectangular hole(s) in specific columns. It is capable of withstanding changes in temperature and humidity which would affect the physical shape of ordinary paper and cause it to jam the machines. Figure 6-2 is a blank Hollerith card with a left corner cut. This cut aids the operator in visually checking to see that all cards in a given deck are facing in the same direction.

FIG. 6-2   A Hollerith card

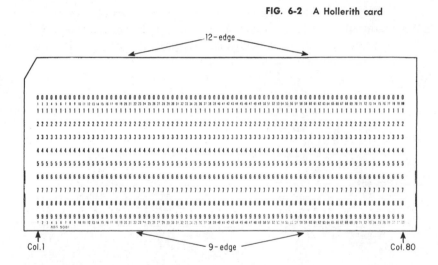

Col.1   9-edge   Col.80

The punched card is a common sight. Many gas and electric companies bill their customers on punched cards. High schools, colleges, and universities use them as class admission cards at the beginning of each term. Paychecks often are printed on them. They frequently are used not only as an input medium but as a source document and as an output medium.

Columns and Rows. The Hollerith card is divided into 80 columns, numbered (left to right) 1 through 80. Since each column can store one character of information, up to 80 characters of information can be stored on each card.

Horizontally, the punched card is divided into 12 punching positions, called *rows*. Row numbers 0 through 9 are shown on the card in Fig. 6-2, and are used to represent numeric data. The remaining two rows are 11 and 12 at the top of the card. Alphabetic information is represented by combining a punch in one of the top three rows with a punch in one of the numeric rows below.

"Edges" and "Faces." Cards are fed into a machine either "12-edge first" or "9-edge first." The top of a punched card is called the 12-edge; the bottom is called the 9-edge (Fig. 6-2).

Because of the positions of their reading brushes, certain machines require that punched cards be fed 12-edge first; other machines read from the 9-edge first.

Certain machines further require that the deck be either "face up" or "face down" in the hopper. The term "12-edge first, face down" means that the top edge of each card is fed through the slot first, with the printed side of the card down.

METHODS OF RECORDING DATA ON PUNCHED CARDS

Data, whether they are numeric (for example, employee number 14060), alphabetic (John Hill), or special (such as characters $, *, &, etc.), are recorded permanently on a card by punching holes in it with a keypunch. These holes code the data in a language understandable to the machines. As the cards pass through the machine, the data are "read" by a reading brush which makes contact with a roller beneath the card whenever one of the punched holes appears. When a hole is detected, the brush makes contact with the roller to complete an electrical circuit (Fig. 6-3). The specific position of the hole

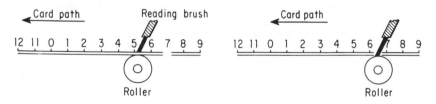

FIG. 6-3 A reading brush before (left) and during the detection of a hole in row 7 of a given column

on the card determines what digit the machine will read. A wired control panel then instructs the machine as to how it is to manipulate this data.

The Card Punching Positions

In order to determine the location of numeric and alphabetic characters on a card, the 12 horizontal card rows are divided into two categories: the digit-punching positions and the zone-punching positions. The digit-punching positions include ten rows in which digits 0 through 9 are stored, respectively. Figure 6-4 shows the locations of these rows.

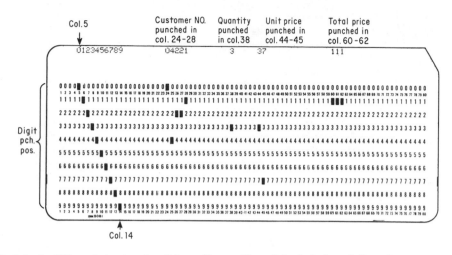

FIG. 6-4 An IBM card showing the digit-punching position—digits 0, 1 through 9, and an example

The zone-punching positions consist of rows 0, 11, and 12. They are used in conjunction with the digit-punching positions, to store alphabetic data. Note that row zero is used for storing either numeric or alphabetic characters in a given column.

Numeric Data Recording

Numbers are recorded in a card by punching *one* hole in any given column for each digit. In Fig. 6-4, a quantity of 3 is recorded in column 38 by punching a hole in row 3 of that column. A unit price of 37 is recorded in columns 44 and 45 by punching a 3 in column 44 and a 7 in column 45.

There are two important points to be noted. First, a value consisting of two or more digits must be punched in two or more *consecutive* columns. Second, one and only one hole should be punched in a given column for each digit. If more than one hole is punched in a column, the machine will not be able to interpret them.

Alphabetic Data Recording

To record alphabetic information in cards, *two* holes must be punched in each column. If the word "student" is to be punched in a card, for example, it will require seven consecutive columns, each of which is punched with two holes, one in the digit-punching position and the other in the zone-punching position. Figure 6-5 shows the zone-punching positions (that is, rows 0, 11, and

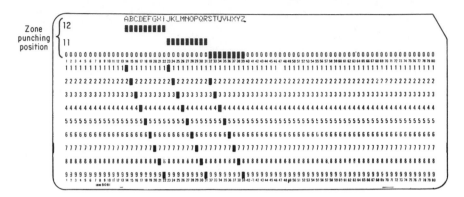

FIG. 6-5 An IBM card showing the zone-punching position and the alphabet

12). Row 11 is often referred to as the *X*-row; row 12 is sometimes called the *Y*-row. The alphabet is punched on columns 15–45.

It should be noted that the zero position can be used either as a zone or as a digit punch. If it stands alone in a given column, it represents a digit and is called a *digit punch*. On the other hand, if a zero punch is used along with another hole in the same column, it signifies an alphabetic code and is called a *zone punch*.

To represent alphabetic information in cards, the 26 letters of the alphabet are divided into three parts. They are: *A* through *I* (9 letters), *J* through *R* (9 letters), and S through Z (8 letters). Each part is coded by one of the three zone rows (that is, 0, 11, 12) and contains one of the remaining 9 rows for nine letters, respectively. This means that a given letter must be represented by two holes in a specific column; one hole in row 12, 11, or 0, and another hole in row 1, 2, 3, 4, 5, 6, 7, 8, or 9.

A through I Coding. The first part of the alphabet consists of the first nine letters: *A, B, C, D, E, F, G, H,* and *I*. Each is coded by a hole punched in row 12 and another hole in rows 1 through 9, respectively. For example, letter *A* is coded by two holes: one hole in row 12 and another hole in row 1 of the same column. Letter *A* is punched in column 15 in Fig. 6-5. Letter *B* is coded by a punch in row 12 and one in row 2, and so on. Figure 6-6 shows the codes of the first nine letters. Note that each of letters *A* through *I* takes a zone punch (row 12) plus a digit punch in that column in one of rows 1 through 9, respectively. Letter *A*, being the first letter, is coded by punches in rows 12 and 1; letter *B*, the second letter, in sequence, is coded by punches in rows 12 and 2; letter *I*, being the last letter in the part containing *A* through *I*, is coded by punches in 12 and 9. Refer to Fig. 6-5 as you check the coding for each of the letters *A* through *I* in Fig. 6-6.

Letter	Zone Punching Position	Digit Punching Position	Word "DEAF" Punched columns 26–29
A	12	1	
B	12	2	
C	12	3	
D	12	4	
E	12	5	
F	12	6	
G	12	7	
H	12	8	
I	12	9	

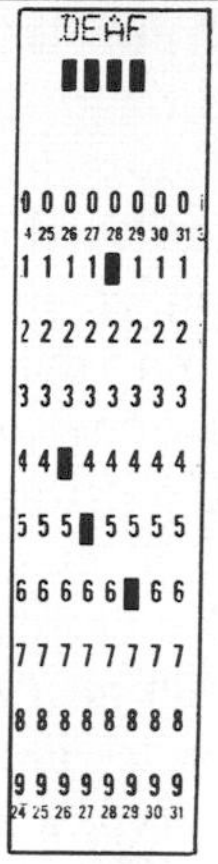

FIG. 6-6 Alphabetic coding table—letters A through I

J through R Coding. The second part of the alphabet contains letters J, K, L, M, N, O, P, Q, and R. The last letter of part 1 (letter I) is coded by a hole in row 9 (the last usable row). It is now necessary to start from the beginning (rows 1 through 9) to code the next 9 letters (that is J through R) by assigning a *different zone punch* to distinguish them from the first nine letters. To do this, a punch in *row 11* for a zone punch is assigned to each of the letters J through R and a punch in rows 1 through 9, respectively, for the digit punch. For example, letter J, the first letter in the J–R group, is coded by a hole in row 11 in a given column (zone-punching position) and another hole in row 1 of that column (digit-punching position) (Fig. 6-7).

FIG. 6-7 Alphabetic coding table—letters J through R

Letter	Zone Punching Position	Digit Punching Position	The Word "PORK" Coded in col. 51–55
J	11	1	
K	11	2	
L	11	3	
M	11	4	
N	11	5	
O	11	6	
P	11	7	
Q	11	8	
R	11	9	

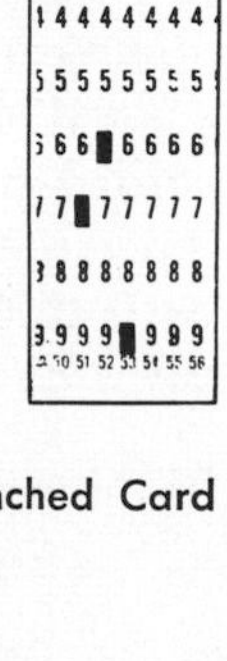

S through Z Coding. The third and last part of the alphabet consists of eight letters only: *S, T, U, V, W, X, Y,* and *Z.* Each of these letters is coded by a punch in row zero (zone punching position) and another punch in rows 2 through 9 (digit-punching position), respectively. Since there are only eight letters in this part, row 1 is left blank and remaining rows (2 through 9) are used for representing letters S through Z. For example, letter S takes a zone punch in row zero and a digit punch in row 2. Both punches must be in the same column. Letter Z, the last letter in part S through Z, is represented by a zone punch (row zero) and a digit punch (row 9). Refer to Fig. 6-8 for the coding of letters S through Z.

It should be noted that any number of consecutive columns in a card can be used to record a given word. In Fig. 6-6, the word *DEAF* is stored in columns 26–29, *STY* (Fig. 6-8) in columns 64–66. The alphabetic and numeric codes are built into the keypunch machine, which is designed somewhat like a typewriter. In order to punch holes in a card representing a digit, a letter, or a group of letters, the operator needs only to depress certain keys on the keyboard.

Letter	Zone Punching Position	Digit Punching Position	Word "sty" punched in columns 64–66
S	0	2	
T	0	3	
U	0	4	
V	0	5	
W	0	6	
X	0	7	
Y	0	8	
Z	0	9	

FIG. 6-8 Alphabetic coding table—letters S through Z

THE UNIT-RECORD PRINCIPLE

A punched card is called a *unit record* because it is used to record information about one transaction only in its 80 columns. Recording only one transaction in a card makes the punched card mobile, in that it can be used later with other cards bearing different, related information, to obtain special reports.

What happens if a transaction contains more characters than can be recorded in a card? Each vertical card column corresponds to a space on a typewriter. If the data to be recorded from an original source document exceed the capacity of the card, it becomes necessary to use more than one card. Every effort is made, however, to avoid this so as to keep all relevant facts on one card. This is done by various methods of coding and condensing data, such as using numeric dates (for example, 071570 instead of July 15, 1970), common abbreviations (for example, "amp" to stand for amplified), and eliminating dollar signs, commas, and decimal points.

Figure 6-9 is an invoice containing six transactions, each of which must be punched in a separate card. The last transaction involving the 50-watt amplifier is punched in a card to illustrate the unit-record principle.

CARD FIELDS

A transaction consists of a number of related details called *units of information*. In Fig. 6-9, each transaction contains a catalog number, quantity sold, name of the item sold, column number, size of the item, unit price and total price: a total of seven units of information. Looking at the punched card in which transaction 6 is recorded, we find that each unit of information is recorded in a number of adjacent, consecutive columns. For example, customer number is recorded in columns 1, 2, 3, 4 and 5. Customer name is punched in columns 6 through 28, and so on. The consecutive columns reserved for storing a specific unit of information are referred to as a *field*.

From the foregoing, then, we can conclude that the punched card in which transaction 6 is punched contains 11 fields in addition to columns 78, 79 and 80, which are left blank. Vertical lines are drawn between the fields for clarity. Card fields for recording identification data such as date, employee number, invoice number are often called *designating* fields. Fields used to record quantities or amounts are called *adding*, or accumulating, fields. The length of a given field varies with the size of the unit of information it contains. It can be as small as one character, in which case it is punched in one card column, or as large as 80 characters, which would occupy the whole card.

Determining the size of a given field(s) is an arbitrary matter. In Fig. 6-8, the customer number field, for example, is punched in columns 1–5. The decision to allow five columns is based on the assumption that the number of customers of Do-It-Yourself, Inc., in the future is likely to exceed 9999 customers and thus will require a 5-digit for recording the 10,000th customer and above. A 5-digit number is judged to be adequate since it is not anticipated that the firm will have more than 99,999 customers within the next decade. Meanwhile, the unused column is filled with a zero as shown in column 1. Therefore, in designing a field, enough columns must be reserved so that the longest anticipated group of digits or alphabetic characters pertaining to that field can be accommodated.

CARD DESIGN

The planning of the arrangement of fields on a card for an application is called *card design*. In designing a card, it is necessary to study the requirements of

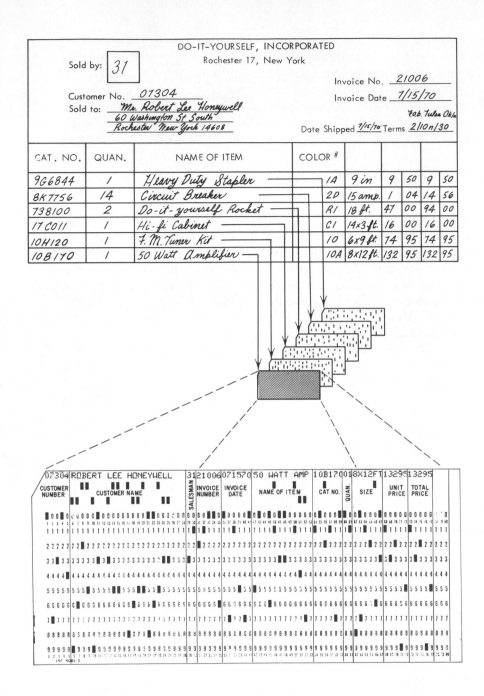

FIG. 6-9 A partial invoice stressing the unit-record principle

the application in order to determine the sequence and size of each field. The proper field sequence is important, especially for keypunching. Fields punched in a card in the same sequence as they appear in the source document make the keypunching operation more convenient to use as well as faster. This is especially true when the reading function is performed manually through the keypunch. In order to standardize and speed up the recording process, it is helpful to keep certain fields common to all cards by placing them in the same position in each card of the deck. For example, if the name-and-address fields are punched in columns 17–56 in one card, all other names and addresses must be punched in the same location in those cards.

As mentioned before, the size of each field must accommodate the longest entry that will be encountered. In the case of a name field consisting of 20 columns, for example, unused columns resulting from shorter names may be left blank. An amount field, on the other hand, may be set up for six digits, total capacity of which is 999,999. Any unused columns *to the left* of a smaller amount (for example, 85968) are often filled with zeros to indicate that no digit was ignored (result 085968).

When the card design is completed, it is customary to have a supply of cards printed with appropriate identification and headings of the various fields for ease of handling. Each card thus becomes a document, supporting details for the processing of a particular application. The various machines used in processing recognize the holes but not the printing on the cards. The printing is for the benefit of the human worker so that recognition of what the code represents will be speeded up.

CARD CLASSIFICATIONS AND TYPES

Cards are classified by use into three major classes: (1) Unit Record (detail), (2) Summary Unit Record (summary) and (3) Master Unit Record (master).

A detail card usually represents one transaction, with pertinent statistical designations. Suppliers, for example, keep a card representing each item sold or shipped to their customers. The card contains information such as customer's name, quantity sold, item code or catalog number, and cost of sale of the item. The card pertaining to transaction 6 in Fig. 6-9 is a detail card.

A summary card contains totals of a group of similar detail cards. This is usually the sum of all sales made to a given customer during a specific period of time. In Fig. 6-9, a summary card may be prepared to include the name of the customer (Robert Lee Honeywell), the total number of items shipped (6), date of the shipment (7/15/70), and the total price ($341.96).

This summary is generally obtained automatically by means of a summary card punch during a tabulating or accumulating operation. For report preparation, a summary card is substituted for a whole host of detail cards, A monthly report of sales by customer, for example, can be prepared from 20 daily summary cards instead of from 2,000 detail cards for each product. This is time-saving and becomes especially important when time and cost of operating the equipment are at a premium.

A master card contains information that is somewhat fixed or permanent in nature. A customer master card, for example, would contain all information associated with one particular customer; that is, name, address, account number, class, codes, etc. The card is punched with an account number, item description, size, cost, selling prices, and other related data. This fixed information may be reproduced into a detail card for a given transaction, thus eliminating manual punching of the fixed data.

There are many types of cards within the three major classifications. Among them are:

(1) Dual Use Cards. A written record from which subsequent punching on a card is made. For example, a time card is manually filled out daily by an employee. At the end of the week, data are copied from the time card and punched in punched cards for use in payroll processing.

(2) Composite Cards. Cards which are used for several different applications or for different uses in the same application. For example, a customer's balance card can be used either to prepare a sales report, to determine the number of items left in stock, or to prepare a statement for billing purposes.

(3) Prepunched Cards. Detail cards partially or completely punched from a master card. For example, a detail payroll card may be prepunched with employee number, department number, name, and card code prior to giving it to the employee for daily use.

(4) Stub Card. A card containing a detachable stub which serves as a receipt. For example, most electric bills come with a tearoff portion or a perforation across the width of the bill. One section is kept for customer's future reference and the other section is sent back with the payment.

(5) Mark-sense or Optical Scanning Card. A card designed for marking amounts with a special pencil. The marks are later converted automatically to punches (holes) in the same card by a special machine (Fig. 6-10). These cards have been used extensively in the retail food industry as an efficient method of reordering stock items.

FIG. 6-10 A mark-sensed card

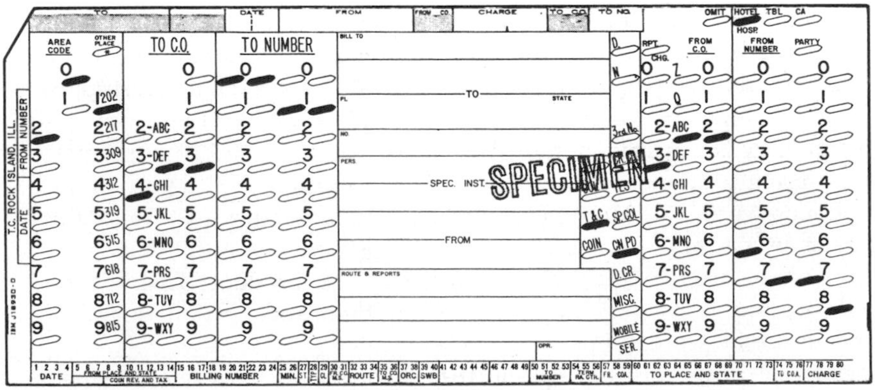

(6) Multiple-use or Tumble Card. A card designed for re-use for data requiring less than the capacity of a standard-size card. For example, in an 80-column card, the first 40 columns are handled as one unit at one time, while the second 40 columns are handled as a second unit at a later time (Fig. 6-11).

(7) Document Cards. Standard or special punch-card forms to prepare checks, bills, toll tickets, airline tickets, purchase orders, etc.

FIG. 6-11 A tumble card

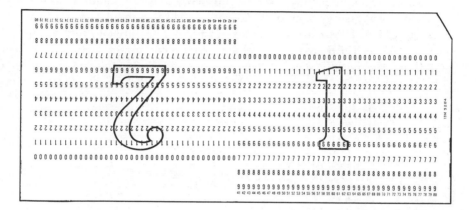

CONTROL PUNCHES

It has been pointed out that holes in cards serve to code numeric, alphabetic, or special characters. There are also other purposes for which code punches are used. A punch or group of punches can be used to instruct a certain machine to do a specific operation. For example, assuming that the control panel is wired properly, a hole in row 11 (*X*-punch) over the units column of a numeric field (a group of consecutive columns reserved for an amount) can be made to cause the entire amount to be treated as a credit (minus). The absence of that hole indicates that the amount is a debit (plus). Control holes are also used to do things such as printing three lines from one card (instead of the usual one line per card) on an accounting machine which is used for accumulating totals and printing reports.

Another common use of an X-punch or control punch is to separate or extract a specific card or a group of cards from a deck for a predetermined operation. For example, in an employee file, female employees may have an X-punched in a specific column to make it possible to extract all their cards from the major file of all employees for a specific event. When the X-punch is made in column 27, for example, of each female employee's card, the machine can be wired to eject in a designated pocket every card it senses having the X-punch in that column. When this operation is completed, the main employee file would be divided into two smaller files or decks: male and female decks.

To conclude, a control punch aids in locating or rearranging a deck of cards into two or more decks, depending on the specific objective in mind.

THE IBM 96-COLUMN CARD

The IBM 96-column card (Fig. 6-12), the first new design in punched cards since the introduction of the Hollerith and Powers cards, was made commercially available in July 1969. Slightly larger than a standard wallet-sized credit card, it measures 3.25 in. × 2.63 in. × .046 in., about one third the size of the 80-column IBM card. It consists of 96 columns, divided into an upper, middle and lower third area of 32 columns each. The upper section contains columns 1-32; the middle section contains columns 33-64; the lower section contains columns 65-96. It has up to 128 positions (4 lines of 32 positions) for printed characters.

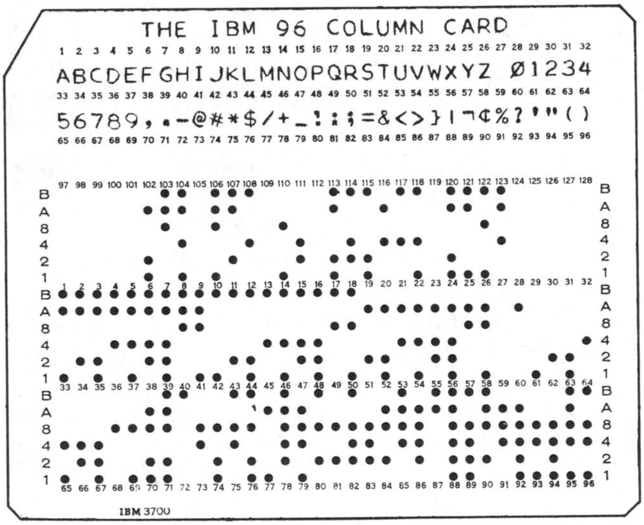

FIG. 6-12

This new, small punched card is a radical departure from the traditional 80-column IBM card which has been the standard of the industry for many years. Unlike the rectangular holes of the 80-column card, the 96-column card holes are circular, much like those of the Remington Rand card holes.

The coding system used for the IBM 96-column card is similar to the IBM System/360—Extended Binary Coded Decimal Interchange Code (to be discussed in a later chapter, titled Coded Data Representation). The four lower positions in each column represent the values of the powers of 2, from 0 to 3, respectively; i.e., the values 1, 2, 4 and 8. Thus numeric coding is accomplished by punching the combination of positions that add up to the desired digit. Alphabetic and special character coding make use of the upper two positions of the column, called the A and B positions, in combination with the four lower positions. The first nine letters of the alphabet (*A-I*) are represented by holes in the A and B positions plus the appropriate hole configuration for the digits 1 through 9. The second nine letters (*J-R*) are composed of a hole in row A and the proper hole configuration for the digits 1 through 9. The last eight letters (*S-Z*) are represented as a hole in row B plus the appropriate hole configuration for the digits 2 through 9. Special Characters are represented by various other combinations of the six positions in a column.

Another feature of the IBM 96-column card, which differentiates it from the 80-column IBM card, is that all the data punched in the card are printed in a maximum of 32 column lines at the top of the card. This differs markedly from the method used in the Hollerith card, where the characters are printed immediately above their respective column(s).

The IBM 96-column card is designed specifically for use with the IBM System/3, which is classified as a small-scale business computer system. More will be said about IBM System/3 in later chapters.

Glossary of Terms

COMPOSITE CARD: A multipurpose data card, or a card that contains data which are needed in the processing of various applications.

CONTROL PUNCH: A specific code punched in a card to cause the machine to perform a specific operation.

DATA PROCESSING CYCLE: The sequence of steps involved in manipulating business information.

DIGIT-PUNCHING POSITION: The area on a punched card reserved to represent a decimal digit.

DOCUMENT CARD: A special card form used in preparing a document such as a check, a purchase order, etc.

FIELD: A specified area of a record used for a particular category of data, e.g., a group of card columns used to represent a wage rate or a set of bit locations in a computer word used to express the address of the operand.

HOLLERITH: A widely used system of encoding alphanumeric information onto cards, hence Hollerith cards is synonymous with punch cards.

9-EDGE: Denotes the bottom edge of a punched card.

PUNCHED CARD: (1) A card punched with a pattern of holes to represent data. (2) A card as in (1) before being punched.

STUB CARD: A card containing a detachable stub to serve as a receipt for future reference.

12-EDGE: A term used to designate the top edge of a punched card.

UNIT RECORD: (1) A separate record that is similar in form and content to other records; e.g., a summary of a particular employee's earnings to date. (2) Sometimes refers to a piece of nontape auxiliary equipment; e.g., card reader, printer, or console typewriter.

X-PUNCH: A punch in the second row, one row above the zero row, on a Hollerith punched card.

ZONE PUNCH: A punch in the O, X, or Y row on a Hollerith punched card.

Questions for Review

1. Explain the steps involved in the punched card data processing cycle. Give an example to illustrate these steps.
2. What are the two main types of punched cards? What is the size of each type?
3. What is the primary difference between the Hollerith and the Powers code?
4. What is a punched card? Give an example of its use.
5. What is meant by "9-edge first, face down"? What is meant by "12-edge first, face up"?
6. How is alphabetic recording of data different from numeric recording in a card? Explain briefly.
7. What is the zone-punching position of each of the following letters? C, S, U, K, F, X, Q, Y.
8. What is the digit-punching position of each of the following chaarcters? 4, S, 7, P, I, 8.
9. What is the unit-record principle? Explain.
10. What is a card field? Give an example.
11. What is the difference between a designating field and an accumulating field? Give an example to illustrate.
12. What factors must be considered in designing a card? Explain.
13. What is the difference between a detail card and a summary card? Give an example.
14. Describe briefly the three main classifications of a punched card.
15. Define the following:
    (a) Composite card
    (b) Stub card
    (c) Mark-sense card
    (d) Tumble card
    (e) Document card.
16. For what reason(s) is a control punch used? Explain.
17. Describe briefly the characteristics of the 96-column IBM card.

chapter seven

INPUT PREPARATION AND ENTRY

ORIGINAL DOCUMENTS FORM the basis for future data processing. They are important because they represent the ultimate proof of a transaction. Each of these documents must go through a process which includes the use of one or more punched card machines before meaningful results can be obtained. The number and type of machines used depend on the kind of work to be performed. A sales invoice, for example, contains source information which is usually handwritten: processing, therefore, must begin with the conversion of the handwritten data into a punched card. This is referred to as the recording function, and is one of the most frequently used steps in the processing cycle. The other steps are classifying, calculating, summarizing and reporting. All these steps will be covered separately in later chapters.

RECORDING BY PUNCHING

As mentioned in earlier chapters, a machine capable of reading and processing handwritten information accurately and completely has yet to become available on a commercial basis. The most common practice today is to record source data by punching them in cards. Once recorded, they can be handled easily by various data processing machines.

THE KEYPUNCH [1]

The recording of data is usually done by machines called keypunches or, in the case of the IBM System /3, a data recorder. It is as easy to keypunch as it is

[1] There are four 80-column keypunches in use today:

IBM 24—punches data in cards but does not print what it punches.
IBM 26—punches data in cards and prints their interpretation on top of card.
IBM 29—has extended code to accommodate the IBM 360 computer system.
UNIVAC 1701—allows operator to rekey data before final punching.

to typewrite on an electric typewriter. Both machines have a keyboard containing numeric, alphabetic and special characters. The mere depression of a certain key causes the character it represents to be recorded. Another similarity is that both machines perform the recording function one character at a time. The typewriter *prints* one character at a time on a sheet of paper as the carriage moves from right to left. The keypunch punches one character at a time in a standard-size card as the card moves from right to left.

Some keypunches (Fig. 7-1) have the optional feature of printing the character on the top of the column at the same time the character is punched.

FIG. 7-1 IBM 029 card punch

This means that a maximum of 80 characters can be printed on the top edge of the card (corresponding to the total number of columns on the card).

The traditional IBM method of keypunching is referred to as the *serial* method. Keys representing certain characters are depressed one key at a time, causing consecutive punching until the job is done. Thus each column is punched serially in accordance with the sequence of key depression.

The other method of keypunching is called the *parallel* method, which is used on the Remington Rand card punch machine. The desired number of characters to be punched in a blank card is "keyed in" first; then, by means of a release key, is punched in the card simultaneously.

The Card Punch Keyboard

The method used in the IBM System /3 data recorder is best described as the "delayed serial" method. As the keys are depressed, the information is recorded in a buffer (in this case, a 96-position, temporary electronic storage unit) on a serial basis. When all the information to be punched has been "keyed in," a release key is depressed and the characters are electronically "read" from the buffer and punched into the card serially.

FIG. 7-2   IBM 029 keyboard

The keyboard of the IBM keypunch (Fig. 7-2) is like a regular typewriter keyboard. If the letters *A-B-E-L* are to be punched, the keypunch operator depresses these four keys consecutively. Every time a given key is depressed, it immediately punches the character in the card.

Unlike a typewriter, however, the arrangement of the numeric keys is such that the operator need use only her right hand to punch them. In Fig. 7-3, keys representing digits 0 through 9 are located close to one another in the right-hand section of the keyboard. In a typewriter keyboard, the numeric keys are located horizontally across the top of the keyboard.

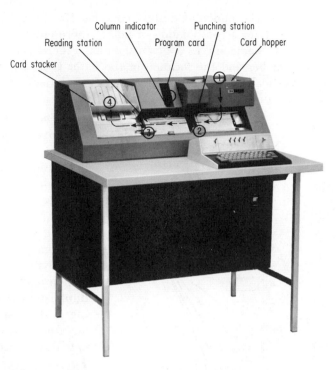

Card stacker   Reading station   Column indicator   Program card   Punching station   Card hopper

FIG. 7-3 Components of the keypunch showing the path of the card through the punch

The Card Path

A blank card becomes a data card after it has been punched with the necessary data. The *card path* begins in the card hopper, where all blank cards are placed, and ends in the card stacker, which holds the recently punched cards (Fig. 7.3).

The Card Hopper. The card hopper located on the right side of the machine, holds approximately 500 cards, which are to be fed through the punching unit one at a time.

The Punching Station. All recording is performed when a card moves to and passes under the punching station (Fig. 7-3). In order to move a card to the punching station, the "Feed" key is depressed, causing the first card in the hopper to drop onto the card bed. The feed key is depressed a second time, causing another card to drop while column 1 of the first card is aligned under the punches. This step sets the stage for the recording (punching) function.

Single cards also may be fed manually under the punching station by depressing the "Reg" key. Once the key is depressed, the first column of the card is aligned under the punches, ready for punching. This method often is preferred when only a few cards are involved.

The punching station contains 12 punches, aligned vertically to punch a hole or a combination of holes (representing a numeric, alphabetic, or special character) in a given column. Figure 7-4 shows the location of the 12 punches and the location of the letter *C* in a card column. The punches are vertically aligned to conform to the locations of the 12 punching positions in each of the 80 columns of a card.

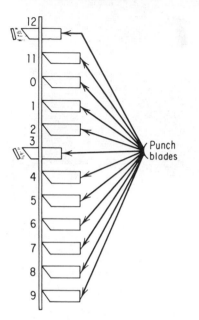

FIG. 7-4   Letter "C" punched in a card column

The Reading Station. After column 80 of a given card passes through the punching station, the card moves under the reading station and the next card moves under the punching station. From this moment on, both cards will move in synchronization; that is, as the first card passes under the reading station, the next one passes under the punching station.

Synchronization between the reading station and the punching station allows for duplication of punching in cards. Duplicating is done simply by depressing a "dup" key for the length of time it takes to duplicate the desired number of columns of data. For example, if it is desired to duplicate columns 1 through 15 from the card under the reading station onto the card under the punching station, the keypunch operator depresses the "dup" key until the column indicator on the keypunch passes column 15.

Duplicating data from one card to another by means of a keypunch is useful and convenient when the number of columns to be duplicated is limited and only a few cards are involved. Mass duplication, or reproducing, from one card into several other cards is done on a machine called *the reproducer.*

The Card Stacker. When column 80 of the card under the reading station is released, it moves horizontally until it is aligned opposite the card stacker and then turned 9-edge up, in the stacker. The card stacker is located on the left side of the keypunch and holds approximately 500 cards (Fig. 7-3).

Automatic Recording on the Keypunch

The keypunch can be "programmed" to do certain routine jobs automatically, thus minimizing the drudgery of manual work that otherwise would be done by the keypunch operator. The device that controls this automatic feature is called the "program control unit" (Fig. 7-3). Through this unit, duplicating, skipping, and shifting can be done automatically.

In order for the program control unit to perform these functions, a blank card must first be punched with the pertinent codes to tell the machine what to do, and when and where to start performing the desired function (Fig. 7-5).

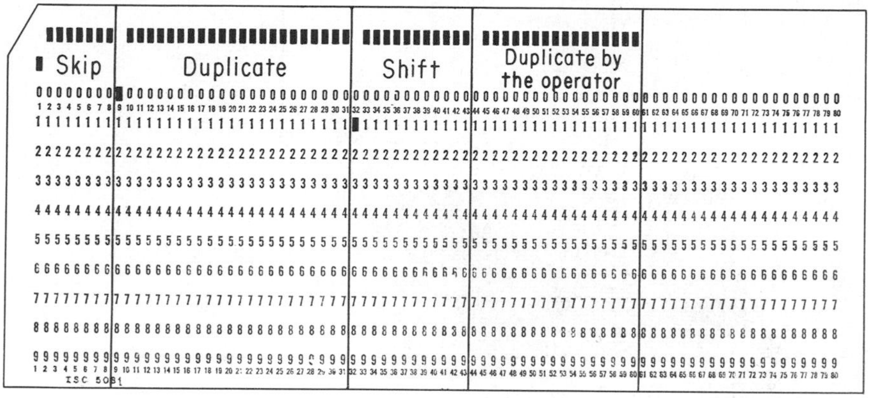

FIG. 7-5 A program card

Next, the coded program card is wrapped around a drum and placed in the program control unit. Duplicating, skipping, shifting to alphabetic mode, and left zero insertion may be performed automatically by appropriate punches in the program card, thus speeding up keypunching operations and reducing the possibility of error. Figure 7-6 shows the program card wrapped around a drum.

In the IBM System /3 data recorder, the punched program cards are read by the data recorder and stored (saved) in the on-line storage unit. The appropriate program is selected or overridden by selecting and depressing the proper function key. The IBM System /3 data recorder is capable of saving four program cards in its storage unit, simultaneously.

FIG. 7-6 An IBM program control drum

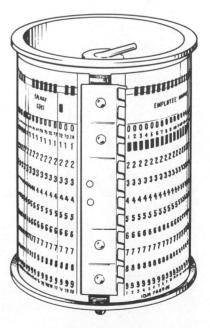

Verification of Recorded Data

Regardless of how well-experienced a keypunch operator is, it is always possible for him to make errors during the keypunching routine. In order to increase the accuracy of recorded data, another machine is used: the *verifier* (Fig. 7-7).

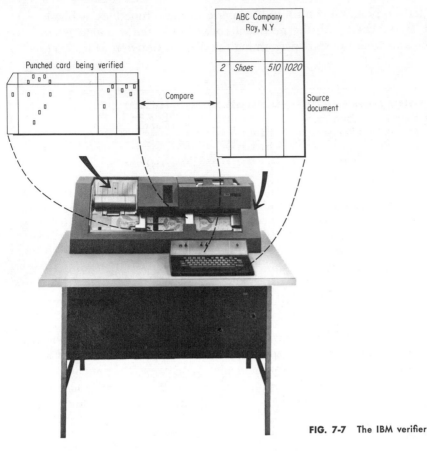

Punched card being verified

ABC Company
Roy, N.Y

| 2 | Shoes | 510 | 1020 |

Compare

Source document

FIG. 7-7 The IBM verifier

The IBM verifier is similar to the keypunch, except that its main function is to check, rather than to punch, data in a card. The verifier operator feeds the data cards into the hopper and keys in the information from the source document (that is, the one from which the cards originally were punched). As the operator keys in the data, a metal plunger passes through (senses) the punched holes. If the holes are not where they should be, meaning that they do not represent the proper character, then an error is indicated by a notch on the top of each incorrectly punched column. If the sensed holes match the correct character, as keyed in by the operator, a notch indicating the correctness of the punched data is made on the right edge of the card, opposite row 1.

Figure 7-8 shows a correctly punched card compared to the source document. Note the notch on the right edge, indicating its verification. Figure 7-9 shows two error notches on the top of columns 33 and 34, where the year (19)70 has been incorrectly punched 07.

Verification for the IBM 96-column card is done on the same machine that punches the data. The data recorder operator flips a switch, which converts the data recorder to a verifier. Then she places the punched cards in the hopper and proceeds in the same manner as when she punched the original. If a

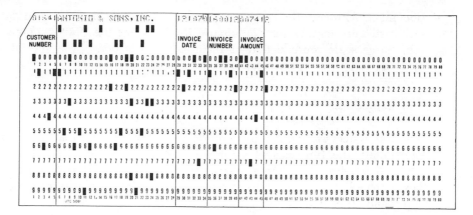

FIG. 7-8   A verified card

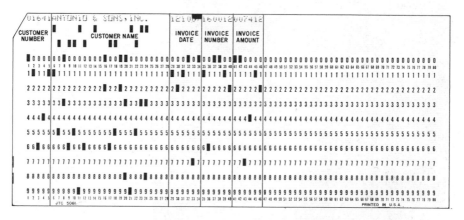

FIG. 7-9   An error notched card

punching error is present, an error light will be displayed and the keyboard will lock. The operator will then attempt to verify the card again. If the error light comes on and the keyboard locks a total of three times, the mistake is verified.

The time taken for verification signifies the importance of having accurate punched data. Errors must be corrected at this stage or inaccurate data will enter the data processing cycle. It would be comparatively more costly and time-consuming to correct errors later.

RECORDING BY REPRODUCING

We have stressed the use of the keypunch to record input data for future processing. Generally, the recording function of the keypunch is considered manual, in that an operator must key in the desired information from a source document. Although the keypunch can be used to duplicate certain data from one card into another card automatically, it is not the best machine for the job. Large scale reproduction of recorded data is done by a special-purpose machine called the *reproducer*.

The Reproducer

The reproducer is a special-purpose document-originating machine capable of performing the functions of duplicating, gang punching, and mark sensing (Fig. 7-10). For duplicating a large number of cards it is favored over the keypunch because of its greater speed and flexibility in the reproduction of input and other data cards.

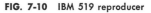
FIG. 7-10 IBM 519 reproducer

Before presenting any details regarding its main functions, it would be helpful to discuss the reproducer's features and main component parts.

The IBM reproducer contains two major units: the reading unit and the punching unit. The primary function of the reading unit is to read data cards and, through a control panel, which is specially wired by the operator or analyst, to cause certain dies to punch the information they contain into blank cards.

Control panels are wired boards which are used by the reproducer and certain other punched-card processors to allow flexibility in the manner with which specific cards are handled. The panel is inserted into the machine by the operator, is easily removed, and may be rewired for different applications.

In order to reproduce cards, data cards are placed in the "Read" hopper 12-edge first, face down, and pass over two sets of reading brushes, each of which contains 80 brushes, corresponding to the 80 columns on a card (Fig. 7-11). The first set, called the *reproducing brushes,* are connected to the control panel, which is wired to perform a specific operation. When a card is read, its data are transferred by the reproducing brushes to the punches through the control panel where an exact duplicate of the data is punched into a blank card. The other reading brushes are called the *comparing brushes,* whose main function is to read the data card and compare it with the data punched into the new card to insure accuracy.

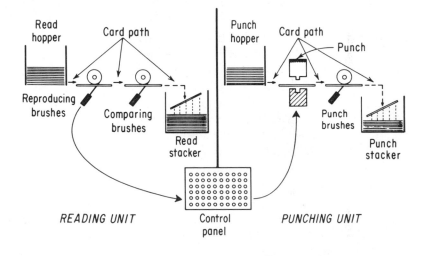

FIG. 7-11   Component parts of the IBM reproducer

The punch unit contains a card hopper in which a deck of blank cards is placed 12-edge first, face down. When a data card is fed through the reproducing brushes in the reading unit, a blank card also is moved under the punch unit where it will be punched with whatever information is received. It is important to remember that both the data card and the blank card move in synchronization; that is, when row 1 on the data card is over the reproducing brushes, row 1 on the blank card is under the punches. This synchronization makes it possible to duplicate data from one card into another.

It should be noted that the reproducer provides the flexibility of being able to copy only selected data from one card into another. Figure 7-12 shows a sales card (left), punched with the customer's account number, name, and the amount sold. The amount sold, punched in columns 35-38, is reproduced into the master card for subsequent calculation of the total balance due. In this case, the control panel is wired to read columns 35-38 and punch their

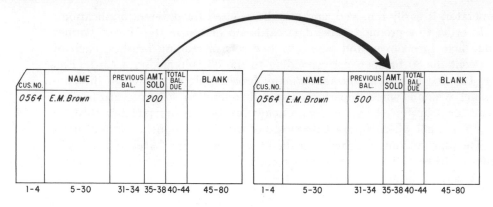

CUS.NO.	NAME	PREVIOUS BAL.	AMT. SOLD	TOTAL BAL. DUE	BLANK		CUS.NO.	NAME	PREVIOUS BAL.	AMT. SOLD	TOTAL BAL. DUE	BLANK
0564	E.M.Brown		200				0564	E.M. Brown	500			
1-4	5-30	31-34	35-38	40-44	45-80		1-4	5-30	31-34	35-38	40-44	45-80

FIG. 7-12 Selected reproduction of data from one card into another—an example

contents in the same location in the master card. The data in the remaining columns are not read for this specific application.

Another point which should be noted is that selected information from the data card (for example, "amount sold" in columns 35-38) may be duplicated in any four consecutive columns in the master card. In this case, the control panel can be wired to read columns 35-38 of the data card and activate dies to punch their contents elsewhere in the master card (for example, columns 50-53). This flexibility is useful in cases where the card being punched does not have the same design or layout as that from which the data are read.

Gang Punching. Gang punching is defined as the automatic copying of punched data from a master card into one or more detail cards following it. This process is accomplished by using the punching unit only, since it is assumed that the blank cards are merged behind their master card(s) in advance of the gang punching operation, thus providing one complete deck to be placed in the "Punch" hopper of the reproducer (Fig. 7-13).

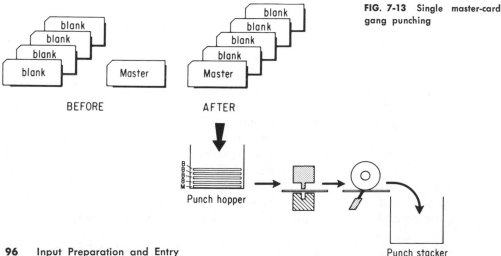

FIG. 7-13 Single master-card gang punching

BEFORE

AFTER

Punch hopper

Punch stacker

In gang punching, the master card moves past the punches and to the punch brushes, followed by the first blank card, which moves under the punches. Through a control panel, wired for a gang punching operation, the desired data read from the master card are punched into the blank card. The master card drops into the stacker, the gang punched card moves to the punch brushes, and a second blank card moves from the punch hopper to the punches to be punched. This operation goes on until the last blank card in the hopper is gang punched and finally dropped into the stacker.

When only one master card is involved, followed by one or more blank cards constituting the deck, the operation is referred to as *single master card gang punching* (Fig. 7-13). However, unlike this set up, in *interspersed gang punching*, the card deck contains two or more master cards, each of which is followed by a number of blank cards to be gang punched. In Fig. 7-14, the

FIG. 7-14   Interspersed gang punching

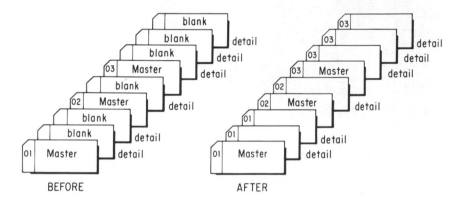

BEFORE   AFTER

first master card and the following two blank cards are gang punched as they would be with the single master card gang punching method. The fourth card (master card 2) is detected by the machine as a master card and is not gang punched as is the blank card but rather moves past the punches and to the punch brushes to activate the gang punching of the blank cards which follow it. The ability of the machine to detect a master card from any other card in the deck by use of a punch in a specific location makes interspersed gang punching possible. Special wiring of the control panel is the key to this operation.

END PRINTING AND MARK SENSING

Besides duplicating and gang punching, the reproducer can also perform the functions of end printing and mark sensing.

The end-printing function of the IBM reproducer is simply that of converting punched information into printing across the end of a card. It is similar to that of *interpreting* punched data which prints across the top of the card. End printing makes it possible to have a quick reference to the data on a given card (Fig. 7-15). This capability is a unique feature of the reproducer and may be performed at the same time that other functions, such as gang punching, summary punching, or mark sensing are performed.

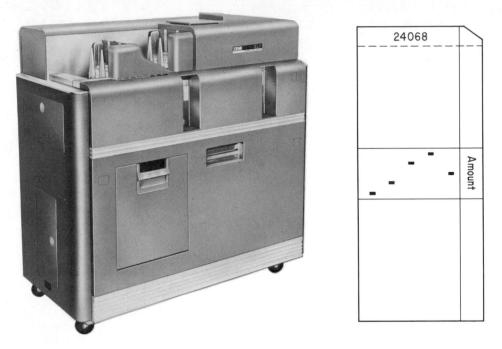

FIG. 7-15 End printing—an example

Mark sensing is a copying process in which the user marks special areas of a punched card with an electrographic pencil to represent (record) data. When these cards are fed into the reproducer, the machine senses the marks and punches their values into the card (Fig. 7-16). Mark-sense cards are placed in the "Punch" hopper and, assuming that the control panel is wired to do this job, the cards are ejected into the punch stacker after they have been punched. This conversion step is necessary before the mark-sensed cards can be processed further.

INTERPRETING

Interpreting is the process of converting punched-card holes into human language. It is done mainly by sensing alphabetic or numeric data punched in a card and printing it on the same card. Often duplicated, gang punched, or otherwise reproduced cards do not give a visual interpretation of the holes punched into them. In order to make it convenient for the user to interpret

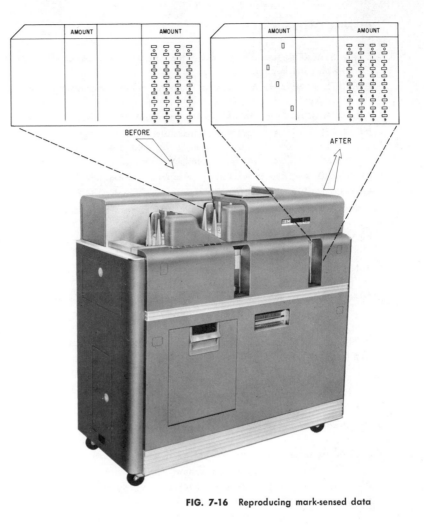

FIG. 7-16 Reproducing mark-sensed data

these holes, the cards are placed in the hopper of the interpreter, and with the insertion of the proper control panel, each card is read. The desired interpretation is printed at the top of the card.

Unlike the keypunch, which is capable of printing the meaning of the character it contains on the top of each column, the interpreter prints across the face of the card, in specific locations and in larger type than the keypunch.

Interpreting is a helpful supplementary aid in the reproducing function. Because many cards are reproduced or gang punched, a person can read them more easily if the cards are first interpreted. Otherwise he has to read the punched holes, a job which is both time-consuming and boring.

Glossary of Terms

CARD STACKER: An output device that accumulates punched cards in a deck. Contrast with card hopper.

CONTROL PANEL: (1) A part of a computer console that contains manual controls. (2) Same as plugboard.

GANG PUNCH: To punch identical or constant information into a group of punched cards.

INTERPRETER: (1) A program that translates and executes each source language expression before translating and executing the next one. (2) A device that prints on a punched card the data already punched in the card.

KEYBOARD: A group of marked levers operated manually for recording characters.

KEYPUNCH: A keyboard-operated device that punches holes in a card to represent data.

MARK-SENSE CARD: A card designed to allow entering data on it with an electrographic pencil.

PROGRAM CARD: A coded card inserted in the program control unit of the keypunch to control operations such as skipping, duplicating, and shifting, automatically.

PUNCHING STATION: The area on the keypunch where a card is aligned for the punching process.

READING STATION: The area on the keypunch where a data card is aligned for reading by a sensing mechanism to duplicate it automatically into another card located in the punching station.

REPRODUCER: A machine that duplicates a punched card by punching another one.

VERIFIER: A device on which a record can be compared or tested for identity character-by-character with a retranscription or copy as it is being prepared.

Questions for Review

1. Give a general description of the keypunch.
2. Compare a keypunch to a typewriter. How are they similar? How are they dissimilar?
3. What is meant by the serial method of keypunching? How is it different from the parallel method?
4. What is the function of the punching station? The reading station?
5. What procedure is usually followed in punching data in a deck of cards?
6. How are data duplicated manually from one card into another card through the use of the keypunch?
7. How are data duplicated automatically on a keypunch?
8. What is the function of a verifier? What happens when an error is detected in a certain column (for example, column 16)? Explain.
9. Describe the reproducer, its functions, and main units.
10. What is gang punching? Explain how data are gang punched.
11. What is mark sensing? What is end printing?
12. What is the difference between interpreting and mark sensing? What machine is used by each process?

chapter eight

CLASSIFYING AND SORTING RECORDED DATA

CHAPTER 7 DESCRIBED the recording process and the methods by which input data are prepared. This chapter brings us a step further into the data processing cycle by introducing the classifying function, the various ways of sorting input data, and the machines used in the preparation of the data for further processing. Classifying is necessary in establishing files of records in a given data processing system.

RECORD HANDLING

Generally, most recorded data are compiled and filed as they are received. In a banking application, for instance, loan installment tickets accepted by the teller are recorded in punched cards in the order in which they are received. Once these "input" data are recorded, they must be *classified* (for example, by loan number or by customer account number), and later merged with the main file to determine the balance outstanding on accounts for which payments have been received.

What is classifying? What machines are involved? What operations are performed on these machines? Answers to these and related questions comprise the subject matter of this chapter.

WHAT IS CLASSIFYING?

Classifying is defined as a process in which like transactions are prepared, in either numeric or alphabetic order, based on the data they contain. Classifying includes sorting, grouping and selecting.

Sorting is the arrangement of numeric or alphabetic data in a given sequence. Although descending sequence is possible, ascending sequence is the more popular method (Figs. 8-1 and 8-2).

FIG. 8-1 Numeric sorting

BEFORE

AFTER

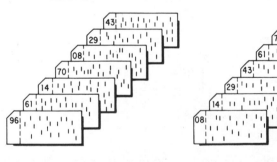

FIG. 8-2 Alphabetic sorting

BEFORE

AFTER

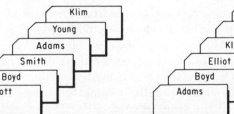

Grouping is the arrangement of a mass of data into related groups, all of which have common characteristics. For example, in a deck of student admission cards arranged by student number, the cards may be rearranged by class, so that each student is identified as freshman, sophomore, junior, or senior. Figure 8-3 shows a deck of student admission cards filed by student number (left), and later grouped by class.

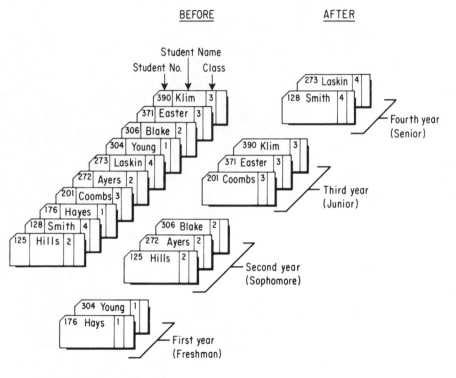

BEFORE   AFTER

FIG. 8-3 Grouping—by class

Selecting is defined as the process of extracting a number of cards from a deck for a specific purpose, without disturbing the sequence in which they originally were filed. The selecting process is widely used in various business applications. Usually, selected cards contain a code (for example, an X-punch) in a specific location. The sorter is set (or wired, in the case of the collator) to detect and extract such cards from the main file and eject them into a separate pocket. If a code is not already punched in the cards to be selected, the sorter can be set to read a specific digit (for example, 2) in a given column and suppress the reading of any other digit or characters punched in that column. In either case, a selection is made and the net results are the same. When the process is completed, the original deck has been separated into two smaller decks: (1) the selected cards and (2) the remaining file (Fig. 8-4).

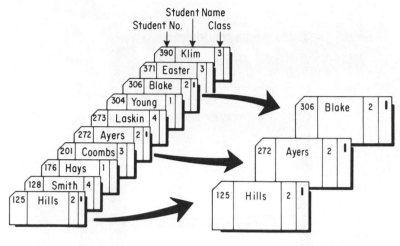

Student No. ┌ Student Name ┐ Class

390	Klim	3
371	Easter	3
306	Blake	2
304	Young	1
273	Laskin	4
272	Ayers	2
201	Coombs	3
176	Hays	1
128	Smith	4
125	Hills	2

306	Blake	2
272	Ayers	2
125	Hills	2

FIG. 8-4 Selecting

SORTING

Unit records are more meaningful when they are arranged as parts of a group of records in a given sequence. Sorting is similar to filing. In a progressive business firm, manual sorting of business records is considered both costly and time-consuming. When a punched card data processing system is in use, it is necessary to integrate a sorter into the system to speed up the process of re-sequencing business records.

Sorters available today operate in a similar manner. Each performs the basic job of rearranging records in a given sequence. The main differences between them are the rate of speed, the method of editing, and the convenience of operation. Rated sort speeds are commonly 650 cards, 1,000 cards, and 2,000 cards per minute.

A Typical Sorter [1]

The IBM 82 (Fig. 8-5) sorter has 13 pockets into which processed cards are ejected. Reading from the right, they are: *Reject,* 12, 11, 0, 1, 2, 3, 4, 5, 6, 7, 8, and 9.

The "reject" pocket usually receives cards that contain an invalid character in the card column being sorted, or cards which do not belong in any of the other 12 pockets, such as a blank column. The remaining pockets conform to the card format and are used for both numeric and alphabetic sorting; that is, pockets 0 through 9 are used in numeric sorting, and pockets 12, 11, and 0 are

---

[1] Newer and faster sorters are available which sort electronically or with "electric eye" contact rather than with brushes. These generally have more efficiently designed machine controls as well. Some feature special devices which provide certain types of computation and statistical functions as well as the primary sorting functions.

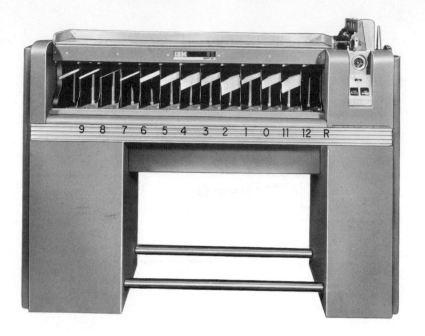

FIG. 8-5 IBM 82 sorter

used in combination with pockets 1 through 9 for alphabetic sorting (Fig. 8-5).

As in other sorters, the IBM 82 follows the reverse-digit method of sorting; that is, sorting begins with the unit's position of a given field and proceeds one column at a time (from right to left) until the field is completely sorted. In numeric sorting, the number of passes required to sort a field is equal to the number of columns it contains, because the sorter sorts only one column at a time.

In a one-column field, card-column 37, containing a punch in row 4, will drop into pocket 4. Before any sorting is done, the card is placed in the hopper. The single sorter brush is moved to align with column 37 and then the "START" button is depressed. This causes the card sorting on column 37 to move under the brush and be ejected into pocket 4. Figure 8-6 shows the single sort brush of the 82 sorter, positioned to sort on column 37.

The reverse-digit method of sorting is applicable on a field of two or more columns. Assume, for instance, that we desire to sort a deck of cards in columns 17–19. First, the deck is placed in the hopper and the sort brush is set at the unit's position of the sort field (or column 19). When the sorter starts, cards move under the sort brush and eject into any one of the 10 pockets (0–9), based on the digit punched in that column; that is, a card punched with digit 8 in column 19 will drop into pocket 8, digit 6 into pocket 6, etc. (Fig. 8-7).

When the machine stops, the cards are taken out of their pockets and reassembled. This marks the end of Pass One. The sort brush is reset to column 18 (the ten's position), and the reassembled deck is placed in the hopper again

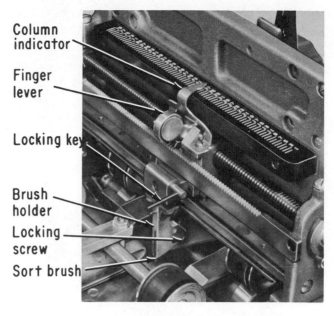

Column indicator

Finger lever

Locking key

Brush holder

Locking screw

Sort brush

FIG. 8-6 Sort brush—IBM 82 sorter

as Pass Two begins. The reassembled deck at the end of Pass Two and the setting of the sort brush on column 17 mark the beginning of Pass Three. After Pass Three is completed, the entire 19-card deck has been sorted into the proper sequence (Fig. 8-7).

Alphabetic sorting requires twice as many passes as numeric sorting. Since each letter is represented by two holes, it takes two passes to sort each alphabetic column: the first pass by digit, and the second pass by zone. To illustrate, suppose we have 26 cards, each of which contains a different letter punched in a given column. To sort these cards into the proper alphabetic sequence, Pass One must sort the 26 cards on the digit portion; that is, the sort brush is directed to read only the holes in the digit-punching positions (0–9). This sort ejects the cards into one of the 0 through 9 pockets. In Fig. 8-8, Pass One causes letter A to drop into pocket 1, B into pocket 2, C into pocket 3, etc.

When the cards are reassembled, they are placed in the hopper and the sort brush is directed to the zone portion (that is, 12, 11, or 0), ignoring any punches in the digit-punching positions. On the second sort, cards punched with letters A through I will drop into pocket 12; letters J through R, into pocket 11; and letters S through Z, into pocket 0. When the cards are taken out of the three pockets and assembled, they will be sorted into the proper alphabetic sequence, A through Z (Fig. 8-8).

In summary, it takes two passes to sort each alphabetic column, compared to one pass to sort a numeric column. Thus, if we wish to sort a four-column field containing alphabetic information, it will take eight passes (4×2) to sort the whole field.

FIG. 8-7 Numeric sorting—reverse digit method

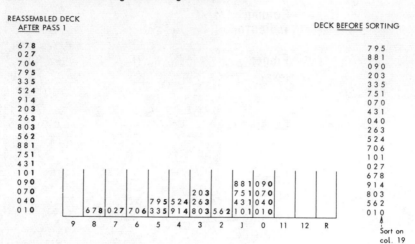

REASSEMBLED DECK
AFTER PASS 1

DECK BEFORE SORTING

REASSEMBLED DECK
AFTER PASS 2

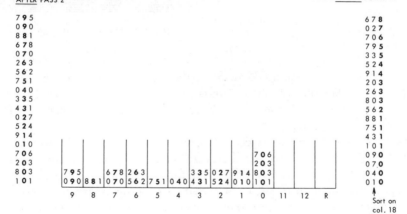

DECK BEFORE SORTING

REASSEMBLED DECK
AFTER PASS 3

DECK BEFORE SORTING

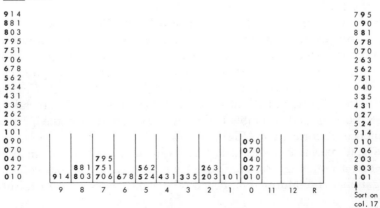

FIG. 8-8 Alphabetic sorting—the IBM 82

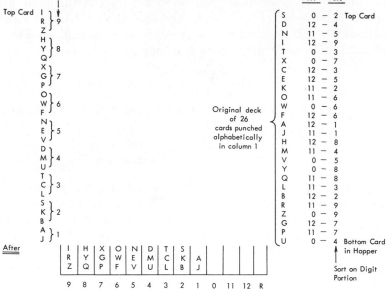

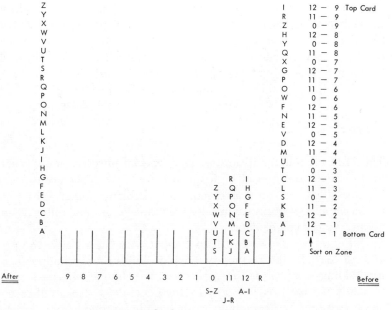

Computation of Sorting Time

Sorting time is computed by multiplying the number of cards to be sorted by the number of passes that must be made, then dividing the product by the speed of the sorter. For example, the time it would take to sort 1,300 cards, each of which is punched with a five-digit numeric field, on a machine capable of sorting 650 cards per minute is computed as follows:

$$\frac{1,300 \times 05}{650} = 10 \text{ minutes}$$

Assuming that we have a five-column alphabetic field in each of 1,300 cards, the sorting time is doubled:

$$\frac{1,300 \times 10}{650} = 20 \text{ minutes}$$

In addition to machine sorting time, it is a common practice to allow some percentage of sorting time for the handling of cards between passes. Approximately 25 percent of the sorting time is considered average. In the case of our last example, *total* sorting time would be $10 + 2.5 = 12.5$ minutes for the numeric sort, and $20 + 5 = 25$ minutes for the alphabetic sort.

THE COLLATOR

Collation of sorted data is accomplished by bringing together (interfiling) two decks of cards in a given order. The sorter is capable of performing this routine on a limited scale provided the merging field is in the same location in each card. This requirement is often difficult to meet, however, because two decks may have the same data punched in different locations to suit the needs of two specific applications. To repunch one deck in order to make it conform to the format of the other deck is both costly and time-consuming. To avoid this, another filing machine has been developed called the collator.

A Typical Collator

The IBM 88 collator is an auxiliary, special-purpose, filing machine designed to do various routines at high speed (Fig. 8-9). These routines include merging, matching, selecting, and sequence checking. Other IBM collators also are available and perform essentially the same functions, differing mainly in rates of speed and type of data.

Figure 8-9 shows two feed hoppers: on the right is the primary hopper, and on the left, the secondary hopper. The primary hopper has an extension for holding more cards than the secondary hopper, because the primary deck of cards normally is larger than the secondary deck. Other components include two sets of 80 reading brushes each (secondary and primary), and five stackers.

FIG. 8-9   IBM 88 collator

Initially, two decks of cards are placed in the primary and secondary hoppers. Cards moving from either of two directions drop into one of the five stackers and pass under their respective reading brushes based on the type of operation in action. The collator carries out a given operation (for example, merging) by comparing a card from the primary with one from the secondary hopper. Based on the way the control panel is wired, it "decides" on the location and the sequence in which the cards must drop.

The Merging Function

Merging is defined as combining two decks of cards into one deck of a given sequence. To perform a merging operation manually involves the use of the eyes and the mind—the eyes to see and read the data, and the mind to determine the sequence into which these data must be placed. Likewise, a collator merges similar data punched in cards through the use of brushes and a control panel. The brushes are the "eyes" of the machine and the control panel is its "mind."

The control panel is wired to merge two decks of cards into one deck of a given sequence, usually an ascending sequence. The two decks, each of which must already be in sequence, are placed in the primary and secondary feed hoppers. When the collator starts, a card from the primary hopper (primary card) moves under the primary reading brushes. At the same time, a card from

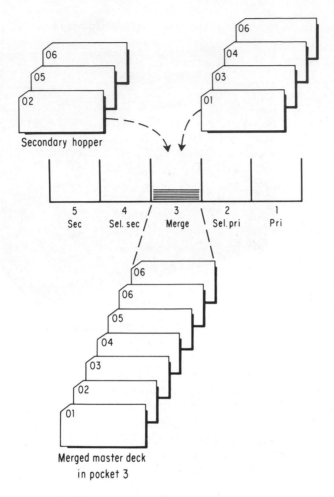

Secondary hopper

| 5 | 4 | 3 | 2 | 1 |
| Sec | Sel. sec | Merge | Sel. pri | Pri |

Merged master deck
in pocket 3

FIG. 8-10 Merging—an example

the secondary feed hopper (secondary card) moves under the secondary reading brushes. A comparison is made between the values in the primary and secondary cards. The card with the smaller value drops into pocket 3 (the middle pocket), followed by another card either equal to or smaller than the value of the card to which it is compared. When the two cards are of equal value, the machine drops the primary card first, followed by the secondary card.

To illustrate, Fig. 8-10 presents a merging operation involving two decks of cards. The deck of three cards (numbers *02, 05,* and *06*) in the secondary hopper is merged with the deck of four cards (numbers *01, 03, 04,* and *06*) in the primary hopper. In merging the two decks, six comparisons are made.

They are:

	Secondary Card No.		Primary Card No.	
1	02	—	01	Primary card *01* drops in pocket 3 and card *03* moves under the primary reading brushes.
2	02	—	03	Secondary card *02* drops in pocket 3 and card *05* moves under the secondary reading brushes.
3	05	—	03	Primary card *03* drops in pocket 3 and card *04* moves under the primary reading brushes.
4	05	—	04	Primary card *04* drops in pocket 3 and card *06* moves under the primary reading brushes.
5	05	—	06	Secondary card *05* drops in pocket 3 and secondary card *06* moves under the secondary reading brushes.
6	06	—	06	Primary card *06* drops in pocket 3 first, followed by secondary card *06*.

The Matching Function

Matching is checking on the equality of a specific field in two decks of cards. To perform this operation, the control panel is rewired from the arrangement used in merging, and the two decks of cards are fed through the primary and secondary hoppers. Next, a card from each deck is compared. If the values are equal, both cards drop into the matched pockets, the primary card into pocket 2 (the matched primary pocket), and the secondary card into pocket 4 (the matched secondary pocket). In an unequal comparison (that is, if the two cards do *not* match), they drop into the pockets 1 and 5 (Fig. 8-11).

Often, a combination of "merge" and "match" operations is performed, whereby two decks of cards are compared. The cards that match are directed to merge into the middle pocket, rather than pockets 2 and 4. Unmatched secondary cards drop into pocket 5, and unmatched primary cards drop into pocket 1. This routine is referred to as the "match-merge" operation.

The Selecting Function

Selecting is defined as extracting certain cards from a deck for a specific purpose. In the match-merging operation, for example, unmatched cards dropping into pocket 1 are said to be *selected* (through control panel wiring) to drop into that pocket. There are situations in which cards are selected because they require special attention; for example, in checking on the proper sequence of a deck of cards, any or all that are out of sequence can be selected to drop into a separate pocket without disturbing remaining cards of the deck.

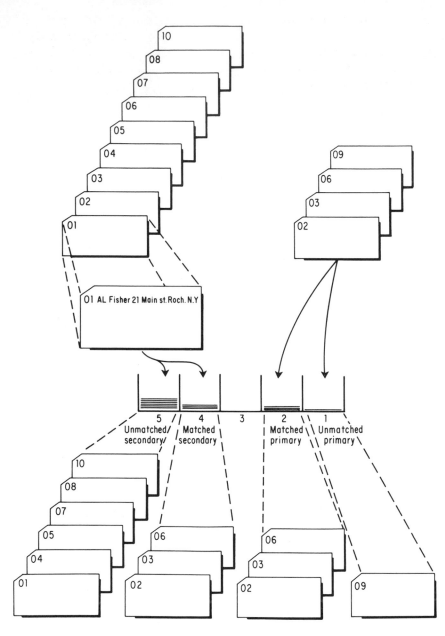

FIG. 8-11 Matching—an example

Other examples of selecting include extracting from a given deck (1) any cards having no specific code, (2) cards that have a zero balance in a given location, (3) cards that have a code, such as an X-punch in a given column, and (4) cards that have a value punched in a specific field which falls between specified limits. For example, in a business application, delinquent accounts between five and ten days from the due date may be extracted from the file for future action. A card is punched with the maximum and minimum date and is fed into the machine as the first card of the deck. With proper control panel wiring, all cards that contain dates within the limits punched in the "lead" card are separated (or selected) into a given pocket.

Sequence checking is the act of determining the order in which the cards of a given deck are filed. In sequence checking, only the primary hopper is used, since the operation involves just one deck of cards. The control panel can be wired to divert cards that are out of sequence into a separate pocket without disturbing the processing routine. Under normal circumstances, however, the machine is wired to stop automatically upon the detection of an "out-of-sequence" card.

Sequence checking is performed by comparing a value in two consecutive cards for one of three possibilities: high sequence, low sequence, or equal sequence. In Figure 8-12, card *01* is compared with card *04*, reflecting a "high sequence." Card *01* drops into the designated pocket, leaving card *04* under the reading brushes to be compared with card *03*.

In a second comparison, the result is "low sequence," meaning that in an ascending-sequence checking operation, card *04* would be considered out of sequence. If the machine is wired to stop automatically as a result of a low-sequence comparison, the machine would be "run out," thus ejecting the two cards (*04* and *03*) into the pocket. The operator at that time re-sequences the two cards manually and then restarts the machine to continue the operation.

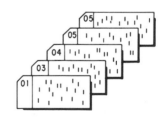

FIG. 8-12 Sequence checking

A third comparison can be made between card *05* and the following card *05*. The result is "equal sequence." Both cards drop into the pocket in the order in which they are fed. Technically, the last two cards are processed after a "Run-out" button is depressed.

Although sequence checking is used as a separate operation, it can be, and usually is, used in conjunction with other operations, such as merging, matching, match-merging, and selecting. While any one of these operations is being performed, the control panel can be wired to sequence-check the cards in each of the two decks simultaneously to make sure they are in the right order. The application of sequence checking with other operations saves time and insures accuracy.

OTHER IBM COLLATORS

The IBM 77, 85 and 88 collators are numeric collators. They are comparable both in operation and control panel wiring. They process only numeric data unless a special alphabetic collating device is installed.

The IBM 87 and 188 collators are capable of processing either numeric or alphabetic data and are called alphabetic collators. Both machines are similar in basic functions performed and in speed. The 188 model, however, is a solid state machine that performs various alphabetic or numeric operations at high speed.

Glossary of Terms

CLASSIFYING: Arranging data in a specific form, usually by sorting, grouping, or extracting.

COLLATOR: A device to collate or merge sets of cards or other documents into a sequence.

GROUPING: Arranging a mass of data into related groups, having common characteristics.

MATCHING: A data processing operation similar to a merge, except that instead of producing a sequence of items made up from the input, sequences are matched against each other on the basis of some key.

MERGE: To combine items into one, sequenced file from two or more similarly sequenced files without changing the order of the items.

SELECTING: Extracting certain cards from a deck for a specific purpose without disturbing the sequence in which they were originally filed.

SEQUENCE CHECK: A data processing operation designed to check the sequence of the items in a file assumed to be already in sequence.

SORTER: A machine capable of sorting punched cards either alphabetically or numerically.

SORTING: Arranging numeric or alphabetic data in a given sequence.

Questions for Review

1. What is meant by classifying? What are its three main types? Explain each type briefly.

2. What is the primary difference between grouping and sorting? Between grouping and selecting?

3. The following is a deck of 8 cards, each of which contains a customer account number in columns 1 and 2. Sort these cards in ascending sequence.

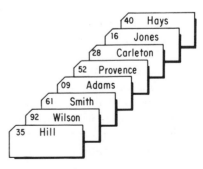

4. Assume the following deck of 20 numbers, each of which represents a card:

(top card)	20	67	10	80	18
	08	75	72	95	26
	20	11	52	33	51
	33	46	07	64	93 (bottom card)

(a) How many passes are required to sort the deck?
(b) Using the reverse-digit method of sorting, present in ascending order a reassembled deck after each pass.

5. Sort the following letters, each representing a card, using the IBM 82 sorter, by showing their location in the proper sorter pockets:

(top card)	Q	T	L	E	F
	S	K	G	V	P
	N	L	C	U	R
	B	J	W	M	Y (bottom card)

6. Suppose we wish to sort 9,000 cards on a four-digit numeric field,
   (a) How many passes would be required to sort the deck?
   (b) Assuming a speed of 650 cards per minute, what is the running time of this sort?
   (c) What is the total sorting time if 10 percent of the running time is allowed for handling?

7. What advantage does a collator have over a sorter?

8. Describe the IBM 88 collator. What are its chief functions?

9. Define the following terms:
   (a) Matching
   (b) Merging
   (c) Selecting
   (d) Sequence checking
   (e) Match-merging
   (f) High sequence
   (g) Equal sequence
   (h) Low sequence.

10. Suppose we wish to merge the following two decks of cards:

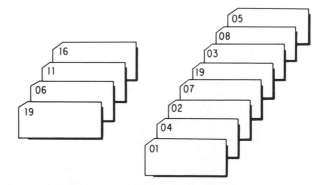

(a) What step(s) must be taken before any merging can take place?
(b) How many comparisons are made by the collator during the merging operation?

11. Assume two decks of data cards: the primary deck consisting of employees' withholding-

tax information, and the secondary deck including the employee's name-and-address cards. In a matching operation:

(a) Which cards (or card) in both decks match?

(b) Which cards (or card) in both decks do not match? In which pocket(s) do they drop?

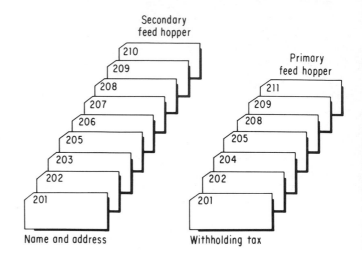

12. Suppose we wish to match-merge the two decks of cards in Problem 11 above with each employee's withholding-tax card behind his name-and-address card. Assuming that the control panel of the collator is wired to perform a match-merge operation,

(a) In which hopper (that is, primary or secondary) is the name-and-address deck placed? Why?

(b) Into which pocket do the merged cards drop?

(c) Into which pocket do the rest of the cards from both decks drop? Specify.

13. What types of cards can be selected out of a deck of punched cards? Explain each type briefly.

chapter nine

THE PREPARATION OF REPORTS

GENERALLY EVERY BUSINESS APPLICATION INVOLVES some calculation on the data it contains. Previous chapters pointed out the stages through which source data must go before they are ready to be calculated and then produced in the form of reports. These stages, in effect, are steps in a process whereby certain information is recorded, sorted, interfiled, and otherwise manipulated toward the ultimate goal of realizing meaningful reports. The results are not considered until after some calculating has been carried out and the reconstructed data, along with other pertinent information, have been summarized and printed.

THE CALCULATING FUNCTION

Most calculations performed in solving business problems involve one or a combination of the four basic arithmetic operations: addition, subtraction, multiplication and division. Considering the thousands of records to be updated periodically, a business firm of average size finds it difficult and costly to calculate them by hand or even with the help of basic mechanical devices. In a punched card data processing installation, a calculator is used, such as the IBM 602 or 604 calculating punch or the IBM 609 calculator (Fig. 9-1).

The IBM punched card calculator determines a result, based on the instructions wired in the machine's control panel. It takes one instruction at a time and carries it out until the answer is obtained. Normally, calculating begins by feeding data cards from the hopper of the punch unit. Next, a field— or several fields—of a card are read and transferred to the calculating unit. If the operation is to multiply one field by another, for example, this arithmetic operation is performed in the calculating unit, and the product promptly transferred to the punches, which punch the answer into a designated location in the same card or into another card following it.

FIG. 9-1   IBM 609 calculator

A typical application involving the use of the calculating punch is payroll. In processing the payroll, several steps are involved, which are divided into substeps for the purpose of simplifying the calculating routine. Gross pay is reduced by federal and other applicable taxes and deductions before arriving at the net pay. Figure 9-2 is a flowchart showing the steps taken in this operation.

All input data must be as accurate and complete as possible, since the accuracy of the results obtained by the calculating unit depends upon the accuracy and validity of the input information.

FIG. 9-2 A flow chart for the calculation of payroll

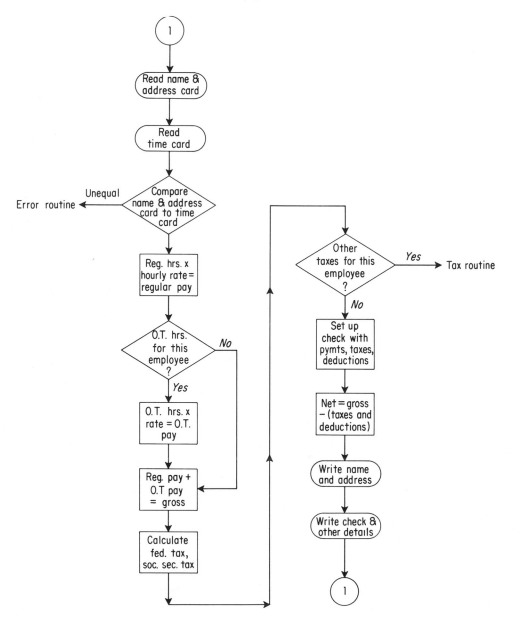

One of the most important steps in the punched card data processing cycle is the printing and preparation of needed reports. Managers cannot function effectively without these reports, since they represent condensed data which often are vital to the overall operation of the business. Furthermore, the functions of recording, classifying, and calculating data (discussed in previous chapters) would be meaningless unless they contribute to the finished product —printed reports.

Reports are prepared on continuous paper forms on an accounting machine, more commonly referred to as a tabulator (Fig. 9-3).

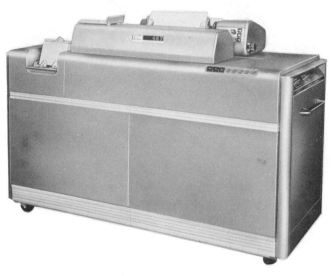

FIG. 9-3 IBM 407 accounting machine

Originally machines did not print; they merely accumulated amounts in counters. The amounts were transcribed manually at the end of the operation. Later, when printing tabulators were developed, two options were provided: (1) to print (list) each card passing through the machine, plus the necessary totals accumulated (added or subtracted) during the run, and (2) to print the totals only (referred to as tabulating or group printing). Alphabetical information, naturally, is only printed, not accumulated as would be the case involving amounts.

A tabulator is capable of reading data by means of its reading brushes and of processing the data it reads. The instructions it receives via a control panel "tells" the tabulator what field(s) to read, what to do with the data read, and where to print them on the paper form.

Figure 9-4 is a control panel inserted in the IBM 407 accounting machine. Printing is "activated" by means of a connection (through the control panel) between the reading brushes and the print wheel (older models print by means of type bars instead of print wheels). A wire causes the connection

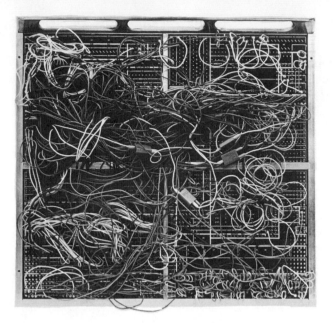

FIG. 9-4 A control panel *(courtesy IBM)*

of a specific reading brush to activate a selected print wheel to print the contents of a given column.

When the deck of cards is fed into the card hopper and the control panel is properly wired and inserted in the machine, the reading brushes read each card, and through the control panel, cause data to be printed on a paper form, one line at a time. This "one-line-at-a-time" printing is referred to as "parallel" printing, which is compared to "serial" printing, an example of which is "typewriting." The operator should take time to look over the printed data to make sure that no obvious errors have been made.

The Summarizing Function

Tabulators perform the functions of summarizing, printing, and summary punching. *Summarizing* is the compression of certain data into a more meaningful and concise form. An income statement *summarizes* the primary revenues and expenses of a given firm for a specific period of time; the balance sheet *summarizes* the chief assets, liabilities, and owners' equities of that firm at a given point in time. Summarizing is accomplished by a number of counters, which are used to accumulate totals as a result of the addition or subtraction of two or more numbers.

The Printing Function

The most important function, and a required role, of the tabulator is its ability to print summarized and other data on a continuous paper form. The form is mounted on sprocket wheels which help to advance it every time a line is printed.

Depending on the model and make, tabulators print either by means of type bars or print wheels. The older IBM 402 alphabetic tabulator employs eighty-eight type bars aligned across the width of the form. When printing is desired, the designated type bars are raised, or positioned, for printing one complete line at a time; that is, all the required type characters are pressed against the paper simultaneously.

The IBM 407 tabulator uses 120 print wheels, arranged in one group to print up to 120 characters within a maximum width of twelve inches. It prints a number of required characters in a specific location on the form. Activated by electrical impulses generated by holes in the punched card, certain print wheels are rotated so that the proper character is aligned to print in the proper position on the line. In actual operation, a *print wheel* rotates to position the desired character to the line, as contrasted to the type bar which moves vertically to position the same character.

Detail and Group Printing. Detail printing, or listing, involves printing one line for each card fed from the hopper. When the tabulator's control panel is wired to detail-print, each card is read and the printing mechanism is activated to print any or all of its data on a line. If we have a deck of ten cards, ten lines will be printed.

Group printing, on the other hand, means printing one line for each *group* of cards having similar characteristics. For example, suppose we have ten punched cards: the first five contain a product number (for example, 714), the number of units sold, and the unit price. The remaining five cards contain a different product number (for example, 800), the quantity sold, and the unit price. The group-printing routine includes that of adding the quantity sold under each of the products (714 and 800), determining the total amount, and printing two lines including the necessary details (Fig. 9-5).

FIG. 9-5 Group printing

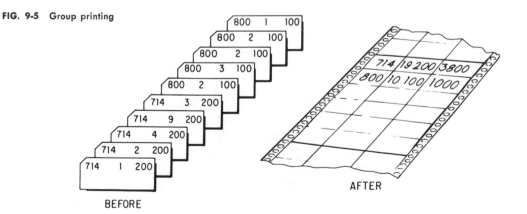

BEFORE

AFTER

The tabulator group-prints by comparing specified columns of each card with the one following it. When two cards are equal they are considered part of a group, and their selected values are accumulated. This process continues until an unequal comparison occurs, denoting the end of one group and the beginning of another. At that time, the tabulator prints the accumulated amount in its counters and begins again, following the same routine on the succeeding group.

Summary Punching

Summary punching is defined as the act of automatically converting data accumulated from detail cards into punched holes. The summarized data group-printed on the form also may be punched into a card or cards through the coordinated use (by a direct connection) of both the accounting machine and the reproducer. While the accounting machine is group printing on a paper form, the reproducer is copying (punching) the same data into blank cards. This function is valuable when group-printed data are required for future processing.

When punched card equipment was first used, the tabulator or accounting machine could perform accumulation, addition, or subtraction while printing information from punched cards. This led to simultaneous summary-card punching by means of linking a punch to the tabulator. Later, when calculators were developed, cards were read, calculations were performed, and results were punched into cards for subsequent tabulating or printing. This, of course, is the punched card approach closest to the electronic data processing system, which also uses magnetic tape and/or drums for high-speed input and output. Punched card equipment includes calculating punches, electronic calculating punches, and electronic punched card computers.

The trend in tabulator design is toward high-speed printing available as part of an integrated system. Machines have been built, and are in use, which produce printed and punched cards; one is called the card punching printer, which prints on both sides of a standard punched card and punches data during the same run. Another development resulted in printing in magnetic ink or printing with special type fonts, acceptable to optical scanners when re-entered into the processing system.

AN APPLICATION OF THE PUNCHED CARD SYSTEM

Typically, a punched card system consists of a keypunch, a sorter, an interpreter, a reproducer, and a tabulator (with summary punch). Assume "Pep-Up, Inc." has such a system. Prepunched item cards (one card for each case of soft drinks) are filed in a tub file, by brand. For each order received, the required number of cards is extracted from the file. The reproducer is used to punch new cards which will be inserted into the file when the company replenishes its stock. In this case, the file represents the actual inventory of cases in the warehouse.

Next, customer cards are taken out of a master customer file and reproduced and merged with the "item" cards to form a customer billing deck. The various billing decks are sorted according to the customer's geographical locations and are fed through the tabulator, which prints out the day's orders in quadruplicate. One copy goes to the sales department; another to a routing clerk, who combines the various orders by truck and route; and two are given to the drivers. One of these is the customer's copy; the other is turned in by the driver with the empty bottles he returns. As the orders are printed by the tabulator, the summary punch creates a gross-charge card for each customer. These are held in a "suspense" file.

Another tub file contains prepunched item cards for empty bottles. A clerk pulls the proper number of cards indicated by the driver on the returned order-copy, and matches them with the gross-charge cards in the suspense file. The combined deck of cards is run through the tabulator to obtain a listing (detail printing). In the same operation, a summary punch creates net-charge cards, which are run through the tabulator to print invoices for each customer. About 5,000 separate orders may be included in these invoices.

Next, the cards are sorted and run through the tabulator to produce an "aged" trial balance of accounts receivable (total dollars owed Pep-Up, Inc.). The result shows the age of any unpaid bill and, as payments are received during the month, the corresponding accounts-receivable cards are removed from the file. (See Fig. 9-6.)

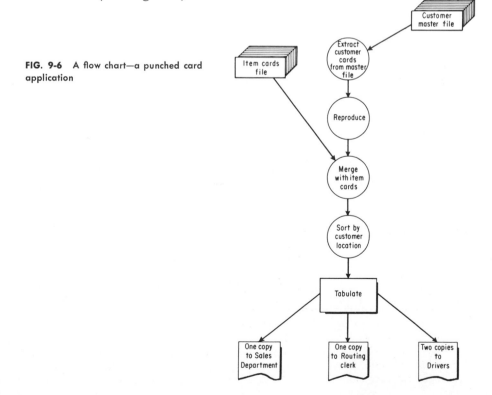

FIG. 9-6 A flow chart—a punched card application

A number of management reports are prepared from the cards created during the foregoing procedure. Among them are the following:

Daily: Sales analysis by item, updated for the month.
Weekly: (a) Customer sales analysis by item, updated for the month.
(b) Salesman's sales analysis by item, updated for the month.
(c) Wholesaler's sales analysis by item, updated for the month.
Monthly: Sales report by item, sales report by brand, sales report by state—all updated for the year. Sales report by customer and item for this year and last year. Sales report by state and item, for this year and last year. Sales report by salesman, updated for the year.

In this instance, we may conclude that the punched card system is primarily responsible for speeding up service to customers, a factor considered vital in today's competitive market.

Glossary of Terms

ACCOUNTING MACHINE: (1) A keyboard actuated machine that prepares accounting records. (2) A machine that reads data from external storage media, such as cards or tapes, and automatically produces accounting records or tabulations, usually on continuous forms.

CALCULATOR: (1) A device capable of performing arithmetic. (2) A calculator as in (1) that requires frequent manual intervention. (3) Generally and historically, a device for carrying out logic and arithmetic digital operations of any kind.

COUNTER: A device such as a register or storage location used to represent the number of occurrences of an event.

DETAIL PRINTING (listing): The printing of one line for each card read by the tabulator.

GROUP PRINTING: A procedure whereby one line is printed for each group of cards having similar characteristics.

SUMMARIZING: Condensing a mass of data into a concise and meaningful form.

SUMMARY PUNCH: A card punch operating in conjunction with another machine, commonly a tabulator, to punch into cards data which have been summarized or calculated by the other machine.

Questions and Problems for Review

1. What is meant by the term *calculate*? Give an example.
2. What are the main arithmetic operations of the IBM punched card calculator? Explain.
3. Explain how the punch and the calculating units are used to calculate a given problem.
4. Show (by giving an example) how new data are created in a "gross-pay" calculation.
5. What factors are needed in calculating federal income-tax withholding? Explain by giving an example.
6. Bob Sanderson, a college student, accepted a summer job with a local contractor to pave driveways. He worked 32 hours a week and was paid at the rate of $4.35 per hour. His year-to-date gross earnings are $4,680. He is single and has no dependents.

Assuming that Bob's employer deducted 25% for federal income-tax withholding and $1.50 for health insurance premium, calculate:

(a) Gross pay

(b) Federal income tax withheld

(c) Net pay.

7. List and explain briefly the main functions of the control panel of an accounting machine.

8. List the four primary functions of an accounting machine. Explain each function briefly.

9. How is summarizing performed in an accounting machine? Illustrate.

10. What is the function of a counter? What is the maximum value which can be stored in a four-position counter?

11. What types of total can be represented or stored in a counter? Define each type and present an illustration of your own, showing their significance and their location on a paper form.

12. How is a final or grand total derived?

13. What are the two methods of printing? Explain and give an example of each method.

14. What is detail printing? What is group printing?

15. A deck containing eight cards (account numbers 201, 202, 203, 203, 204, 205, 205, and 206) are placed in the card hopper of an accounting machine. Assuming that detail printing is desired, how many lines would the machine print? How many lines would be group-printed? Why?

16. What is summary punching? On what machine(s) is it used? Why?

ELECTRONIC
DATA PROCESSING

ELECTRONIC DATA PROCESSING SYSTEMS

IN THE PRECEDING CHAPTERS we discussed data processing methods which require punched card equipment. As business firms expand, their needs increase for processing data faster. Although punched card data processing is a major improvement over manual systems, it has some limitations. Intercommunication between the machines in the system is somewhat limited. The machines are not capable of handling exceptions within a normal routine so a firm must occasionally return to manual processing. The punched card system is also limited because of its inability to "make decisions" in the course of processing. Complex problems must be solved in pieces, or fractions, rather than in one continuous process.

Unlike a punched card installation, which requires the punched card as a primary unit record, the computer is capable of processing data received through a number of other types of devices. Moreover, it performs faster and more economically. Wiring panels are not required by most computers; instructions are received by a program which is loaded into the machine. The program performs the same function as the wired control panel in a punched card machine.

A punched card system includes a series of individual pieces of equipment, each of which processes the same unit record (or a summarized form of that record) in different ways. Certain equipment sorts; other equipment calculates, prints, and so on. A computer system, on the other hand, includes equipment which processes the unit record *under control of a central unit* (called a *processor*). All individual units are tied to the processor; they either accept or produce records as a result of the logic it imposes upon them. Although both systems are made up of many individual pieces of equipment, the punched card system is not under a central automatic control as is the computer system.

The computer system is more flexible. The punched card system reads the cards, sequences them, accumulates them, and finally prints out summary reports. The computer system, on the other hand, performs the same routine, but with greatly extended capabilities. That is, it can add, subtract, multiply and divide; verify the accuracy of incoming information; reject certain cards if they contain invalid coding; and use a preplanned set of logic to deal with output data before a final printout is made.

BASIC TYPES OF COMPUTERS

Analog and Digital Computers

Electronic computation can be achieved by using digital or analog methods. A digital computer counts, using strings of digits to represent numbers. An analog computer measures, representing numbers by physical magnitudes, such as pressure, temperature, voltage, and current. Analog computers are physical systems which behave in a way analogous to some other physical or abstract system. A slide rule is an analog device, with length serving as the analog of the logarithm of the numbers; a desk calculator is a digital machine, with cogged wheels serving as digits.

In an electronic analog computer, the analog of a number generally is a voltage, a resistance, or some similar electrical quantity. Computations are performed by combining these quantities. Simple circuits can be built to add, subtract, multiply, divide, and otherwise combine electrical quantities. Networks of these circuits can compute very complicated mathematical expressions.

A continuous-variable function in an analog computer can be represented in a digital computer by a sequence of discrete numbers in the same way that a distribution function is represented by a bar graph; with enough digits, the agreement of the analog and digital forms can be as close as is required. The digital process sometimes may be slower than its analog counterpart, but the net result will be the same. A digital computer can even be made to behave as if it were an analog computer by equipping it with devices to convert the input from analog to digital form and to convert the output from digital to analog form.

The greater accuracy of digital computation gives it an advantage over analog computation. The precision with which a voltage can be measured limits the accuracy of an analog computer; an accuracy of better than one part in 1,000 is very difficult to achieve. Digital computation, on the other hand, is accomplished electronically by digits. A digital computer can get any required accuracy by using as many digits as it needs (or, to phrase it differently, by carrying the solution to as many decimal places as necessary).

Analog computers are well suited to some types of problems, notably those in which the inputs and outputs are complex functions of time and in which the system being studied is producing inputs to the computer by reacting to its own outputs (that is, acting as part of a *feedback loop*). Thus analog computers have been used effectively in studying human tracking performance, in building flight simulators, and in network simulation. For business applications, however, analog computers are generally not used.

Hybrid Computers

Although both digital and analog computers have been extensively used and widely accepted in various sectors of industry, an attempt has been made to design a computer which combines the best features of digital and analog computers. This computer is referred to as the *hybrid* computer. Being a special purpose machine, it promises great potential in solving problems with greater accuracy than an analog computer and solving them faster than a digital computer.

Special Purpose and General Purpose Computers

The computers we have already discussed are general purpose machines. They differ in detail, but they are basically similar in arrangement and logical design. They are built to do a variety of jobs through the use of the stored program. Because of this, they have sacrificed certain aspects of speed or efficiency, which may be extremely desirable for one customer but have little benefit for another. General purpose computers have the advantage of lower cost, better service, and longer and more extensive testing during production to eliminate "bugs."

In contrast, the special purpose machine is built for a specific operation, and usually for a single customer. It may incorporate many of the features of a general purpose machine, but its applicability to a particular problem is a function of design rather than of program. Naturally, it lacks the flexibility of the general purpose machine.

Examples of successful special purpose systems are devices for the collection of highway tolls, for air traffic control (which receives such flight information as departure time, destination, route, payload, etc., via teletype), and for airline reservations systems. Another important special purpose computer is the ERMA system, originally built by General Electric Company and Stanford Research Institute for the Bank of America. With ERMA, checks and deposit slips are read, using magnetic-ink character recognition (MICR) to identify account numbers.

Classification of general purpose digital computers is determined by the power and the speed of the equipment, measured in terms of data handling and storage capacities and a variety of input-output possibilities. Internal computer speeds are measured by the time required to perform specific operations (for example, add or multiply) and are stated in terms of milliseconds (thousandths), microseconds (millionths), nanoseconds (billionths), or picoseconds (trillionths).

ELEMENTS OF AN ELECTRONIC DATA PROCESSING SYSTEM

The primary elements of an overall computer system center around procedures and equipment (referred to as *hardware*); programs (called *software*); and personnel (called *peopleware*). In this text, a *system* is defined as a group of procedures and/or physical devices which, when combined into a well-organized, logical relationship, produce desired results, with emphasis on efficiency and economy of operation.

Hardware

For a computer system to function efficiently, it must be supported by additional devices to feed input data and to produce output results. Thus, of necessity, it must be supported by primary and peripheral devices to accomplish preplanned objectives.

The hardware element relates to the physical components which perform data preparation,[1] data input, data storage (primary and secondary), data computation and control, and data output (Fig. 10-1). These operations are performed by input and output devices, controlled by the central processing unit.

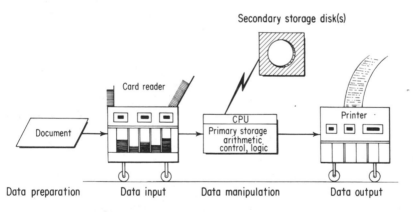

FIG. 10-1 Elements of a computer system

For each computer system, a particular *procedure*(s) is followed in the preparation, manipulation, and production of data, including formal routines to be taken in the event of equipment failure or error detection.

Input Devices. A typical computer is designed to work on input data after they have been converted into electrical impulses. This conversion stage is made after the data have been transferred from source documents to accept-

[1] Usually called *offline* equipment, since it is not connected to the computer system. All other components are referred to as *online* equipment.

able media such as punched cards, magnetic tape, magnetic disks. Currently, more input devices are being used which allow direct entry of source data into the computer. It is likely that these devices will become even more prevalent in the future. Details on input devices are presented in Chapter 13.

Output Devices. Just as the computer requires data input in the form of electrical impulses, it also produces results in the same form. Because of the limited ability of most users to read output data in machine language, a printer (output device) was designed exclusively for converting output from machine language to human language. Output data can also be punched in cards or recorded on magnetic tape or magnetic disks for further processing by the computer. Output devices are discussed in detail in Chapter 13.

Primary Storage. Primary storage retains the data which will be used during processing. It is called "internal memory," owing to its similarity in function to human memory. Primary storage, or "memory," is used during the processing of a problem to act upon the data being manipulated, just as the human memory is used to "think out" the logical solution to a given problem. Like the human brain, the computer's memory is not used to retain all answers, nor to retain all the elements of a problem. Answers usually are written down, rather than committed to memory permanently; in other words, computer memory is based on the temporary retention of information, or data. This does not imply that the physical aspects of the memory allow the information to fade away or be lost after a while. On the contrary, once data are written into memory, they are retained permanently unless purposely or accidentally destroyed. Data are retained as long as they are being processed. When another problem is fed into the processor, the data it contains replace the data of the previous problem.

Information in computer memory can be numeric, alphabetic, or alphanumeric. A single piece of information in digital or alphabetic form is called a *character*. For the logic of the computer to locate any information it desires, the "character-oriented" computer is designed so that each character position in its memory can be located by an *address* or a location number. A computer having 5,000 character positions of primary storage, for instance, is capable of storing 5,000 alphabetic or numeric characters in all. The address of the first character of a 5,000-character memory is 0000; the last address is 4999.

In Fig. 10-2, 7,912 is stored in position numbers 2401-2404. Number 2401 is the address of digit 7; 2402, the address of digit 9; 2403, of digit 1; and 2404, of digit 2.

Picture a large bank of post-office boxes. Each of the boxes has a number and is assigned to a particular individual. A person receives his mail by going to the box which bears his assigned number or address. It should be noted that the address is not the mail it contains, but merely a location number to aid the owner in finding his mail.

FIG. 10-2

7	9	1	2
2	2	2	2
4	4	4	4
0	0	0	0
1	2	3	4

Computer memories are similar in structure. Each character in storage is assigned an address. This address has nothing to do with the information it represents.

Computer memories are divided into two basic categories: character-oriented and word-oriented memories. Most of the early computers had memories which were divided into sections called "words." Each word had a location number, and contained enough bits of binary digits to hold a 10 or perhaps 11 numeric positions (the word-size was determined by the manufacturer). These machines lent themselves easily to mathematical or scientific problems, since a word containing a large number could be manipulated as rapidly as one containing a small number. As most scientific and engineering problems deal with a wide range of numbers and usually do not deal with alphabetic information, word machines fit the need of these problems most conveniently.

The inconvenience of programming word-oriented machines for business data processing led to the development of the "character-oriented" computer. In a character-oriented computer, addresses do not refer to a group of positions, but to only one position, so that field sizes may vary from one character to many. Memory can accommodate fields just as they appear on a punched card, as a string of characters divided into fields of various sizes.

Generally speaking, word-oriented machines are best suited for scientific or mathematical applications; character-oriented memories appear to be more efficient for business data processing applications, although either type of application can be performed on both types of computers. Ideally, a combination of word and character memories would be best. The newer computers are utilizing such memories in an attempt to consolidate both types of problems on the same general purpose machine. There appear to be definite economical advantages to such an arrangement.

Types of Internal Memory Devices. Early in computer development, there were two basic primary-storage devices: Acoustic Delay Line (for example, Univac I) and Electrostatic Storage (for example, the IBM 701 and 702). The methods of these machines were considered adequate for their time, but have been replaced by less expensive, faster, and more reliable types of machines.

Magnetic cores. To speed up access time and to make it the same regardless of the location of any particular information in storage, another storage technique is in common use: the magnetic core (Fig. 10-3). Magnetic cores,

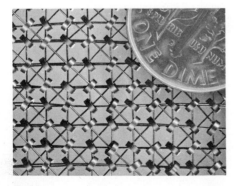

FIG. 10-3 Plane of magnetic cores

similar to tiny doughnuts, are ferrite rings capable of being magnetized in one of two states. Each core is equivalent to a bit. Combinations of these cores, strung together, represent numbers or other characters in the same manner as those on a magnetic drum.

Magnetization, or polarity, in the core is made either clockwise or counterclockwise. By convention, when magnetized clockwise, the core is said to be turned "on" or to represent a binary "one." When magnetized counterclockwise, the core is said to be "off," representing a binary "zero." In order to induce magnetization, or change direction of polarity, the cores are strung on ultrathin wires, forming grids or "planes." An additional wire runs through the core for the purpose of "reading" its direction of polarity (Fig. 10-4).

Electric current passing through each core is able to set and "read" the status of its polarity. The direction of polarity will depend on the direction of the current in the two wires that cross in the center of the core. This bistable nature of the core network enables it to flip from one direction of polarity to the other quite easily by changing the direction of the electricity in the wires (Fig. 10-5).

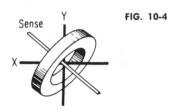

FIG. 10-4

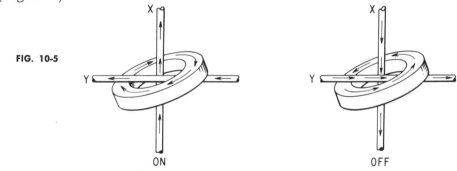

FIG. 10-5

ON   OFF

Cores are set up in the form of planes connected to the central processor. The number of planes varies with the size and cost of the computer, but they are stacked in a series to form a basic module of memory (Fig. 10-6). Computer capacity often may be increased simply by adding new memory modules to the same computer.

Core memory is referred to as "non-volatile," meaning that once information is placed in core memory, it remains there until new information replaces it. Further, there is no physical wear on a core since there are no moving or rotating parts to cause friction, as is the case with a drum.

In addition to the advantages of permanent storage of data and durability of cores, other major advantages of core memories include their compact size, low power consumption, low heat dissipation, and adaptability to word-oriented or character-oriented computers.

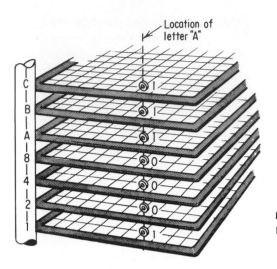

Location of
letter "A"

C
B
A
8
4
2
1

1
1
1
0
0
0
1

FIG. 10-6   Schematic of character in storage—even parity

Parity checking.   In fast core memories, one method of checking takes the form of an extra bit, called a *parity bit*. The parity bit serves to check whether bits have changed accidentally.

A manufacturer using a fixed number of binary bits to code data may decide arbitrarily to set an even number of bits to represent any given character. Codes using an even number of "one-bits" are called *even parity*. Codes using an odd number of "one-bits" are called *odd parity*. For instance, decimal-digit one (1) is coded 0000001. This representation satisfies the requirements of odd parity, since the number of one-bits that stand for digit "one" is odd. However, in even-parity coding, another "one" must be added in the parity bit (left bit) to make the total number of one-bits even (therefore, 1000001).

Consequently, in this particular system, any time that information is received, the parity bit is turned on or left off, as the case may be, based on what character is represented. Assuming that the information in memory is all even parity, the wiring logic immediately discovers the error whenever a single bit in any character is dropped or an extra bit is picked up.

Accuracy in computers is of prime importance. In listening to the radio or listening to music played from a reel of tape, the absence of a few sound "bits" is barely noticeable. Fidelity is important, but not crucial. In computers, however, accuracy is both important and crucial. The loss of one bit of information can cause distortion in processing. Parity bits aid in detecting errors in data representation.

Thin film.   Basically, thin film memory is a thin plane of glass with ferrite rectangles taking the place of the familiar ferrite cores strung on wires (Fig. 10-7).

One of the newest thin-film memories is a 2.7 in. × 1.7 in. glass plane, .008 in. thick. On this small glass are rectangles of a nickel ferrite substance which are 1,200 angstroms thick (one angstrom is one one-hundred millionth of a centimeter). On this small plane, there is room for 768 rectangles, each representing one bit of storage, a total capacity of 128 character positions of memory.

The first thin-film planes made were done by hand. If one bit was not up to standard, the entire plane had to be discarded. Consequently, the initial price of a plane was about a dollar per bit. With new techniques of vacuum depositing, the present cost has brought the thin-film memory into a practical price range. Undoubtedly, there will be further improvements and miniaturization of the films. Since the size for particular computer memory is often based on the practical cost for the system, and since it is desirable to have more memory than is made available, a cheaper method of primary storage is constantly being sought.

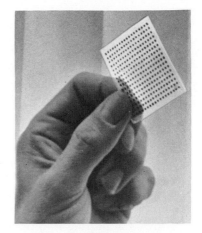

FIG. 10-7 A thin film memory (courtesy Univac Division, Sperry Rand Corp.)

Cryogenic memory.   The latest development involves *cryogenics,* a term derived from a word relevant to the study of cold temperatures. A cryogenic memory is a superconducting memory set at a very low temperature. Extremely fast and small, it is at this time considered too expensive to be marketed competitively.

Photo-digital memory.   This is a memory system designed by IBM Corporation for the U.S. Atomic Energy Commission. The system, basically, employs an electron beam to record binary data on 1.3 in. by 2.7 in. pieces of film. The film, then, is developed by an internal automated "film laboratory," transported in plastic cells through a series of pneumatic tubes, and filed for later retrieval. Reading of the data is accomplished by a flying spot scanner. This unique and highly expensive form of memory serves to illustrate the types of research and development being conducted in the area of computer memory.

Software

Critical to the proper and effective use of the hardware are the programs and other operating aids (usually available to the user by the manufacturer) which extend the capabilities of a specific computer system. These programs are generally referred to as *software* and are commonly used in such tasks as printing out machine-readable records and in sequencing, organizing, and updating files.

Generalized programs written by the user are made up of instructions that tell the computer what to do for processing a given application. While the manufacturer provides some of these programs for certain tasks, the user finds himself required to write a number of programs for various projects.

Peopleware

The term *peopleware* refers to computer operators, programmers, and systems analysts whose job is to perform whatever tasks necessary to achieve desired results for the user. The computer operator's tasks are relatively well-defined ones that require limited knowledge of programming or the internal workings of the computer system.

By contrast, the programmer is expected to have specialized skills in writing and preparing the instructions for computer use. Unlike programmers or computer operators, the systems analyst is expected to have adequate educational background and broad knowledge of business organizations and the internal workings of the departments involved.

Given the foregoing elements of a computer system, certain steps are followed in putting it to practical use.

1. *Problem diagnosis.* Deciding on the type and frequency of processing of certain information.
2. *System design and logic.* Determining in advance the manner in which a given project will be processed.
3. *Programming.* Preparing well-debugged instructions in a form understandable to the computer.
4. *Preparation of input data.* Recording data to be processed in a form (e.g., punched cards) which can be read by the computer system.
5. *Program loading and processing.* Loading the program in primary computer storage and processing the data (as dictated by the program) for obtaining desired output.

Glossary of Terms

ACCESS TIME: (1) The time interval between the instant at which data are called for from a storage device and the instant that delivery is completed, i.e., the *read* time. (2) The time interval between the instant at which data are requested to be stored and the instant at which storage is completed, i.e., the *write* time.

ADDRESS: (1) An identification, represented by a name, label, or number, for a register, location in storage, or any other data source or destination, such as the location of a station in a communication network. (2) Loosely, any part of an instruction that specifies the location of an operand for the instruction.

ANALOG COMPUTER: A computer which represents variables by physical analogies. Thus any computer which solves problems by translating physical conditions such as flow, temperature, pressure, angular position, or voltage into related mechanical or electrical quantities and uses mechanical or electrical equivalent circuits as an analog for the physical phenomenon being investigated. In general, a computer which uses an analog for each variable and produces analogs as output. Thus an analog computer measures continuously whereas a digital computer counts discretely.

AUXILIARY STORAGE: Storage which is outside the central-processing unit but is controlled by it.

BINARY: (1) Pertaining to a characteristic or property involving a selection, choice, or condition in which there are two possibilities. (2) Pertaining to the number representation system with a radix of two.

BIT: (1) An abbreviation of *binary digit*. (2) A single character in a binary number. (3) A single pulse in a group of pulses. (4) A unit of information capacity of a storage device.

CHARACTER: An elementary mark or event used to represent data. A character is often in the form of a graphic spatial arrangement of connected or adjacent strokes.

COMPUTER WORD: A sequence of bits or characters treated as a unit. Synonymous with machine word.

CRYOGENICS: The study and use of devices utilizing properties of materials near absolute zero in temperature.

DIGITAL COMPUTER: Operates on discrete data by performing arithmetic and logic processes on these data. Contrast with analog computer.

GENERAL PURPOSE COMPUTER: Designed to solve a wide class of problems.

MAGNETIC CORE: A configuration of magnetic material that is, or is intended to be, placed in a spatial relationship to current-carrying conductors and whose magnetic properties are essential to its use. It may be used to concentrate an induced magnetic field as in a transformer induction coil, or armature, to retain a magnetic polarization for the purpose of storing data, or for its nonlinear properties as in a logic element. It may be made of such material as iron, iron oxide, or ferrite, and in such shapes as wires and tapes.

MEMORY: (1) Pertaining to a device into which data can be entered, in which it can be held, and from which it can be retrieved at a later time. (2) Loosely, any device that can store data.

PARITY CHECK: A check that tests whether the number of ones (or zeros) in an array of binary digits is odd or even. Synonymous with odd-even check.

PROCESS: A general term covering such terms as assemble, compile, generate, interpret, and compute.

SOFTWARE: Programs and other operating aids which extend the capabilities of the computer.

SPECIAL-PURPOSE COMPUTER: A computer that is designed to solve a restricted class of problems.

Questions for Review

1. What are some of the chief limitations of a punched card data processing system?
2. What are some of the unique characteristics of the punched card and the computer systems?
3. List and explain briefly the primary elements of an electronic data processing system.
4. What are the basic types of storage? Explain.
5. List and explain the basic components of a digital computer.
6. What is an address? A character? Give an example to illustrate each.
7. If the amount 946742 is stored in primary storage in location numbers 801 to 806, what is the address of digit 7? 2? 9?
8. What are the primary storage devices? Explain.
9. What is the difference between hardware and software? How are they related?
10. Describe a magnetic core. How does it store information?
11. What is meant by parity check? What is the difference between even- and odd-parity check?
12. What is thin-film memory? Explain.
13. List and describe briefly the basic types of computers.
14. What is the difference between an analog and a digital computer?
15. What is the difference between special purpose and general purpose computers?

chapter eleven

CODED DATA REPRESENTATION

To SIMPLIFY THE HANDLING OF DATA ELECTRONICALLY, it was important to develop methods of coding decimal and alphabetic information into a form that could be used by computers. Just as punched cards are a form of coded information employing one of two states (either a hole or no hole in a particular position), so electronic computers employ the state of a particular location to represent information. This may be indicated by the direction of a magnetic field, by an open or closed relay, or by a ferrite core magnetized clockwise or counterclockwise. Such schemes of "yes or no," "on or off," and "zero or one" introduce the important concepts of the binary numbering system. Combinations of the zero- and 1-symbols (bits) are basic to the representation of digits, letters, and/or special characters in primary storage.

NUMERICAL DATA REPRESENTATION

For the convenience of the user, especially in business data processing, input to the computer is written or printed in standard decimal or alphabetic form. It should be remembered, however, that these characters are first converted into codes by the computer, based on the binary numbering system used within the computer. Next, the coded data are reconverted to decimal and alphabetic characters when printing the output results (Fig. 11-1). Although few people except the microprogrammer need to work in terms of these binary codes, it is desirable to understand something about them and their ability to represent data in computer storage.

To understand the binary system, a review of the basic characteristics of the decimal system would be helpful. Our decimal system probably is used because man's fingers are the most convenient tools nature has provided for

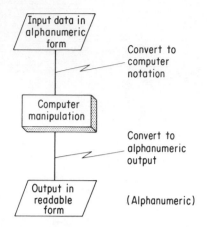

Convert to computer notation

Convert to alphanumeric output

(Alphanumeric)

FIG. 11-1 Steps involved in converting data into, and out of, a computer system

counting. The decimal system involves the use of ten different digits: 0 through 9. To represent any amount greater than 9, the proper decimal numbers are positioned side by side. Each position has a value which is a multiple of 10, as these digits are placed from right to left. In Fig. 11-2 each box represents one decimal digit and its appropriate power. The decimal value 1 5 6 2 3, then, is the sum of each of the individual numbers after each has been multiplied by the value of its position:

$$
\begin{array}{rrr}
3 \times & 1 = & 3 \\
2 \times & 10 = & 20 \\
6 \times & 100 = & 600 \\
5 \times & 1000 = & 5000 \\
1 \times & 10000 = & 10000 \\
\hline
& & 15623
\end{array}
$$

The answer might seem obvious, since we are accustomed to dealing with decimal numbers. This technique will be helpful in understanding binary figures, however.

In binary, the only acceptable numbers are 0 and 1. Since "bi" means *two*, such a system is called *binary*. With these two symbols we can represent the equivalent of any decimal digit by placing the two symbols in certain mathematical combinations. The binary numbering system lends itself most easily and economically to the design and function of digital computers.

10^4	10^3	10^2	10^1	10^0
10,000	1000	100	10	1
1	5	6	2	3

FIG. 11-2

To represent decimal data greater than 1 in binary, the next higher binary number is formed by adding 1 to its predecessor (Fig. 11-3). In other words, from right to left, the value of each binary digit is a greater power of two (2^0, 2^1, 2^2, etc.), just as the decimal system increases by multiples of ten. In Fig. 11-4, the binary powers of two are placed from right to left. To represent decimal amount 10 in binary, for instance, digit 1 is placed in the box of the approximate binary power; that is, it is determined as shown in Fig. 11-4.

Decimal	Binary	Decimal	Binary
1	1	11	1011
2	10	12	1100
3	11	13	1101
4	100	14	1110
5	101	15	1111
6	110	16	10000
7	111	17	10001
8	1000	18	10010
9	1001	19	10011
10	1010	20	10100

FIG. 11-3

As mentioned earlier, most electronic data-processing equipment operates in a binary mode. The devices used in computers are essentially in either of two states: conducting or nonconducting. This stage is analogous to an electric light bulb which is turned either "ON" or "OFF." It is easy to realize, then, that when the device in computer storage is conducting, it has the effect of representing one binary bit; and when it is nonconducting, it represents a zero bit.

FIG. 11-4

binary power		binary bit		decimal equivalent
8	X	1	=	8
plus				
4	X	0	=	0
plus				
2	X	1	=	2
plus				
1	X	0	=	0
				10

32	16	8	4	2	1

(before)

32	16	8	4	2	1
		1	0	1	0

(after)

For example, in Fig. 11-5, decimal value 5 is represented by two light bulbs turned on in binary place values 4 and 1. That is, 5 in decimal is determined by the sum of:

FIG. 11-5

$$4 \times 1 = 4$$

and

$$1 \times 1 = 1$$

$$\overline{5} \text{ (or 0 1 0 1 in binary)}$$

A popular method of converting decimal to binary is to divide the decimal amount successively by two. The remainder of each of the successive divisions, reading up, constitutes the binary equivalent (see Fig. 11-6).

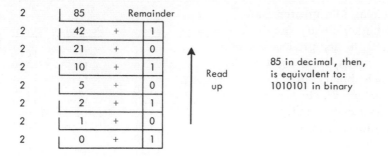

FIG. 11-6 Decimal to binary conversion

Binary-to-decimal conversion follows exactly the opposite routine. That is, to convert a binary value to a decimal equivalent, each binary digit (beginning at the left) is multiplied by two, and its product is added to the number until the entire binary amount is converted. For example, in converting binary amount 1 1 1 0 1 0, we proceed as shown in Fig. 11-7.

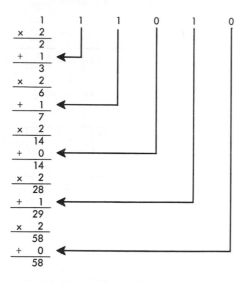

Therefore, 111010 in binary is equivalent to 58 in decimal

FIG. 11-7 Binary to decimal conversion

Some computers, particularly those which are constructed chiefly for scientific and engineering purposes, represent numbers in a pure binary fashion. In such cases, decimal input is converted to binary, manipulated, and usually converted back into decimal for output. A disadvantage of binary over decimal numbering is that bits (binary digits) require more positions; however, without binary, decimal numbers would have to be represented by ten different quantities of electricity, rather than a simple "on-off" state. This would present many problems of control and reliability to the engineers.

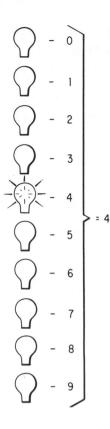

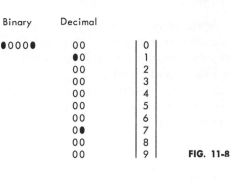

Binary	Decimal	
●0000	00	0
	●0	1
	00	2
	00	3
	00	4
	00	5
	00	6
	0●	7
	00	8
	00	9

FIG. 11-8

Binary is a way to represent decimal digits without being concerned about the quantity of electricity. On a punched card, for example, the numbers 0 through 9 are represented by a hole in a particular position in the column. A similar approach would involve the use of 10 light bulbs, each one representing a decimal number. When one of the lights is turned on, it represents the particular digit for which it is reserved (Fig. 11-8). By installing these "columns" side by side, one could represent a large decimal number.

Figure 11-8 shows that decimal-digit 17 would be represented by two columns of bulbs in straight decimal representation, as compared to a binary representation of the same amount. Whereas the binary code requires five places (five light bulbs) to represent decimal value 17, the decimal system (although it uses only two places) requires 20. From the human point of view, it might be better to use the extra "light bulbs" and eliminate the binary-to-decimal conversion, but it should be remembered that this conversion is done automatically by a computer at a great rate of speed. For simplicity, the filled-in zeros in Fig. 11-8 represent "on" light bulbs.

OPERATOR NOTATION

It can be concluded from the foregoing discussion of binary data representation that any number can be represented by a set of binary digits or bits. However, due to the design and circuitry of various computers, the number of binary digits to be used in representing a number must be specified either in terms of a *fixed* number of bits (ranging in size from 16-60) or a *variable* number of bit sets (ranging in size from 4 to 8 bits each set). The former requirement fits the description of a fixed word length computer, whereas the latter requirement fits the description of a variable word length computer.

In representing numbers by fixed set of bits, the computer operator often finds it cumbersome to work with or read a series of binary digits. More effective computer notations have been developed. Currently emphasized are the octal and the hexadecimal.

Numbers represented by a variable number of bit sets refer to the binary coded decimal system (a binary based system of coding) explained in a later section in the chapter.

Octal

The octal (or base eight) system uses three fixed bits for number representation. The three bits (when each bit consists of one) represent a total of 7, i.e., in the octal system, there are only the digits 0 through 7. The numbers 8 and 9 are never used.

To represent decimal-digit 8 or more, another position is added to the left of its predecessor, thus increasing by a multiple of eight, compared to the decimal system, which increases by a multiple of 10, or the binary system, which increases by a multiple of two (see Fig. 11-9).

FIG. 11-9   Numerical coding systems

Decimal Digit	Binary	Octal
0	0	0
1	1	1
2	10	2
3	11	3
4	100	4
5	101	5
6	110	6
7	111	7
8	1000	10
9	1001	11

In manual conversion, an octal coded number may be converted into decimal by multiplying each octal digit by 8 (beginning with the left-most digit) and adding its product to the digit to the right until the whole number is included. For instance, 721 in octal is converted to decimal as follows:

```
                    7   2   1
Multiply      × 8
              ─────
               56
Add           + 2  ◄─┘
              ─────
               58
Multiply      × 8
              ─────
              464
Add           + 1  ◄───────┘
              ─────
              465
```

Therefore, 721 in octal is equal to 465 in decimal.

Octal coded numbers are also converted into decimal by multiplying each octal value by its positional value. Using the same example, octal number 7 2 1 is converted to decimal as follows:

octal   7   2   1

$$1 \times 8^0 = 1$$
$$2 \times 8^1 = 8$$
$$7 \times 8^2 = 448$$
$$\overline{465} \quad \text{Decimal equivalent}$$

Another way of expressing 721_8 is as follows:

$$(7 \times 8^2) + (2 \times 8^1) + (1 \times 8^0).$$

A decimal value is converted to octal by dividing it successively by 8. The remainder of each division stands for an octal number. For example, the decimal value 6 1 4 is converted into octal as follows:

Remainder

8	614	
8	76	6
8	9	4
8	1	1
8	0	1 → 1 1 4 6 (octal equivalent)

The octal system provides a simple "shorthand" for representing long binary numbers.

Octal coded numbers may be easily converted into binary by assigning a fixed number of three binary digits to each octal digit. For instance, octal number 7 2 1 is converted to binary as follows:

octal   7   2   1
binary equivalent   111   010   001

Hexadecimal

The representation of large numbers in binary is often cumbersome to interpret and to manipulate. The hexadecimal system is used to handle such large numbers, since each hexadecimal digit represents four binary bits.

The hexadecimal numbering system uses a base of 16, unlike base 10 of the decimal system, base 8 of the octal, or base 2 of the binary system. Since the decimal system provides only ten digits to represent the first ten values of the hexadecimal system (0–9), the remaining six hexadecimal values are arbitrarily represented by the first six letters of the alphabet, A, B, C, D, E and F. Thus, the entire symbolic set of the hexadecimal numbering system consists of 0, 1, 2, 3, 4, 5, 6, 7, 8, 9, A, B, C, D, E, F. In this sequence, letter A represents a decimal value of 10, letter B, a decimal value of 11, . . . , and letter F, a decimal value of 15 (Fig. 11-10). Note that when the decimal number 10 is reached, a "carry" to the next most significant position takes place. In the case of the hexadecimal system, when hexadecimal number 16 is reached, there is a "carry" to the next most significant position.

Decimal	Binary	Octal	Hexadecimal	FIG. 11-10
0	0	0	0	
1	1	1	1	
2	10	2	2	
3	11	3	3	
4	100	4	4	
5	101	5	5	
6	110	6	6	
7	111	7	7	
8	1000	10	8	
9	1001	11	9	
10	1010	12	A	
11	1011	13	B	
12	1100	14	C	
13	1101	15	D	
14	1110	16	E	
15	1111	17	F	
16	10000	20	10	
17	10001	21	11	
25	11001	31	19	
26	11010	32	1A	
27	11011	33	1B	
28	11100	34	1C	
29	11101	35	1D	
30	11110	36	1E	
31	11111	37	1F	

Since a hexadecimal digit represents a fixed set of four binary digits, the conversion of hexadecimal to and from binary is relatively simple. Hexadecimal to binary conversion is made by replacing each hexadecimal digit by the equivalent set of four binary digits. For example, hexadecimal number E 7 A is converted to binary as follows:

hexadecimal   (E)   (7)   (A)
binary equivalent   1110   0111   1010

A binary number is converted into hexadecimal by separating the binary digits (starting with the rightmost digit) into fixed sets of four digits. If the last set is less than four digits, leading zeros are added. Once established, the equivalent hexadecimal digit for each set is substituted. For example, the binary number 010111001011 is converted to hexadecimal as follows:

binary   010111001011

hexadecimal equivalent   (5) (C) (B)

A decimal number is converted to hexadecimal by dividing successively by 16. The remainder of each division stands for a hexadecimal number. The remainders 10 through 15 must be converted to their hexadecimal notation of A through F, respectively. For example, the decimal value 1 9 7 0 is converted into hexadecimal as follows:

Remainder

16	1970	
16	123	2
16	7 (11)	B
16	0	7

7 B 2   (the hexadecimal equivalent of 1970).

Conversion from hexadecimal to decimal is simply performed by a series of multiplications and additions.

1. Multiply the most significant (leftmost) hexadecimal digit by 16.
2. Add the next most significant hexadecimal digit to the product and multiply the sum by 16.
3. Continue the add and multiply procedure until the least significant (leftmost) hexadecimal digit has been added to the last product.

Using the hexadecimal result (7 B 2) in the example above, we proceed as follows:

```
                          7  B  2  Hexadecimal
        Multiply     ×   16
                        112
        Add          +   11
                        123
        Multiply     ×   16
                       1968
        Add          +    2
                       1970
```

7 B 2 in hexadecimal, then, is equivalent to a decimal value of 1970.

Binary Coded Decimal (BCD)

In its most common usage, the BCD code was originally a four-bit code for representing decimal numbers in binary format. It is used for business-oriented computers. Although it simplifies the programming phase of computer applications and the input/output conversion, it sacrifices internal operating speeds.

The BCD representation is detected by the presence of a 1-bit in the appropriate box, or level. Figure 11-11 shows the most popular type of BCD code, based on four binary bits. These are more than adequate to represent any decimal digit (0 through 9); that is, with each of the four positions containing a 1-bit (turned on), the maximum value would be $(8 \times 1) + (4 \times 1) + (2 \times 1) + (1 \times 1) = 15$ (Fig. 11-12).

The 4-bit BCD code is used to represent one decimal digit at a time. If two or more decimal digits are represented, two or more 4-bit combinations are required: one to represent the unit's position, another to represent the ten's position, and so on. For instance, decimal amount 271 is shown in Fig. 11-13. Therefore, the decimal value can be determined in terms of powers of ten by the position of the bit in the BCD code. A bit in the top position is worth eight; the next, four; then, two; and the bottom position, one.

A binary-coded number is converted into octal simply by dividing the binary value (beginning from the right digit) into an equal portion of three bits each. If the last (left) digit (or digits) does not total 3 in number, add zero(s). For example, binary number 1 1 0 0 1 is converted into octal as follows:

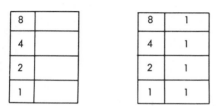

FIG. 11-11   The BCD code   FIG. 11-12

BCD		Decimal	
	2	7	1
8	0	0	0
4	0	1	0
2	1	1	0
1	0	1	1

FIG. 11-13

binary	0 1 1	0 0 1
octal	3	1

Alphanumeric Data Representation

In modern electronic data processing, the need for the central processor to represent alphabetic as well as numeric information has become very important. To be able to do this, manufacturers have settled on an internal representation, a 6-bit alphanumeric code system, which is similar in most computers. This code utilizes a six-bit grouping called a *frame*, in which the lower four bits are the BCD 8, 4, 2, and 1. These four bits alone are sufficient to represent numeric data, but to represent alphabetic data, two more bits are added (bits A and B). Their combination with 8, 4, 2, and 1 in forming alphabetic characters is similar in approach to alphabetic coding in the punched card (through the use of the zone-punching positions). Each computer has its

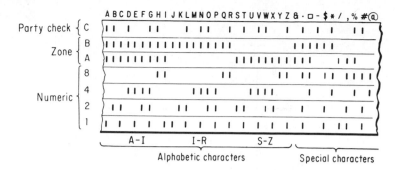

FIG. 11-14 Alphanumeric data representation

own coding scheme for combining the A- and B- (zone) bits with the numeric bits to form alphanumeric characters.

In one popular code (Fig. 11-14), letters A through Z are represented as follows: letters A through I are represented by the A- and B-zone bits, in addition to numeric bits 1 through 9. Letters J through R are represented by the B-zone bit only, in addition to numeric bits 1 through 9. Letters S through Z are represented by the A-zone bit, along with numeric bits 2 through 9. The A- and B-bits together perform the same function as the 12-punch in a card; the B-bit is the same as the 11-punch; and the A-bit is similar to the 0-punch.

Special characters representing blank, asterisk, comma, slash, etc., are arbitrarily established by the computer manufacturer and are coded in such a way as to distinguish them from one another. The seventh bit (C-bit) is added in this scheme for parity checking.

To summarize, the foregoing presentation shows that although the user is interested only in decimal numbers as output, the internal operation of electronic computers is based on digits in various binary forms. Having a comprehensive understanding of these forms would give a more meaningful conception of the output realized.

Alphanumeric characters can be represented as binary-coded characters in one of three ways. One approach (explained above) is to expand the four bit BCD code into a 6-bit code to represent the alphabetic and special characters. This is typical of a second-generation computer as the IBM 1401 system (Fig. 11-15). The second approach is to use two 4-bit (BCD) sets, one set representing alphabetic character and the other set representing special character (Fig. 11-16).

The third approach is a variation of the first two approaches and is quite common in third generation computers. It uses an 8-bit byte [1] which can represent either an alphanumeric or two numeric characters. As shown in Fig. 11-17, in alphanumeric representation, four digits of the 8-bit byte can be used to represent a numeric digit, while the other four bit set can be used to represent a zone (alphabetic) digit.

[1] A byte is a string of digits, operated on as a unit. In most cases, it is 8 bits long.

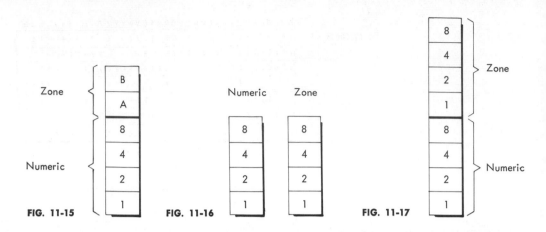

FIG. 11-15   FIG. 11-16   FIG. 11-17

Extended Binary Coded Decimal Interchange Code (EBCDIC)

The nature of data processing is such that it is necessary that a computer system be capable of manipulating data made up of alphabetic, numeric and special characters. To facilitate representation of the desired data for computer use, these characters are coded as sets of binary digits which are compatible with digital computer operation, and the first common method of representing a full range of characters was the binary coded decimal (BCD) code. The expansion of character requirements puts a damper on the adequacy of the BCD format, which led to the development of Extended Binary Coded Decimal Interchange Code (EBCDIC) and American Standard Code for Information Interchange (ASCII).

EBCDIC employs an eight-bit unit byte for data representation. This coding structure as well as the ASCII code are similar to the third variation introduced earlier. The use of eight bits, instead of the previously used six, has several advantages. First, the use of eight bit units represents a maximum of 256 distinct characters, which makes it feasible to represent numeric, alphabetic (upper-case and lower-case), and special characters. Especially significant in the growing use of communication-based computer systems is the availability of bit configurations in excess of those required for alphabetic, numeric, and special characters. This allows the characters necessary for the control of remote terminal devices to be uniquely represented, minimizing the possibility of undetected device activity.

Another major advantage of an eight bit configuration for character representation has to do with numeric characters, which remain the most common form of data. Since a decimal digit may be represented by only four binary digits (and, consequently, by a set of four bits), an eight bit configuration allows the representation of two decimal digits. This is commonly referred to as a "packed" format. The rightmost four bits are used to represent the decimal value and the leftmost four bits are used for sign designation.

In EBCDIC, an unsigned digit is assumed positive and is represented by 1 1 1 1 in the leftmost four bits. The 1 1 1 1 format was chosen to make certain that numeric characters would be the highest in the collating sequence of

156

characters. A plus sign is represented by 1 1 0 0 and a minus sign by 1 1 0 1. Usually, the sign occupies the leftmost four bits of the least significant digit and the remaining digits occupy 1 1 1 1 in the leftmost four bits. In the "packed" format, however, the sign occupies the least significant (rightmost) four bits and all other sign designations are eliminated. Selected bit configurations for EBCDIC are presented in Fig. 11-18.

American Standard Code for Information Interchange (ASCII)

ASCII was originally in the form of a seven-bit standard code promulgated by the American Standards Association (now the American National Standards Institute) in 1966. Today's version of ASCII is a modification of the seven-bit standard code which uses eight bits. The concept and advantages of eight-bit ASCII are identical to those of EBCDIC. The difference lies in the bit configurations chosen to represent alphabetic, numeric and special characters. Selected bit configurations for ASCII-8 are comparatively represented in Fig. 11-18.

FIG. 11-18

Character	EBCDIC	Bit Representation	Configuration ASC11-8	Bit Representation
0	1111	0000	0101	0000
1	1111	0001	0101	0001
2	1111	0010	0101	0010
3	1111	0011	0101	0011
4	1111	0100	0101	0100
5	1111	0101	0101	0101
6	1111	0110	0101	0110
7	1111	0111	0101	0111
8	1111	1000	0101	1000
9	1111	1001	0101	1001
A	1100	0001	1010	0001
B	1100	0010	1010	0010
C	1100	0011	1010	0011
D	1100	0100	1010	0100
E	1100	0101	1010	0101
F	1100	0110	1010	0110
G	1100	0111	1010	0111
H	1100	1000	1010	1000
I	1100	1001	1010	1001
J	1101	0001	1010	1010
K	1101	0010	1010	1011
L	1101	0011	1010	1100
M	1101	0100	1010	1101
N	1101	0101	1010	1110
O	1101	0110	1010	1111
P	1101	0111	1011	0000
Q	1101	1000	1011	0001
R	1101	1001	1011	0010
S	1110	0010	1011	0011
T	1110	0011	1011	0100
U	1110	0100	1011	0101
V	1110	0101	1011	0110
W	1110	0110	1011	0111
X	1110	0111	1011	1000
Y	1110	1000	1011	1001
Z	1110	1001	1011	1010

157

FLOATING POINT BASICS

Most electronic data processing systems operate within a fixed range involving data representation. This constraint is governed by the capacity of the system and the size of the data word(s) to be accommodated. The job of relying on the computer to keep track of decimal points in calculative problems and values of different sizes in a given application becomes extremely important. The programmer no longer needs to check on sizes of different data and maintain proper alignment with the computer's storage and register capacity. This job is done by computers that use a system of notations called a *floating-point* number representation.

A floating-point number is, basically, a representation of a value that is made up of two numbers: a numeric fraction between .1 and 1 and a power of the base of the number system used. In the decimal number system, a floating-point number is composed of a numeric fraction and a power of 10; in binary, a numeric fraction and a power of 2; in octal, a numeric fraction and a power of 8, and in hexadecimal, a numeric fraction and a power of 16.

The number represented by the floating-point notation is obtained by multiplying the two component numbers. For example, decimal number 795,362 is represented in floating-point notation as $.795362 \times 10^6$ and the decimal number 0.00513 is represented in floating-point notation as $.513 \times 10^{-2}$. This method of number representation is called *scientific notation* when it is used outside the context of data processing.

Glossary of Terms

BINARY-CODED DECIMAL: A decimal notation in which the individual decimal digits are each represented by a group of binary digits; e.g., in the 8-4-2-1 binary-coded decimal notation, the number 23 is represented as 0010 0011, whereas in binary notation, 23 is represented as 10111.

ASCII: American Standard Code for Information Interchange—now called USASCII.

BYTE: A string of digits, operated on as a unit. In most cases, it is 8 bits long.

FLOATING-POINT: Usually a representation of numbers and a method of performing arithmetic. The point is at a location defined by the number itself.

HEXADECIMAL: A number representation system using base 16.

OCTAL: A number representation system using base 8.

Questions for Review

1. Convert the following values from decimal to binary: (a) 4; (b) 9; (c) 11; (d) 17; (e) 25; (f) 64; (g) 126.
2. Convert the following values from binary to decimal:
   (a) 1 0 1   (b) 1 0 0 0 1   (c) 1 0 0 1   (d) 1 1 1   (e) 1 1 1 0 1
   (f) 1 0 1 1 1   (g) 1 1 1 0 1   (h) 1 0 0 1 1 0 0

3. "The decimal system uses base ten whereas the binary system uses base two." Explain this statement. Give an example to illustrate.
4. What is a *coding system?*
5. What is the difference between straight binary and binary-coded decimal representation?
6. What is the octal code? Represent decimal values 62 and 74 in octal.
7. Show how the following values are represented in (1) straight binary; (2) BCD; (3) octal; and (4) hexadecimal: (a) 3; (b) 4; (c) 8; (d) 13; (e) 89; (f) 98; (g) 106; (h) 890.
8. Perform the following conversions: (a) 3780 to octal; (b) 321_8 to decimal; (c) 110000-1111010 to octal; (d) 416_8 to binary.
9. Convert the following octal numbers to binary: (a) 133; (b) 302; (c) 704.
10. Convert the following hexadecimal numbers to binary: (a) CB; (b) 29; (c) FA; (d) 1A.
11. Use the numbers in Question 10 and convert them to decimal.

chapter twelve

THE ARITHMETIC AND CONTROL UNITS

161

MUCH HAS BEEN SAID regarding the role and function of primary storage in electronic data processing. For it to perform an active and effective role in a computer system, supporting devices such as the arithmetic and control units are integrated to achieve the correct result. Harmonious coordination between these devices is imperative since neither device is capable of working alone. Primary storage has been shown to store the data being processed and retain the results until needed. However, in order to get these results, the arithmetic unit must be both present and active for the execution of the various required arithmetic operations.

PARALLEL ADDER

The arithmetic unit is defined as that part of the computer which performs the basic arithmetic functions of addition, subtraction, multiplication, and division under the direction of the control unit. It is composed of adder circuits, electronic devices which perform all arithmetic and logical operations. The adder is like the mechanical wheels of an adding machine, except that computer adders are electronic, rather than mechanical.

Adders are of two kinds: serial and parallel. Since a fixed word-length computer deals with information in groups of several digits at a time, it is necessary to have an adder which is capable of (1) adding a full word of digits to another full word of digits; (2) allowing the result to be accumulated at the same time; and (3) taking care of the carryover from one decimal position to another. Adders which add several bits simultaneously are called parallel adders.

In addition to a parallel adder, a computer also includes an electronic device called an *accumulator*. Its function is to store values (sums) temporarily. For example, when two numbers are added, an accumulator first is cleared and the first number is stored in it. Next, through the adder, the second number is added to the contents of the accumulator, which also shows the final sum. When the final total is reached, the result is moved back into the computer memory (Fig. 12-1). Later improvements in this concept move the final

FIG. 12-1 Parallel adder—adding two numbers

Step 1.   Clear the accumulator.

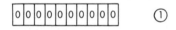

Step 2.   Move the first amount from
          computer memory into the
          accumulator.

Step 3.   Add contents of second
          amount to it (5719818117).

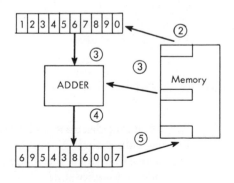

Step 4.   Result stored temporarily in
          the accumulator.

Step 5.   Move the sum to computer.

Step 6.   The sum still shows in the
          accumulator until cleared when
          another addition is made.

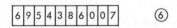

sum directly into computer memory the moment it is realized, thus eliminating the need for its temporary storage in the accumulator. This is referred to as the "add-to-storage" concept (Fig. 12-2).

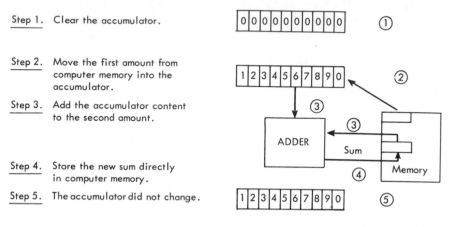

Step 1.   Clear the accumulator.

Step 2.   Move the first amount from computer memory into the accumulator.

Step 3.   Add the accumulator content to the second amount.

Step 4.   Store the new sum directly in computer memory.

Step 5.   The accumulator did not change.

FIG. 12-2   Add to storage concept

SERIAL ADDER

With the character-oriented or the variable word-length computer, the parallel adder is not practical. Since fields are of varying lengths, there is no requirement for a specific number of digits involving the adder or the accumulator.

Essentially, a serial adder is a one-digit adder. When two fields are to be added together, the low-order (right-hand) position of the first field is put into the adder. The low-order position of the second field is added to it. The sum is put back directly into computer memory in the low-order position of the area reserved for storing the sum. The arithmetic unit continues this process until all the digits of the two fields (amounts) have been added (Fig. 12-3). The serial adder utilizes the "add-to-storage" concept, and makes the need for an accumulator unnecessary.

BINARY ADDITION

The foregoing discussion illustrates the arithmetic unit's capability of adding decimal values through the use of adders and accumulators. Binary addition also is feasible since the electronic state of the computer would provide for the one-versus-zero state.

Addition is performed on binary digits following the same basic rules as those used in the decimal system. It should be noted that a "carry" occurs in binary when a total exceeds one; a carry occurs in decimal after 9 is reached. The rules for binary addition are as follows:

$$0 + 0 = 0$$
$$1 + 0 = 1$$
$$0 + 1 = 1$$
$$1 + 1 = 0 \text{ with a carry-over of } 1$$

Step 1.

1. Add the two low-order digits together (3 + 8)
2. Store the sum.
3. Note the carry following step 1.

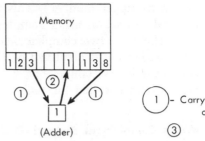

Step 2.

4. Add the next two digits (2 + 3) and the carry of 1.
5. Store the sum with carry from step 1. (Note carry off following Step 2)

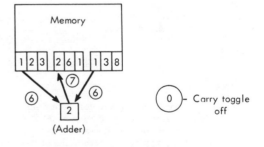

Step 3.

6. Add the last two digits (1 + 1).
7. Store the sum

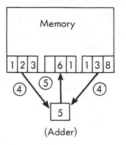

FIG. 12-3   Serial adder

For example, the binary addition of 1 0 1 0 and 1 0 1 1 would be performed as follows:

Binary	Decimal
1 0 1 0	10
1 0 1 1	11
1 0 1 0 1	21

The sum of 1 0 1 0 (ten) and 1 0 1 1 (eleven) in binary, then, is equal to 1 0 1 0 1, or 21 in decimal.

DECIMAL SUBTRACTION

Most digital computers perform binary subtraction first by complementing the subtrahend (lower number) and then adding the complement to the minuend (upper number). This may be best understood by comparing it to decimal subraction using complements.

There are two complements of interest associated with a decimal digit: one complement is identified by the base of the decimal system, less one. It is called the nine's complement. The other is related to the base of the decimal system, and is called the ten's complement.

Nine's Complement Method—Decimal System

In the nine's system, each decimal digit in the subtrahend is first subtracted from 9. The nine's complement of digit 5 is 4; of digit 6, 3; of digit 7, 2. Subtraction proceeds by adding the complemented subtrahend to the minuend, as shown in Fig. 12-4.

```
      Minuend   + 3 8 9 5            The manual
                 -                   subtraction
                                     method.
      Subtrahend  +   6 4 2
                  +   3 2 5 3    Remainder
```

Step 1. Determine the nine's complement of the subtrahend and add.

```
                              BEFORE            AFTER
              Minuend       + 3 8 9 5          + 3 8 9 5
                             -              +
              Subtrahend    + 0 6 4 2          + 9 3 5 7

(9999 - 0642 = 9357)                           1 3 2 5 2
```

Note: For complementing purposes, both fields used in subtraction must be of equal length. If one field is shorter than another, zero(s) are added in the high-order positions to equalize the length.

Step 2. The end-around carry (encircled) is added to the lower-order position:

```
                                      ①3 2 5 2
                                           ➤ 1
                                      3 2 5 3   Remainder
```

FIG. 12-4

However, if no carry is realized in the high-order position, it means that the remainder is in complement form and is also negative. A recomplement is necessary to obtain the true remainder. For example, in subtracting $6 - 8$, we proceed as follows:

Step 1. Complement the subtrahend and add.

	Before	After	
	6	6	Minuend
	-8	$+1$	Complemented subtrahend
		$\overline{7}$	Remainder in complement form

Step 2. Since there is no carry, 7 must be recomplemented and a minus $(-)$ sign added.

$$\begin{array}{r} 9 \\ -7 \\ \hline -2 \end{array} \text{ The true remainder}$$

Therefore, $6 - 8 = -2$.

Ten's Complement Method—Decimal System

In the 10's complement method, a similar procedure is followed: that is, the 10's complement of the subtrahend is determined and added to the minuend, replacing any end-around carry with a plus $(+)$ sign. The 10's complement of digit 6 is 4; of 7 is 3; of 8 is 2; etc. For example, suppose we wish to subtract 17 from 25, using the 10's complement method. We proceed as follows:

Manual Method

Minuend	25
Subtrahend	-17
	$\overline{08}$ Remainder

Step 1. Determine the ten's complement of the subtrahend.

$$(100 - 17 = 83)$$

Step 2. Add the complemented subtrahend to the minuend.

Minuend	25
	$+83$
	$\overline{①08}$

Step 3. The encircled digit is a carry, and is changed to a plus $(+)$ sign.

Minuend	25
Subtrahend	$+83$
	$+\overline{08}$ True remainder

If no carry is realized, a recomplement of the remainder must be made and a negative sign added denoting a negative remainder. For example:

17 Minuend
-25 Subtrahend   The manual method of subtraction.
$\overline{-08}$

Step 1. Determine the ten's complement of the subtrahend.

$$(100 - 25 = 75)$$

Step 2. Add the complemented subtrahend to the minuend.

$$
\begin{array}{ll}
17 & \text{Minuend} \\
+\,75 & \text{Complemented subtrahend} \\
\hline
+\,92 & \text{Remainder in complement form}
\end{array}
$$

Step 3. Since there is no carry, the remainder should be complemented and a negative sign added, denoting that it is a negative remainder.

$$(100 - 92 = 08)$$ Adding the negative sign, 08 becomes −08.

BINARY SUBTRACTION

One's Complement Method—Binary System

Binary subtraction is performed by reversing the binary state of the subtrahend which gives us the one's complement, adding it to the minuend, and adding any resulting carry to the sum. For example, to subtract 1 0 0 1 (9) from 1 1 0 0 (12), we proceed as follows:

Step 1. Reverse the subtrahend to its opposite state. That is, all 1's are changed to 0's and all 0's changed to 1's. *This is the one's complement.*

Decimal	*Binary* *(before)*	*Binary* *(after)*
12	1 1 0 0	1 1 0 0
09	1 0 0 1	0 1 1 0
03		

Step 2. Add

$$
\begin{array}{l}
1\,1\,0\,0 \\
0\,1\,1\,0 \\
\hline
\textcircled{1}\,0\,0\,1\,0
\end{array}
$$

Step 3. If a carry results in the high-order position, it is added to the unit's position, thus:
1 0 0 1 0 becomes

$$
\begin{array}{l}
\textcircled{1}\,0\,0\,1\,0 \\
\qquad\qquad\searrow 1 \\
\hline
+\,0\,0\,1\,1
\end{array}
$$

Two's Complement Method—Binary System

Binary subtraction may be performed by using the two's complement. As with the 10's complement method an end-around carry is replaced with a (+)

sign. If no carry occurs the result must be recomplemented and given a minus sign. For example, suppose we wish to subtract 0101(5) from 1001(9) using the two's complement method. We proceed as follows:

Step 1. Determine the two's complement of the subtrahend.

$$(10000 - 0101) = 1011$$

Decimal	Binary (before)	Binary (after)
9	1 0 0 1	1 0 0 1
− 5	0 1 0 1	1 0 1 1
4		

Step 2. Add.

$$\begin{array}{r} 1\ 0\ 0\ 1 \\ 1\ 0\ 1\ 1 \\ \hline ①0\ 1\ 0\ 0 \end{array}$$

Step 3. The encircled digit is a carry, and is changed to a plus (+) sign.

$$\begin{array}{r} 1\ 0\ 0\ 1 \\ 1\ 0\ 1\ 1 \\ \hline +0\ 1\ 0\ 0 \end{array}$$

If no carry is realized, the complement of the remainder must be taken with a negative sign added denoting a negative remainder. For example, to subtract 9 from 5:

Step 1. Determine the two's complement of the subtrahend.

$$(10000 - 1001) = 0111$$

Decimal	Binary (before)	Binary (after)
5	0 1 0 1	0 1 0 1
− 9	1 0 0 1	0 1 1 1
− 4		

Step 2. Add.

$$\begin{array}{r} 0\ 1\ 0\ 1 \\ 0\ 1\ 1\ 1 \\ \hline 1\ 1\ 0\ 0 \end{array}$$

Step 3. Since there is no carry the remainder should be recomplemented and given a negative sign.

$$(10000 - 1100) = 0100$$

Adding the negative sign, 0100 becomes −0100.

DECIMAL MULTIPLICATION

Multiplication simply is a series of additions, plus some shifting. Look at the following example:

$$
\begin{array}{rr}
\text{Multiplicand} & 1\,2\,3 \\
\text{Multiplier} & 3\,2 \\
\hline
& 2\,4\,6 \\
& 3\,6\,9 \\
\hline
& 3\,9\,3\,6 \quad \text{The product}
\end{array}
$$

Upon receiving the instruction to perform a multiplication, the arithmetic unit first takes the low-order digit of the multiplier (2) and adds the multiplicand to itself twice, arriving at 246. This sum is put aside temporarily. Second, the next high-order position of the multiplier (3) is used to determine the number of times the multiplicand will be added to itself. Each time the next high-order position of the multiplier is used (as in the case of the multiplier-digit 3), the multiplicand is shifted one position to the left, with a zero filling in on the right. Thus, the second operation in this example adds the multiplicand (which is now 1230) to itself three times, as indicated by the next position in the multiplier (3). This sum will be 3690. The first sum (246) plus the second sum (3690) gives the proper answer (3936).

Any two numbers, regardless of their size, may be multiplied. Each time a digit in the multiplier is used, the multiplicand has one more zero added to its right. Each time a new sum is developed, it is added to the previous one until all multiplier digits have been used.

BINARY MULTIPLICATION

Binary multiplication follows the method used in decimal multiplication. The binary multiplication table is short and consists of four entries:

$$
\begin{array}{l}
0 \times 0 = 0 \\
1 \times 0 = 0 \\
0 \times 1 = 0 \\
1 \times 1 = 1
\end{array}
$$

For example, 1 1 1 (seven) multiplied by 1 0 1 (five) equals 1 0 0 0 1 1, as follows:

$$
\begin{array}{cc}
& \textit{Decimal} \\
\begin{array}{r}
1\,1\,1 \\
1\,0\,1 \\
\hline
1\,1\,1 \\
0\,0\,0 \\
1\,1\,1 \\
\hline
1\,0\,0\,0\,1\,1
\end{array}
& \quad
\begin{array}{r}
7 \\
\times\,5 \\
\hline
35 \quad \text{Product}
\end{array}
\end{array}
$$

1 0 0 0 1 1 (35 in decimal)

Division is a combination of successive subtractions just as multiplication is a series of successive additions. In subtraction, however, there also is the use of the complementing process. Complementing must be done first, and then additions take place. However, assuming that complementing is done every time subtraction is made, division is shown as follows:

The manual division method.	No. of Subtractions

```
                4    Quotient          20
Divisor    5    20   Dividend         −5       1
               20                    ────
               00                     15
                                     −5        1
                                    ────
                                     10
                                     −5        1
                                    ────
                                     −5        1
                                    ────      ──
                                      0        4
```

BINARY DIVISION

Like the decimal division method, binary division is performed on the basis of the following table:

$$0 \div 1 = 0$$
$$1 \div 1 = 1$$

For example:

```
            1001              9
    11    11011       3      27
          11                 27
         ─────              ───
          00011              00
          11
         ────
          00
```

HEXADECIMAL ADDITION

Hexadecimal addition is governed by the same rules that apply to decimal and binary addition. Basically, the primary difference among the three types of addition is the point at which a "carry" occurs. In performing decimal addition, when the sum of a series of decimal digits exceeds 9, there is a carry to the next higher order digit position. A carry in binary addition takes place when the sum of binary digits exceeds one. In hexadecimal addition, the carry takes place when the sum of digits exceeds F (equivalent to 15 in decimal). For example, $7 + 8 = F$ (not 15), $7 + 9 = 10$ (equivalent of decimal 16), and $B + 4 = F$ in hexadecimal. Table 12-1 presents the hexadecimal addition of 15×15 matrix or 256 entries.

TABLE 12-1

HEXADECIMAL ADDITION MATRIX

	1	2	3	4	5	6	7	8	9	A	B	C	D	E	F
1	02	03	04	05	06	07	08	09	0A	0B	0C	0D	0E	0F	10
2	03	04	05	06	07	08	09	0A	0B	0C	0D	0E	0F	10	11
3	04	05	06	07	08	09	0A	0B	0C	0D	0E	0F	10	11	12
4	05	06	07	08	09	0A	0B	0C	0D	0E	0F	10	11	12	13
5	06	07	08	09	0A	0B	0C	0D	0E	0F	10	11	12	13	14
6	07	08	09	0A	0B	0C	0D	0E	0F	10	11	12	13	14	15
7	08	09	0A	0B	0C	0D	0E	0F	10	11	12	13	14	15	16
8	09	0A	0B	0C	0D	0E	0F	10	11	12	13	14	15	16	17
9	0A	0B	0C	0D	0E	0F	10	11	12	13	14	15	16	17	18
A	0B	0C	0D	0E	0F	10	11	12	13	14	15	16	17	18	19
B	0C	0D	0E	0F	10	11	12	13	14	15	16	17	18	19	1A
C	0D	0E	0F	10	11	12	13	14	15	16	17	18	19	1A	1B
D	0E	0F	10	11	12	13	14	15	16	17	18	19	1A	1B	1C
E	0F	10	11	12	13	14	15	16	17	18	19	1A	1B	1C	1D
F	10	11	12	13	14	15	16	17	18	19	1A	1B	1C	1D	1E

In using the table, two hexadecimal digits (one digit in a row and another digit in a column) are selected. The sum is found at their intersection. For example, the last digit in each of the 16 rows and columns is F. The sum of $F + F = 1E$ (intersection). 1E is equal to $(1 \times 16) + (14) = 30$ in decimal.

HEXADECIMAL SUBTRACTION

Hexadecimal subtraction follows a similar routine to decimal and binary subtraction. The primary difference relates to the point that a carry of 1 in hexadecimal represents decimal 16. The following examples illustrate two ways in which subtraction is performed:

Example 1. The conventional method

high order digit ⌐ ⌐ low order digit

```
  7  A  7   Minuend
- 2  E  A   Subtrahend
  ─────────
  4  B  D   Difference
```

Step 1. Begin with the low-order (right) digit and subtract A from 7. Since A (equivalent of decimal 10) is greater than 7, 1 (equivalent of decimal 16) is borrowed from A, increasing 7 to 17 (equivalent of decimal 23). Next, subtract A from 17. The remainder is D (equivalent of decimal 13). A (having been decreased by 1) becomes 9.

Step 2. Subtract E (14 in decimal) from 9. Since E is greater than 9, 1 is borrowed from 7 (third hexadecimal digit), increasing 9 to 19. Now, subtract E from 19. The remainder is B. The high order digit 7 becomes 6.

Step 3. Subtract 2 from the high order digit 6, leaving 4. Therefore, the final remainder is 4 B D.

Example 2.   The Paycheck Method

$$
\begin{array}{rccccl}
 & 2 & 5 & 2 & B & 1 & \text{Minuend} \\
- & & D & 3 & 2 & C & \text{Subtrahend} \\
 & 1 & 1 & & 1 & & \text{Carry} \\
\hline
 & 1 & 7 & F & 8 & 5 & \text{Difference}
\end{array}
$$

Step 1. Begin with the low-order digit and subtract C from 1. Since C (equivalent of decimal 12) is greater than 1, 1 is borrowed from B, increasing 1 to 11 (equivalent of decimal 17). Now, subtract C from 11. The remainder is 5.

Step 2. Add a carry of 1 to 2 (the next higher-order subtrahend), making it 3. Subtract 3 from B. The remainder is 8.

Step 3. Subtract 3 from 2. Since 3 is greater than 2, 1 is borrowed from 5, increasing 2 to 12 (equivalent of decimal 18). The remainder is F.

Step 4. Add a carry of 1 to D, making it E. Subtract E from 5. Since E is greater than 5, 1 is borrowed from 2, increasing 5 to 15 (equivalent of decimal 21). The remainder is 7.

Step 5. Subtract a carry of 1 from 2. The remainder is 1.

HEXADECIMAL MULTIPLICATION

Hexadecimal multiplication is subject to the same rules that apply to decimal and binary multiplication. In order to simplify the complex procedure followed, the following hexadecimal multiplication table is presented.

TABLE 12-2

HEXADECIMAL MULTIPLICATION MATRIX

	2	3	4	5	6	7	8	9	A	B	C	D	E	F
2	04	06	08	0A	0C	0E	10	12	14	16	18	1A	1C	1E
3	06	09	0C	0F	12	15	18	1B	1E	21	24	27	2A	2D
4	08	0C	10	14	18	1C	20	24	28	2C	30	34	38	3C
5	0A	0F	14	19	1E	23	28	2D	32	37	3C	41	46	4B
6	0C	12	18	1E	24	2A	30	36	3C	42	48	4E	54	5A
7	0E	15	1C	23	2A	31	38	3F	46	4D	54	5B	62	69
8	10	18	20	28	30	38	40	48	50	58	60	68	70	78
9	12	1B	24	2D	36	3F	48	51	5A	63	6C	75	7E	87
A	14	1E	28	32	3C	46	50	5A	64	6E	78	82	8C	96
B	16	21	2C	37	42	4D	58	63	6E	79	84	8F	9A	A5
C	18	24	30	3C	48	54	60	6C	78	84	90	9C	A8	B4
D	1A	27	34	41	4E	5B	68	75	82	8F	9C	A9	B6	C3
E	1C	2A	38	46	54	62	70	7E	8C	9A	A8	B6	C4	D2
F	1E	2D	3C	4B	5A	69	78	87	96	A5	B4	C3	D2	E1

The following example illustrates the procedure used in hexadecimal multiplication.[1]

		6	A	4	Multiplicand
×			3	B	Multiplier
			2	C	B × 4 ⎞
		6	E		B × A ⎬ The product of the first
	4	2			B × 6 ⎠ multiplier digit
			C		3 × 4 ⎞
	1	E			3 × A ⎬ The product of the second
1	2				3 × 6 ⎠ multiplier digit
Carry	1	1			
1	8	7	C	C	Final product

Note that one multiplier digit is handled at a time and, by shifting, the product of the two multiplier digits is added as shown above.

LOGIC

Another function of the arithmetic unit is to perform the logic of the computer system. It is generally accepted that one of the primary differences between a typical calculating device and a computer is the computer's logical ability. A computer's logic is relatively simple compared to the complex logical thinking of the human brain. However, the speed of the computer logic, plus its capacity for "remembering" its former steps in reaching a goal or problem solution, compensate for the basic simplicity of its logical operations and make it efficient in the processing of data.

Generally, logical decisions made by computers include the ability to tell (1) if two numbers or characters are equal or unequal, (2) if one number is greater or less than another, and (3) if a quantity is positive, negative, or zero. Decisions made by most computers are based on simple comparisons. For instance, if we have a deck of punched cards, each punched with digit 3 in column 1, we can direct the computer to check the presence of the punched digit in each card. Despite the fact that a computer does not "know" a 3 in the same manner we do, it still is able to "tell" us whether column 1 of each card has a 3 punched in it. To do this involves storing in the computer memory the proper instructions as a part of the program it receives.

A computer determines the equality of two values by comparison. Using the deck of cards in the previous example and assuming the storage of digit 3 in memory location 0006, the computer can be instructed to compare the content of column 1 of each card with that of address 0006 in memory. Further, based on the subtraction of one number from another, the computer can determine whether the remainder is negative or positive. If the result is negative,

---

[1] The procedure introduced in this section is adapted from F. R. Crawford, *Introduction to Data Processing*, Prentice-Hall, Inc., Englewood Cliffs, N.J., 1968, pages 126-29.

it can be concluded that the column containing the number is less than 3. If the remainder is zero, it indicates that both numbers (fields) are the same. If the result is positive, the contents of the card column are greater than digit 3 in memory.

How does the computer compare values? The computer contains indicators (on-off bits used only by the arithmetic unit and not part of primary storage) which have special purposes. Generally, there is a "high-low" toggle (or indicator), "equal/unequal" indicator, "minus" indicator, and "zero/non-zero" indicator. When a computer is asked to test any of these functions (one function at a time), the appropriate indicator is set. The result determined by this setting may be used to provide the desired information.

THE CONTROL UNIT

The third major part of the central processor is called the control unit. The control unit causes the arithmetic unit and primary storage to be used in a logical fashion. With every computer system, there is a prewired set of instructions, or commands. Electronic circuitry is provided for each of the functions desired in that particular system. For instance, there is an individual circuit to add, to subtract, to divide, to multiply, to compare, to test for plus or minus, etc. Each of these circuits is given an individual number, and the programmer is told what these numbers are. In computer terminology, they are called operation codes (or op-codes). This list of operation codes is furnished to the user by the manufacturer and differs from computer to computer. An operation code of 7 may mean for one computer to add, but it may mean for another computer to compare.

In dealing with the problem within the internal mechanism of a computer, two elements are stressed: the operation to be performed and the data upon which the operation will take place. The operation to be performed is called the *op-code;* the data are referred to as the *operand*. The sequence of instructions determines the manner in which the problem is to be solved. A complete list of instructions is called a *program*. People trained to write the computer instructions are called *programmers*. Since operation codes and primary storage vary from one computer to another, the actual format of the instruction varies also. Regardless of the computer system used, however, an instruction contains at least an operation code and a reference to an operand.

Registers

A register is a device in the computer which is used for storing temporarily a specific amount of information, an example of which is the accumulator. To illustrate the use of registers, assume the availability of a fixed word-length computer that holds ten BCD positions in each word and consists of 5,000 words. First it will be necessary to have some registers. In addition to an accumulator, another type of register called an "R-register" is used. The accumulator and the R-register each can hold ten digits. The R-register also may be used as an extension register; for example, multiplying a 10-digit number by a 10-digit number produces a 20-digit result, thus utilizing the accumulator and the R-register. The accumulator holds the ten high-order (right-most) digits of the product; the R-register holds the ten low-order digits.

Assuming the use of the same computer, other registers also are needed. One is the Instruction Register (I-register), which retains each instruction (both operation codes and operand) until it is executed. The size of the I-address register is equal to the length of the word in memory (in this illustration, it is ten BCD digits).

A sequence Register (S-register) controls the sequence of the instructions; that is, it refers to the location of each instruction as it is used. It requires only a four-digit position, since the memory addresses of the computer are 0000 through 4999 (Fig. 12-5).

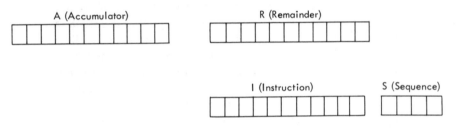

FIG. 12-5 Major registers in a hypothetical computer

Each instruction in this hypothetical machine occupies ten positions or a complete word in storage. The first two positions hold the operation code. The last four positions hold the operand (the location, address, or other specific related data). Assume for the moment that the middle four positions are not used. When the necessary instructions are placed (loaded) into the primary storage, the program is ready to process data.

In executing a program, the first step involves the console (the unit on the central processor which displays the registers in their BCD form), where the sequence register is set to 0000. When the operator pushes a certain console button, all other registers are cleared to zero to be sure that the accumulator doesn't have any "leftovers" from a previous program (Fig. 12-6). When this is done, the "Clear" button causes the "Fetch" light to turn on. This means that the computer is in a "fetch" phase for retrieving an instruction specified by the sequence register.

Upon the depression of the "Step" button, the contents of the memory location indicated by the sequence register (which is the first instruction) are picked up by the control unit and placed in the instruction register (I-register). Once this is accomplished, the sequence register is incremented automatically by one (to the next word), thus making sure that instructions are

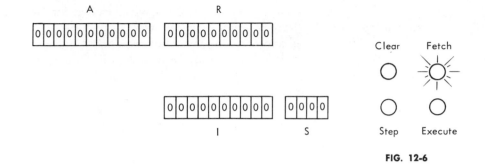

FIG. 12-6

being retrieved, one at a time, in a predetermined sequence. Thereafter, the content of the sequence register will increase by one each time an instruction is executed to show that it is ready for the next instruction (0001 in this case) to be fetched.

At this point, the control unit manipulates the first instruction through an execute phase as indicated by the "Execute" light (Fig. 12-7). The execute light tells us that the processor is now ready to execute the instruction loaded in the I-register. Once this is done, the execute light is turned off automatically and the "Fetch" light is turned on instead, ready for retrieving the next instruction in sequence (Fig. 12-8). This process continues until the whole program is loaded and its instructions are executed.

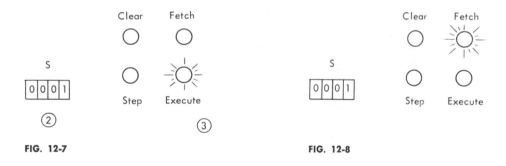

FIG. 12-7   FIG. 12-8

Assuming the use of cards for input, information is "read" into memory from the card, some calculations are performed on the data from each card, and a new card is usually punched out or a line is printed (one at a time) in its final form. This is done by a duplication of some of the information from the input side, plus the calculated answer. The process of "read a card into memory, calculate, punch out new card" is an example of a *program cycle*.

Branching

A program is usually written to perform as if there were only one input card to be considered. At the point where the instruction has been given to punch out a new card, it is necessary to repeat exactly the same program steps for the next card in the input deck. If a separate program were needed for each of these program cycles and a large number of cards were to be read, much memory space would be required and programmers would run out of memory space in a very short time. Instead, all computers are provided with a branching, or jump, instruction which takes the program out of its normal sequence (S) and to another instruction instead, resetting the S-register.

Computers must have this branching ability to turn away from a sequential path in the program, not only to enable them to repeat the same program over and over again, but also to deviate from the normal path (the main-line routine) and branch off in another direction. The fact that there are "compare" instructions in a computer indicates the presence of alternative paths provided by the programmer.

To summarize the foregoing description: a computer is able to distinguish between an instruction and the data because (1) the programmer tells the computer where the first instruction is located, and (2) through the use of the fetch and executive controls in connection with the sequence register, instructions are fetched to the instruction register automatically and then executed. If the programmer does not set up the program and data locations properly, it is possible for the computer to treat the data as a series of instructions. Ultimately, however, it would get an invalid operation and code, causing the computer to stop.

INSTRUCTION FORMATS

Computer systems differ from one another in terms of requirements and the manner in which they are programmed. In addition to the requirement for different operation codes, they also must be programmed according to a specific instruction format built into the machine. At present, there are four common variations in instruction formats. The ones with which the industry is most familiar are single-address, two-address, three-address, and one-plus address systems.

In a single-address instruction, each instruction word contains only one memory reference, or operand address (Fig. 12-9). To do addition, for example, requires three instructions: (1) an instruction to place a quantity into the accumulator; (2) an instruction to add the second amount to the accumulator; and (3) an instruction to move the result from the accumulator and store it into a selected memory location.

With a two-address machine, one instruction is used (rather than three) to add the contents of one address to the contents of another. The accumulator is not used by the programmer. Both the address of the first quantity and the address of the second are in the instruction word. The result of the addition replaces the second quantity in memory (Fig. 12-10).

A three-address instruction provides for three addresses in the instruction word. For an "ADD" instruction, the contents at the first address are added to the contents of the second address and the sum is stored in the third address (Fig. 12-11).

Generally speaking, the word length (number of bits) in multiple-address computers is longer than in single-address machines to accommodate the additional addresses. This is compensated for by the fact that fewer instructions will be needed to do a job. Multiple-address systems also are employed in character-oriented computers. The length of their instructions is not fixed by the length of a word. In one popular machine, the instructions may vary from one to eight characters in length.

The one-plus system is utilized on some drum-memory computer systems to take advantage of the rotation of the drum. If instructions are stored sequentially on a drum, a minimum of one revolution to fetch each instruction would be necessary. An instruction could not possibly be executed before the very next instruction has been passed over, so the one-plus system, in effect, carries its own sequence register in the instruction. Basically, the instruction is a single-address instruction as far as reference to an operand is concerned. However, it carries along with it the address of the next instruction to be fetched, which is not necessarily the next instruction on the drum itself (Fig. 12-12).

A programmer might calculate that an "add" can be performed in half the revolution time of the drum. If this were the case, the next instruction to be fetched could be stored half a revolution around the drum. This is called *optimizing* the program, and is not an easy thing to do. If instructions are misplaced, for example, as much as a full revolution can be missed. It takes a skilled person to time out each of the instruction executions so that the next command is properly spaced.

Op.Code	Address

FIG. 12-9 Single-address instruction format

Op. Code	Address 1	Address 2

FIG. 12-10 Two-address instruction format

Op. Code	Address 1	Address 2	Address 3

FIG. 12-11 Three-address instruction format

Op. Code	Address 1	Address of next instruction

FIG. 12-12 One-plus instruction format

Glossary of Terms

ACCUMULATOR: A register in which the result of an arithmetic or logic operation is formed.

ADDER: A device whose output is a representation of the sum of the quantities represented by its inputs.

BRANCHING: The selection of one or more alternative actions in a program based on a specific condition.

LOGIC: (1) The science dealing with the criteria or formal principles of reasoning and thought. (2) The systematic scheme which defines the interactions of signals in the design of an automatic data-processing system. (3) The basic principles and application of truth tables and interconnection between logical elements required for arithmetic computation in an automatic data-processing system.

OPERAND: That which is operated upon. An operand is usually identified by an address part of an instruction.

OPERATION CODE: The part of an instruction which tells the computer which operation is to be performed.

PROGRAM: (1) A plan for solving a problem. (2) Loosely, a routine. (3) To devise a plan for solving a problem. (4) Loosely, to write a routine.

REGISTER: A device capable of storing a specified amount of data, such as one word.

TOGGLE: (1) Same as flip-flop. (2) Pertaining to any device having two stable states.

Questions for Review

1. Explain the difference between a parallel and a serial adder. Illustrate.

2. Add the following values in binary. Check by converting to decimal.

   (a) 100 (b) 011 (c) 101 (d) 101 (e) 101
       011   101   011   110   100

   (f) 111 (g) 10111 (h) 11011 (i) 10111 (j) 11111
       111   11011   11110   01011   11111

3. Subtract the following problems in binary. Check by converting to decimal.

   (a) 10 (b) 11 (c) 11 (d) 01 (e) 101 (f) 010
       01   10   01   10   100   101

   (g) 1011 (h) 0100 (i) 1111
       0100   1101   1000

4. Multiply the following problems in binary. Check by converting to decimal.

   (a) 100 (b) 101 (c) 111 (d) 111 (e) 1011
       11   11   11   111   1101

5. Multiply each of the problems in Problem 4, using the shift method.

6. Divide the following:

   (a) 100/10 (b) 110/10 (c) 111/10 (d) 1001/11
   (e) 10010/11 (f) 11110/110 (g) 11101/101

7. How does a computer compare two values? Explain.

8. Describe the control unit of the central processor.

9. What are the two parts of an instruction? Describe each part briefly.

10. What is a register? A sequence register? An I-register? A data register?

11. What is meant by a "program cycle"?

12. Describe briefly the four common variations in instruction formats. Illustrate.

chapter thirteen

INPUT/OUTPUT DEVICES— PART 1

THE POWER OF A COMPUTER is determined by the capabilities and characteristics of the central processing unit. But, as mentioned in previous chapters, the central processor cannot function alone. A company owning a computer is more concerned with the overall operation of a system than with the central processor alone. Auxiliary media and devices are needed to transfer the data from secondary storage to the computer (input) or to receive processed data from the computer and store it externally until needed (output).

Input units, regardless of the type of medium they employ, perform the function of transferring human or machine language to the central processing unit, where it is retained either temporarily or permanently. In the case of human language, the input unit must be capable of translating it into computer language. Output units, on the other hand, are designed to take the processed results from the computer and make them available to the user or to another machine for further processing. Like an input device, output units must be capable of translating output from computer language to human language before the data can be used effectively. Figure 13-1 illustrates the activity of input and output devices in the processing of information. While buffering is not shown in this particular illustration, buffering per se usually cuts down on the idle time (no activity space shown in Fig. 13-1) between phases, thus speeding up the rate of operation of the system. Details on buffering are presented in Chapter 14.

This illustration points out the fact that input and output devices are, in effect, communication links that make it possible for the computer to process the necessary facts and contribute favorably to the solution of the problems

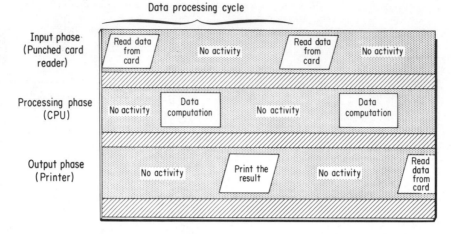

FIG. 13-1 The role of input and output devices in electronics

encountered. In the search for more comprehensive and more satisfactory ways of handling computer input and output data, the industry has developed a large number of solutions, some general in purpose and others serving specific needs only. At present, there are several input and ouput devices available to an electronic data processing system. Table 13-1 presents in condensed form details regarding these devices.

TABLE 13-1

INPUT/OUTPUT DEVICES

	Device	Medium Used	Speed Range	
			Low　High	
Input Devices	Card reader	Punch card	300– 1,600	Cards per minute
	CRT display	Cathode Ray Tube	250–10,000	Characters per second
	Optical scanner	Special paper	70– 2,400	Characters per second
	Paper tape reader	Paper tape	350– 1,000	Characters per second
	Typewriter	Special paper	6– 16	Characters per second
Output Devices	Card punch	Punch card	100– 500	Cards per second
	CRT display	Cathode Ray Tube	250–10,000	Characters per second
	Printer	Special paper	300– 1,500	Lines per minute
	Paper tape punch	Paper tape	20– 150	Characters per minute
	Typewriter	Special paper	6– 16	Characters per second

The Punched Card Reader

The card reader is one of the most common devices used in small- to medium-size computer systems. It is designed to recognize holes punched in a card and to transmit their meaning to the central processor. Once punched card data "enter" the computer, they are stored internally in a computer language. The language used depends on the make and type of computer. Only valid characters are transferred to and stored in the computer. A card reader (see Fig. 13-2) usually has a built-in device to discontinue reading when an invalid character is sensed. In this case, the operator must check the type of error and correct it before any further reading can be done.

Depending on the technique used, card reading employs one of two methods: serial or parallel. The *serial* method is a *column-by-column* reading (columns 1-80); the *parallel* method reads either rows 12 through 9 (when the card enters 12-edge first), or rows 9 through 12 (when it enters 9-edge first).

With the parallel method, the entire card must be read before any meaning can be realized from any of the columns. That is, there are no distinguishing punches until all the rows have been read and reassembled into columns. A hole is judged to be a particular character, based on its distance from the leading edge of the card and the amount of time it takes the reading brushes to reach that hole. Assuming a constant card-reading speed, the holes in the 0-row, for instance, are read at zero time (zero being a prescribed amount of time away from the leading edge of the card).

FIG. 13-2   High speed card reader

Serial reading has been popular for several years, even though the parallel method has been in use longer. It is felt to be more practical to read one column at a time, since the information punched in each column is a complete character.

Physically, the reading process is done in one of two ways: (1) via the brush-type reader or (2) via the brushless-type reader. The brush-type method of reading punched data is the same as that used in most punched card data processing equipment; that is, a reading brush on the top of a card makes contact with a roller beneath the card every time a hole is detected. This contact activates a circuit which manipulates the data based on the instructions stored in the unit (Fig. 13-3).

FIG. 13-3 Reading a punched card—the brush type

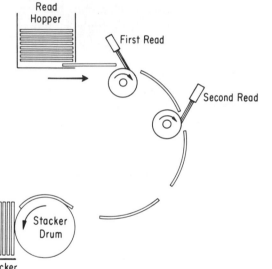

The brushless type is simply a light-sensing device, shining light on the face of the card passing under it. Holes in the card allow the light to shine through them, thus establishing contact with photoelectric cells (Fig. 13-4). Light sensing is less likely to cause a "misread" since there are no brushes to get caught, cause jamming, or cause possible subsequent intermittent reading failures.

Output Card Punch

Punching is done by a set of punches which make holes in certain locations in a card, based on the information they receive (Fig. 13-5). Other methods, such as burning, have been tried, but none has proved as effective as the punch.

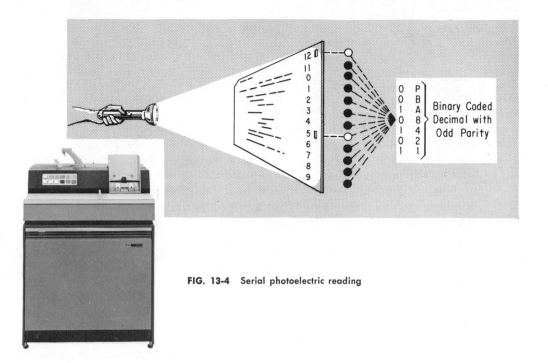

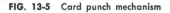

FIG. 13-4 Serial photoelectric reading

Punching, like reading, can be either serial or parallel. The internal codes of the computer are translated into standard punched card codes before the information is transferred to the punch. Since the equipment is mechanical in design, punches operate at a limited speed, a feature which restricts the effectiveness of punching a card as output compared to the use of other devices.

In a typical computer system, the card punch moves blank cards (one card at a time) from the hopper to the punches, which punch according to pulses received from the computer memory. Next the punched columns are read at a reading station (brush-type) to check on the accuracy of the punched data. If no errors are detected, the punched card is ejected into its designated pocket (Fig. 13-5). Depending on the make and type of equipment used, some card-punch devices are integrated as a part of the card reader.

FIG. 13-5 Card punch mechanism

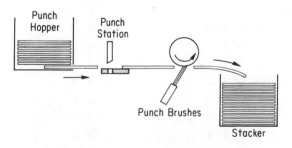

Printers

One of the devices on a typical data processing system is the printer. By comparison, all other devices can be considered "data collection" devices. They are used to collect, sort and update information which is kept in the computer. Although the printer has none of these capabilities, it is considered a most important device because of its role in communicating results (through printing) from the computer to the user on continuous paper forms.

The two main purposes of a business data processing installation are to provide customer service and to keep management informed on the status of the business. In order to perform either of these functions, pertinent reports must be communicated to management and customers in the fastest and clearest possible form. Therefore, the printer is the most valuable output device for human communication.

A printer translates the computer's internal character representations into alphabetic or numeric information understandable to the human eye. There are three basic kinds of printers:

1. Character-at-a-time printers, which print each character serially, a position at a time, similar to the way a typewriter prints.
2. Line-at-a-time printers, which print all characters on a given line simultaneously.
3. Other machines employing various, less common printing techniques.

Character-at-a-time Printers

Matrix Printer. A matrix printer consists of pins placed in a 5 x 7 array. Characters are formed by causing the appropriate pins to strike against the paper. This is a relatively fast technique, providing there is a matrix for each print position. Speeds of 900 lines per minute are not unusual. The characters shown in Fig. 13-6 represent 1 and A.

Teletype Printer. The teletype printer operates by printing one character at a time and presents type in a square block (Fig. 13-7). This type square

FIG. 13-6 The matrix printer (schematic)—digit 1 and letter A

FIG. 13-7 Teletype printer—(schematic)

A	B	C	D	E	F	G
H	I	J	K	L	M	N
O	P	Q	R	S	T	U
V	W	X	Y	Z		0
1	2	3	4	5	6	7
8	9		#	.	,	/
@	*	⌗	&	–	%	$

moves from left to right, positioning the proper character at each print position. As it stops at each position, a hammer behind the character in the matrix strikes it from behind, depressing it against an inked ribbon, which in turn imprints the character on the paper form. Maximum speed for this type of printing is approximately 10 characters per second.

Console Printer. Several computer systems are provided with an auxiliary output printer called a console, message, or supervisory printer. Normally, it is a typewriter device used by the computer for relaying messages to the operator. For instance, a program may be written to check for specific codes on card input. When an error card is sensed, the console printer will print a message describing the nature of the error. Because of its relatively low cost, such printers are most frequently used for small-volume output.

Line-at-a-time Printers

The Bar Printer. One printer of the impact type is that which uses type bars. This model, still in use today in most types of general accounting machines, consists of a series of type bars, positioned side by side, with one type bar for each print position across the line. The number of print positions varies from one model to another, numbering usually 55-88.

A printer using type bars is a relatively slow one, because of the mechanical positioning of the bars. A rated speed of 150 lines per minute is about average for straight numeric printing. Alphabetic information is restricted to a section of the type bars, further reducing the printing speed to 100 lines per minute.

The Wheel Printer. The wheel printer is an improvement over the bar printer. It is similar in design, except that the bars are replaced by a disk (wheel) around which all characters are embossed. Generally 120 print positions are available with alphabetic, numeric, and special characters being printed. It has a rated speed of 150 lines per minute, which makes it a faster printer than the type-bar printer, despite the fact that the number of characters on each wheel far exceeds that of a type bar, because there is less mechanical effort in activating a circular wheel than in activating a vertical moving type bar.

Drum Printer. A drum printer employs a solid cylindrical drum, around which characters are embossed (Fig. 13-8). The drum rotates at a constant speed. As the A-row passes the line to be printed, hammers behind the paper strike the paper against the drum, causing one or more A's to be printed. As

FIG. 13-8 The drum printer—schematic diagram

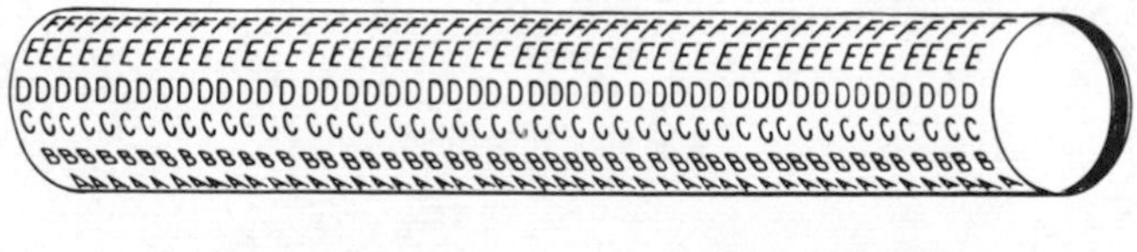

the *B*-row moves into place, any print position requiring the letter *B* is printed in the same manner. One complete revolution of the drum is required to print each line. Drum printer speeds range from 700 to 1,600 lines per minute.

Chain Printer. A chain printer consists of a series of "links," arranged side by side (Fig. 13-9). In a five-part chain, for instance, a complete set of alphabetic, numeric, and special characters is included on each part. The chain is mounted horizontally, so that it revolves from left to right at constant speed. As the chain rotates, hammers behind the paper are timed to select the desired characters and strike the back of the paper to force it against the designated character. The inked ribbon between the character and the form leaves an imprint of the selected character. Speeds range from 600 to 1,300 lines per minute.

Comb Printer. As the name suggests, this printing mechanism resembles a comb. A complete set of characters is mounted on a solid bar, and the bar is placed horizontally in front of the paper form so that it slides from left to right. As the bar passes in front of the paper, hammers strike the desired character(s) onto the form. When the bar has passed over the width of the paper, it returns to a home position to print another line. The comb printer was developed as an inexpensive device, since the entire comb contains 47 pieces of type, compared to the same number for each print position required by a wheel printer. Speed averages 150 lines per minute for mixed alphabetic and numeric data.

FIG. 13-9 The chain printer (courtesy IBM)

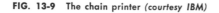

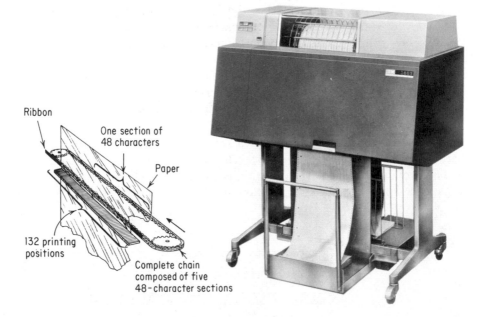

Ribbon

One section of 48 characters

Paper

132 printing positions

Complete chain composed of five 48-character sections

Electrostatic Printing. The electrostatic method is considered the fastest method of printing since it is limited only by the speed at which paper can be moved. The printing process involves placing "spots" of electricity on a special paper backed with a coating which allows the paper to hold a charge. These spots are assembled in matrix form. Next, the paper moves through a powdered ink bath, which clings to the paper wherever a character has been placed, before moving to a high-temperature area, where the ink is permanently melted on it. Speeds of 2,000–5,000 lines per minute are typical. The major disadvantages are the expense of the special paper and the fact that only one copy can be produced.

Other printing devices have been developed, including Addressograph plates, which are used to print an entire four-line address at one time. Other information can be combined with it from punched cards. Photographic reproductions through cathode-tube or Xerox processes are also in use.

MAGNETIC TAPE INPUT/OUTPUT

A major departure from punched card input and output has been provided by the recording of data on *magnetic tape.* In medium- to large-scale computer systems, magnetic tape is the most widely used source of secondary storage and high-speed read-in and write-out. In addition to the speed with which it transfers data to and from internal storage, magnetic tape's main advantage lies in the relatively reduced data-storage space requirements. That tape may be erased and reused repetitively further qualifies it as one of the most economical and versatile forms of storage.

Magnetic tape used in home tape recorders was developed many years prior to its application for computer data storage. The principle of the two applications is quite similar. In recording a human voice, a tape-recorder head forms magnetic patterns on a tape. During playback, the same patterns are amplified to duplicate the original sound. A computer tape unit does much the same thing, recording bits of information sent from the central processing unit in patterns on the tape. Once stored, the information can be "read" back to the computer at a later time. Like sound recording, magnetic-computer tape recording may be "read" again and again without destroying the information it contains. It can be erased and reused indefinitely for rewriting new information.

Physical Characteristics of Magnetic Tape

Although early magnetic tapes were made of metal, all popular tapes are now made of plastic, coated on one side with a metallic oxide about the same color as the tape used in home tape recorders. The metallic oxide can be easily magnetized and retains its magnetism indefinitely. Bits of information in the form of magnetic fields, referred to as *magnetic spots,* are recorded on the oxide side of the tape by the read-write heads of the tape unit. The spots, which are invisible to the eye, are placed across the width of the tape on parallel tracks running along its entire length. Each track is assigned a read-write head for later recording.

In a more expensive tape, a very thin coat of polyester on top of the oxide inhibits wear. Despite this added feature on "sandwich" tape, it is likely to have a certain amount of wear over a long period of time.

Magnetic tape is manufactured to meet rigid specifications. It is wound on spools, called reels, which are kept in dust resistant plastic cases while in storage. Although tape length on the individual reels varies from system to system, it usually comes in either 2,400 or 3,600 foot reels. The width of the tape varies also; however, one-half inch, three-quarter inch, and one inch widths are the most common sizes.

Data Representation

Although the number of tracks on magnetic tape varies with its width, a seven or nine channel tape is used today with a tape width of one-half inch. The pattern of the magnetized spots across the width and along the length of the tape is a *coded representation* of the data stored on it. These spots are magnetized in one of two directions of polarity, indicating either a zero-bit or a one-bit to correspond with the pulses received from the computer.

Across the width of the tape, the seven tracks provide one column of data (frame) or simply one character (Fig. 13-10). The presence of a dash or

FIG. 13-10 Magnetic tape—the seven-channel code

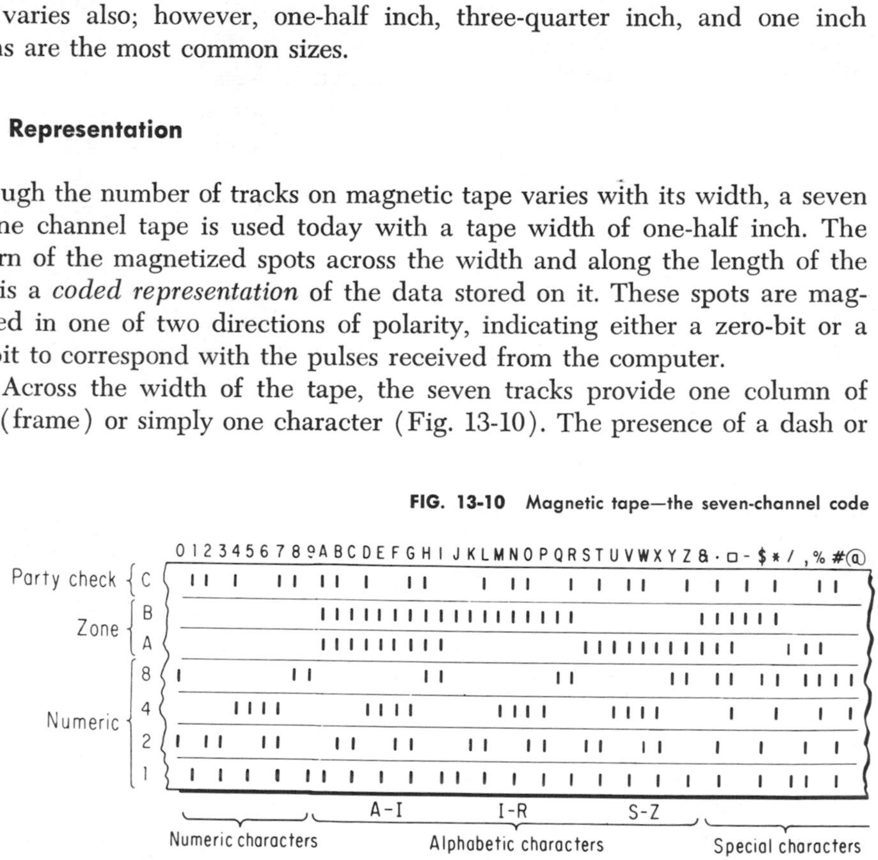

a short line stands for one bit of information which, combined with zero-bits (the absence of a dash) in a seven-channel code, can represent a letter, a digit, or a special character. In the nine-channel coding (Fig. 13-11), each column of data (called a byte) is capable of representing an alphabetic, numeric, or a special character, or part of a data word.

Characters are recorded on tape serially; that is, one or more characters

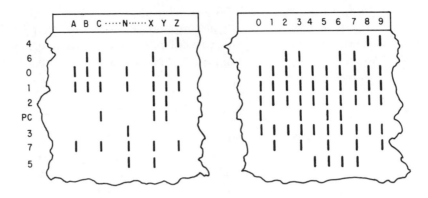

FIG. 13-11 The nine-channel code

at a time, as the tape passes by the read-write heads. In the tape system illustrated one complete character is read at a time since there are seven read-write heads across the channels on the tape. On other tapes, more than a single character may be read at a time depending on the number of tape channels and the coding format.

Tape Units

Reading from and writing on tape is performed by a tape unit (Fig. 13-12) at a constant rate of speed. The transfer rate of information to and from tape depends largely on two factors: (1) the actual movement of the tape across the read-write heads, and (2) the number of characters that can be stored on an inch of tape, referred to as its *packing density*. For example, assume a tape movement speed of 100 inches per second and a density of 400 characters to the inch. At those rates, the character transfer rate would be 40,000 characters per second. In typical systems on the market today, tape speed is about 90 inches per second, with a common packing density of 800 characters per inch, giving a transfer rate of approximately 72,000 characters per second. In the early tape systems, transfer rates commonly

FIG. 13-12 Tape unit
(courtesy IBM)

were in the 6,000 to 15,000 character-per-second range. Each year brings improved methods of tape handling and packing, however, so that today tape systems are marketed with transfer rates of more than 200,000 characters per second. Table 13-2 summarizes key characteristics of the IBM 2400 tape unit models.

TABLE 13-2

THE IBM 2400 MODELS—KEY CHARACTERISTICS *

	TAPE UNIT					
	2401		2402		2403	
ITEM	7-track	9-track	7-track	9-track	7-track	9-track
Density (bytes/inch)	200 556 800	800	200 556 800	800	200 556 800	800
Data rate (bytes/second)	7,500 20,850 30,000	30,000	15,000 41,700 60,000	60,000	22,500 62,500 90,000	90,000
Speed (inches/second)	37½	37½	75	75	112½	112½
Interblock gap (inches)	0.6	0.75	0.6	0.75	0.6	0.75

* Adapted from F. R. Crawford, *Introduction to Data Processing*, Englewood Cliffs, N.J.: Prentice-Hall, Inc., 1968, p. 184.

Several methods have been employed to move the tape across the read-write heads in a fast, yet synchronized, manner to prevent breakage. The sudden burst of speed in starting a tape and the abrupt jolt when the tape stops have been "softened" by the provision of slack in the tape at areas in which breakage is likely to occur. Most tape units are designed to include vacuum columns to house a loop of tape on both sides of the read-write head which take up and give the required slack before and after recording is done.

The loop in each vacuum column acts as a buffer to prevent high-speed starts and stops from breaking the tape. Vacuum-activated switches in the columns allow the file reel and take-up reel to act independently. The file reel *feeds* tape when the loop in the left chamber reaches a minimum point, and the take-up reel *winds* tape when the loop in the right chamber reaches a minimum point. During the rewinding or backspacing of tape, the two reels simply reverse their roles. The vacuum action is the same, although rewinding speeds generally are faster than reading or writing speeds.

Other methods provide slack in the tape before it moves across the read-write head. A file reel and a take-up reel are mounted on the tape unit, followed by the threading of the tape through the tape transport mechanism. Recently, automatic tape threading has been developed, by which tape cartridges are mounted in the tape drive mechanism and self-threading by the machine takes place. Some tape units use pinch rollers to move the tape; others make use of suction only, with rotating capstans to pull the tape past the read-write heads. Some machines read the tape in one direction only; others are capable of reading in the reverse direction as well. During operation, tape is fed from the file tape, down through the vacuum chamber, across the read-write heads, down through the right vacuum chamber, and up to the take-up reel (Fig. 13-13).

Major safety features are built into magnetic-tape units to prevent accidental erasure of data while reading is taking place. A common one consists of a plastic ring (Fig. 13-14). When installed in its groove, reading or writing may take place. When writing is to be suppressed to safeguard the recorded data from being overwritten inadvertently, the plastic ring is removed. This aspect is well-known among tape operators, whose jargon is "no ring, no write."

FIG. 13-13 Magnetic tape mechanism—schematic diagram

FIG. 13-14 IBM file protection device

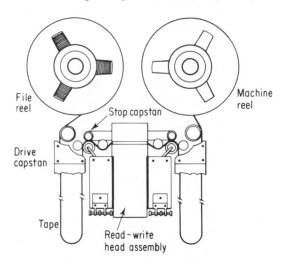

File reel

Stop capstan

Machine reel

Drive capstan

Tape

Read-write head assembly

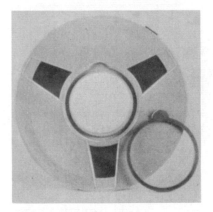

Accuracy Control

Data characters stored on magnetic tape must be checked constantly for accuracy and for any possibility of accidental erasure of magnetized bits that constitute a part of a given character or characters. To maintain accuracy, manufacturers have built into the tape unit one or more of three basic safeguards: parity checking, dual recording, and the dual-gap read-write heads.

Parity Checking

Parity checking is a technique whereby the machine counts the total number of one-bits representing each character on tape. Fig. 13-15 shows the tape channel which is reversed for parity checking, with emphasis on even parity. Even parity involves the maintenance of an even number of one-bits representing each character on tape. If a given character is represented by an odd number of one-bits, an extra one-bit is added to the parity-check track to make the total even. For instance, the digit "seven" ordinarily is represented by three one-bits in frames 4, 2, and 1. Under an even-parity code, a fourth one-bit is added to make the total one-bit count even (Fig. 13-15). When this is accomplished, the accidental loss of one of the four bits would signal an error in future processing, since the remaining bit count would be odd. If you look at the characters in Fig. 13-15, you will find that each and every character is represented by an even number of one-bits.

FIG. 13-15 Even-parity checking

Vertical Parity Check
Even Parity

Before

	1	3	4	5	9	2	7
C							
B	0	0	0	0	0	0	0
A	0	0	0	0	0	0	0
8	0	0	0	0	1	0	0
4	0	0	1	1	0	0	1
2	0	1	0	0	0	1	1
1	1	1	0	1	1	0	1

After

	1	3	4	5	9	2	7
C	1	0	1	0	0	1	1
B	0	0	0	0	0	0	0
A	0	0	0	0	0	0	0
8	0	0	0	0	1	0	0
4	0	0	1	1	0	0	1
2	0	1	0	0	0	1	1
1	1	1	0	1	1	0	1

Odd parity is the reverse of even parity. A character is represented by an odd number of one-bits. A parity check bit (1-bit) is added to each character which originally is coded with an even number of one-bits.

The foregoing discussion is related to lateral or vertical parity check. That is, the number of one-bits is counted across the width of the tape, representing an individual frame. The tape unit is further designed to take a horizontal, or longitudinal, parity check at the end of a segment of tape, usually at the end of a record. Horizontal parity checks assure the number of one-bits in each of the channels used to represent alphabetic, numeric, or special characters. If the check is for even parity, an extra bit is added to each channel that contains an odd number of one-bits (to make it even); it is vice versa in the case of odd parity check.

Horizontal parity checking is performed to double-check the accuracy of recorded data, since it is possible that two bits could be reversed in a single frame and remain undetected under a system using only vertical parity checking.

Dual Recording and Dual-Gap Read-Write Heads

In *dual recording systems,* a character is written twice in each frame across the width of the tape. It is compared for equality when it is being written and again when it is being read. This method is used only on tape systems with enough channels to record two characters side by side.

To insure the accuracy of data recorded on tape, *dual-gap read-write heads* are also used. A character written on tape is immediately "read" by a read head to verify its validity and readability. If the character is not readable, an error signal is given. Under the direct control of the computer, the tape can be backspaced and instructed to rewrite the proper data. Even then, the dual-gap feature will check the accuracy of the rewrite before any further recording continues.

The main causes of tape errors stem from physical and environmental factors. Flaws in the tape itself due to faulty manufacturing processes probably are the most common causes of error. Also, tape normally wears out after a certain amount of repetitive use, and this, plus a drastic change in temperature and/or humidity, may cause chipping of the oxide on which the magnetized spots are made. Dust particles or a weakness in the magnetic field of the recorded bits often contribute to poor results and frustrations in the processing cycle.

The correction of errors during the reading phase usually requires backspacing a portion of the tape to be read again. If the cause of the reading difficulty is dust or a weak magnetic signal, corrected reading often resumes after the second or third try. Manufacturers have developed schemes for internally correcting "uncorrectable" errors on tape; the usual alternative is to rerun the program that created the tape containing the errors. In most cases, however, tapes have proven very reliable and this alternative is seldom necessary.

Tape Records

Related data usually are written on tape as a group or as a complete unit of information, called a *record.* In an accounts-receivable application, for example, each customer's account, including such data as previous balance, current receipts, and outstanding balance, may be considered a record. Information received from the central processor continues to be written on tape until a special character or mechanism built into the computer signals the transmission of information to stop. Some tape systems use a fixed block of characters in each record; however, the more common practice is to write variable-length records, limited primarily by practical considerations of available space and the storage capacity of the central processing unit.

Each record is separated from the succeeding one by an "interrecord gap." Gaps vary from about half an inch to an inch (Fig. 13-16). Once the size of the interrecord gap is determined for a particular tape system, it is not likely to change. Interrecord gaps are created automatically when data are written on tape, and no information is recorded within them. Their presence also allows the tape unit to accelerate and decelerate when starting or stopping, without failing to read or record the desired information. Encountering an interrecord gap causes the unit to stop reading; that is, it denotes the end of a physical record. Decelerating to a stop takes place within the interrecord gap, taking approximately half the length of the gap. The remaining half is used upon acceleration before the next sequential record is read. A new "read" command from the central processor initiates the tape to move again, and by the time it reaches the next tape record, it is at the proper speed to read and transfer the stored data to the computer.

Many records in data processing activity are not of great length. Records of 50 characters and a recording density of 556 characters per inch of tape, for instance, are written on a fraction of one inch of tape, allowing a constant three fourths of an inch for the interrecord gap (the size of the gap depends

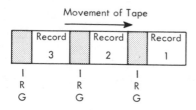

FIG. 13-16   The interrecord gap

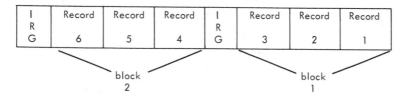

FIG. 13-17   Blocked records

on the manufacturer). This clearly is a waste of tape and a problem which has been solved by "blocking" such short records. Blocking consists of grouping more than one logical record into a physical record separated from the next block by an interrecord gap. Figure 13-17 shows two blocks of three records each. The interrecord gap used between records in Fig. 13-16 is eliminated, thus realizing a saving of tape.

An even more important saving is that of computer time, since the central processor is not waiting constantly while the tape stops and starts between records. Reading a blocked record proceeds from one gap to another, making it possible to read into computer memory several individual records with a single "read" instruction. Once read, records within each block are separated by the program in the primary storage of the computer. Related blocks make up a complete application, which may be a fraction of, or in excess of, one reel of tape.

PAPER TAPE READER

A paper tape reader provides direct input to a computer by reading prepunched data in paper tape. It also provides output from a computer by punching output information in the same medium. Paper tape systems are used most often in systems where information is received over wire communication circuits and in scientific applications involving limited input and output. In the past, paper tape has not been widely used as an input/output medium due to the lack of tape preparation devices. Most of the tapes had to be prepared manually or, in some cases, punched by units which provided limited flexibility. Presently, this difficulty has been overcome with relative success through the introduction of better punching devices. Although still comparatively less popular than other input/output media, paper tape currently is being used more effectively than in the past.

Recording on paper tape is done by machines that punch data by a direct connection to a typewriter or a keypunch. Other machines are used to transmit data punched into paper tape over telephone or telegraph lines in order to produce a duplicate tape at the other end of the line, where the newly punched paper tape can be used for further processing.

Data stored on paper tape are recorded in patterns of round punched holes, located in parallel tracks (channels) along the length of the tape. A character is represented by a combination of punches across the width of the tape. Paper tapes vary according to the number of channels they contain. Most of them are either five or eight channels wide. Consequently, the methods of coding data also vary. Punched paper tape has the advantage of easy and relatively compact storage. It takes less space for storage than does the punched card. Being light in weight, it is easier to handle and cheaper to mail. It also is more economical to use than punched cards because of the low cost of the tape and the transport units.

Compared to more advanced media, however, punched paper tape has been found to be as impractical as the punched card. Coded information being punched into it manually allows considerable possibility of error. Like the punched card, it is relatively slow. Because it is made of paper, it is more likely to break during processing (giving rise to the expression, a "torn-tape system"). Other disadvantages include the fact that paper tape cannot be split apart for sorting, collating, and other related operations as can punched cards. Visual reading of punched paper tape is a problem for someone who is untrained, although there are certain machines which can interpret and print the characters on the paper tape in the same fashion that cards may be interpreted.

DIRECT/RANDOM ACCESS DEVICES

The advantages of magnetic tape as an input/output and auxiliary storage medium account for its widespread use in almost all types of computer systems. However, since data are recorded and processed serially, individual records are referenced only after scanning the records preceding them. Thus, magnetic tape-oriented operation is applicable mostly to batch processing where the records to be processed are in a predetermined sequence and are in line with additional data used for updating the file.

The foregoing constraint led to the development of input/output storage devices with random access as well as sequential capabilities. Random access (arbitrarily called direct access) means that any record in the file is accessible and can be replaced anywhere in the existing file, with no particular regard to the sequence in which the file is arranged. For example, if record number 400 in a file were needed for updating purposes, the use of a random access device would allow the record to be obtained without first reading the preceding 399 records, and the updated record could be rewritten in its proper position without rewriting the entire file.

Similar to magnetic tape characteristics, random access devices can have sequential access features when such an operation becomes necessary. Currently, there are three types of random access magnetic storage devices: magnetic disk, magnetic drum, and mass storage devices.

Magnetic Disk Devices

Magnetic disk devices are one of today's most popular, general purpose random access devices and are normally used as input/output auxiliary devices in medium- to large-scale computer systems or for applications requiring large-volume data with immediate accessibility (Fig. 13-18).

Physically, the magnetic disk unit is similar to the 45 rpm juke box record which was once popular. It consists of a single disk or a series of disks arranged vertically on a spindle. Some disk models have permanently attached disk(s) while others (the more popular models) accommodate detachable sets of disks, called *disk packs*. The disk pack is popular because it allows a user to conveniently move the data stored in one disk file to another place so that it can be processed on various computer systems. Replacement of one disk pack by another is a job that takes less than one minute.

Each disk face is divided into a number of concentric circles called *tracks*. Depending on the size of the disk, each track is capable of storing strings of characters within a predefined limit. Each track is divided into records separated from one another by interrecord gaps.

FIG. 13-18   A current paper tape reader

FIG. 13-19   IBM 2311 magnetic disk storage device

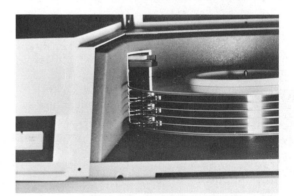

A magnetic disk is separated from adjacent disks to allow enough room for the movement of read/write heads. One head serves to read from and write information on the top surface of the disk and the other head serves the same function on the bottom surface, thus utilizing both sides of the disk at all times (Fig. 13-19). Like magnetic tape recording, there is no limit on the number of times data are recorded on disk. Old data are automatically replaced by the data being recorded. Once recorded, the data can be read as often as necessary.

Since the disks are arranged vertically on a spindle, a given track is in the same relative position on all recording surfaces. This positioning is important because once the read/write heads are positioned to read data from one track in a particular "cylinder," all the other tracks in the "cylinder" can be read without repositioning the read/write heads. This means that up to eighteen tracks of data can be read or written with a single move of the read/write heads. This is a capability of some importance, since access time is the most significant factor in using disk drives.

Four factors have a direct bearing on the speed with which data is transferred from disk to primary storage.

(1) *Access motion time*. The amount of time it takes to position the read/write heads at the cylinder containing the desired record. If the heads are already positioned at the correct cylinder, the access motion time is zero. The access motion time reaches its maximum when the heads must travel from the first cylinder to the last or vice versa. Access motion time, then, is a function of the number of cylinders moved.

(2) *Head activation time*. The amount of time required to electronically select the proper read/write head of the access mechanism. It is generally considered to be negligible in most cases.

(3) *Rotational delay*. The amount of time required for the desired data to reach the read/write head so that actual reading or writing may begin. Rotational delay ranges from zero to one complete revolution of the disk. Rotational delay depends upon how fast the disk is rotating and the location of the data in relation to the read/write head.

(4) *Data transfer time*. The amount of time required to transfer the data from the storage device to the primary storage (memory) of the computer. It is a function of the rotational speed and the density of the recorded data and is usually expressed in thousands of characters (or bytes) per second.

Magnetic disk storage devices are potentially powerful and efficient devices for a great many applications. However, in some applications it is necessary or desirable to access a smaller volume of data very quickly. In this situation, magnetic drum storage would probably be used.

Magnetic Drum

The magnetic drum (Fig. 13-20) is a metal drum coated with magnetically sensitive material on its outer surface. The surface is divided into a number of tracks. Each track has single or multiple read/write heads, depending on whether data transfer is serial (bit by bit) or parallel (multiple bits at a time).

The presence of one or more read/write heads for each track eliminates any access motion time associated with the access of data stored on a magnetic drum. Since the only timing factors pertinent to drum operation are head selection time (which is negligible), rotational delay, and data transfer, the use of the magnetic drum as a storage device provides faster and more efficient operation than other direct access storage devices. However, the size constraint of the drum compromises its storage capacity compared to other auxiliary storage devices. That is, what the drum storage device offers in terms

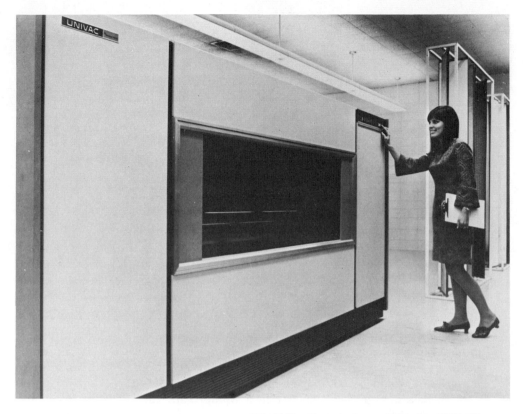

FIG. 13-20 Magnetic drum unit *(courtesy UNIVAC)*

of speed, it falls short of in storage capacity. Neither the drum nor the disk storage device quite satisfies the user who needs large random access storage capacity and is relatively unconcerned with access speed. For such a user mass random access storage devices were developed.

Mass Storage Files

Much has been done to supplement primary storage. Secondary storage devices have been used to hold related data until they are needed by the computer. When they are needed, they are transferred to the computer's primary storage for processing. Data stored in primary storage are considered temporary and generally remain there only during the operation of the program; if certain information must be stored for a longer period of time, it is transferred to a secondary storage medium for that purpose. Magnetic tape and punched cards are examples of secondary storage media.

A *mass-storage file* (Fig. 13-21) is a unique type of temporary secondary storage designed to supply the computer with the required facts for an immediate up-to-date report on a given account. A direct, rather permanent hookup (on-line) to the computer system is required. Insurance companies

FIG. 13-21 Mass storage file *(courtesy IBM)*

utilize this system, usually through a direct-access device, to satisfy customers' inquiries regarding policy billing information. This service can be provided manually, but because of the thousands of policyholders and hundreds of daily inquiries, it would be both costly and inefficient.

A mass-storage file is similar to a library card catalog. When someone wishes to know about a particular book, he searches in the card file, which normally is arranged alphabetically either by subject or by author. New book information may be added to the file with little difficulty. The cards for lost books may be removed from the file with relative ease. Such flexibility and convenience also are desired in a computer mass-storage device. It must be large enough to accommodate new data, as well as being capable of dropping or altering old data.

Data File

The first devices made for mass storage, called *data files,* were produced by the Burroughs Corporation for its 205 computer system and are still being used today. The data file is a large coffinlike box which contains 50 individual pieces of nonremovable magnetic tape, each of which is 250 feet in length, draped over a center bar which runs the length of the file. Lengthwise, the tapes are divided into two lanes, each of which contains 1,000 "blocks." A block is large enough to accommodate 20 words of 10 digits each, plus the sign. In one complete unit (called a bin), there are 100 lanes containing 100,000 blocks, two million words, or a total of 20 million digits of information. On the Burroughs 205 computer system, there can be a maximum of 10 bins, thus providing a total secondary storage of 200 million digits.

To transfer data from the bin to primary storage, read/write heads move along the bar and stop on a designated lane. The tape is positioned either forward or backward to the desired block on that lane. The data stored in the block are then transferred to the computer for processing.

Magnetic Card Storage

Some of the known magnetic card or strip storage devices include the IBM Data Cell and the NCR CRAM (Card Random Access Memory). (See Fig. 13-22.) While they are slower than magnetic disk storage devices, they allow direct access to data and are relatively inexpensive. The CRAM package consists of a removable cartridge containing 256 magnetic cards of material similar to magnetic tape. These cards store magnetic bits of information totaling 5.6 million characters per cartridge. Cards drop from the cartridge onto a cylinder drum, at which time reading or writing takes place (Fig. 13-22). Sixteen cartridges, or 89 million characters, can be on-line at one time. The IBM Data Cell Drive is somewhat similar to the CRAM unit. It is made up of an array of "cells," divided into 20 subcells each. A subcell contains 10 magnetic strips of tape with a magnetically sensitive coating on one side. When a magnetic

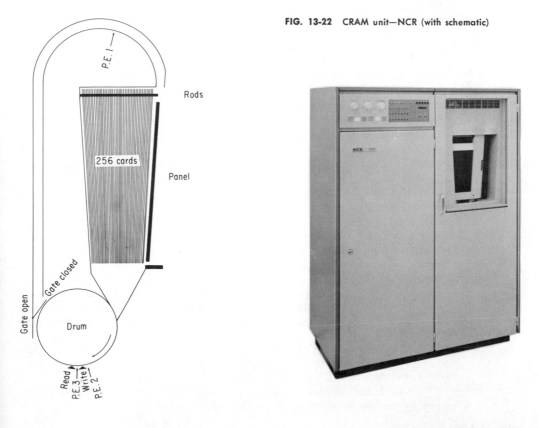

FIG. 13-22   CRAM unit—NCR (with schematic)

strip has been selected, the pickup arm withdraws the strip from the subcell and wraps it around the drum. As the strip revolves it passes a set of 20 read/write heads. Each of these heads services five of the one hundred "tracks" on the strip. The strips are returned to the subcell by reversing the rotation of the drum (see Fig. 13-21).

In summary, we note that direct access devices are useful in terms of their ability to hold large amounts of data at reasonable cost, and in forms prescribed for processing. A business firm integrating direct access devices into its system must maintain an efficient balance between storage volume and unit cost of storage. Compared to magnetic tape, however, these devices have certain disadvantages in the way of control and are comparatively higher in cost. As cost is reduced, direct access devices are likely to be the most popular form of secondary storage in the future.

Glossary of Terms

BAR PRINTER: A printing device that uses several type bars positioned side by side across the line. Printing data on a line involves activating specific bars to move vertically until the characters they contain are properly aligned. Then, the data are printed simultaneously.

BLOCK: A set of things, such as words, characters, or digits, handled as a unit.

CHAIN PRINTER: A device which uses a chain of several links, each of which contains alphabetic and numeric characters. The chain rotates horizontally at constant speed. Hammers from the back of the paper are timed to fire against selected characters on the chain, causing the printing of a line.

COMB PRINTER: A device which consists of a set of characters mounted on a bar facing a paper form. As the bar passes over the paper (left to right), hammers strike the selected characters onto the form. When the bar reaches the right edge of the form, it returns to a home position to print another line.

CONSOLE PRINTER: An auxiliary output printer used in several computer systems for relaying messages to the computer operator.

CRAM: Card Random-Access Memory, a mass-storage device that consists of a number of removable magnetic cards, each of which is capable of storing magnetic bits of data.

DRUM PRINTER: A printing device which uses a drum embossed with alphabetic and numeric characters. As the drum rotates, a hammer strikes the paper (from behind) at a time when the desired character(s) on the drum passes the line to be printed. To complete printing a given line, further rotation of the drum containing the remaining characters is necessary.

DUAL-GAP READ-WRITE HEAD: Used in magnetic-tape data processing to insure the accuracy of recorded data on tape. A character written on tape is read immediately by a read head to verify its validity.

ELECTROSTATIC PRINTER: A device that prints an optical image on special paper. Spots of electricity are placed in matrix form on paper. When the paper is dusted with powdered ink material, the particles cling to the electrically charged characters. Later, they are moved to a high-temperature zone where the ink is melted and is permanently fixed to the paper.

INTERRECORD GAP: An interval of space or time, deliberately left between recording portions of data or records. Such spacing is used to prevent errors through loss of data or overwriting, and permits tape stop-start operations.

MAGNETIC DRUG: A right circular cylinder with a magnetic surface on which data can be stored by selective magnetization of portions of the curved surface.

MASS-STORAGE FILE: A type of temporary secondary storage that supplies the computer with the necessary data for an immediate up-to-date report on a given account.

MATRIX PRINTER: Synonymous with *wire printer*. A high speed printer that prints character-like configurations of dots through the proper selection of wire-ends from a matrix of wire-ends, rather than conventional characters through the selection of type faces.

ON-LINE INPUT: A system in which the input device transmits certain data directly to (and under control of) the central processing unit.

PACKING DENSITY: The number of useful storage elements per unit of dimension, e.g., the number of bits per inch stored on a magnetic tape or drum track.

PARALLEL READING: "Row-by-row" reading of a data card.

PARITY CHECK: A check that tests whether the number of ones (or zeros) in an array of binary digits is odd or even. Synonymous with odd-even check.

RAMAC: Random-Access Method of Accounting and Control, a mass-storage device that consists of a number of rotating disks stacked one on top of another to make up a data file.

RECORD: A collection of related items of data, treated as a unit.

SERIAL READING: "Column-by-column" reading of a data card.

TELETYPE PRINTER: A device that presents type in a square block. The type square moves from left to right and positions one character at a time. When this happens, a hammer strikes the character from behind, depressing it against the inked ribbon that faces the paper form.

WHEEL PRINTER: Similar in method of operation to the bar printer except that the type bars are replaced by wheels around which all the necessary characters are embossed.

Questions and Problems for Review

1. What is the primary function of an input unit?
2. What basic input techniques are available to computer systems? Explain.
3. Describe the operation of a punched-card reader.
4. What is the difference between the serial and the parallel method of card reading? Include in your answer any advantages or limitations of each method.
5. Contrast the brush-type and the brushless-type readers.
6. What is the primary function of the output card punch? Explain.
7. Discuss the functions, uses, types, and methods of reading and recording data on (a) punched paper tape, (b) magnetic tape.
8. What are the advantages and limitations of paper tape?
9. What is a magnetic tape? Present some of its physical characteristics.
10. How are data represented on tape? Illustrate.
11. What is meant by packing density?
12. Describe briefly the methods by which reading from and writing on tape are performed.
13. What is a parity check? Even parity? Odd parity?
14. What are some of the main causes of tape errors? Explain.
15. Define the following terms:
    (a) Logical record   (c) Single read block
    (b) Interrecord gap   (d) Multiple record block.
16. Describe briefly the 7- and the 9-channel coding systems.
17. Under what conditions is random access more effective than sequential access (magnetic tape) processing?
18. Explain the features and uses of magnetic disk devices.
19. What factors are considered in data transfer from magnetic disk to primary storage?
20. Explain briefly the features and uses of mass storage devices (files). How are they different from magnetic core storage?

chapter fourteen

INPUT/OUTPUT DEVICES— PART 2

MAGNETIC INK CHARACTER RECOGNITION (MICR)

OPTICAL READERS

CHARACTER RECOGNITION EQUIPMENT
The Bar Code Reader
Mark Sense Reader
The "Stylized" Font Reader
The "Generalized" Font Reader

DATA COMMUNICATIONS
Data Set

INPUT/OUTPUT TERMINAL DEVICES
Touch Tone Devices
Card Dialer
Call-A-Matic
Voice Response
Visual Display (CRT) Devices

THE MICROFILM (COM) SYSTEM

OTHER TYPES OF INPUT/OUTPUT TERMINAL DEVICES
Keyboard-to-Tape
Keyboard Printer
Punched Card or Paper Tape
Magnetic Tape
Buffering

In Chapter 13 we considered some of the more traditional types of input/output media and devices. In addition to these, other available devices are designed to make the data processing function faster, easier, and more accurate. Table 14-1 (see end of chapter) summarizes the devices presented in this chapter.

MAGNETIC INK CHARACTER RECOGNITION (MICR)

The widespread use of magnetic ink character recognition (MICR) by banking institutions deserves special mention as a major breakthrough in standardized documents for automated input. In 1955 the American Bankers Association recognized a need for some way to automate the processing of the mounting volume of bank paperwork. Either the check, which is the basis for most bank transactions, had to be used, or some new document must be developed as input to an automated system.

Even though they are used successfully by the government and other agencies, punched card checks require standard sizes and thicknesses. The size requirement of a punched card check was unsatisfactory to the personal checking accounts carried by commercial and other banks, since their printed checks come in various sizes, shapes, and thicknesses. A check written on a particular bank may be processed by as many as four other banks before it is received by the bank on which it originally was drawn. If you look at a used personal check, you will notice on the back the names of all the banks through which the check has passed. Consequently, it is necessary that any approach to automation must be acceptable and agreeable to all banks concerned.

After some research, it was proposed, and later agreed, that coding the desired information on the check in magnetic ink would be a suitable solution to the problem. Magnetic ink, in this case, solves three major problems: (1) the original document can be used directly as input to the computer so that no substitute document has to be prepared; (2) the necessary information can be coded on checks of any size within a reasonable range; (3) the information is easily readable by persons handling the document.

For several months, committees discussed all possible type font characteristics and discarded many as being unusable, impractical, or of poor quality. Finally, the E 13B type font (Fig. 14-1) was agreed upon and was adopted. The E 13B type font was selected because the characters are visually readable, and each of them can be distinguished through electronic reading devices; that is, a 0 cannot be mistaken for an 8, etc. There are fourteen different characters in E 13B; digits 0 through 9, and the four special characters illustrated in Fig. 14-1. Magnetic ink character recognition (MICR) cannot be used in many data processing problems since the alphabetic characters were not considered. However, the MICR characters meet the operating needs of most types of financial institutions.

Since MICR was developed to enable banks to process information automatically through computer systems, manufacturers of these systems were busy developing the equipment to read MICR documents. A

FIG. 14-1 The E 13B type font

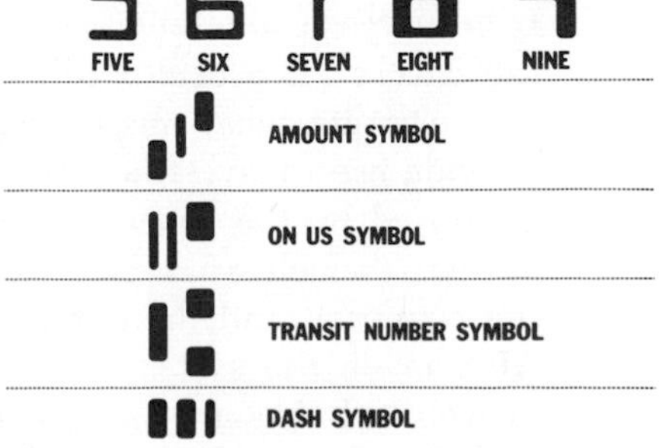

MAGNETIC INK CHARACTER RECOGNITION CHART

| ZERO | ONE | TWO | THREE | FOUR |

| FIVE | SIX | SEVEN | EIGHT | NINE |

AMOUNT SYMBOL

ON US SYMBOL

TRANSIT NUMBER SYMBOL

DASH SYMBOL

FIG. 14-2 Magnetic character reader

popular machine for this purpose, called the *reader-sorter* (Fig. 14-2), is designed to read checks of various length, width, height, and thickness, and transmit the information to the memory of the central processor, which is used later to update the customers' accounts. In addition, the reader-sorter is capable of sorting the check to any one of its pockets. Eventually, all checks must be sorted by account number so that they can be returned to the person who wrote them; therefore, the reader-sorter performs the dual function of reading information for automatic processing and physically sorting the checks. It may either be hooked up to the central processor, whereby information is transferred directly to memory (on-line), or be connected to tape units for data storage on magnetic tape, which can be processed later by the computer. Physical sorting of checks can be performed by the reader-sorter whether or not information is transferred to magnetic tape or to the computer. This is done by detaching the machine from the computer system (off-line processing).

The reader-sorter is the final judge of the proper coding of documents. Any unreadable information goes to a separate pocket, called the *reject pocket*. If an unreasonable number of documents are rejecting, it is an indication that the checks have been badly coded.

Despite what might seem like overwhelming odds against MICR, it is in wide use today. Much credit goes to the diligent efforts of the committees organized by the American Bankers Association (ABA), the Federal Reserve System (which at present is utilizing successful automatic systems all over the country), and the equipment manufacturers, whose cooperation with the ABA made the system possible. Consequently, savings and loan institutions as well as banks are using MICR satisfactorily, processing items as quickly as 1,600 checks per minute. In England, the British Bank Association has accepted the E 13B type font as a standard. It could very well be true that MICR in its present form will become something of an international symbolic banking language in the future.

OPTICAL READERS

Optical readers offer the most efficient direct reading of typed, printed, and handwritten data without manual operation. Basically, such an operation is the translation of printed or handwritten characters into machine language. The reader is called an optical character recognition (OCR) reader and consists of (1) transport unit, (2) a scanning unit, and (3) a recognition unit. (See Fig. 14-3.) It converts the characters into a "picture" through the use of a photoelectric eye. The circuitry is designed to break up this image into pulses which identify the specific character(s). Internally stored reference patterns guide the recognition unit to verify (match) the patterns held by the scanning unit. Generally, the matching process is made either on the basis of the line formation of each character or (in the case of handwritten characters) on the outline of the character. Any unmatched character patterns cause the document to be rejected. The reject rate runs around 5 percent of the total documents scanned.

FIG. 14-3   The primary elements of an optical character reader

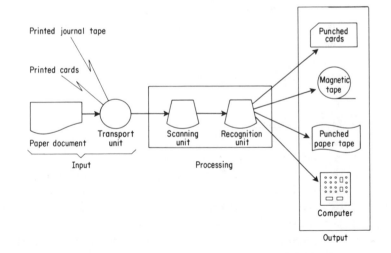

Some difficulty is still encountered in optical reading. Diversity in hand-printed characters and in the type and quality of printed styles are continuously being adjusted. Today, fewer documents are rejected, indicating reduction in error rate and improvement in optical scanning techniques.

Pure OCR equipment has been in commercial use since 1956. While its use has not grown by leaps and bounds, all indications point to increasing future use. OCR equipment is generally categorized on the basis of the types of documents it accepts and the classes and complexity of type fonts it will handle.

Three generalized classes of document handling mechanisms are used:

1. *Document reader,* capable of reading a maximum of three lines of information on a document, regardless of the size of the document.
2. *Journal tape reader,* designed to read paper tapes such as those used in cash registers or adding machines.
3. *Page reader,* capable of reading multiple lines of typed or printed material from a normal page layout, usually measuring 8½ x 11" or 8½ x 14".

Three classes of font capability are also used.

The Bar Code Reader

The optical character reader explained earlier is one of three classes of optical readers. The other two readers are the mark sense reader and the bar code reader. Although they all operate on the principle of detecting difference in contrast, their method of recognition differs somewhat.

A bar code reader reads a given numeric character set by indirect recognition of associated bar codes. These codes are normally printed on paper by a keyboard imprinter or by embossed cards. The reader is comparable in reliability to that of the OCR, despite the limited feature of resorting and the need for preparatory devices such as embossed cards for performing the job.

Mark Sense Reader

As indicated earlier, magnetic ink character recognition is especially useful in specialized organizations such as financial institutions. However, the MICR's limited direct document reading led to the development of other types of devices, which add more versatility to optical scanning. One of these devices is the mark sense reader.

Mark sensing is the machine reading of pencil marks placed in predetermined positions on a paper document. In its early use, a special "electrostatic" pencil was required so that the marks would be electrically conductive. The advent of sensing mechanisms based on optical techniques led to the use of light sources to detect character presence, diminishing the need for special pencils.

Mark representation is determined by its position on the document. Each position is preassigned a value which remains fixed for that type of document. The preassigned value may be any of the characters acceptable to the equipment being used.

Mark sensing has been widely used in the administration and scoring of examinations. It is well suited to multiple-choice or true-false type exams and does much to ease the drudgery of scoring. However, the necessity of pre-assigning values to be coded limits its application to other areas of information processing.

The "Stylized" Font Reader

This device is capable of reading one or more fonts specifically designed for machine and human legibility. The font may be restricted to numerics or, in some machines, full alphanumeric sets may be accepted. In any case, the shape and size of the characters in any of the "stylized" fonts are governed by specifications of limited flexibility. Deviations from these specifications generally produce unreadable characters.

The "Generalized" Font Reader

This reader is designed to read a minimum of several standard typewriter or printed fonts (both upper and lower case). Some devices even accept hand-printed alphabetic characters. Unlike the "stylized" font reader, the "generalized" font reader eliminates the need for equipment to produce the specially designed "stylized" font on input forms. This flexibility allows the preparation of input on currently available equipment.

OCR equipment, then, is designed to minimize the amount of transcription (reducing the error rate) necessary in preparing source data for machine input and to increase the flow of information into the computer system. The trend of OCR readers supports this view.

Journal tape readers were developed in response to the retailers' need for a faster and more efficient method of processing daily sales information. The use of cash registers capable of recording data in the proper font allows these organizations to obtain machine ready input as a byproduct of a normal retail merchandising function, realizing substantial savings in keypunching and other data preparation costs.

Great interest has been expressed in recent years in developing OCR equipment capable of accepting handwritten characters. This interest stems from the realization that by using this technique data could be prepared in machine acceptable format at its source with no additional recording or transcription. Its potential use is significant in organizations where source data are produced in branch or field locations. Although there is the technology for the production of this type of OCR equipment, production costs remain prohibitive. As these costs diminish, it is likely that increased usage of OCR equipment will lead to the demise of the "keypunch."

DATA COMMUNICATIONS

Data communications is a key area in data processing and is currently the subject of much technological development. While the process is generally known as the transmission of bits of data from one point to another, data communications assume a more precise and definite meaning. It is the transmission of specially coded data utilizing special purpose transmission components.

In their present use, data communications make extensive use of the wide transmission capabilities maintained by telephone and telegraph companies. The techniques and associated equipment are geared to subvoice grade, voice grade, or broad-band (including microwave) channels. A voice grade channel is suitable for speech, digital or analog data, or facsimile transmission. Transmission is made at a frequency of 300-3,000 cycles per second. Since the device converts data into machine-oriented electrical impulses or wave patterns, it becomes necessary to link these devices between the transmission equipment and the input/output equipment for human reading.

Data Set

The device which performs the translation function is called a *data set* (Fig. 14-4). Its primary function is to alter the characteristics of the wave patterns generated by the appended equipment so that they conform to the wave patterns of the transmission component(s) or vice versa. The process of making a machine signal compatible with a communications signal is called *modulation;* the process of retrieving the original signal from the modulated carrier wave or translating the communications signal back into a machine signal is called *demodulation.* The data set is capable of performing all these functions and transmits in either serial or parallel mode. In serial transmission, one bit of information at a time is sent; in parallel transmission, one complete character is sent.

The type of transmission facilities used is also a subject of choice. Transmission facilities may be used either on a pay-as-you-use basis, or leased, or purchased. On a pay-as-you-use basis, normal transmission lines are utilized. This requires adding telephone equipment to the data set since initiation of line use requires dial-up of the other point in the linkup. The connection is then routed over existing lines in the same manner as a normal telephone call.

One advantage of leasing or purchasing transmission lines is the convenience of direct connections, dedicated usage, and constant availability of transmission paths.

INPUT/OUTPUT TERMINAL DEVICES

The increased reliance of business organizations on computer produced output has generated demand for paperless output devices which produce data in a quiet and fast manner and minimize waste of management time. Among these new devices are the touch tone, voice response, and visual display.

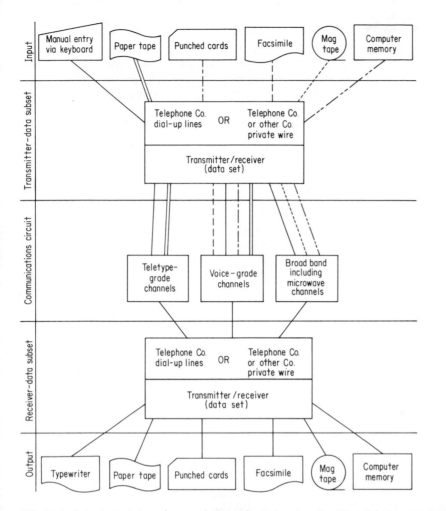

| Input | Manual entry via keyboard | Paper tape | Punched cards | Facsimile | Mag tape | Computer memory |

Transmitter-data subset

Telephone Co. dial-up lines OR Telephone Co. or other Co. private wire

Transmitter/receiver (data set)

Communications circuit

Teletype-grade channels   Voice-grade channels   Broad band including microwave channels

Receiver-data subset

Telephone Co. dial-up lines OR Telephone Co. or other Co. private wire

Transmitter/receiver (data set)

| Output | Typewriter | Paper tape | Punched cards | Facsimile | Mag tape | Computer memory |

FIG. 14-4 Data transmission *above* and data phone *(courtesy American Telephone and Telegraph) below*

Touch Tone Devices

Recently, business organizations have been resorting to a new type of telephone, called touch tone devices, to improve their telephone service and boost their data transmission system through the use of the equipment available by the American Telephone and Telegraph Company.

Card Dialer. One type of touch tone device, called the *card dialer,* reads prepunched holes in a plastic card at the rate of 8-9 characters per second. The combination of the card and the card dialer is ideally used in information retrieval and in applications that require entry of fixed information such as the account number punched in a gasoline credit card.

Call-A-Matic. The *Call-A-Matic,* another touch tone device, stores (on-line) several hundred entries in a magnetic belt by means of a telephone dial. To read the information into the telephone network, the user depresses a button after verifying the entry displayed at the window. In this system, off-line loading of digits on the magnetic belt is feasible.

Voice Response

One of the latest breakthroughs in computer technology has been the development of the computer's ability to "talk" with the user, called *audio response* or *voice output.* Earlier aspects of this technique are now well developed and involve the user's transmitting a coded message to a central processing unit and in return receiving a voice reply. For it to do so, the computer gains access to a prerecorded vocabulary which it uses in giving out a certain answer.

Voice response systems are currently used in many business activities. A bank teller, for example, uses a special terminal unit to talk to the computer about the status of a customer's account (say account number 5678). The computer locates and answers back in an audible voice a message such as: "Account number 5678 balance to date seven eight nine point one one." The answer is usually heard through the receiver or through a loudspeaker nearby.

Visual Display (CRT) Devices

One of the more popular terminal devices, the TV-like CRT display (Fig. 14-5) is used as an input and ouput device and consists of a Cathode Ray Tube (TV set) equipped with a keyboard. Data are displayed on the face of the tube immediately after they are entered from the keyboard or received from the computer.

The alphanumeric type of CRT device displays data in textual form on the tube. The editing facilities that go with it allow the operator flexibility of keying in data and modifying previously displayed information. This device is used extensively in inquiry/response type situations where data are required for immediate information purposes. Unless it is attached to a printing device, no permanent record of displayed data is kept.

The graphic display (or line drawing) device (Fig. 14-6) is used primarily by engineers and scientists to display pictorial information. It is capable of drawing complex charts or designs.

FIG. 14-5 CRT display—alphanumeric device

FIG. 14-6 Graphic display unit

THE MICROFILM (COM) SYSTEM

Considered an off-line system, a microfilm system records data (in the form of digital signals) from magnetic tape or the central processing unit on a 16-mm film in an understandable human language. This *computer on microfilm* (COM) system (Fig. 14-7) consists of magnetic tape unit, microfilm components, a film processor, and viewer-printers. While it is in a relatively new technology, it is gaining acceptance due to its high speed and fine quality.

FIG. 14-7 Computer on microfilm system

OTHER TYPES OF INPUT/OUTPUT TERMINAL DEVICES

Keyboard-to-Tape

The operator records source data by keying in the information on magnetic tape through a typewriter or a keypunch. The device consists of a keyboard, a buffer memory, and a magnetic tape unit. It is normally used to replace keypunching operation or to capture data directly at the source, resulting in substantial savings to the user. The increased popularity of the system is explained by its reliability, speed of feeding source data, and unique editing features. Knowledge of its operation is required, due to the magnetic tape controls connected with keying in source data.

Keyboard Printer

This device is designed to function as both an input and an output terminal. Input is generated by depressing the keys which are generally similar to those of the typewriter. The depression of the key generates a unique electrical signal which is then transmitted over the communications system. On the output phase, receipt of a signal by the device activates an appropriate type bar, causing printout of the desired character on a paper form. Printout is achieved by electronically activating the type bars connected with the operation.

Punched Card or Paper Tape

These devices may have input-only, output-only, or input and output capability. However, regardless of their capability, the media used are the same. Each device consists of a signal converter and a reading and/or punching mechanism. For the input phase, punched cards or paper tapes (prepunched with the desired data) are read by the device. The signal converter senses the impulses received and activates the appropriate punching mechanism.

Magnetic Tape

Magnetic tape works on the same principles as the punched card or paper tape devices except that magnetic spots on the tape take the place of the holes of the punched card or punched tape.

Buffering

A computer system requires that the component units work together in a compatible and harmonious manner so that meaningful results can be expected. No individual unit is capable of functioning effectively unless it becomes a part of the whole system. Cables are used to connect the auxiliary units to the central processing unit which controls their work and the extent to which they are used in getting the job done.

A *buffer* is a device used on most computers to hold temporary information being transmitted between external- and internal-storage units, or between input/output devices and internal storage. An unbuffered system performs a "read-compute-write" cycle in serial fashion; that is, one operation

after another: READ-COMPUTE-WRITE. A buffered system allows all three
operations to proceed simultaneously:

Read	A	B	C	D	E	etc.
Compute		A	B	C	D	etc.
Write			A	B	C	etc.

The need for buffers is readily apparent when the timing of a computer
system is considered. Today's electronic computers execute instructions at
nanosecond speeds, while most input and output equipment (being mechanical) still operates relatively slowly. There is no compatibility, for instance,
between a computer executing an instruction in as little as 10 microseconds
(ten millionths of a second), and a card reader that reads data to the computer in 75 milliseconds, or 7,500 times as slow. A buffer is designed to compensate for this imbalance. It can be described as an electronic memory device,
connected directly to the main computer memory but not available to the
programmer.

In the system illustrated (Fig. 14-8), two buffers are added: an input
buffer with a holding capacity of 80 characters (one punched card) between
the card reader and the computer; and an output buffer, one line of print
between the computer and the printer. Electronic in nature, this device makes
it much faster to transfer the 80 characters in the buffer to another electronic
device (the computer) than it is to transfer the same positions directly from
the card reader to the computer. The computer will be processing one record
while the next record is filling the buffer from the card reader.

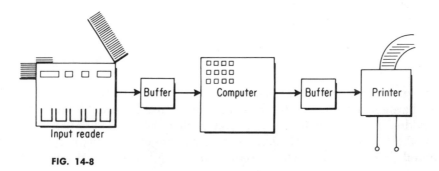

FIG. 14-8

To illustrate the role of a buffer when integrated into a computer system,
the following is a step-by-step process of a card deck with printed data as
output:

1. Input deck is fed into the card reader.
2. Information from the first card goes automatically into the *input buffer*.
3. The stored program calls for a card to be read. Information from the buffer is transferred to memory.
4. Card 2 begins to transfer automatically to the buffer.
5. Card 1 is processed while the buffer contains the data from card 2.
6. Processed information from card 1 is sent to the *output buffer*.
7. The stored program calls for another card to be read. Information from the buffer (card 2) is transferred to memory.
8. Card 3 begins to transfer automatically to the input buffer.
9. Output buffer is automatically sending processed data of card 1 to the printer.
10. Information from card 2 is processed, while the input buffer fills with the next card's contents.

At the end of this processing, card 1 has been completely read, processed, and printed. The information from card 2 is ready to be sent to the output buffer, and the data of card 3 are available in the input buffer. The process between steps 6 through 10 continues until the entire deck of cards is processed. You will note that at the input stage, a card is always being prepared ahead of time by moving it into the buffer while the card ahead of it is being processed. Likewise, at the output stage, a card is always in the process of being printed while the card preceding it is being processed. Through the use of such overlapping with buffers a great deal of total processing (throughput) time is saved.

In brief, the use of a buffer aids the mechanically driven input or output units to keep up with the electronic computer, thus maximizing the efficiency of the system. This includes the primary functions of speed change and time sharing. Other functions involve the buffer's ability to change a code from machine to human language or vice versa, and to change the mode of data transmission; i.e., from serial to parallel or from parallel to serial transmission.

Buffering has been employed in a slightly different concept with the advent of Cathode Ray Tube display terminals. The image on the CRT is produced by an electron beam which sensitizes the material on the inside of the tube according to the signals it receives. The sensitized areas on the tube are not permanent and will degenerate quickly if they are not reinforced. Reinforcement involves reissuing the appropriate signal to the electron beam scanner as long as the image is needed. In an unbuffered CRT device, this reissuing of signals must be done by the central processing unit; this absorbs valuable processing time. In a buffered CRT device, the data are transferred once from the CPU to a buffer located in the CRT device. Then, the signal to the electron beam scanner is reissued as needed by circuitry within the CRT device.

TABLE 14-1

SUMMARY OF SOURCE DATA EQUIPMENT *

EQUIP-MENT	Primary Functions	Application Areas	MEDIA		Data Volume	Primary Advantages	Primary Limitations
			Input	Output			
MICR Readers	Direct reading of magnetic ink characters or magnetic ink	Banking industry Credit cards Ticketing systems Retail merchandising	Magnetic ink documents Magnetic mark cards	Tab cards Punched paper tape Magnetic tape	180-1,800 documents per minute	High reliability of reading Reduced forgery possibility	Document must be preprinted and specially prepared Magnetic cards can't be read by humans Limited character set
Optical Readers	Direct reading of printed handwritten documents	Postal sorting Bank checks Stock checks Credit cards Billing cards Ticket sales Publications	Printed paper documents Printed cards Printed journal tape	Punched cards Punched paper tape Magnetic tape Direct to computer	18-1,800 documents	No immediate data preparation Direct online input	High initial cost Multiple font costs Limitations on input and character sets High volume required
Touch Tone Devices	Translating and recording data received from a touch tone telephone	Retail sales Dispatching Stock transactions Credit card sales	Plastic card Manual Cash register Punched paper tape	Direct to computer Machine readable magnetic tape or paper tape	Limited to 3,000 bits per second	Real-time applications Use of common carrier facilities Good low-speed data transmission	Special optional equipment Limited throughout

TABLE 14-1 (continued)

EQUIP-MENT	Primary Functions	Application Areas	MEDIA		Data Volume	Primary Advantages	Primary Limitations
			Input	Output			
CRT Devices	Displaying (via CRT) data received from remote computer or keyboard entry; transmitting to computer for storage or other media output	Text editing Computer input File maintenance Stock quotations Air traffic control	Computer Keyboard Punched tape	Video display Punched paper tape Direct to computer	Limited by message length and transmission facilities	Real-time file Minimal training Response time	Common carrier facility costs Limited character set and display capacity
Keyboard to Tape	Keying data on tape	Inventory control Sales ordering and analysis Quality control inspection Replace keypunch	Keyboard	Printed documents Punched paper tape Edge-punched cards Tab cards Magnetic tape	100 documents with 500 characters prepunched	Direct conversion to machine language Cost reduction Speed increase	For large volume (greater than 8 units) Cost is competitive with OCR techniques Complex controls

* SOURCE: *Data Processing Magazine* (September 1969), pp. 28-29.

Glossary of Terms

BUFFER: A storage device used to compensate for a difference in rate of flow of data, or time of occurrence of events, when transmitting data from one device to another.

MICR: Magnetic Ink Character Recognition, a process involving the use of a device that senses and encodes into a machine language characters printed with an ink containing magnetized particles.

OFF-LINE: Pertaining to equipment or devices not under direct control of the central processing unit.

ON-LINE: Pertaining to peripheral equipment or devices in direct communication with the central processing unit.

OPTICAL SCANNING: Translation of printed or handwritten characters into machine language.

Questions and Problems for Review

1. What is magnetic-ink character recognition? How does it aid banks in processing information? Explain.
2. What is optical reading? Explain its operation and use in business data processing.
3. Distinguish the primary characteristics of recognition equipment.
4. What is the primary difference between modulation and demodulation?
5. Explain briefly the uses and characteristics of (a) terminal devices, (b) visual display devices, and (c) the microfilm system.
6. What is meant by buffering? Why is it used? What are its advantages?

chapter fifteen

REPRESENTATIVE COMPUTER SYSTEMS

IN THE PRECEDING CHAPTERS WE DISCUSSED the basic concepts and components of representative computer systems in use today. A system is determined by computer size: small, medium-size, and large-scale computer systems. A small computer system rents for as little as $1,000 per month; a large-scale system rents for over $100,000 per month. We shall now examine the three systems separately.

SMALL COMPUTER SYSTEMS

The UNIVAC 9200

A small computer system, such as the UNIVAC 9200 (Fig. 15-1), is generally

FIG. 15-1   The UNIVAC 9200 system

card-oriented; data, master files and pertinent inactive programs are stored in punched cards. Batch processing is followed on data files and involves many sorting, merging, and collating operations using sorters and collators. Primary storage capacity is in the neighborhood of 4,000 characters. Monthly rental on the small version varies between $1,250 and $3,000, while more efficient systems cost up to $5,000 per month.

Processing of data files stored in punched cards is slow and combersome. Many small computer systems are designed to manipulate data files stored on magnetic disks or magnetic tape (Fig. 15-2).

FIG. 15-2 Disk and tape-oriented small computer system

One restriction in processing data stored on magnetic tape is that the data must be in the same sequence as the master file prior to processing. However, small computers using removable disk pack storage offer the advantage of processing data files regardless of their sequence (Fig. 15-3).

FIG. 15-3 IBM disk

The IBM System/3 is specifically designed for marginal computer users whose volume and/or financial resources are not sufficient to support a full-scale computer installation, but who nevertheless could benefit from automated information processing techniques. In the absence of such a system, these users would have been prime candidates for adoption of unit record (TAB) equipment. The gradual phasing out of tab equipment has encouraged computer manufacturers to build small-size computers to fill the gap (Fig. 15-4).

FIG. 15-4 IBM system/3 computer system

The Central Processing Unit (CPU). The main processing component of IBM System/3 uses Monolithic Systems Technology as its basis. It is an integrated circuit which allows a maximum of five circuits in a module and switching speeds of 8 to 12 nanoseconds. The CPU consists of primary storage, arithmetic and logic units, a control system (including registers for sequencing instructions and initiating communication between memory and I/O devices), an inquiry and control console, and (as an option) a "dual program" feature. (See Fig. 15-4.) Primary storage is made up of the traditional ferrite core structure and ranges in capacity from 8,192 to 32,768 bytes. The internal machine code is EBCDIC (described in Chapter 11) with a memory cycle (the time it takes to access and store one byte) of 1.52 microseconds.

The optional dual program feature (used with disk versions of System/3) allows concurrent loading and running of two independent programs. That is, when one program is undergoing an input or output function, the CPU is processing details for the other program, thus putting the CPU to more efficient use.

I/O Devices. The I/O devices for System/3 include Multifunction Card Units (MFCU), printers, and disk storage units. The MFCU, a single machine, is capable of multiple functions. It is designed to read, punch, collate, sort, and print cards in a single path without intermediate operator handling. Reading and punching are done on the 96 column card (unique to IBM System/3) with speeds of 250 and 60 cards per minute, respectively.

Models of the IBM System/3 printer operate at the rate of 100 or 200 lines per minute with a 48 character print set and 98 print positions. As option, the user can order a Universal Character Set which extends its character set to a maximum of 120 and the number of print positions to 132. Similar to the Selectric-type typewriter and capable of both input and output functions, the system's printer-keyboard is available for supporting inquiry, data entry, or operator communications applications or may be used as a second printer.

Disk Storage Units. The basic disk storage unit of System/3 consists of one fixed and one removable disk cartridge on a single drive. Four alternative disk storage unit configurations are available: (1) a single drive configuration with two 14 inch disks having 2.45 million characters of available storage with an average access time of 153 milliseconds; (2) a single drive configuration with two disks having 4.90 million characters of available storage and an average access time of 269 milliseconds; (3) a dual drive configuration with three disks (one fixed and two removable), having 7.35 million characters of available storage with an average access time of 269 milliseconds; and (4) a dual drive configuration with four disks (two fixed and two removable) having 9.80 million characters of storage and 269 milliseconds access time.

Offline Devices. In an auxiliary role, sorters using photoelectric sensing elements are available for off-line use. They are capable of handling 1,000 or 1,500 cards per minute, with special features for sorting numeric and alphabetic data at reduced number of passes. A magnetic character reader (IBM 1255) also can be acquired which is designed to process up to 500 checks and other related bank documents per minute.

Programming. The programming language for System/3 is called RPG II, a modified version of System/360 RPG (Report Program Generator). Programs are written in English-like statements on special specification sheets, which describe information such as the format of the input data, the functions and ways in which the computer is expected to perform, and the format of the desired output. Once the information on the specification sheets is punched into cards, the source program is ready to be entered into the computer. Other programs available for the IBM System/3 include a sort program, a utility program, and a system control program.

The UNIVAC 9400 (Fig. 15-5) is UNIVAC's latest entry in its 9000 series of computers, first announced in 1966. It complements the previously announced 9200 and 9300 models and extends the series into the intermediate class of computers.

The Central Processing Unit

The general design of the 9400 computer is comparable to that of the IBM System/360 computer system. While its CPU uses monolithic circuitry, it features the use of plated wire memory rather than the traditional ferrite cores. This unique type of memory consists of strands of specially coated wires divided into extremely small segments, each segment representing one bit of primary storage.

The 9400 computer uses the eight bit (plus a parity bit) byte to store data. The internal machine code can be either EBCDIC or ASCII, depending on the mode of the program-controlled flip-flop circuit. Primary storage ranges from approximately 24,000 to 131,000 characters.[1] The CPU area consists of

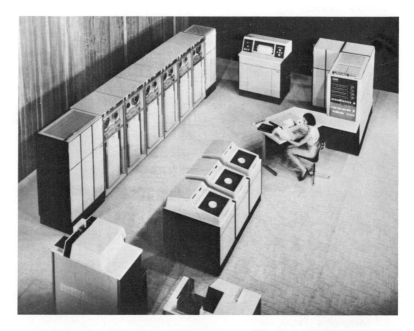

FIG. 15-5 UNIVAC 9400

[1] Memory cycle time is 0.6 microseconds (600 nanoseconds) for accessing and storing 2 bytes. The first 512 bytes of main storage are reserved for use in the handling of interrupts, indexing, I/O, and other control functions.

two sets of 16 general purpose registers, one set for user-defined use and one set for control purposes. It provides a maximum of four I/O interrupt control registers, an interval timer, seven levels of processor interrupts, and write storage protection.

The 9400 CPU can be either in Supervisor or in Standard State. The software operating system uses the Supervisor State to perform vital functions. Within this state, all available instructions are valid and executable and the sixteen "control" general registers are used along with the 512 bytes of its addressable reserved storage. The Standard State, on the other hand, is used to execute user programs. During this state, the "Supervisor instructions" are not valid, allowing the exclusive use of the sixteen "User" general registers. Reserved storage also is not addressable. The two mutually-exclusive sets of general registers increase the efficiency of the operating systems since they eliminate the requirement of storing the contents of the user registers prior to entering the Supervisor State.

Attached to the CPU is a system console which provides communication between the operator and operating system. The console includes a keyboard (similar to that of a standard typewriter), a printer, and system control switches and indicators.

I/O Devices

A relatively wide variety of I/O devices is available for use with the 9400 system. The user can include a card reader; a card punch; two printers; three magnetic tape "subsystems"; two disk storage subsystems; a paper tape subsystem; on line 1004/1005, 9200, or 9300 processors; and/or three data communications subsystems. The system is also capable of accommodating remote terminal devices such as the Uniscope 300 and the DCT 2000.

Paper-Oriented Devices

The card reader is a key device that reads about 600 cards per minute, with a stub card and a read punch option. The card punch component operates at 250 cards per minute, while line printers operate at either 900/1100 lines or 1200/1600 lines per minute. The paper tape subsystem, however, reads at the rate of 300 characters per second, punches at 110 characters per second, and is capable of handling tape with 5, 6, 7, or 8 channels.

Magnetic Tape Units

Three distinct tape subsystems are also available: Uniservo VIC; Uniservo 12; and Uniservo 16 (Fig. 15-6). Each subsystem provides 7 or 9 track formats and the transfer rate ranges from 8,540 bytes per second (for the Uniservo VIC 7-track tape with a 200 bits per inch [bpi] recording density) to 192,000 bytes per second (for the Uniservo 16 9-track tape with a recording density of 1600 bpi).

Disk Storage Units

The primary disk storage unit used with the UNIVAC 9400 computer system is the UNIVAC 8411 Direct Access Storage Subsystem (Fig. 15-7). Up to eight disk drives can be installed. Each drive has removable disk packs of six disks, or 10 recording surfaces. Each disk pack has a maximum capacity of 7.25 million bytes, giving the 8411 subsystem a maximum total storage capacity of 58 million bytes.[2]

FIG. 15-6   Uniservo 12

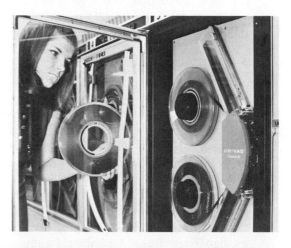

FIG. 15-7   UNIVAC 8411 direct access storage sub-system

[2] The access motion time of each drive ranges from 25 to 135 milliseconds and the rotational delay time ranges from 0 to 25 milliseconds. The maximum data transfer rate is 156,000 bytes per second.

Data Communications

Communication-based data processing is one of the stronger features of the 9400 system. It is capable of servicing up to four Data Communication Subsystems (DCS) through a Communications Adapter. Each DCS can accommodate 1, 4, or 16 full-duplex communications lines, providing a maximum communication capacity of 4, 16, or 64 full-duplex lines. The DCS also includes circuitry for controlling data transmission between the CPU and the line terminals and establishes priorities for individual lines when simultaneous service requests are made.

The UNIVAC 9400 system executes instructions concurrently: i.e., one machine instruction, one high-speed data transfer per Selector Channel, and up to eight low speed I/O operations. Once I/O operations are initiated by the CPU, they are taken over by I/O control units.

Programming

The UNIVAC 9400 offers software support in the areas of Supervisor, Data Management, Job Control, Message Control, and Language Processors. The *Supervisor* handles five level multiprogramming, time allocation, simulated day clock, interval timer services, storage protection, transient area management, automatic buffering, and program checkpoint. The *Data Management* software provides for Sequential Access, Direct Access, and Index Sequential Access Methods. The *Job Control* program provides Control Stream Buffering and Program Restart; the *Message Control* program has Queud communications control capability. Among *Language Processors* and support programs available are Basic Assembler Language, COBOL, FORTRAN, RPG, Sort/Merge, Library Services, Linkage Editor, Utility Programs, and Program Testing Aids.

LARGE COMPUTER SYSTEMS—CONTROL DATA CORP. 7600

The CDC 7600 is one of the largest computer systems commercially available today. Other computer systems have a separate CPU unit, but the processing component of the 7600 system (Fig. 15-8) is composed of a CPU and a number of Peripheral Processing Units (PPU). The PPU communicate with the CPU over high speed data links. That is, they serve as a communication and message switching link between the CPU and individual peripheral equipment controllers. All data enter or leave the system at one of the programmable peripheral equipment controllers. The PPU gather input from the equipment controllers for delivery to the CPU and distribute data to the equipment controllers for output devices. Communication between PPU on one hand, and an equipment controller or the CPU, on the other, is made through a 12 bit full-duplex channel, capable of simultaneous data transference in both directions.

FIG. 15-8   The CDC 7600 computer system

The Central Processing Unit

The CPU of the CDC 7600 is considered an integrated data processing unit. It consists of internal core memory, computation section, and input-output section, operating in a synchronous mode with a clock period of 27.5 nanoseconds.

CPU Core Memory

Internal core memory is either small core memory (SCM), or large core memory (LCM). SCM is arranged in thirty-two banks of 2,048, 60-bit words in each bank, providing a total capacity of 65,536 words or about 650,000 characters. The LCM, on the other hand, is composed of eight banks of 64,000 words each, providing a total capacity of 512,000 words or about 5 million characters. Being the basic working storage for the CPU, the LCM's object programs are assembled for execution in the CPU and all data files are buffered through LCM for the object programs.

Computation Section

The computation section is made up of nine segmented arithmetic units, twenty-four operating registers, and a 12-word instruction stack. These units combine to execute a CPU program stored in SCM. The data move into and out of the computation section through the eight 60-bit X operating registers, which are the basic data handling registers. Eight 18-bit A registers are used primarily as operand address registers, while eight 18-bit B registers are used as index registers to control program execution. Furthermore, there are nine functional units. Each unit, a specialized arithmetic unit, has algorithms for part of the CPU instructions and operates independently. Computation is in binary, either in fixed or floating point.

CPU Input/Output Section

The I/O section contains the mechanism to buffer data to or from the directly connected PPU. There are fifteen channels, each channel having a SCM buffer for incoming data and a separate SCM buffer for outgoing data.

Peripheral Processing Units

The PPU also have core memory, a computation section, and an input-output section. The computation section uses a 12-bit internal word, does binary computation in fixed point, and has synchronous internal logic with a 27.5 nanosecond clock period. The PPU core memory is composed of two banks of 2,048 12-bit words, each giving a total capacity of 4,096 words.

I/O Devices

The CDC 7600 computer system uses card readers and punches, magnetic tape units, line printers, disk drives, and CRT displays. The most significant component is the Disk/Drum Subsystem, which includes a controller and a 7600 Disk File with two storage units, or a maximum of two 7600 Drums.

The 7600 Disk File is made of two double-ended spindles which rotate asynchronously. Each of the four half-spindles contains 18 disks with 32 recording surfaces. Two hydraulic access assemblies service a pair of half-spindles each. Each assembly has two groups of 16 arms, horizontally opposed; on each arm are two head pads, each containing one magnetic read/write head. Thus, there is one read/write head for each recording surface. The Disk Subsystem stores a maximum of 5,072,486,400 bits.

The 7600 Drum Unit is a rotating drum (coated with a magnetic material) and the associated read, write, and head select electronics. There are 128 groups of 16 heads. The total maximum storage capacity of the device is 158 million bits.

The controller contains two read/write control units and is operated by a PPU through two I/O channels, one for data and one for control. Each of the read/write control units operates either one disk file or one drum.

Programming

The three basic software systems used in the CDC 7600 are COMPASS, FORTRAN, and 7600 LOADER. COMPASS is the assembly language of the 7600. It provides a symbolic programming language which efficiently uses the computer resources while the user maintains maximum control over program construction. FORTRAN is a procedural language designed for solving mathematical or scientific problems. The 7600 LOADER loads absolute and relocatable binary programs, links separately compiled or assembled programs, loads library subprograms and links them to user programs, detects errors and provides diagnostics, produces a memory map, and generates overlays.

A Commercial Software Product Set is available for the CDC 7600. It includes COBOL, SORT Information System, Table Generator, and Report Generator. COBOL (Common Business Oriented Language) is a language designed for use in commercial situations and is based on the English language commonly used in business. 7600 SORT is a program that sorts and/or merges files of data. The Report Generator formats raw data (as it is retrieved from the files) into desired reports. Information System is a set of languages which allow the user to create, amend, and retrieve data from files. Table Generator is a generalized program which creates any number of tables from files consisting of fixed and/or variable length records. Finally, CDC 7600 EXPORT/IMPORT programs allow multiaccess from remote locations in batch job processing mode. Users at the remote sites submit jobs and receive output just as they would at stations local to the computer. The EXPORT/IMPORT System is connected to the computer by voice grade or broad band communications links.

Questions and Problems for Review

1. Explain briefly the characteristics of a small computer system.
2. In what respect does the IBM System/3 replace and outweigh the advantages of a punched card data processing system? Explain.
3. Explain briefly the features and peripheral devices that can be used with the IBM System/3.
4. What are the primary characteristics of an intermediate computer system? How is it different from a small computer system?
5. Discuss briefly the features and characteristics of a large computer system. How is it different from an intermediate computer system?

COMPUTER
PROGRAMMING
AND
SYSTEMS DESIGN

4

THE PROGRAMMING CYCLE

DIRECTING A SYSTEM in processing business data involves the specialized field of "programming" and the people (programmers) who perform this function. Generally, a program is defined as a set of instructions. The term *program* is not new, nor is it applicable only to computers. Any activity—social, economic, or political—has its own program. For example, an athletic field day provides a program for the spectators as a guide to the events and the participants. It outlines the steps that will be followed, one after another, during the day. Likewise, computer data processing is conducted according to a program or set of events (instructions).

Preparing the computer program and checking it out are both critical and time-consuming operations. Every single detail must be carefully considered, every possible contingency provided for, and the whole operation reduced to computer instructions written in computer language. Although the final computer run often is quite short, usually a great deal of time-consuming work is done in analyzing, programming, and coding before the run. *Analyzing* is performed in order to determine the overall method of solving the problem; *programming* consists of developing the detailed procedures necessary to implement the method of problem solution (determined in the analysis step) and of documenting the procedures for use in coding. *Coding* is the translation of those detailed procedures into a language acceptable to the computer. The dividing lines between these functions are not always clear or well defined in the total solution of the problem.

SYSTEMS FLOW CHART

A programmer first becomes acquainted with the systems flow chart of the job to be done (Fig. 16-1). This chart describes the overall requirements of

○   ○   ○
DIAGRAMMING AND CHARTING WORKSHEET   Form X24-6413-0
                                                      Printed U.S.A.

Application _Order-inventory-invoice application_ Date _March 7, 197–_ Page _1_ of _1_

Procedure _Work flow chart_   Drawn by _____GDR_____

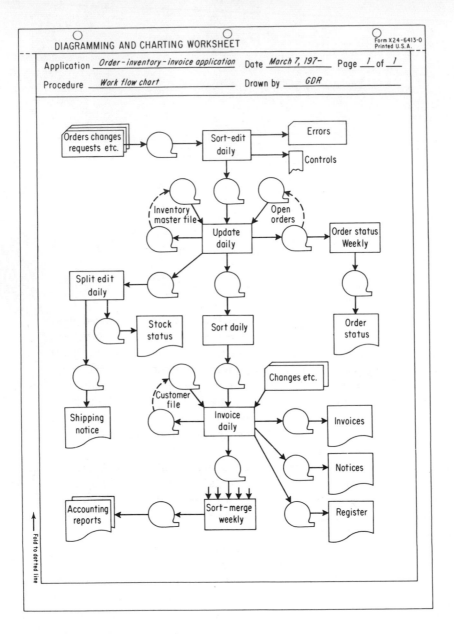

FIG. 16-1   System flow chart

the application and indicates how the data are expected to pass from one
stage to the next. Of course he must be familiar with the system flow chart
symbols used.

At this time the programmer is prompted to ask pertinent questions,
such as: How will the input data for this run appear? What medium is to be
used (that is, punched cards, magnetic or paper tape, etc.)? How many

different files of input data are available? Is the format of these data (their internal arrangement) to be the programmer's decision or is it fixed by a previous operation? With regard to the required output data, what medium is to be used (cards, magnetic tapes or disks, printed reports, etc.)? How many different output files are required? How are the output data to be arranged for reading purposes (in case of reports) or for later computer runs (in the case of machine-readable output)? Regarding the particular processing required in the computer run, the programmer wants to know what must be done to change the files of input data into the required output files: what rules or guidelines of the business is he to implement?

This last factor is very important. The programmer must be aware of the arithmetical and logical choices involved in the situation. To illustrate an *arithmetic* choice, suppose a programmer's job is to prepare bills for the firm's customers. The question arises: Are any customers entitled to a discount? If so, how much? In such a case, the programmer needs to integrate a step into the program to tell the computer that it must multiply the selling price by the discount percentage to arrive at the amount of the discount. The discount then must be subtracted from the selling price to obtain the net billing amount for the customer. This illustration, like many others, involves basic arithmetic.

An example of a *logical* choice related to the same billing situation arises when a discount is allowed for volume purchases (say, more than 100 units). The programmer can include instructions in his program to compare the total order quantity to 100. In this case, the comparison is relatively simple and can be easily stated.

The important thing to note at this stage of programming is that the programmer is attempting to settle, right at the outset, the "rules" of the job. These should be well defined in advance and fixed by operating management. Even though the arithmetic operations appear lengthy at times, they are broken down into a number of simple sequential steps involving basic addition, subtraction, multiplication, or division.

After the programmer has determined how to process *normal* situations, he checks to see if any *exceptions* are expected and plans in advance the steps to be taken to handle each exception. If several alternative courses of action are possible or desirable, a particular alternative usually is specified for him to implement. In the billing illustration, for instance, a transaction from today's file may indicate a customer for whom no record exists in the master file. The procedure to follow might be one of the following alternatives:

1. If the customer is new, a new record should be inserted in the output master file and a regular bill should be produced. Also an additional message should be written out to draw the attention of the sales department to the situation.
2. The transaction could be withheld from processing as a regular bill, pending investigation. It could be written out as it appears onto a separate output exception file and be given special consideration in another computer run.

It should be remembered that this particular phase of problem definition by the programmer is the most difficult and is highly susceptible to error. The error usually results from a failure to account for all the possible exceptions, rather than from a poor choice in how to handle one. An exception may not come up at the beginning, but when it does occur later, major time losses can result in an attempt to rectify the situation. The programmer must be alert to the types of exceptions which are likely to occur in the future processing of a given application.

DATA DESCRIPTION

Having obtained satisfactory answers to his questions, the programmer is now ready to begin his detailed work. The outward appearance of the "working" programmer can be very deceptive, in that there is limited evidence of physical activity. He does most of his work alone, away from the machines, and often over a relatively long period of time.

To organize his thinking, a programmer first records the manner in which the data are to appear at the various stages of processing. He writes down pertinent information regarding any input files to be used, including the number and type of records they contain. Although a rough draft is prepared first, the final format is written on a special preprinted form similar to the one shown in Fig. 16-2. Likewise, when printed reports are desired as output,

File Sheet   **FIG. 16-2** File sheet

FILE NAME Line item file				FILE NO. F 3404.1			
LOCATION Tab room			STORAGE MEDIUM Card tub file				
ACCESS REQUIREMENTS Data for order must be available within 2 minutes.							
SEQUENCED BY Stockroom location within customer number.							
CONTENT QUALIFICATIONS Name and address cards and line item cards for picking tickets							
in process or back – ordered.							
HOW CURRENT 1 to 5 hours old when entered. Remain in file until stockroom has							
attempted to fill picking ticket.							
RETENTION CHARACTERISTICS Data normally removed upon receipt of picking ticket.							
Special purge run once every 2 weeks.							
LABELS ———							
REMARKS ———							
CONTENTS							
SEQUENCE NO.	MESSAGE NAME	VOLUME		CHARACTERS PER MESSAGE	CHARACTERS PER FILE		
		AVG.	PEAK		AVG.	PEAK	
01	Customer name card (R 3001)	320	400	61	19,520	24,400	
02	Customer address cards (R 3004)	640	800	65	41,600	52,000	
03	Line item cards (R 3008)	2250	2800	62	139,500	173,600	
	TOTALS	3210	4000	188	200,620	250,000	

DATE ————   ANALYST ————   SOURCE ————   PAGE ————
STUDY ————

the printed format is determined in advance and laid out on a special form used for that purpose (Fig. 16-3).

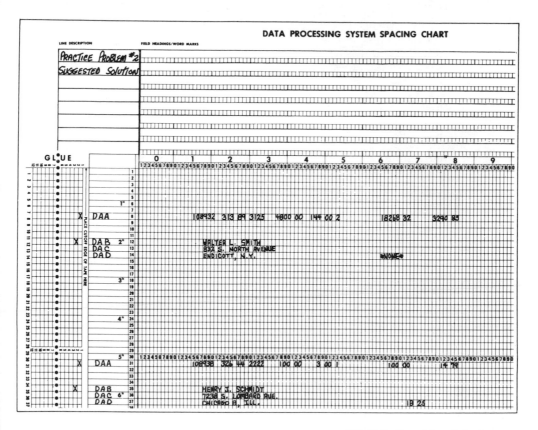

FIG. 16-3   Report format sheet

LOGIC DESCRIPTION

Before any processing can be performed, the programmer records the processing sequence of the operation by *programming flow charts, decision tables,* or both, in several stages. These are considered the two most common descriptive methods, and since the programmer's task is to write down precise instructions for each machine step, these diagramming stages begin at a very broad level of "general logic" and proceed to a level which breaks down broad functions into individual elements. Figure 16-4 is considered a rather broad presentation of the necessary elements for a payroll application. By contrast, Fig. 16-5 is a detailed chart, since it shows the steps performed during the processing of only one block (block *40*) of the previous chart. This shows that the elements included in any given flow chart depend upon the extent and type of details which the programmer feels should be included in the actual processing.

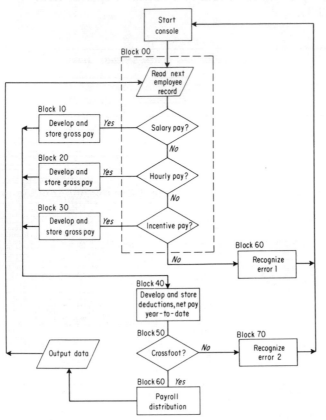

FIG. 16-4 Systems flow chart—payroll

THE INITIAL CODING STEP

After file descriptions, record descriptions, storage maps, and logic diagrams have been prepared, the programmer begins coding. Special forms are used in coding and require that certain data be written in special designated areas on the form. Different computers require the use of different languages and this, in turn, requires the use of different coding forms.

COBOL (Common Business Oriented Language) is a language that can be used on most computer systems, and for this, a special form also is provided (Fig. 16-6). FORTRAN (Formula Translator), a procedure-oriented language used mainly in pro-

FIG. 16-5 Systems flow chart—block 40

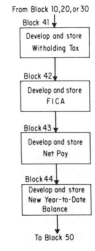

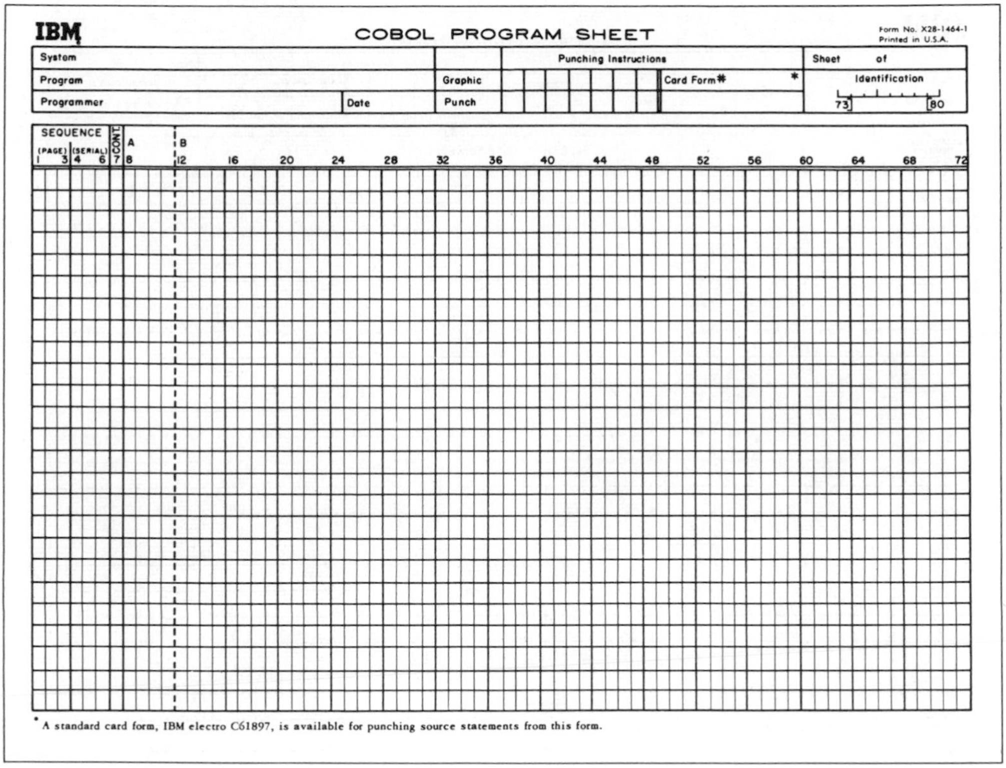

| IBM | COBOL PROGRAM SHEET | | Form No. X28-1464-1 |
| | | | Printed in U.S.A. |

FIG. 16-6 COBOL programming sheet

gramming scientific applications, also is a "common" language for which special coding sheets are provided (Fig. 16-7).

Any programming language will look and sound strange to the layman. However, the programmer is well trained in the particular language he employs in writing computer instructions. A considerable amount of time usually is consumed between the job definition stage and the completion of initial coding. This ranges from several hours to several months, depending on the complexity of the computer run and on the coding languages used. When the programmer has completed the coding stage, he is ready to use the computer.

PRECOMPILE PREPARATION

When a program initially is coded in a special language (not directly that of the computer), the computer translates this symbolic language into one it can understand (a machine language). The process is called *compiling*.

In compiling, the various coding sheets are turned over to a keypunch

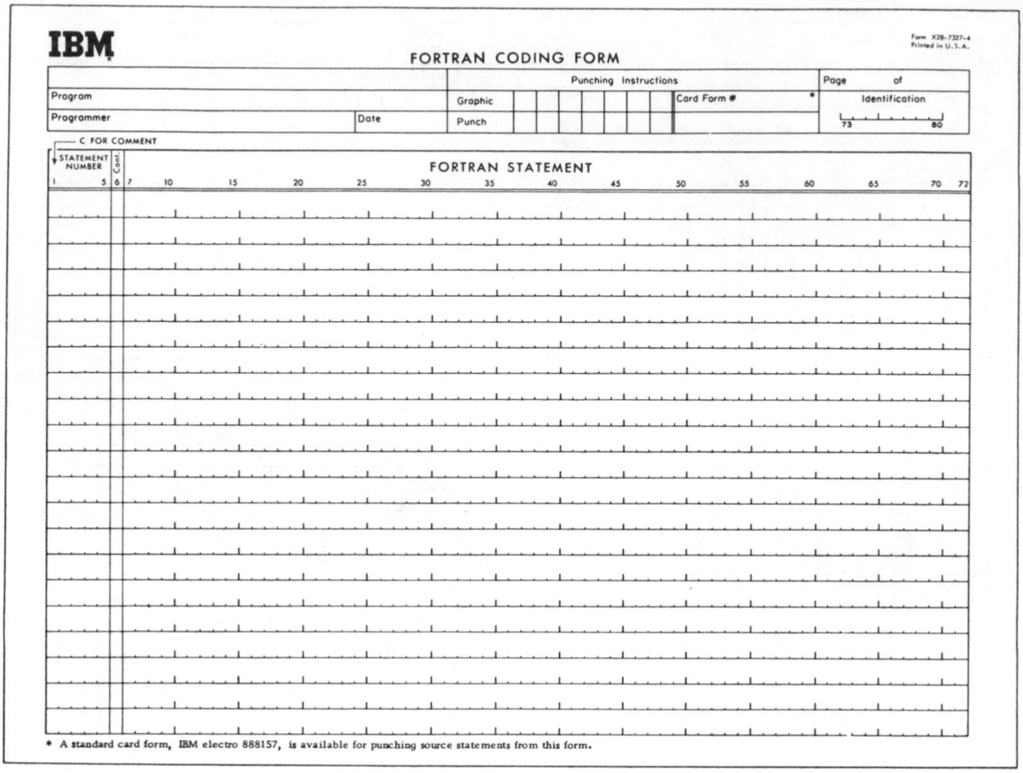
IBM

FORTRAN CODING FORM

Form X28-7327-4
Printed in U.S.A.

Program | Punching Instructions | Graphic | Punch | Card Form # * | Page of | Identification 73 80

Programmer | Date

C FOR COMMENT

STATEMENT NUMBER | Cont. | FORTRAN STATEMENT

1 5 6 7 10 15 20 25 30 35 40 45 50 55 60 65 70 72

* A standard card form, IBM electro 888157, is available for punching source statements from this form.

FIG. 16-7 FORTRAN programming sheet

operator, who punches the data from each line onto a separate card, in exactly the same way in which they are written on the coding form. If the coding sheet contains 16 lines (instructions), then 16 cards are punched, constituting the overall program (Fig. 16-8). In keypunching, the operator punches data into the card in specific locations, just as they appear on the coding sheet. For example, page number 001 is shown in the top left corner of the coding sheet. Digits 1 and 3 in that box refer to the column numbers in which the page number must be punched. The keypunch operator then punches 001 in columns 1, 2, and 3 as shown in Fig. 16-8. This procedure also applies to the remaining characters on that line and to the remaining lines to be punched in their respective cards. Details of COBOL programming are presented in Chapter 21.

LISTING THE PUNCHED PROGRAM

When the deck of cards representing the program (called the *source program*) has been keypunched, it is run through the computer system to produce a *listing* (printing). The listing usually shows what has been punched into the cards, and often other information related to the deck, such as the total number of cards in the deck, the amount of storage the program will occupy, and even the identification of those areas where there has been an obvious misuse of the language (for example, unintelligible symbols, spaces where there should be none, etc.). (See Fig. 16-9.)

The programmer thoroughly reviews the listing to make sure that no clerical or mechanical errors have been made in the program. He evaluates the messages supplied in the listing, corrects his original coding sheets in places where language errors have been made, pulls the corresponding cards out of the card deck, and replaces them with new cards punched with the corrected codes. A second listing usually is made of the corrected deck for future reference.

COMPILING

The prepared deck of source program cards is taken to the computer, and a separate program, called a *compiler,* is first read (loaded) into the machine.

FIG. 16-8 Punched COBOL instructions

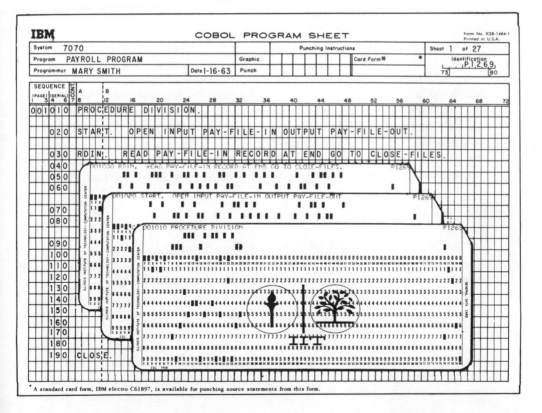

```
AG05        *            DESCRIPTION OF TEMPORARY STORAGE FIELDS
AG06    WORKAREA     DA    1
AG07    GROSSPAY           03,09A5.2
AG08    TAX                13,19A5.2
AG09    FICA               25,29A3.2
AG10    TFICA              35,39A3.2
AG11    NETPAY             43,49A5.2
AG12        *
AG13    ERMESSAGE    DC    -RDW
AG14                       'MASTER IS MISSING FOR MANNUMBER'
AG15    ERRORNO            '            '
AG16        *
AG17        *    PROGRAM
AG18    IOPEN        OPEN  IMASTER,DETAIL,MASTEROUT,CHECKTAPE
AG19    START        GET   DETAIL
AG20    NEXTMASTER   GET   IMASTER
AG21                 COMP  DMANNUMBER,IMANNUMBER,NOMASTER,,NODETAIL
AG22                 ARITH GROSSPAY=IPAYRATE*DHOURS+DSALES*ICOMISRATE
AG23                 ARITH TAX=.18*(GROSSPAY-IDEPENDNTS*13.00)
AG24                 ZSIGN TAX,,,ZEROTAX
AG25    FICATEST     ARITH FICA=GROSSPAY*.03
AH01                 ARITH TFICA=IYTDFICA+FICA-144.00
AH02                 ZSIGN TFICA,FICALC,,FICALC
AH03                 ARITH FICA=FICA-FFICA
AH04    FICALC       ARITH IYTDFICA=IYTDFICA+FICA
AH05                 ARITH IYTDPAY=IYTDPAY+GROSSPAY
AH06                 ARITH NETPAY=GROSSPAY-TAX-FICA
AH07                 EDMOV IMANNUMBER TO CMANNUMBER,INAME TO CNAME,NETPAY TO
AH08                       CNETPAY
```

FIG. 16-9 Source program listing—an example

The compiler program is stored on disks, punched cards or on a reel of tape kept in the installation's library. Once the compiler program is loaded into primary storage, control is transferred to it automatically and the programmer's deck of cards is read in as input data for the compiler program.

The compiler program converts the programmer's punched instructions to machine language instructions. Output begins to develop from the computer, in the form of punched cards, paper tape, magnetic tape, printed listings, console-typewriter messages, or any combination thereof. Figure 16-10 shows a listing of the program produced in a machine language. The instructions as written by the programmer (*source* program) are on the left and the resulting machine-coded instructions (*object* program) are on the right.

MESSAGE ANALYSIS

A listing provides several advantages. First, in addition to a printed copy of the recorded instructions in the input deck, it also shows several columns of numbers. One of these columns represents a sequential numbering of each output line in the listing. Another represents the machine language coding of the instructions. A third represents the machine addresses of the locations reserved for these instructions.

The listing also includes notes to the programmer regarding the validity and correctness of his coding. He examines each note and takes appropriate action where necessary. For example, a correction usually involves making changes in the coding sheet, repunching the corrected instruction in a new

CDREF	LABEL	OP	OPERAND		CDNO	FD	LOC	INSTRUCTION	REF
AG05	*		DESCRIPTION OF TEMPORARY STORAGE FIELDS						
AG06	WORKAREA	DA	1			39	1724	+0017241728	1724
AG07	GROSSPAY		03,09A5.2			39	1725		1725
AG08	TAX		13,19A5.2			59	1726		1726
AG09	FICA		25,29A3.2			59	1727		1727
AG10	TFICA		35,39A3.2			39	1728		1728
AG11	NETPAY		43,49A5.2						
AG12	*				00232		1729	+0017291738	1729
AG13	ERMESSAGE	DC	-RDW		00233	09	1730	-0017301738	1730
AG14 X			'MASTER IS MISSING FOR MANNUMBER'			09	1731	'7900698200	1731
X						09	1732	'7469828269	1732
X						09	1733	'7567006676	1733
X						09	1734	'7900746175	1734
X					00234	09	1735	'7584746265	1735
AG15	ERRORNO					01	1736	'79	1736
X						29	1736	' 00000000	
X						09	1737	'0000000000	1737
AG16	*					01	1738	'00	1738
AG17	*	PROGRAM							
AG18	IOPEN	OPEN	IMASTER,DETAIL,MASTEROUT,CHECKTAPE		00235		1739	+0200040578	
	IOPEN	BLX	IOCSIXG,IOC,IOPEN				1740	+0100091327	
X		B	TAPEFILEIM				1741	+0100091345	
X		B	TAPEFILEDI		00257		1742	+0100091336	
X		B	TAPEFILEMO				1848	+0110092109	
	M,23		M,22-3+MACREG,O2		00257		1849	+3200891611	
X		ST3	CNETPAY(0,1)				1850	+3300672121	
X		ZA3	COMAREA,A(6,7)				1851	+3200011612	
X		ST3	CNETPAY(2,3)				1852	+3300892121	
X		ZA3	COMAREA,A(8,9)				1853	+3200231612	
X		ST3	CNETPAY(4,5)		00258		1854	+3300452127	
X		ZA3	','				1855	+3300451612	
X		ST3	CNETPAY(6,7)				1856	+3300012122	
X		ZA3	COMAREA,A(10,11)				1857	+3200671612	
X		ST3	CNETPAY(8,9)				1858	+3300232122	
X		ZA3	COMAREA,A(12,13)		00259		1859	+3200891612	
X		ST3	CNETPAY(10,11)				1860	+3300452122	
*X		ZA3	COMAREA,A(14,15)				1861	+3200011613	
X		ST3	CNETPAY(12,13)				1862	+3300012127	
X		ZA3	','		00260		1863	+3200231613	
X		ST3	CNETPAY(14,15)				1864	+3300672122	
X		ZA3	COMAREA,A(16,17)				1865	+3200451613	
X		ST3	CNETPAY(16,17)				1866	+3300892122	
X		ZA3	COMAREA,A(18,19)				1867	+3200671613	
X		ST3	CNETPAY(18,19)						
AH08A	*		PREPARE TAPE RECORD FOR PRINTING CHECKS OFFLINE						

FIG. 16-10 Listing—source and object program

253

card, and inserting it in the program deck. After corrections are made, the revised input deck is taken back to the computer and the compiling routine is repeated until the output messages during this compiling stage indicate that there are no more obvious errors in the program. After compilation, the output listing represents the compiled (object) program in machine language form and is presented either on a reel of magnetic tape, on paper tape, or as a deck of punched cards.

TESTING AND "DEBUGGING"

The machine language deck (the *object* program) is tested for accuracy by using it in the processing of sample data. This process is called "debugging" the program. It is here that "bugs" in the program logic and coding should be discovered by testing the results of all possible types of transactions and alternatives that could occur in using "live" data. Once debugged, the program is tested with "live" data, a process which is necessary to allow the computer, under the control of the object program, to process data previously processed manually, and compare the results of the two methods. This parallel operation is called *cutover*.

Cutover may also include the conversion of input files to the form used by the new computer method. This usually involves keypunching and special computer runs.

The programmer observes the testing operation, making corrections, and with his management, reviews the results. It is at this time in particular that the importance of identifying all exceptions during the job definition stage is brought into focus. If the job definition was well done, no "surprises" are likely to occur. However, if an exception is detected for which no provision has been made, *patching* or updating of the program must be done.

PRODUCTION

Before a computer run is initiated, instructions are given to the machine operators to tell them how the computer components should be set up for the job, what to do when any particular message is typed out, and where output is to be forwarded and filed. When this is done, the installation is ready to use the object program over and over again whenever the application for which it was written is repeated. The job of carrying out the daily production is turned over to the operating personnel, and the programmer is now ready to begin a new project.

The foregoing cycle (problem definition to production) points out that no end result could be accomplished without the creative and ingenious efforts of human beings. Although a powerful tool, the computer could not, for example, change time card information into an employee's paycheck, create customer bills, or do any other routine without the advance preparation and loading of a program which can "tell" it what to do. Man is still the "master" and the computer is the "slave."

Glossary of Terms

COBOL: Common *Business-Oriented Language*. A computer language used in business data processing to prepare a program.

CODING: The translation of flow diagrams into the language of the computer.

COMPILE: To prepare a machine language program from a computer program written in another programming language by making use of the overall logic structure of the program, generating more than one machine instruction for each symbolic statement, or both, as well as performing the function of an assembler.

DEBUG: To detect, locate, and remove mistakes from a routine or malfunctions from a computer. Synonymous with *troubleshoot*.

FLOW CHART: A graphical representation for the definition, analysis, or solution of a problem in which symbols are used to represent operations, data, flow, and equipment.

FORTRAN: *Formula Translator*. Any of several specific procedure-oriented programming languages.

OBJECT PROGRAM: The program which is the output of an automatic coding system. Often the object program is a machine language program ready for execution, but it may well be an intermediate language.

SOURCE PROGRAM: A program written in a source language. A language that is an input to a given translation process.

STORAGE MAP: A pictorial aid used by the programmer for estimating the proportion of storage capacity to be allocated to data.

TROUBLESHOOT: See *debug*.

Questions for Review

1. What is a program? Give an example.
2. What are the steps involved in the preparation of a program? Explain fully.
3. What is a storage map? Why is it used?
4. List and describe the advantages of listing program instructions prior to their use in a computer run.
5. What factors are involved in the testing and "debugging" stage?

chapter seventeen

CONTROL AND
THE STORED PROGRAM

THE STORED PROGRAM CONCEPT
Stored Program Computer Design

INSTRUCTIONS

A SAMPLE PROGRAM

CONTROL IS DEFINED as mastery over starting or stopping the computer system, either manually or automatically. Manual control often is used when it is necessary to load input data or machine instructions. Certain buttons are depressed which cause an input device to read-in or "load" the data into primary storage; then the computer is started manually. From this point on, the instructions stored in the computer control its operations automatically. This is referred to as *program control*. The instructions placed in primary storage are called the *stored program*.

The control unit consists of computer elements which aid in executing the stored instructions in a logical sequence. They interpret each instruction in the order given by the programmer and execute the command, depending on the type of interpretation made. Without this, no instruction could be executed automatically; neither could any interpretation be applied toward the achievement of the required output.

THE STORED PROGRAM CONCEPT

The stored program concept is explained by the notion that the entire computer program is available in the CPU during the processing phase. Early electronic computers did not have stored program capability. When processing was desired, program instructions were read sequentially into the CPU from punched cards, paper tape, or early forms of magnetic tape. This method of program execution did not allow for any deviation from the predefined nature of the program, minimizing the logical capability of the computer.

In today's computers, the presence of the entire set of program instructions in primary storage means that deviation from the sequential execution

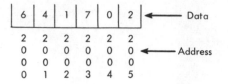

(A) An example of a variable word length.

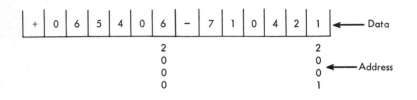

(B) An example of a fixed word-length.

FIG. 17-1

path based on selected conditions is feasible. Stored program computers are designed to choose alternate or nonsequential execution paths based on a logical determination of conditional states. This flexibility accounts for the true significance of the stored program concept and is the factor which has contributed most to the growth of computer usage.

Stored Program Computer Design

The availability of machine instructions as well as other data in primary storage makes it necessary to have some means of determining the location of specific instructions or data. Traditionally, the method used is to divide primary storage into separate locations, each capable of storing a predetermined number of characters, and assign an individual address for each location. The data each location contains are referred to as a *word*. A *word* may contain either program data or an instruction.

If the *word* contains data to be processed, it is called a *data word;* if it contains an instruction, it is called an *instruction word.*

A *computer word* is the basic unit of information in a computer. In some machines, it is of a fixed length; that is, the number of characters it contains is limited to a predetermined size and is handled as a group. This is referred to as *fixed word length.*

Other machines that do not impose a limit on the length of a given word are called *variable word length,* or "character" machines. Figure 17-1A shows an example of a *variable word length.* Each character has its own address (location number); for example, digit 2 is located in *2005* and digit 4 is located in *2001.* Figure 17-1B illustrates a *fixed word length* and defines the length of a word as six characters, plus its sign. These characters are addressed by one address only; for example, the word containing −710421 is addressed as a group by *2001* and the word containing +065406 is addressed as a group by *2000*.

Fixed word length computers have the following chief characteristics:

1. No storage positions are required to define fields. Since the length of each transmission is determined by the computer itself, the fixed-word concept automatically defines the fields.
2. Since the instructions are of fixed length, parallel access is possible. All fixed-word machines have this capability.
3. Fixed-word machines usually have higher speed because of their parallel access characteristics; in some machines, since arithmetic circuits also can be parallel, the speed can be many times faster than in others.
4. Storage may be pure binary or in some other code structure.

By comparison, in *variable word length* computers, each position in storage (whether a digit or character) is individually addressable. Units of transfer are governed only by the practical limits of total storage. Fields or records are usually defined by a special character in the high-order position (left column) of a given record to separate it from an adjacent one. This character is called a flag bit or a word mark.

In order to code data in the BCD or other codes, the computer converts decimal representation at the input stage to the required computer code for processing. At the end of the processing, a converter transforms the coded output back into decimal representation, understandable by the programmer or the user.

Finally, arithmetic circuitry usually is serial, by digit. The variable nature of the fields makes it difficult to design parallel devices. In the previous illustration, it also is assumed that each location is identified by a three-digit address (again, an arbitrary size selected for the purpose of the example). The address itself is not physically labeled in storage; the address simply is a label determined by those who designed and built the machine.

INSTRUCTIONS

A stored program consists of a set of *instructions* (commands) to put the computer into a cycle for executing each instruction, one after the other, until the job is done. It has been mentioned that both data and instructions are stored in primary storage. Through the stored program the control unit can decide whether a particular word is a data word or an instruction word.

At the beginning of each instruction cycle, an instruction word is channeled to the control unit, where designated electrical equivalents of the digit values cause circuits to be set up to control the next part of the cycle. In the next part of the cycle, another data word generally is brought out to the arithmetic unit, where other circuits are affected and a result is established in a specific register. Then the cycle is repeated, and normally the sequential organization of the program directs that the instruction word following the previously used instruction word will be called into the control unit. Again, the electrical analysis is effected and the rest of the cycle goes on as before, acting upon one instruction at a time automatically.

Although electronic speeds give the impression that many things are happening at the same time, a look into the design of the computer shows the contrary. In most computers each cycle representing an instruction is carried out independently and alone. The word which reaches the control unit at the beginning of the cycle is interpreted as an instruction. The next word in storage will be used as the next instruction unless the effect of the first instruction causes a transfer or change in the normal sequence. It remains for the programmer to take advantage of these facts and organize both instructions and data in storage to do useful work.

An instruction, then, is contained in a word transmitted from primary storage to the control unit at the beginning of a machine cycle. Its function is to set up the necessary circuits so that the rest of the cycle can perform some useful purpose. In order to carry out this function, an instruction affects the control unit by its two parts: the *operation code* and the *operand* or address portion (Fig. 17-2).

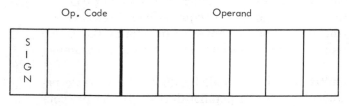

FIG. 17-2 The instruction format

The effect of the operation code is to set up what is to be done during the rest of the cycle. The operand portion specifies the part of the computer system to be used in that operation. When a computer is being designed, the manufacturer has several choices to make concerning the instructions, but the important choice is the number of circuits that should be built in to handle the number of desired operations. The final decision is related to (1) the cost of incorporating the necessary circuits, (2) the cost involved in programming it with fewer instructions, and (3) the cost at object time in carrying out the operations. The final choice results in the *instruction set* of the machine. An example of an instruction set is shown in the sample program later in this chapter.

There are other factors which the designer must consider in developing an instruction set for a computer. For example, let us consider the function of addition. To add, a computer must (1) clear a register of any previous contents; (2) move a word from storage to that register; (3) add another word to the first, so that the sum ends up in the register; and (4) store the sum in a specific location in primary storage. It is quite possible to build circuits to perform one, two, three, or all four functions in one cycle. Whatever the designer decides will have a bearing on the cost of the equipment, the amount of programming time that will be required, and the execution time for the completion of a given application.

Once this decision is made, other matters begin to require attention. For example, if an instruction set of more than ten separate operations is decided upon (0–9), then the number of digits in the word needed to represent the operation code will have to be a minimum of two digits (assuming that only numeric codes are used). This allowance makes it possible to have a unique code for 100 different operations (00–99). If 100 operations are too many, however, then a protection device must be built into the control unit to recognize invalid codes. The net result is to come up with a well-defined "instruction set" considering the codes used and any problems created as a result of this choice.

When one is given the designer's decisions, the concept of storing a program, and the definition of an instruction, another fact becomes clear: since instructions and data are stored in the same place and in the same way, and since an instruction can cause an operation on any word in storage, it follows that one instruction can operate on another. This ability represents the real power of the stored program. When one sequence of instructions recognizes certain facts about the data being processed, other sequences of instructions can be altered, at object time, to cause different operations to occur. This capability brings about a remarkable expansion of the power available to the programmer, although it also requires that he be careful and precise in his logic and in the type of instructions he writes for the computer to execute.

The computer *console* (Fig. 17-3) is used to perform two main functions:

FIG. 17-3   IBM 360 console

(1) To initiate the execution of the stored program, and (2) to provide a communication link between the operator and the system after the stored program is under way.

To aid in communicating data between man and machine, the console is equipped with buttons, switches, and related circuits for (1) inserting a missing or needed word into storage manually, (2) accessing a particular word as the first cycle begins, and (3) setting up an impulse for starting the first cycle. To load the program, the operator depresses some keys on the console and places specific instructions in storage. These instructions are called a *load program*. The load program now takes over and causes the object program to be read through the proper input unit into a specific area in storage. The last instruction of the load program causes the sequence of instructions to transfer to the word containing the first instruction of the object program just stored. From then on, the object program is in direct control. This process is called *program loading*.

As the object program begins to function, the flow of data to be processed proceeds from the input units to storage, through the processing sections, and then to the output units. It is continuous and automatic. The role of each of these components is known and clear to the programmer. The input unit(s), for instance, supply the data records, one or more at a time, as requested by the program through the control unit. The storage unit holds the data received from the input unit as well as the program for the use of the control unit as processing progresses. The arithmetic unit combines words in a specified fashion as established by the instructions in the control unit. The output unit(s) accepts the complete data records at times selected by the program through the control unit. Throughout this whole process, the console provides a monitoring station to observe signals sent from the control unit, indicating the current state of the processing routine.

A SAMPLE PROGRAM

The following program is presented to illustrate the basic functions of a computer system as operated by a stored program. For the illustration several assumptions are made, as follows:

> *Input Units:* one card reader.
> *Output Units:* one printer.
> *Control Unit:* normal circuits and four indicators called high, low, equal, and end-of-file, each of which has two settings (on or off).
> *Console:* has button for word entry, a CLEAR button to clear all storage to blanks, and a typewriter.
> *Storage:* 1,000 eight-character words, with signs, location addresses running from 000 to 999.
> *Arithmetic Unit:* one eight-digit register, with sign.
> *Instruction Set:* In the following section, the name of the operation is given

first, followed by the manner in which this instruction would appear in storage. Letters *AAA* are used to represent any three-digit address. Finally, a description of the function performed is given. All instructions are made up as shown in Fig. 17-2; that is, the sign is shown in the sign column, the next two digits represent the operation part (operation code), and the remaining six digits represent the operand part.

READ: +01 000AAA, read one 80-column card from the input unit into a 10-word storage area beginning in location AAA. (Ten words would be necessary for storage of all 80 columns.)

WRITE: +02 000AAA, write one record of 10 words beginning in location AAA on the output unit (80 characters sent to printer).

CLEAR AND ADD: +03 000AAA, clear the contents of the arithmetic register (accumulator), and then add into the register the word located at AAA.

ADD: +04 000AAA, add the word located at AAA to the word in the arithmetic register. Place the sum in the arithmetic register.

SUBTRACT: +05 000AAA, subtract the word located at AAA from the word in the arithmetic register. Place the difference in the arithmetic register.

MULTIPLY: +06 000AAA, multiply the word in the arithmetic register by the word located at AAA. Place the product in the arithmetic register.

DIVIDE: +07 000AAA, divide the word in the arithmetic register by the word located at AAA. Place the quotient in the arithmetic register.

COMPARE: +08 000AAA, compare the value of the word located at AAA with the word in the arithmetic register. If the number in the arithmetic register is higher, set the "HIGH" indicator in the control unit "ON." If the word in the arithmetic register is lower, set the "LOW" indicator "ON." If the two words are exactly the same, set the "EQUAL" indicator "ON."

BRANCH: +09 000AAA, instead of using the next sequential word as the next instruction, use the word located at AAA as the next instruction.

TEST BRANCH HIGH: +10 000AAA, if the "HIGH" indicator is "ON," turn it "OFF" and take the word at AAA as the next instruction.

TEST BRANCH LOW: +11 000AAA, if the "LOW" indicator is "ON," turn it "OFF" and take the word at AAA as the next instruction.

TEST BRANCH EQUAL: +12 000AAA, if the "EQUAL" indicator is "ON," turn it "OFF" and take the word at AAA as the next instruction.

BRANCH END OF FILE: +13 000AAA, if the "END OF FILE" indicator has been turned "ON" because the last input record has been read, turn it "OFF" and take the word at AAA as the next instruction.

STORE: +14 000AAA, replace the word at AAA by the contents of the arithmetic unit register.

HALT: +15 000AAA, stop the machine and type the digits AAA on the console.

Given the computer specifications and instruction set above, the programmer is asked to add two numbers from each input record and print the sum. When the last sum is printed, the grand total of all the sums is to be printed, preceded by the word "TOTAL." As the records are processed, a check is made to insure that the deck is in ascending sequence. If any card is out of order, the run is to be terminated and the operator is to be informed.

In this case, cards would be resequenced and the entire run started over. These steps are shown graphically in Fig. 17-4.

Another step in programming this problem calls for the programmer to prepare a more detailed flow chart showing the exact functions which the computer must perform to process the data (Fig. 17-5).

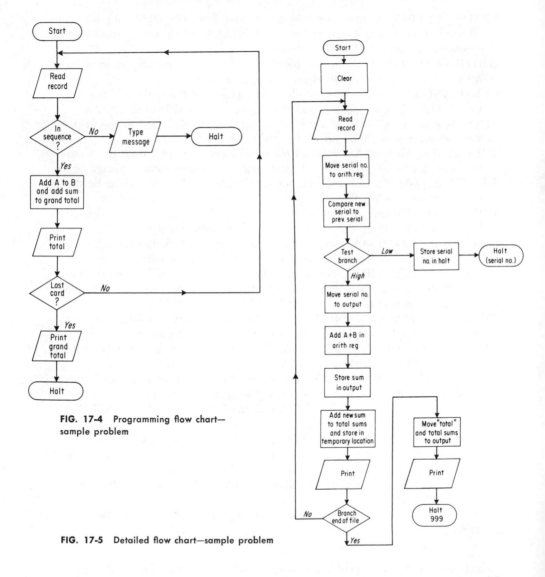

FIG. 17-4 Programming flow chart—sample problem

FIG. 17-5 Detailed flow chart—sample problem

The memory allocation is determined next to ascertain the availability of space for input records, output area, and the stored program (Fig. 17-6).

The layout of the records as they should appear in the cards and on the printed page are shown in Figs. 17-7 and 17-8, respectively.

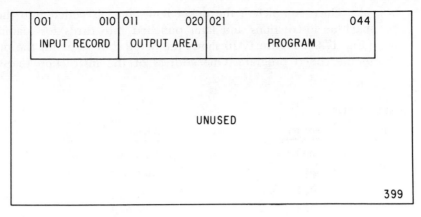

FIG. 17-6 Memory allocation

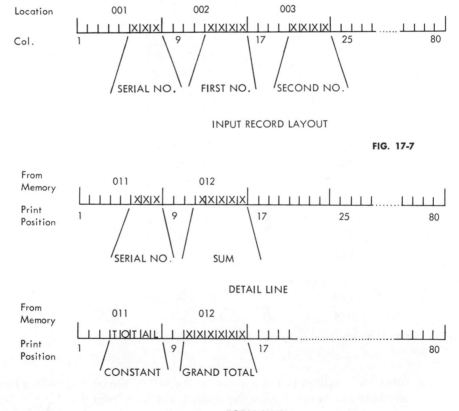

INPUT RECORD LAYOUT

FIG. 17-7

DETAIL LINE

TOTAL LINE

OUTPUT RECORD LAYOUT

FIG. 17-8

Once completed, the detail flow chart is coded into the proper set of machine instructions and later punched into cards for loading the program (Fig. 17-9). Figure 17-10 shows the detail flow chart for the processing, keyed to the coded program. One address of the instruction that carries out the

INSTRUCTIONS

Address	Contents
021	+01 000 001
022	+03 000 001
023	+08 000 011
024	+11 000 040
025	+14 000 011
026	+03 000 002
027	+04 000 003
028	+14 000 012
029	+04 000 043
030	+14 000 043
031	+02 000 011
032	+13 000 034
033	+09 000 021
034	+03 000 044
035	+14 000 011
036	+03 000 043
037	+14 000 012
038	+02 000 011
039	+15 000 999
040	+04 000 042
041	+14 000 042
042	+15 000 (000)

Constants	
043	+00 000 000
044	Total

FIG. 17-9 Machine language flow chart—sample problem

function is written just above and to the left of the corresponding block. These numbers are inserted after the coding has been completed.

In examining the sequence of coding performed, we find that the first instruction is "read." The programmer then determines the way in which he can check the sequence. Except for the first record, the serial number of the previous record can always be found in the first word of the output area.

When the first record is being processed, location 011 should be blank (as a result of a previous clearing of the memory) so that the compare instruction can be addressed to location 011.

The next instruction breaks the sequence if a record is found out of place. When the programmer writes the instruction, he is not really sure how many locations will be necessary for the normal processing. His procedure is to leave the last three digits unfilled and to underline them to remind himself that these must be filled in later (Fig. 17-9).

Instructions located in 025, 026, 027, and 028 perform the detail arithmetic required. The next two instructions (in locations 029 and 030) are used for storing the running grand total. When he comes to these instructions, the programmer knows that he can use any word in storage located outside either the record area or the instruction area for this purpose. He leaves the address part of the instruction blank, underlines it, and goes on.

The next instruction (031) causes a detail line to be printed. Instructions 032 and 033 are included to test for the last record. If the last card read is the last record, then instruction 033 is skipped and instruction 034 is executed, resulting in branching to print the TOTAL as output (instruction 044), and then HALT. However, if the last card read is *not* the last record, instruction 033 is executed, which in effect branches the program to the top instruction (021), which is to read the next record in sequence. It should be noted that by using the word "TOTAL," the programmer has the facility to load the word along with the letters "TOTAL" at the same time he is loading the program. This type of word is called a *constant* to differentiate it from the instructions and the data.

Instructions at 036 to 038 complete the preparation of the grand total line and execute its printing. As shown in Fig. 17-9, instruction 036 refers to the running total location, which still is not fixed. This causes the programmer to underline the address for future reference. When the instruction at 039 is reached, the job is completed. The message "999," a common convention among programmers, is typed to inform the operator of the end of the operation. These digits fill out the "HALT" instruction.

At this time, the programmer may write an instruction to check whether a record is out of sequence. Now that he knows the exact instruction address, he goes back on the coding sheet and fills out the instruction 024 with the digits "040." Instruction 041 stores the contents of the next instruction (042) which is a "halt" instruction. The instruction located at 042 is written on the coding sheet as + 15 000 (000). The parentheses serve as a reminder that the address will be modified before it is executed. These parentheses are not keypunched.

The programmer has now completed all the necessary instruction coding except for filling in the address portions of those to be located at 029, 030, 034, and 036. These refer to the two constant words needed. The word at 043 is assigned to hold the running total; at program loading time, this is started out as "all zeros." The word at 044 is to be loaded with the word "TOTAL." These locations often are referred to as *variable constants* and

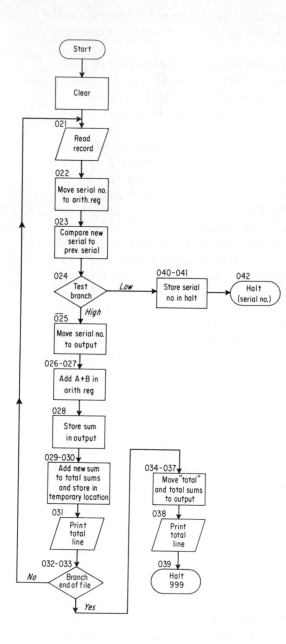

FIG. 17-10 Detailed flow chart for processing—sample program

fixed constants, respectively. The word at 043, a variable constant, will change in value as the program progresses. The word "TOTAL" will not change and is an example of a fixed constant.

The programmer fills in the proper addresses in the instructions to be completed. His coding is now finished and he is ready to begin his testing.

Until higher level symbolic programming languages were developed, all programming required the type of detailed coding illustrated in the foregoing sample program. Modern programming languages allow more flexibility and do not require the attention to clerical detail described above. This has greatly simplified the programming task. (For an explanation of "Programming Systems," see Chapter 19.)

Glossary of Terms

CONTROL: (1) The part of a digital computer or processor which determines the execution and interpretation of instructions in proper sequence, including the decoding of each instruction and the application of the proper signals to the arithmetic unit and other registers in accordance with the decoded information. (2) Frequently, it is one or more of the components in any mechanism responsible for interpreting and carrying out manually-initiated directions. Sometimes it is called manual control. (3) In some business applications, a mathematical check. (4) In programming, instructions which determine conditional jumps are often referred to as control instructions, and the time sequence of execution of instructions is called the flow of control.

DATA WORD: A word which may be primarily regarded as part of the information manipulated by a given program. A data word may be used to modify a program instruction, or to be arithmetically combined with other data words.

FIXED WORD LENGTH: Having the property that a machine word always contains the same number of characters or digits.

INSTRUCTION CODE: See *operation code*.

INSTRUCTION WORD: A computer word which contains an instruction.

OBJECT TIME: The time span during which a stored program is in active control of a specific application.

OPERATION CODE: A code that represents specific operations. Synonymous with *instruction code*.

STORED PROGRAM: A series of instructions in storage to direct the step-by-step operation of the machine.

VARIABLE WORD LENGTH: Having the property that a machine word may have a variable number of characters. It may be applied either to a single entry whose information content may be changed from time to time, or to a group of functionally similar entries whose corresponding components are of different length.

WORD: An ordered set of characters which occupies one storage location and is treated by the computer circuits as a unit and transferred as such. Ordinarily a word is treated by the control unit as an instruction, and by the arithmetic unit as a quantity. Word lengths may be fixed or variable depending on the particular computer.

WORD LENGTH: The number of bits or other characters in a word.

Questions for Review

1. What is meant by control? By automatic control?
2. Describe the main function(s) of the stored program.
3. What are the two main parts of an instruction? Describe each fully. Give an example.
4. How does the control unit carry out the interpretation of instructions?
5. Discuss the role of the console in the processing of data.
6. What is meant by program loading? How is a program loaded in the computer?

PROGRAM PREPARATION

CERTAIN PREPARATORY ROUTINES are often necessary before the coding phase of a programming application can be initiated. As has been pointed out, in addition to the coding phase, some analysis and programming routines are involved. The programming phase includes translating the general solution, developed in the analysis phase, into the detailed procedural descriptions necessary to facilitate coding. Although some applications make it possible for the programmer to mentally keep a record of the procedural details of the project, it is, nevertheless, important to have a written record and documentation for future reference.

Over the years, many "shorthand" methods of procedure development and documentation have been developed. Among others, flow charting and decision tables have been most popular.

FLOW CHARTING

A flow chart or diagram is a means of expressing a solution to a given problem. Flow charts are commonly used in several fields (physics, architecture, business, etc.) and are a basic step in programming procedure.

Before programming an application, it is important to undertake the major step of developing a logic to be used in solving the various factors which the problem encompasses. This approach is similar to that of "laying out" a long motor trip in advance, or of diagramming a football play before the game is played.

To flow chart correctly and properly, a programmer must be acquainted with basic techniques and be familiar with selected symbols, each of which represents a specific action. Once completed, the flow chart can be converted into a machine language program, ready to process data.

In programming applications, flow charts are used to represent two distinct types of "flow": (1) The flow of data through the various parts of the system, called the *systems flow*, and (2) the procedural description of a specific program within the system, called a *program flow*.

Each type of flow chart comprises symbols used to represent functions or operations. The basic ones are *input/output, processing, annotation,* and *flowline* symbols (Fig. 18-1). *Specialized* input/output and processing symbols are also used (see Fig. 18-2, page 274).

Input/output   Processing   Flowlines   Annotation

FIG. 18-1 Basic symbols

Basic Symbols

Input/output symbol (parallelogram). It represents any I/O function—either to represent information for processing (input) or to record processed information (output).

Processing symbol (rectangle). It represents any action to be taken by the computer while working on the input data. For example, "Add A + B," "Move data to punch," and "Multiply B × C" are three examples of processing instructions which usually are shown somewhere between the input and output symbols.

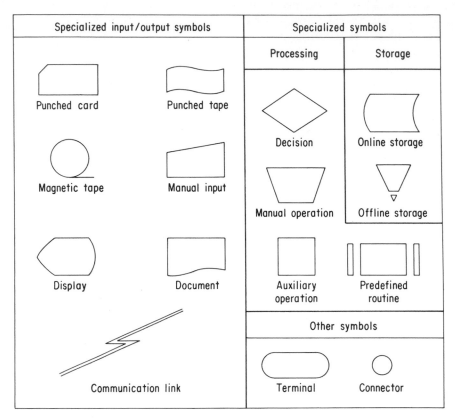

Specialized input/output symbols		Specialized symbols	
		Processing	Storage
Punched card	Punched tape	Decision	Online storage
Magnetic tape	Manual input	Manual operation	Offline storage
Display	Document	Auxiliary operation	Predefined routine
		Other symbols	
Communication link		Terminal	Connector

FIG. 18-2 Specialized flow charting symbols

Flowline symbol (straight line). It is used to link symbols and to indicate the sequence of operations. Flowlines may cross or form junctions which define logical relationships. Conventionally, every flowline entering or leaving a junction should have arrowheads near the junction point.

Annotation symbol (open-ended rectangle with a broken line connecting the Annotation Symbol to any other symbol at the point where the Annotation is desired). It is used to provide descriptive comments or explanatory notes for clarification.

Input/Output Symbols

Several specialized symbols have been developed which, in addition to representing the I/O function, represent the medium in which the information is recorded and/or the method of handling the information (Fig. 18-2). In the absence of any suitable specialized symbol, the basic symbol is normally used.

Punched card symbol. Used to represent an I/O function using any type of punched card, including mark sense cards, stub cards, deck of cards, etc. Additional specialized versions of the punched card symbol represent a deck (collection) of punched cards or a file of punched cards (a collection of related punched card records).

Punched tape symbol. Represents a punched tape routine.

Magnetic tape symbol. Represents a magnetic tape routine.

Manual input symbol. Represents an *input* function in which information is entered manually at the time of processing by means of keyboards, switches, buttons, etc.

Display symbol. Represents an I/O function in which the information is displayed for human use at the time of processing by means of video devices, console printers, plotters, etc.

Document symbol. Represents a printed document format.

Communication link symbol. Represents data transmitted automatically from one source to another.

Storage Symbols

On-line storage symbol. Represents an I/O function using any type of storage such as magnetic tape, drum, or disk.

Off-line storage symbol. Refers to any storage not directly accessible by the computer system.

Specialized Processing Symbols

Specialized process symbols (Fig. 18-2) represent, in addition to the processing function, the specific type of operation to be performed on the information.

Decision symbol. Denotes any action to be taken by the computer while working on the input data. It involves the "thinking" part of a program. "Is it the last card?" "Is *A* greater than *B*?" "Is year-to-date gross pay equal to or greater than $5,000?"

A decision symbol also relates to algebraic notations used to test a given relationship. These tests are:

Compare A to B ($A:B$)
A less than B ($A < B$)
A greater than B ($A > B$)
A less than or equal to B ($A \leq B$)
A greater than or equal to B ($A \geq B$)

Manual operation symbol. Represents any off-line process to be performed manually without the use of mechanical aids.

Auxiliary operation symbol. Represents an off-line operation performed on equipment not under the direct control of the CPU.

Predefined process symbol. Represents a named process consisting of one or more operations or program steps that are specified in an area other than the set of flow charts in which the symbol is used.

Preparation symbol. Represents a modification of an instruction or group of instructions which changes the program, such as the setting of a switch, or the modification of an index register.

Sort symbol. Represents the function of arranging a set of items into a particular sequence.

Collate symbol. Represents the function of forming two or more sets of items from two or more other sets.

Other Symbols

Several additional specialized symbols are designed to improve the clarity of flow charts (Fig. 18-2).

Connector symbol. Denotes an exit to or an entry from another part of the flow chart.

Terminal symbol. Represents any terminal point in a flow chart, e.g., stop, halt, delay, or interrupt.

Parallel mode symbol. Represents the beginning or the end of two or more simultaneous operations.

Flow Direction

The flow direction of the flow chart is represented by the flowlines drawn between symbols. The normal direction of flow is from left to right and from top to bottom. If the flow direction is not normal, open arrowheads should be placed on the flowlines to indicate direction. Open arrowheads also may be placed on normal flowlines for added clarity. If the flow is bidirectional, either single or double lines may be used. In either case, however, arrowheads should be used to indicate both directions of flow.

Flow Charting in General

Although programs differ, depending on the work to be performed and the characteristics of the data involved, there is a basic similarity among them. Figure 18-3 shows a flow chart of a typical program, illustrating commonly used block-diagramming symbols. Although other ideas are involved, it should be remembered that each step in the logic diagram represents useful work and may call for any number of machine instructions. The diagram can be used to define terms and to describe some common techniques.

In Fig. 18-3, the sequence of steps from *A* to *E* (top to bottom) represents the typical idea flow of all programs, and is referred to as the *main line*. This is the sequence normally followed in representing the major job to be accomplished, and indicates the proper way in which to read a flow chart. The steps following each of the symbols *B*, *C*, and *D* indicate the presence of a logical decision in which circumstances can cause a deviation from the main line. In a more detailed chart of an actual program, these "decision points" may total several hundred steps. Since the main line of the program is the most important sequence in solving the principal problem, however, the programmer pays special attention to the way in which he implements it. The goal is to minimize the time required to execute the main line, thus producing a workable and efficient program.

FIG. 18-3 Sample flow chart—main line and subroutine

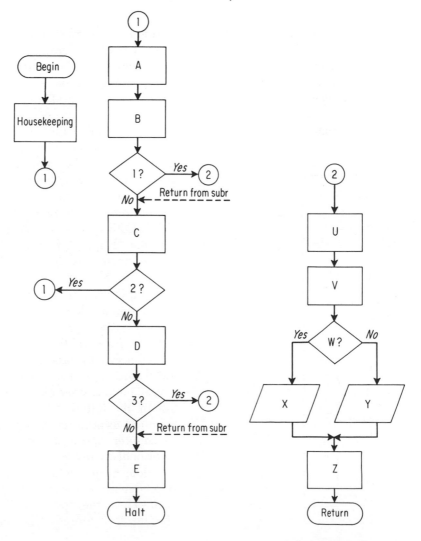

Housekeeping

In every program, a certain amount of "housekeeping" is necessary. This requirement involves setting up basic steps in the computer's internal registers or storage areas, such as steps to clear certain areas to blank or to zero, reading in the input record, resetting accumulators, etc. A programmer usually is aware of the importance of the housekeeping (initialization) stage, since it might be required more than once during processing, especially if it is necessary to restart the program. When this happens, the tedious routine of reloading the entire program becomes unnecessary.

Looping

Certain calculations involve the repetition of a number of instructions over and over again. The programmer can avoid wasted storage space and effort by writing out one set of instructions in which the last instruction directs the control unit to "branch" back (or repeat) the process, rather than writing a complete set of instructions for each record read. This repetitive operation is termed *looping*.

Figure 18-4 shows a flow chart which simply calls for an input card to be read, its contents to be moved to the punch area, and then the data to be punched in a blank card. In a 1,000-card input deck, this flow chart (through the branch instruction at the bottom) would be used repetitively until the 1,000th card has been processed. Without the "looping" feature, the programmer would have to write out a 3,000-step program, duplicating the first three steps for each input card in the same deck. Every time the program flow-charted in Fig. 18-4 is looped back to process another card, it executes a *pass*. In this example, it will take 1,000 passes to process the entire deck of 1,000 cards fed in for processing.

The necessary elements for a loop consist of the initial data and the instructions required to perform the operation, some sort of counter, and a storage location in which intermediate results are temporarily stored. The loop begins when a counter is fed with a predetermined beginning value, usually 1 or 0. Then, the operation is performed and the result is stored. The counter is tested

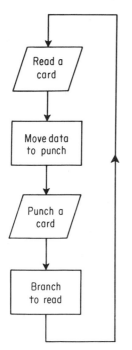

FIG. 18-4 A simple flow chart—an example

against a predetermined value, and if the comparison does not indicate the end of the operation, a fixed amount is added to the counter, typically +1, while the whole process is repeated. When the counter reaches the end value, the loop is broken and the program continues.

Subroutines

A major attempt to reduce programming cost and compiling time has been made through the use of *subroutines*. A subroutine occupies a secondary or a subordinate function within the overall program, and one of its main features is that it can be written separately from the main program and be kept in a "library" until it is needed, at which time it is integrated into the main program for proper use.

A subroutine is a set of instructions which varies in size, ranging from a few to several hundred instructions. When it is in operation, a subroutine derives its information (input) from the main program, performs the required steps within its capacity, and then furnishes its results (output) back to the main program. These inputs to and outputs from a subroutine often are referred to as *entrance parameters* and *exit parameters*.

To illustrate, Fig. 18-3 shows a subroutine in the set of symbols beginning with block U and ending in block Z. Looking at Fig. 18-5, we see that there is a slight difference between its O-to-T sequence and the U-to-Z sequence in Fig. 18-3. Blocks U to Z use more core storage. Since the subroutine can be initiated from several places in the program, provision must be made to be sure control is returned to the proper instruction. If entry is made from decision point 1, for instance, control will return to block C, but if decision point 3 returns control to the subroutine, it will be to block E. For this reason, the use of a subroutine requires that certain information be supplied to it: the location of the instruction which caused the *branching* (change of control sequence).

Some of the most common subroutines are completely generalized; for example, in the subroutine used to evaluate the square root of a number, not only must the instruction location be indicated, but also the variable number or numbers (parameters). For these reasons, the subroutine usually uses slightly more core storage than the one written in Fig. 18-5; however, the multiple use of the same subroutine results in the saving of valuable storage space. Due to the problem of branching back and forth to a common subroutine, the object-time execution of the subroutine can be expected to be slightly longer than that needed to execute a specially written routine. It is up to the programmer to choose between the economics of saving space and that of saving time.

No attempt has been made thus far to describe the operation to be performed, since the diagram can be thought of as describing any number of real programs. Through the use of the input/output symbols (X and Y in Fig. 18-3), the illustration represents a very common use of the subroutine to cause all input/output operations. Only 18 blocks have been shown in this example,

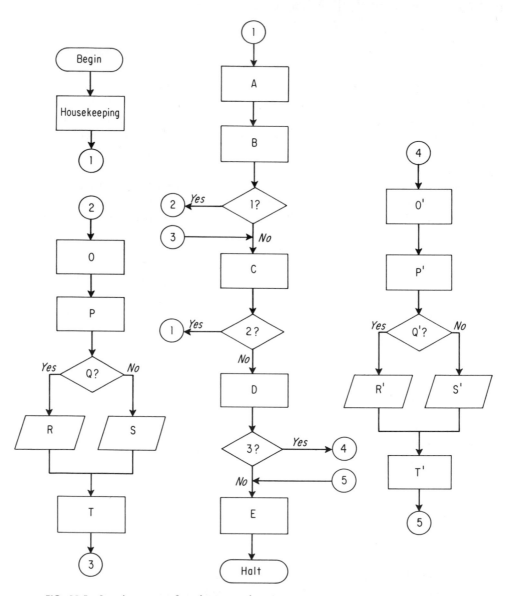

FIG. 18-5 Sample program flow chart—no subroutine

and from this, one can assume that it represents a very broad level of logic. As the programmer works out the flow chart, the reader could expect it to fill several pages; for example, the block labeled *X*, which might indicate input operations, could be expanded to several hundred operations in detail.

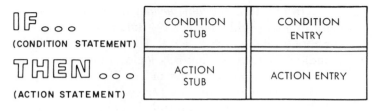

IF... (CONDITION STATEMENT)	CONDITION STUB	CONDITION ENTRY
THEN... (ACTION STATEMENT)	ACTION STUB	ACTION ENTRY

FIG. 18-6   A decision table—basic elements

DECISION TABLES

A *decision table* is an effective substitute for, or an auxiliary aid to, a block diagram. It is an excellent notation for expressing the logic required in the definition of business data processing problems. It is used in situations that involve complex decision logic because it presents the original condition and the course of action to be taken if the conditions are met in a tabular form.

A decision table is divided into two main sections (Fig. 18-6). The upper section questions or *conditions* what must be done, and the lower section presents the *action* to be taken. The left part of each of these sections is called the stub (that is, *condition stub, action stub*). The right part is called the entry (*condition entry, action entry*).

Further elements of a decision table include a line (row) for each condition or action. Several columns are added to show certain rules or instructions, each of which pertains to a specific condition and the manner in which the condition is acted upon (Fig. 18-7).

FIG. 18-7   Further elements of a decision table

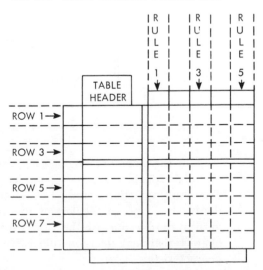

In Fig. 18-2, the *table header* shows the table number and/or table name (for example, table number 1). *Rule reference* indicates the rule number (for example, rule 1, rule 2, etc.). The *condition stub* describes all or part of a condition statement. That is, a logical question, or relational or state condition that is answerable by a yes or no. The *condition entry* provides completion of the condition statement (extended entry) or Y(yes), N(no), or *blank* (limited entry). The *action stub* describes all or part of an action statement, or an explicit statement of where to go next for each rule, if it is not specified in the table header. Finally, the *action entry* shows completion of the action statement (extended entry), or X, or blank (limited entry).

A general rule governing the use of decision tables is that the "actions" must be carried out in the order they are written. This is done so that the logic of the procedure is always in the proper order. A condition entry is left blank only if the condition is not applicable or if the presence of other conditions makes the specific condition of no concern.

An Example—Design Engineering

With this general background on decision tables, let us see how they can be profitably applied to *design engineering*. Initially, a decision table skeleton is prepared. Customer specifications are shown in the condition area of the table and the product characteristics are shown in the stub. Names of the specifications and names of the characteristics are shown in the stub, while various values for those names are displayed in the entry area (Fig. 18-8).

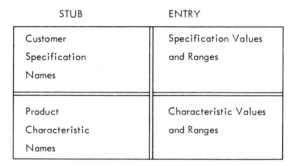

FIG. 18-8   Skeleton structure of an engineering decision table

In the filled-out engineering decision table shown in Fig. 18-9, various customer specifications (e.g., service, application, etc.) are listed on the left. The resulting action (product characteristics) is presented below the horizontal double line and to the left of the vertical double line. To the right of the vertical double line are the values for the customer specifications and product characteristics. A decision rule is a unique combination of specifications and characteristics.

Reading a part or parts of a decision table is relatively easy. For example, in Fig. 18-9, rule 1 reads: "IF the service is DC, and the application is temperature, and the rating units are MV and the number of phases is 1, THEN the armature is a moving coil type and the number of windings is 1 and the part number is 012526 and the assembly drawing number is A 26 and the next table is 2."

Table No. 1	Rule 1	Rule 2	Rule 3	Rule 4
Service	DC	DC	AC	AC
Application	Temperature	Speed		
Rating Units	MV	MV	MV	MA
Number of Phases	1	1	1	1
Type of Armature	Moving Coil	Moving Coil	Electrodynamic	Inductive
Number of Windings	1	2	2	1 + Number of Phases
Part No.	012526	012526A	012530	012535
Assembly Drawing No.	A26	A26A	B30	B30A
Next table	2	2	2	10

FIG. 18-9 Engineering decision table—filled out

Types of Tables

Tables are usually classified by the type of information recorded in the entries.

Limited-Entry. Probably the most widely used type, this form requires a fixed type of information in each quadrant. The condition entries are limited to Y(yes), N(no), or blank. Similarly, the action entries are limited to X's. To facilitate these types of entries, the condition stub must be written so that it is either true or false and the action stub must *completely* describe action to be taken (Fig. 18-10).

Being limited to a Yes or No pattern as is the case in binary logic, limited-entry tables are well suited to computer processing and computer-oriented application.

Extended-Entry. In this type of table, the entry portion of the table is an extension of the stub portion. In other words, the stub portion describes the variables whose values are placed in the entry portion. This type is especially well suited to problems with a few variables which may have many values. When it comes to programming, extended-entry tables are often converted to limited-entry form (Fig. 18-11).

Decision Table	Date: 12/10/70 Operation: Toll fare Drafted by: A. Johns			
Vehicle/Toll	1	2	3	4
Is Vehicle a pick up truck?	Y	Y	N	N
Is Vehicle towing a trailer?	Y	N	Y	N
Charge $2.50	X			
Charge 1.00		X		
Charge .85			X	
Charge 3.00				X

FIG. 18-10   A limited entry table—an example

Decision Table	Date: 12/10/70 Operation: Toll fare Drafted by: A. Johns			
Vehicle/Toll	1	2	3	4
Type of Vehicle?	Pick up	Pick up	Passenger	Truck
Is Vehicle towing a trailer?	Trailer	No Trailer	Trailer	No Trailer
Toll Fare	A	B	C	D

Toll
 A $2.50
 B   1.00
 C   .85
 D   3.00

FIG. 18-11   An extended entry table—an example

Mixed-Entry. As its name indicates, it is a combination of rows with limited entries and rows of extended entries. However, while the rows may be mixed, all entries in a given row must be either limited or extended (Fig. 18-12).

Open and Closed Tables

In complex decision patterns it is often difficult to completely describe the operation pattern in a single table. Therefore, some method of controlled linkage of multiple tables is provided. This controlled linkage takes the form of either *open* or *closed* tables.

Decision Table	Date: 12/10/70 Operation: Toll fare Drafted by: A. Johns			
Vehicle/Toll	1	2	3	4
Type of Vehicle?	Pick up	Pick up	Passenger	Truck
Vehicle Towing a trailer?	Trailer	No Trailer	Trailer	No Trailer
Charge $2.50	X			
Charge 1.00		X		
Charge .85			X	
Charge 3.00				X

FIG. 18-12 A mixed entry table—an example

In an *open table,* the last action of each rule is to proceed to the next table to be used. The statement is expressed by the words *Go to,* followed by the name or number of the appropriate table. In a limited-entry table, the name or number of the referenced table appears as part of the statement, while in an extended-entry table, the name or number appears in the entry.

Sometimes it is desirable to pass control temporarily to another table, which then returns control to the original table. A *closed table* is one which does not end with a specific directive of where to proceed next. When a closed table has been completely executed, control reverts to the table which originally issued the directive. Control is passed to a closed table by use of a *Do* statement followed by the name or number of the closed table. Return of control to the previous table is usually indicated by the word *closed* in the table header or by an action entry such as *exit* or *return.* Control is returned to the same rule in the same table which released control, and the next indicated action is taken. Thus, the use of closed tables eliminates the need for repeating action or condition element to more than one table and allows re-entry to a given area within the table without reverting to the normal point at the top of the table.

OTHER CHARTS

In addition to flow charts and decision tables, the systems analyst and the programmer use layout and grid charts as tools in planning and analyzing programs for various computer applications.

Layout Charts

Layout charts are preprinted forms depicting input/output data records and/or location of key information in storage. Among these are storage layout, card layout, tape and disk layout.

IBM

INTERNATIONAL BUSINESS MACHINES CORPORATION

RECORD FORMAT

X20-1702-0 U/M 025
Printed in U.S.A.

Application _____ Record Name _____ By _____ Date _____ Page ___ of ___

FIELD NAME

CHARACTERISTICS*

RELATIVE POSITION

File Description
Recording Mode
Records per Block
Characters per Record
Label Records are
File Identification
File Serial Number
Reel Sequence Number
Creation Date
Retention Cycle

Remarks

Major 1
2
3
4
5
6
SORTING 7
FIELDS 8
9
10
11
12
13
14
15
Minor 16

FOOTNOTES

* Characteristics
Alphabetic or Blank ___ A
Alphanumeric ___ X
Numeric ___ 9
Assumed Decimal Point ___ V
Examples of Signed Fields
X9999   9999X
X999V99   9999V9X

REVISIONS

Date | By

Fold to Here

FIG. 18-13 A storage layout form

Storage charts (also referred to as memory maps) are used by programmers who deal with computers that have fixed storage areas. The layout indicates the position of constants, input/output data, and the work area in primary storage. Some second generation computers (e.g., the IBM 1401 series) make the use of storage layout a necessary tool for organizing and manipulating various types of information.

A card layout is designed to help the user plan the location of various data (alphabetic and numeric) within the constraints of the IBM card. Using this, the processing staff can be more certain that the information is processed properly and fully.

Tape and disk layouts indicate the manner in which data are written on a magnetic tape or a magnetic disk. Unlike the card layout, which is limited to 80 columns, tape and disk layouts are bound only by the length of the tape and dimensions of the disk which accommodate the contents of hundreds of punched cards (Fig. 18-13).

Grid Charts

A grid chart is another tool used for summarizing the relationship between two key variables. It is useful in situations where duplicate information is present in various reports. The systems analyst can refer to the chart and take steps to discard unnecessary reports or to simplify the ones in current use (Fig. 18-14).

FIG. 18-14 A grid chart—an example

Item \ Report	Sales Report	Salesman Performance	Delinquency Report
Cust. Number	✓	✓	✓
Cust. Name		✓	✓
Cust. Address			✓
Cust. Rating		✓	✓

Glossary of Terms

BRANCH: A set of instructions that is executed between two successive decision instructions.

HOUSEKEEPING: For a computer program, housekeeping involves the setting up of constants and variables to be used in the program.

LIBRARY SUBROUTINE: A set of tested subroutines available on file for use when needed.

LOOP: A sequence of instructions that is repeated until a terminal condition prevails.

PARAMETER: A variable that is given a constant value for a specific purpose or process.

SUBROUTINE: A routine that can be part of another routine.

Questions for Review

1. Explain a flow chart. Give an example.
2. What are the basic flow-charting symbols?
3. What part of a flow chart is called the main line? Illustrate.
4. What is involved in a housekeeping routine? Where in the program is it located?
5. What is meant by looping a program? Illustrate.
6. What is a subroutine? A library subroutine? Explain.
7. Define the terms "parameter," "branching," and "decision table."
8. Why is a decision table used? Explain in detail its parts, types, and their functions. Give an example to illustrate.
9. What is the primary purpose of the storage, card, and tape layout?

chapter nineteen

PROGRAMMING SYSTEMS

MACHINE LANGUAGE CODING

THE PROCESSOR PROGRAM

LANGUAGES—FORMATS AND TYPES

SYMBOLIC LANGUAGE—ASSEMBLER

MACRO LANGUAGES

PROCEDURE-ORIENTED LANGUAGES

GENERALIZED PROGRAMMING AIDS

ASSEMBLERS AND COMPILERS

INPUT/OUTPUT CONTROL SYSTEMS

OPERATING SYSTEMS

UTILITIES

MACHINE LANGUAGE CODING

THE LANGUAGE OF THE COMPUTER is predominantly numeric and is highly dependent on the design and requirements of the particular computer being used. These conditions make the process of writing programs in computer language (referred to as machine language coding) complicated and often tedious. Some of the problems are:

1. The programmer works almost exclusively with numbers. For example, when he needs to add a value to the arithmetic unit register, he must determine the correct numeric operation code for that operation. This might not be much of a problem when it involves few instructions. However, it takes on major proportions when the instructions number in the hundreds.

2. A significant feature of machine language coding is that all references to data or instructions are referenced by their storage address. This complicates the work of the programmer, because frequently in coding instructions, references are made to data or instructions which are not coded until some later stage in the program. That is, the storage address of referenced data or instructions may not be known and the instruction calling the reference must be left incomplete until the storage address is determined. This type of procedure is time-consuming and highly prone to error.

3. The notion that data and instructions are referenced by their storage address implies that, in order not to lose track of the program logic, the programmer must maintain several lists that coordinate data with their addresses. Some of the common lists include those of instruction locations, constant locations, data locations, and storage locations used and available.

A programmer also has to translate the descriptions he writes on the program flow charts into the numerical language of operation codes and storage addresses. He has to see that the resulting coding is transcribed into machine readable form so that it can be loaded into storage when needed.

Since the early 1940s, programmers have been thinking about better ways of transcribing source programs into machine readable form and reducing coding errors. This has led to the development of programming aids. The functions mentioned above can be performed by using a computer; what is needed is simply a program to do them. Such a program is called a *processor program*.

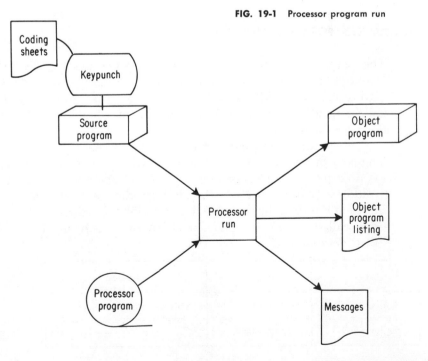

FIG. 19-1 Processor program run

THE PROCESSOR PROGRAM

As input, the processor program uses the recorded coding of the programmer, presented in a language similar to English. This language is commonly called "symbolic" language. Loaded along with the processor program are fixed and variable constants to be used for translation and for recording the assignment of addresses in the object program (the program when coded in a machine language). The processor program can produce the object program in the necessary machine readable form, as well as in a printed form. It also can supply the storage map and certain messages concerning any clerical errors which may have occurred in transcribing the source coding (Fig. 19-1).

It should be noted that the processor program performs very little arithmetic. Its major work consists of reading the lines of coding (which have been punched into cards), treating them as input records, comparing the operation code with a table to find the right machine code, comparing the address portion with symbolic addresses to find the proper machine address, assembling the instructions for output, and then writing the necessary output. As a precautionary measure, many exceptions are provided for, an approach considered desirable in all programs.

This points out the programming economy realized in the use of processor programs. Computer manufacturers employ a large staff of programmers for this purpose. When a new computer is announced today, it is expected that the total computer system will include not only the equipment hardware, but also the accompanying processor programs ("software").

LANGUAGES—FORMATS AND TYPES

The programmer who uses a processor program is expected to specify the layout of his input and output records. Most importantly, he must specify what kind of characters will be recognized and in what order they should be read and/or handled. This specification results in what is called the *language* of the processor system.

Since the language of the processor program is to be translated into the language of the machine, the format will have some similarity. The three required parts of an instruction are (1) the operation code, (2) the operand or address portion, and (3) the location address of the instruction itself. As shown in Fig. 19-2 the terms used to describe these three parts are *label* (sometimes called a tag), *op-code* (or operation code), and *operand* (sometimes called *data address*).

Label	Op Code	Operand
(Basically, the address of the instruction)	(The symbol describing what is to be done)	(The description of the things to be operated upon)

FIG. 19-2 Coding sheet for processor language

The first level of language described for a class of processor programs is called the *symbolic, assembly,* or "one-for-one" language. As the third term indicates, the characteristic of this language is that there is one line of coding for each machine instruction as it finally appears in the object program. This type of language and its corresponding processor programs were the first type defined years ago.

The use of a symbolic language provides the programmer with several conveniences. One is the use of op-codes (operation codes) similar to the English language. Figure 19-3 shows the way this would be specified for the

Name	Op Code	Machine Code
Read	Read	+ 01
Write	Write	+ 02
Clear and Add	Cladd	+ 03
Add	Add	+ 04
Subtract	Subt	+ 05
Multiply	Mult	+ 06
Divide	Div	+ 07
Compare	Comp	+ 08
Branch	Br	+ 09
Test Branch High	Brhi	+ 10
Test Branch Low	Brlo	+ 11
Test Branch Equal	Breq	+ 12
Branch End of File	Breof	+ 13
Store	Store	+ 14
Halt	Halt	+ 15

FIG. 19-3 Mnemonic op-codes

computer explained in Chapter 17. The op-code suggests the function to be performed. Since internal storage space is limited, the writer of the processor program must decide how many characters can be allotted to op-codes and still provide some mnemonic function (the use of symbols). In this illustration, it is decided that no more than five characters are to be used to represent any op-codes; for example, the words *Clear and Add* are condensed into *CLADD* to conform to the five-character requirement. This common type of contraction leads a newcomer to comprehend the meaning rather easily. When a person uses symbolic language for some time, he becomes very familiar with the symbols.

A second accommodation symbolic language affords the programmer is that of facilitating references to other instructions by using symbolic names rather than numbers. Once again, the author of the processor program must decide how large these symbols should be and where they must appear in input records. As shown in Fig. 19-2, the usual order is *Label, Op-Code, Operand.* Labels commonly are restricted to five, six, or seven characters, depending on the specifications stored in the processor program.

Another consideration is the kind of characters to be used. To protect the programmer from confusion and the processor program from unnecessary difficulty, one restriction might be to prohibit the use of the op-code symbols as labels. Another restriction might be that the first character of the label-symbol should be a letter of the alphabet. In this way, the author of the processor program would reserve anything beginning with a digit for other purposes, usually constants or actual machine-word locations.

It is obvious that the author of the processor program has many decisions to make regarding the instruction format and, in particular, the format of input records to be processed by the program. After these decisions are made, however, the rules must be communicated to user programmers for proper application. Learning these language rules is one of the first requirements faced by those who want to program a particular computer system.

Providing a way to write symbolic labels and op-codes leaves only the need to do the same thing for data and constants. This is performed through a device commonly called the *declarative operation,* a coding sequence made up of a symbolic label, a declarative operation code, and an operand. Figure 19-3 shows the use of a declarative operation code symbolized as *DA.* This type of operation code differs from the ones previously described in that it represents a signal to the processor program that the items associated with it are to be entered into one of the address lists for later reference. Such an operation is not to be performed at object time as are operations like ADD, STORE, etc.

The sample coding shown in Fig. 19-4 is interpreted by the processor program as follows: the first line indicates that an area 10 words long is to be reserved. This whole area then can be addressed by using the symbol *INPUT.*

FIG. 19-4 Declarative operations

Label	Op Code	Operand
Input	DA	10
Serial		1
Fact 1		2
Fact 2		3
		4, 10
Output	DA	10
Outser		1
Sum		2
		3, 10

The areas of storage for the object program are assigned according to the order in which the various coding sequences are "read-in" during the processor run (Fig. 19-1). For instance, if line 1 is the first one read, the area 000 to 009 will be reserved and "INPUT" will be entered in a list indicating that it represents 000. Later, if a READ INPUT instruction is encountered, the machine instruction will be +01000000.

Next, line 2 is interpreted. Since there is no operation code, it is interpreted as one of the data items within the area *INPUT*, and is the first word (operand = 1) tagged by the symbol *SERIAL*. Machine location 000 will be associated with this symbol. Line 3 associates the symbol *FACT 1* with machine location 001, and line 4 assigns 002 to *FACT 2*. Line 5 simply means that the remaining seven words of the area are not used, but should be saved because of the special type of read instruction designed into the equipment. The sixth line begins the same sequence for the *OUTPUT* area as the one for the *INPUT* area. Figure 19-5 presents a fully coded program showing the symbolic lan-

FIG. 19-5 Fully coded program

Label	Op Code	Operand	Loc	Word Contents
	Coding			Object Program
Input	DA	10	000	
Serial		1	000	
Fact 1		2	001	
Fact 2		3	002	
		4, 10		
Output	DA	10	010	
Outser		1	010	
Sum		2	011	
		3, 10		
Runsum	DC	+ 00 000 000	020	+ 00 000 000
Word	DC	Total	021	Total
Begin	Read	Input	022	+ 01 000 000
	Cladd	Serial	023	+ 03 000 000
	Comp	Outser	024	+ 08 000 010
	Brlo	Seqchk	025	+ 11 000 041
	Store	Outser	026	+ 14 000 010
	Cladd	Fact 1	027	+ 03 000 001
	Add	Fact 2	028	+ 04 000 002
	Store	Sum	029	+ 14 000 011
	Add	Runsum	030	+ 04 000 020
	Store	Runsum	031	+ 14 000 020
	Write	Output	032	+ 02 000 010
	Breof	Exit	033	+ 13 000 035
	Br	Begin	034	+ 09 000 022
Exit	Cladd	Word	035	+ 03 000 021
	Store	Outser	036	+ 14 000 010
	Cladd	Runsum	037	+ 03 000 020
	Store	Sum	038	+ 14 000 011
	Write	Output	039	+ 02 000 010
	Halt	999	040	+ 15 000 999
Seqchk	Add	Hltseq	041	+ 04 000 043
	Store	Hltseq	042	+ 14 000 043
Hltseq	Halt	000	043	+ 15 000 (000)

guage written by the programmer. The three left columns usually are referred to as the "source program," and the machine language equivalent (the two right columns), is called the "object program."

MACRO LANGUAGES

The next level of languages takes the coding idea one step further. Programmers began to notice that certain sequences of instructions had a tendency to be repetitive. The most common example is the one which moves a word from one place in storage to another (CLADD, STORE). Since this is such a common instruction, two choices were available: (1) To change the design of the equipment so that two address instructions were available, a change that has been made in many modern computers; or (2) to expand the function of the processor program beyond the strict one-for-one situation.

If one could predict what combination of machine instructions would be needed in these common instances, it would be relatively simple to add new operation codes to the processor program vocabulary. Such operation codes are called *macro operation codes,* or simply *"macros."* Macros differ from the symbolic one-for-one in that more than one object-program machine instruction can be produced for the use of each macro instruction.

The languages that evolved from this thinking were a combination of declarative op-codes, symbolic one-for-one op-codes, and macros. The sample macro instructions shown in Fig. 19-6 could be easily added to our basic processor language. Once again, the format of the input record (the instruction) must be fixed. The format is shown first to the left; the equivalent symbolic one-for-one instructions, to the right. Given this facility, the processing part of the coding for our example program is shown in Fig. 19-7.

Comparing Figs. 19-6, 19-7, and 19-8, one begins to appreciate what this

FIG. 19-6 Macro instructions—a sample

Macro Formal	Equivalent Symbolics	
Move A, B	Cladd	A
(Meaning – Move word at A to loc B)	Store	B
Accum A, B, C	Cladd	A
(Meaning – Add word at A to word	Add	B
at B and store sum in loc C)	Store	C
Cmpar A, B, H, L, E	Cladd	A
(Meaning – Compare value of	Comp	B
word at A with word at B, if A is	Brhi	H
high, branch to H, if low to L,	Brlo	L
and if equal to E)	Breq	E

Label	Op Code	Operand
Begin	Read	Input
	Cmpar	Serial, Outser, Next, Seqchk, Next
Next	Store	Outser
	Accum	Fact 1, Fact 2, Sum
	Accum	Sum, Runsum, Runsum
	Write	Output
	Breof	Exit
	Br	Begin
Exit	Move	Word, Outser
	Move	Runsum, Sum
	Write	Output
	Halt	999
Seqchk	Accum	Serial, Hltseq, Hltseq
Hltseq	Halt	000

FIG. 19-7 Example program using macro instructions

FIG. 19-8 Program coding in COBOL

COBOL PROGRAM SHEET

PAGE 1 3 006	PROGRAM PROBLEM –13	FOR 1401	SYSTEM 1401	SHEET 6 OF 7
	PROGRAMMER		DATE 11/15/70	IDENT. 73 P,R,O,B, ,1,3 80

```
SERIAL   A   B
4  6  8  12  16  20  24  28  32  36  40  44  48  52  56  60  64  68  72
0,1,0  PROCEDURE, DIVISION.,
0,2,0  HOUSEKEEPING, SECTION.,
0,3,0  HK.. OPEN, INPUT, MASTER-FILE, TRANSACTION-FILE, OUTPUT, OUTPUT-FILE,
0,4,0      ORDERS-CANCELLED-FILE, ERROR-OUT.. MOVE, ZERO, TO, SKIPIT,
0,5,0  BEGIN.. READ, MASTER-FILE, AT, END, GO, TO, CLOSEM.. GO, TO, SWITCH-OFF,
0,6,0      DEPENDING, ON, SKIPIT.. DEAD, TRANSACTION-FILE, AT, END, GO, TO,
0,7,0      CLOSET.
0,8,0  PRE-TEST.. IF, CANCEL-ORDER, GO, TO, TEST-AGAIN.
0,9,0  CMP.. IF, ADDITIONAL-QTY, AND, MOD-ORD-NO, EQUAL, TO, TMOD-ORD-NO, NEXT,
1,0,0      SENTENCE, ELSE, GO, TO, TEST.. ADD, NEW-QTY, TO, QUANTITY.,
1,1,0  OUT.. WRITE, MASTER-OUTPUT, FROM, MASTER.. GO, TO, BEGIN..
1,2,0  TEST.. IF, QTY-CANCELLED, AND, MOD-ORD-NO, EQUAL, TO, TMOD-ORD-NO, NEXT,
1,3,0      SENTENCE, ELSE, GO, TO, TEST-AGAIN.. SUBTRACT, NEW-QTY, FROM,
1,4,0      QUANTITY.. IF, QUANTITY, IS, NEGATIVE, NEXT, SENTENCE, ELSE, GO, TO,
1,5,0      OUT..
1,6,0  CANCEL-IT.. WRITE, CANCEL-RECORD, FROM, MASTER, GO, TO, BEGIN..
1,7,0  TEST-AGAIN.. IF, CANCEL-ORDER, AND, MOD-ORD-NO, EQUAL, TO, TMOD-ORD-NO2,
1,8,0      GO, TO, CANCEL-IT.. IF, TMOD-ORD-NO2, IS, GREATER, THAN, MOD-ORD-
1,9,0      NO, MOVE, 1, TO, SKIPIT, GO, TO, OUT, ELSE, WRITE, ER-OR, FROM, MASTER,
2,0,0      GO, TO, BEGIN..
```

development is really designed to do. Basically, it is designed to conserve the energy of the creative worker—the programmer—so that he can accomplish his work more quickly and with less chance of error.

There are other improvements in this macro-language idea. For example, looking at the second instruction in Fig. 19-7, we learn that if we are using a language with the format and results shown in Fig. 19-6, the equivalent symbolic instructions to this statement would be:

BEFORE: CMPAR   SERIAL, OUTSER, NEXT, SEQCHK, NEXT

                translated as

AFTER: CLADD   SERIAL
          COMP   OUTSER
          BRHI   NEXT
          BRLO   SEQCHK
          BREQ   NEXT

A reference to Fig. 19-5 shows that this translation results in two more instructions (the third and fifth above) than we had felt necessary in the one-for-one coding.

A common way to avoid this apparent waste of storage and time in the object program is to change the description of the macro instruction slightly. Then the processor program is changed accordingly so that the proper instructions are produced. In this case, the definition of CMPAR is stated:

        CMPAR   A, B, H, L, E

        Meaning: Compare value of the word at A with the word at B. If A is high, branch to location H; if low, branch to location L; if equal, branch to location E. If, however, any particular branch possibility is not anticipated, omit any symbol between commas.

With this definition, we now can write:

        CMPAR   SERIAL, OUTSER, SEQCHK

It is translated as:

        CLADD   SERIAL
        COMP   OUTSER
        BRLO   SEQCHK

This is what originally was wanted.

Variations on this theme are many. When approaching a new language, it is important to be familiar with its rules. Because it comes closer to the kind of language we use in everyday life, the macro language is easy to learn and use.

PROCEDURE-ORIENTED LANGUAGES

The obvious goal of these programming languages is to come as close as possible to our common language. There have been many approaches to this idea of "procedure-oriented" languages. Those which are best known and are being used most widely today are COBOL, FORTRAN, and ALGOL. COBOL (Common Business Oriented Language) is designed for use in normal commercial, nonscientific situations. FORTRAN (Formula Translator) is particularly suited to the needs of the scientist and engineer for the statement of solutions to arithmetic problems. ALGOL (Algorithmic-Oriented Language) has basically the same function as FORTRAN with some additional features.

Figure 19-8 shows a page of coding from the processing part of a program stated in COBOL. Figure 19-9 shows a similar section of coding for a separate problem written in FORTRAN. Figure 19-10 shows a sample ALGOL problem. Processor programs to translate COBOL, FORTRAN, and ALGOL statements into machine-coded object programs have been prepared for many of today's computer systems.

C FOR COMMENT

STATEMENT NUMBER	Cont.	FORTRAN STATEMENT
C		DETERMINATION OF CURRENT IN AC CIRCUIT
7		READ 1,OHM,FREQ,HENRY
100		READ 2,FRD1,FRDFIN
101		PRINT 1,OHM,FREQ,HENRY
102		VOLT =1.0
9		PRINT 1, VOLT
103		FARAD =FRD1
5		AMP = VOLT/SQRTF(OHM**2 +(6.2832*FREQ*HENRY
	1	-1./(6.2832*FREQ*FARAD))**2)
104		PRINT 2,FARAD,AMP
105		IF(FARAD-FRDFIN)3,4,4
3		FARAD =FARAD +0.000 000 01
106		GO TO 5
4		IF(VOLT-3.0) 6,7,7
6		VOLT = VOLT+0.5
107		GO TO 9
1		FORMAT (3F14.5)
2		FORMAT (2E14.5)

FIG. 19-9 Program coding in FORTRAN

Although there appears to be a tremendous difference between the work of the programmer using a symbolic language and one using a procedure-oriented language, a search for similarities is revealing. The most striking similarity is the sequential nature of the thinking involved. This is primarily because of the design of the equipment to be used. Although the language tends to look less and less similar to the machine equivalent, the programmer still thinks about one step at a time. Whether the free form of COBOL or the stylized, rigid format of a one-for-one language is used, the sequential nature of the processing section of coding remains evident.

```
Comment quadratic equation Y equals 5X squared plus
6X plus 7 for values of X from 1 through 11;

begin

     integer X, Y;
     for X: = 1 step 1 under 11 do

          begin

               Y: = ((5X + 6) X + 7);
               print (X, Y)

     end

end
```

FIG. 19-10 Program coding in ALGOL

There is even greater similarity when we look at the coding required to define the data. In fact, this part of the work is the most difficult to separate from machine considerations. FORTRAN and COBOL are discussed in more details in the next two chapters.

GENERALIZED PROGRAMMING AIDS

Over the past several years, certain programs have been extremely common to most business operations. Consequently, computer manufacturers have organized their own programming staffs to develop these programs in the best possible way and to make these programs available to their customers. This approach makes efficient use of the best talent available. Programmers in "user" installations can take advantake of the generalized routines available from the manufacturer and direct their attention to problems peculiar to their own industry or company.

ASSEMBLERS AND COMPILERS

The following section describes the basic characteristics of common processor packages supplied by manufacturers and gives an indication of their current state. To review, processor programs are used to take care of translating programmer's language to machine language. The terms "compiler" and "assembler" have different meanings. A *compiler* permits statements which produce whole subroutines, while an *assembler* works only on one-for-one statements. In fact, a complete compiler program usually is made up of several parts, the last of which is an assembler. The first phases of the compiler break down the source statements and call from an internal library the one-for-one statements which make up the necessary subroutine. These statements are then passed on to the assembler phase, where translation to machine language and assignment of locations are performed.

The procedure-oriented languages are examples of compiler programs. Today, the creation of good assemblers and compilers is taken for granted. Almost every machine system on the market has an associated assembler. In addition, it is expected that the system will have at least one business language compiler (most often COBOL), and one scientific language compiler (usually FORTRAN), or one designed for both (PL/1). Some machine systems also are available with another macro-level compiler using a language specifically chosen to take advantage of the design elements of the equipment.

The result of all this work is to provide tools for programmer use which permit programmers to concentrate on the job at hand and describe their solutions to problems in a language close to their own. Through the skill of the programmers who design and implement these processor programs, the application programmer can obtain the proper balance between two economic measures: space and time. The "space" referred to is that available in the various types of storage: magnetic core, magnetic tape, magnetic disk, magnetic drum, or punched cards. The "time" refers to programming time, compiling run time, or object-program run time. The extent to which a compiler or assembler provides a good choice to the programmer is the best measure of its usefulness.

INPUT/OUTPUT CONTROL SYSTEMS

A special element of a processing system is the section which accommodates input and output requirements. As explained earlier, getting information into and out of the central processor is relatively more time-consuming than internal calculations. The use of buffers, channels, and multiplexors has helped the situation in terms of time but has made programming more complicated. Their complexities must be minimized. Fortunately, things to be done with input/output devices are predictable. Following is a list of the operations to be handled and a very brief description of the type of operation:

1. SEEK-READ-WRITE: These are the obvious elements of introducing data into central storage and of recording the results after processing.
2. BLOCK-DEBLOCK: In several of the input/output (I/O) media, it is most efficient to group logical records into blocks of information to save time. When such blocks are read into storage, they are separated into logical records for processing and then reblocked before writing.
3. SCHEDULING: Now that it is possible to carry out processing, input and/or output simultaneously overlapping, it is necessary to schedule the de-

mands on the input/output devices to achieve maximum use of all equipment. Although this is complicated and calls for great precision on the part of the program, it nevertheless is completely feasible and can be generalized.

4. ERROR PROCESSING: Many factors can contribute to errors in the I/O operations. Often it is a human error (mounting a wrong tape reel, error made in keypunching, or using a control card that is out of sequence), but other times, it is equipment trouble (dust deposits on a recording surface, oxide flaking off, etc.). The main requirement of an I/O routine is to correct the error, if possible, within the minimum period of time.

5. END OF REEL–END OF FILE: Special consideration must be made when either an element of a file or the entire file has reached an end. One of the major jobs at "end-of-reel" time is to switch to an alternate device where the next reel should have been mounted by an operator. To eliminate the chance of operator error and to provide auditing controls, it is common to check the sequence number of the next reel, the total records on the reel just finished, the date when the next reel was written, and so on.

6. CHECKPOINT–RESTART: When a computing run takes a long time, it becomes expensive to start all over again if something happens to interrupt. For this reason, a *checkpoint* record is written periodically, the purpose of which is to record the vital elements of the system at a particular moment. Then if something happens, the only necessary step is to activate the *restart* program (a special program which reads in the last checkpoint record, re-establishes the central storage, repositions the input/output devices at their proper positions, and transfers control to the processing program).

The items in the foregoing list represent at least 40 percent of the total job in most business programming activities. These functions can be programmed basically as subroutines and made available to the compiler. The language usually is designed so that the programmer can describe his records and files in a "check-list" manner. In his file lists, he usually indicates what optional subroutines he would like compiled, keeping in mind the space–time equation. After that, he can forget this part of the work and think of the records as being available to his program one at a time and in proper sequence. This greatly simplifies the total job.

Present-day compilers include very efficient I/O sections. Because of its importance, this programming of I/O subroutines usually is included even in assemblers. The major difference between the two processors is that the programmer using the compiler writes statements such as "GET IN RECORD" or "FILE PAY LINE," while the assembler language requires the programmer to write a few "bridging" instructions to transfer from his main line of coding to the preassembled subroutines.

OPERATING SYSTEMS

Over the past decade, computer manufacturers have been trying hard to improve and advance the capabilities of computers of various types. As more sophisticated computers were designed, some concern was voiced regarding the efficiency of their use. Extensive manual control of computer operations (e.g., the manual initiation of each program loading procedure) could seriously affect the efficiency of most high-speed computers. This problem was met by the development of specialized programming systems, called *operating systems*, which automatically perform many of the functions formerly performed manually. While their capability ranges from very elementary to extremely sophisticated routines, operating systems are also capable of routines which are not possible under manual control. In any case, the primary use of an operating system is to maximize the use of the speed and "power" of sophisticated computer systems.

Some of the capabilities which operating systems may provide include:

1. *Multiprogramming.* Allows multiple programs to be executed concurrently. Generally, primary storage is divided into sections occupied by several programs. With the operating system controlling their execution, it switches a new program into action whenever a given program is idle due to an I/O operation. When the new program pauses for an I/O operation, the operating system switches again, and so on, until the whole operation is completed.

2. *Dynamic Priority Scheduling.* Multiple programs are entered into the computer system at one time and are stored in direct access secondary storage. The operating system then selects programs for execution on the basis of their preassigned priorities. If during execution a program of high priority is entered, the operating system schedules it ahead of all previously entered programs of a lower priority.

3. *"Job Stacking."* Multiple programs to be executed are "stacked" one behind the other in the input device. A manual loading procedure is required only for the first program in the stack. Once initiated, succeeding programs are loaded and executed in sequence by the operating system. Thus, the contributions of operating systems to operational efficiency make them a key element of computer systems.

UTILITIES

Many common jobs recur frequently. These are serviced by a set of programs referred to as *utility programs* or *utilities*. Their function is to aid in the production of programs for the computer system. Some of these include:

1. Card to tape, tape to card, tape to printer. These are programs used to transfer data from one medium to another.

2. Memory print—used to write out complete areas of central storage up to and including the entire storage capacity. The program also is referred to as a "dump."

3. Program loader—introduces a new program into storage.

4. Tape duplication—this program permits the user to reproduce a reel of tape on another reel.
5. File routines—the use of large capacity, random-access files requires the user to copy the information from these files onto magnetic tapes with some regularity for protection purposes. With so much of a firm's active data in these files, it is necessary to be sure that the files can be reconstructed if a major stoppage occurs. This is similar in concept to the checkpoint previously discussed.

Naturally, there are many other utilities; however, the foregoing list should give the reader an idea as to the kind of work they can do. Almost all of these utilities take a common form: each is supplied as an assembled program, ready to run. The user puts it to work either through some well-defined console operation or a combination of the console and a control card(s) which contains initializing data. For example, the Memory Print program usually requires the programmer to specify the locations in storage which are the boundaries of the area to be written. These are punched into specific columns of a control card. After the Memory Print program is loaded, the card is read; the program is initialized; and the printing takes place.

There are several computer users' organizations which have common interests. These organizations maintain whole libraries of generalized programs. Thousands of them are available. The best advice one can give to any learning programmer is to make sure that he becomes aware of what others have done and are doing. Much valuable time can be saved by such sharing.

Glossary of Terms

ALGOL: Algorithmic-oriented language. An international procedure-oriented language.

ASSEMBLE: To prepare a machine language program from a symbolic language program by substituting absolute operation codes for symbolic operation codes and absolute relocatable addresses for symbolic addresses.

DECLARATIVE OPERATION: A coding sequence which involves writing symbolic labels and operation codes for data and constants. It is made up of a symbolic label, a declarative operation code, and an operand.

HARDWARE: Physical equipment, e.g., mechanical, magnetic, electrical, or electronic devices. Contrasts with software.

LABEL: One or more characters used to identify an item of data. Synonymous with key.

MACRO INSTRUCTION: (1) An instruction consisting of a sequence of micro instructions which are inserted into the object routine for performing a specific operation. (2) The more powerful instructions which combine several operations in one instruction.

PROCESSOR PROGRAM: A programming aid which prepares an object program first by reading symbolic instructions and then by comparing and converting the instructions into a suitable computer language.

PROGRAMMING LANGUAGE ONE: A new, high level procedure-oriented language designed to satisfy the needs of business and scientific applications as well as processor programming.

SOFTWARE: (1) The collection of programs and routines associated with a computer, e.g., compilers, library routines. (2) All the documents associated with a computer, e.g., manuals, circuit diagrams. (3) Contrasts with *hardware*.

Questions for Review

1. What are some of the complications involving the job of a programmer? Explain.
2. What is a processor program? How is programming economy realized through the use of a processor program? Explain.
3. List and describe the three parts of a symbolic language instruction.
4. What is meant by "one-for-one" language?
5. What accommodations does a symbolic language provide a programmer?
6. What is a macro language? How do macros differ from the "one-for-one" language?
7. List and explain three main "procedure-oriented" languages.
8. What similarities are there between a symbolic language and a procedure-oriented language?
9. List and explain briefly five operations handled by input/output devices.
10. What is a utility program? Why is it used? Give three examples of utility programs.

FORTRAN CONCEPTS

THIS CHAPTER EXAMINES one of the more popular "high-level" programming languages, FORTRAN. In general, high-level programming languages are oriented toward the solution of problems or the development of procedures rather than toward a particular computer. Thus, FORTRAN is machine-independent and is specifically oriented to the solution of mathematical-types of problems. The language consists of a set of symbols and words and specific rules for writing procedural instructions.

FORTRAN, an acronym for *For*mula *Trans*lator, was originally developed in 1957 by a group of thirteen men from IBM, to simplify the work of scientists and engineers in stating their problems for machine solution. Since its initial development, it has progressed through several versions (where version is taken to mean an improvement over the previous state rather than a major modification in concept). The current version is FORTRAN IV, which has stabilized sufficiently to lead the American National Standards Institute to develop a standard FORTRAN IV. For brevity, it will be referred to in this chapter as FORTRAN.

THE FORTRAN PROGRAM CARD

In preparing a FORTRAN program, statements (the equivalent of natural-language sentences) are written on a FORTRAN coding sheet with a format similar to that of the program card (Fig. 20-1). Each line of the coding sheet represents an instruction and is punched in a separate 80-column card. Unlike data cards in which data can be punched in any of the 80 columns, a FORTRAN program card is divided into areas reserved for specific types of information. See Fig. 16-7 for a sample of the FORTRAN coding sheet.

Briefly, column 1 is punched with letter *C* (meaning comment) when the card contains explanatory (versus instructional) information and is not a part

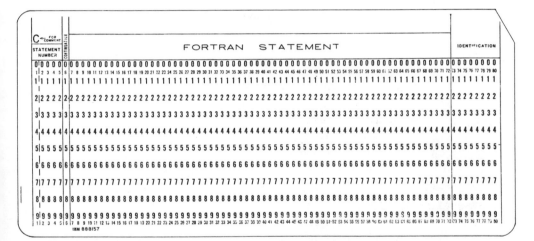

FIG. 20-1 Fortran program card

of the operating program. The computer ignores the contents when the object program is executed. In most FORTRAN programs, however, column 1 is used with columns 2-5 to store a statement number for later reference. A statement number identifies the statement so that it can be used later in the program in a branching or other out-of-sequence situations. It should be kept in mind that while any numeric value may be used as a statement number, no two statement numbers within a given routine may be the same.

Column 6 is usually left blank, unless a program instruction requires additional cards. In this case, a punch (other than zero) is made to tell the computer that the remaining part of the instruction is punched in the succeeding card.

Columns 7-72 are reserved for punching a program instruction. An instruction requiring more than one card is continued (beginning in column 7) in each succeeding card.

Columns 73-80 are reserved for punching such information as the sequence numbers of the cards of the program or other legal characters. This field is ignored by the computer during processing.

BASIC ELEMENTS OF FORTRAN

Like any other language, FORTRAN is composed of key elements which serve to define its formal structure. They are:

(a) The character set
(b) Constants
(c) Variables
     Array variables and subscripts
(d) Dimension statements
(e) Arithmetic statements
     Arithmetic assignment statements
(f) Input/output statements
(g) Format statement
(h) Control statements
(i) Imperative statements
     The DO statement
     The CONTINUE statement
     STOP and END statements

The Character Set

The FORTRAN character set consists of decimal digits 0 though 9, letters A through Z (upper case), the period, the comma, and the parentheses.

Constants

A constant is any specific value (e.g., 27) or a number that does not change during the execution of the program. Two valid types of numeric constants are used: (1) integer, or (2) real. An *integer* (or fixed-point) constant is one or more decimal digits containing no decimal point and may be preceded by a + or a − sign. In the absence of either sign, the constant is assumed to be positive. Examples of valid constants are:

341, +101, −40 (not −4.0), 10211 (not 102.11)

A *real* (or floating point) constant is a number (0-9) written with a decimal point. The decimal point can be placed between any two digits, preceding or following the string of digits. For example:

$$0. \qquad 1. \qquad .020 \qquad 3.02141$$

represent the *fixed* format of a real constant. The *floating-point* format is an adaptation of "scientific notation" and is represented as a real constant followed by the letter E and a one- or two-digit integer constant. The letter E and the integer constant comprise the exponent which represents the power of ten by which the real constant is to be multiplied. For example:

$$7.0E3 \text{ means } 7.0 \times 10^3, \text{ or } 7,000$$

The maximum value of the exponent is determined by the specific computer used. Other examples of valid real constants are:

$$56.58, \ -.0061, \ +5., \ 35.1E20, \ 7.E + 10, \ 3.24E - 9, \ -18.E - 8$$

Examples of invalid real constants are:

4E10 (no decimal point present), 2,100.7 (no comma allowed), 11.0E674 (more than two digits in the exponent is not allowed), .18E1.1 (exponent is not in the integer).

Variables are symbolic of different value representation. For example, in the formula ($Y = 7X^3 + 4X^2 + 2X + 3$), digits 7, 4, 2, and 3 are constants, while Y and X are variables. It is common for programmers to use variables which clearly indicate the represented quantities. For example:

$$\text{VALUE} = \text{UNITS} * \text{PRICE}$$

Thus, they can be considered as names of memory locations. They remain unchanged throughout the program, even though the contents of the memory locations they represent change frequently.

A variable name must begin with a letter and may be composed of no more than six alphameric characters. For example, 7C14 is not a valid variable name because it begins with a digit. Likewise, MULTIPLY is not a valid variable name because it contains more than six characters.

Value representation can be either integer or real depending on whether the value represented is integer or real. An *integer variable* is a series of alphameric characters with the first letter being I, J, K, L, M, or N. Some examples are:

IMAX, JOLT, KLARK, LEM10, MR121, NSUM

I J K L M N

A *real variable,* on the other hand, is a series of alphameric characters with the first letter being any letter other than *I* through *N.* Some examples are:

XMIN, SUM, PAY1, A9999

While the programmer exercises freedom in deciding on the variable name(s) to be used, there are certain predefined names (processes) which are reserved and must be avoided. For example, SQRT (abbreviation of square root) is a reserved word for the generalized square root subroutine and is incorporated in the FORTRAN computer for his convenience.

Array Variables and Subscripts. It was mentioned earlier that a real or an integer variable name may be used as the name of a memory location. The term *array* is used in this section to refer to any *dimensioned* (or array) variable. A dimensioned variable represents one or more memory cells specified in a dimensioned statement, and appears as the first statement in the program.

Arrays are either lists of values or matrices (Fig. 20-2).

In Fig. 20-2 we have an array, arbitrarily named COST. If we wish to refer to the third value, for example, we would write the FORTRAN notation COST(3), 3 being the *subscript* which must be enclosed in parentheses and follow the variable name. Reference to any of the elements of the array requires the use of subscript I, e.g., COST(I), where I is equal to any element of the array set.

The above figure also shows a 3 × 3 matrix (3 × 3 referred to as the dimensions of the matrix), arbitrarily called MINI. If we wish to refer to the value 1 in row 3 and column 2 (the elements of the intersection) we write the notation MINI(3, 2), where 3 and 2 are the subscripts. The first digit always refers to the row number and the second digit refers to the column number. The two digits are separated by a comma and enclosed in parentheses following the variable name. Reference to the 9 values of the matrix is written as follows:

	Row No.	Col. No.	Value
MINI	(1,1)		4
MINI	(1,2)		2
MINI	(1,3)		3
MINI	(2,1)		1
MINI	(2,2)		3
MINI	(2,3)		7
MINI	(3,1)		4
MINI	(3,2)		1
MINI	(3,3)		2

In FORTRAN, any element of a given two-dimensional matrix is represented by the subscripts *I* and *J.* Thus, in the matrix named MINI, the

FORTRAN notation is written as MINI (I,J), where *I* represents values in rows 1, 2, and 3 and *J* represents values in columns 1, 2, and 3.

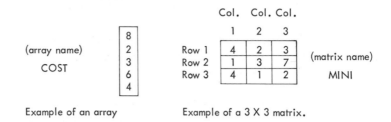

Example of an array   Example of a 3 X 3 matrix.

FIG. 20-2 Arrays and matrices

Dimension Statements

In FORTRAN programming, when a series of memory locations are reserved for array variables, a dimension statement (first statement of the program) is used to specify the dimensions of the variable(s) involved.[1] Referring to Fig. 20-2, the dimension statement for the array and another for the matrix are written as follows:

DIMENSION COSTS(5)
DIMENSION MINI(3, 3)[2]

DIMENSION COSTS(5) tells the computer that the array, named COST, consists of 5 elements. DIMENSION MINI(3, 3) tells the computer that the dimensions (size) of the matrix, named MINI, consists of 3 rows and 3 columns, respectively.

Arithmetic Statement

In constructing a FORTRAN program, various elements of the language (i.e., constants, variables, subscripts, or operation symbols) are combined in some predefined manner to form statements or expressions. One of the more commonly used statements is the arithmetic statement. It ranges from the simple form of a single operand (i.e., real or integer variable or constant) to a relatively complex mathematical expression. In cases where more than one operand is present, arithmetic operators are used to "tie" the operands together into a valid arithmetic expression. The operands and operators are used in the same way as one would build a normal mathematical equation. The operation symbols are as follows:

---

[1] If no array variables are used, then no dimension statement is necessary.
[2] The two statements can be written on one line with a comma separating them. Thus:
       DIMENSION COST(5), MINI(3, 3)

$$+ \quad \text{addition}$$
$$- \quad \text{subtraction}$$
$$* \quad \text{multiplication}$$
$$/ \quad \text{division}$$
$$** \quad \text{exponentiation}$$

Arithmetic operators have predetermined priority concerning the order in which operations will be performed. Thus, a statement is scanned from left to right, and executed as follows:

1. All exponentiations are performed first.
2. All multiplications and divisions are performed next.
3. All additions and subtractions are performed last.

For example, the statement:

$$\frac{A}{B^2}+2+CXD+E^3$$

is expressed as A/B**2+C*D+E**3 and is treated as

$$\left(A/(B^{**}2) \right) + \left(C^*D \right) + \left(E^{**}3 \right)$$

The innermost parenthetical expressions are evaluated first, leading to the evaluation of the outermost expressions. All equal levels of groupings are evaluated before moving to the next higher level.

In the case of multiple operations of equal priority [3] operations are performed in order from left to right. For example, A + B + C is treated as (A + B) + C. One exception to this rule is the case of exponentiation. In an expression consisting entirely of exponentiations, the operations are performed from right to left. For example, the expression E**F**G would be equivalent to E**(F**G). It is important to note that parentheses may be used to override the implied priority of the operators. When parentheses are used, the expressions within the parentheses are first evaluated from innermost to outermost. Thus, parentheses are useful in clarifying an expression to avoid any probability of misinterpretation or ambiguity.

Other rules are also followed.

1. All FORTRAN expressions must be clearly stated. For example, if we wish to multiply A by B, the statement is written as A * B. Any other expression (e.g., AB) is interpreted as a variable name.
2. Only one operator is permitted between two valid characters. Two or more consecutive operators require the use of parentheses; e.g., the expression ISUM + −5 is not valid because of the presence of two consecutive operators between ISUM and 5. It must be rewritten as ISUM + (−5).

[3] It should be kept in mind that multiply and divide have the same priority. Add and subtract also have the same priority.

3. Operands in any arithmetic expression must be of the same type—integer or real constants. No mixed mode arithmetic may be performed.[4]

Arithmetic Assignment Statement. This statement has the general form VARIABLE = EXPRESSION and, in effect, replaces the value of the single variable on the left by the computed value of the expression on the right. Although arithmetic assignment is represented by an "equal sign," the sign does not have the same connotation in FORTRAN as it does in mathematics. In mathematics, the equal sign means "is identical to" or "has the same magnitude as." In FORTRAN, however, the equal sign is interpreted as "replaced by." In other words, the expression A = B + C actually means to compute the sum of the values of the variables B and C and place the sum in the storage location assigned to the variable A. Thus, we see that in FORTRAN the expression I = I + 1 is completely legitimate and means "take the contents of the storage location assigned to the variable I, add 1 to that content, and place the sum in the storage location assigned to the variable I." Thus, if the value of I were 3 prior to execution of the arithmetic assignment, it would be 4 after execution. It should be obvious, then, why the left side of the statement can only be a single variable.

Generally, both sides of the statement are of the same type; that is, either integer or real. However, there is no rule against mixing types for the two sides. In the case where an expression (expressed in floating-point) is assigned to an integer variable, it is converted to a real result (with a fractional part of zero) before the assignment. Then, the fractional part of the real result will be dropped before final assignment. On the other hand, if an integer expression is assigned to a real variable, the expression is converted to a real configuration in its final assignment. For example, assume the assignment I = X/Y where X = 5.0 and Y = 2.0; the real result of the division would be 2.5 but the value assigned to I would be 2. (fraction dropped).

Input/Output Statements

Input/output statements instruct the computer on the steps to be taken (read a card, print a line, punch a card, etc.); how to arrange data for input/output (that is, what *format* is to be used); and what data (reference to variable name), to manipulate. Thus, input/output statements manipulate the transfer of data between the computer's primary storage and external (input and output) devices.

Each input/output word (READ, WRITE) is followed by an input device number and a format statement number (separated by a comma), and a list of variable names. READ statements initiate the transfer of input data from the punched cards to the computer's primary storage for processing. The WRITE statement actuates the printer to printout the result of certain computations (output data).

---

[4] Based on ANSI Standard FORTRAN IV.

The READ satement takes the form:

$$READ \ (integer, \ integer) \ LIST$$

Using the array in Fig. 20-2, the READ statement would be written:

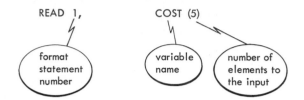

The statement instructs the computer to read from an input device number 1, five elements into a storage location named COST according to a format specified in a statement having reference number 10. Thus, the first integer of the READ instruction refers to the input device number and the second integer refers to the format statement number. The LIST specifies the variable name and the quantities to be transferred into computer memory. Any number of quantities may be included in a given LIST.

The WRITE statement instructs the computer to print output results on the printer. As many successive lines are printed (guided by the FORMAT statement specifications) as are variables in the LIST.

The WRITE statement takes the form:

$$WRITE \ (integer, \ integer) \ LIST$$

For example:

$$WRITE \ (3, 5) \quad COST \ (5)$$

Like other input/output statements, execution of the WRITE statement is based on the FORMAT statement specifications. It should be noted that up to 120 or 132 characters (depending on the printer used) can be printed on one line.[5]

FORMAT Statements

FORMAT statements are nonexecutable and serve input/output statements to specify the arrangement of data in an external medium (such as punched cards, magnetic tapes, or on printed paper). Its form is:

$$FORMAT \ (specifications)$$

[5] The first character on the line is reserved for printer-control symbols and is not available for printing a data character. The symbols used in Column 1 are:

(1) blank—tells the printer to print single space.
(2) 0 —tells the printer to print double space.
(3) 1 —tells the printer to eject the page.

The list of specifications must be enclosed in parentheses and separated by commas.

In this section, two broad classes of data and the way they are specified are discussed. They are numeric and alphameric data. Numeric data may be (1) integer data, (2) real data in fixed-point form, or (3) real data in floating-point form.

I Specifications. The FORMAT specification for integer data is called I [6] *FORMAT Specification* and is given in the form:

Iw, where I signifies that the number to be read is an integer and

w denotes the field or the number of character positions to be assigned (including a + or a − sign and any required blanks).

Several rules must be followed: (1) Leading zeros are replaced by blanks on output. (2) Blank card columns are interpreted as zeros on input (a zero value is not affected). (3) Available data are right-justified. (4) Input data exceeding w positions are lost and an asterisk is printed. However, if the data is less than the specified w position unfilled positions are indicated by blanks.

For example, assume the following data are punched in Columns 1-11:

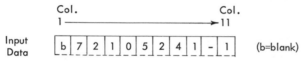

The input I specifications (4I1, I2, I3, I2) [7] show the values in seven memory locations as:

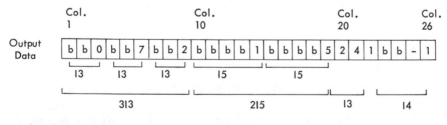

Given the output I specifications:

$$(3I3,\ 2I5,\ I3,\ I4)$$

the output would be punched in Columns 1-26 as follows:

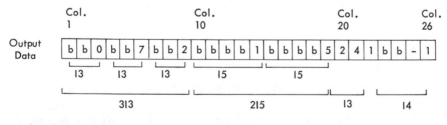

[6] I stands for integer.
[7] 4I1 means 4 fields, each consisting of one integer character.
I2 means 1 field consisting of two integer characters.
I3 means 1 field consisting of three integer characters.
I2 means 1 field consisting of two integer characters.

F Specifications. The F (meaning floating-point) specifications statement takes a given field read from an input medium as a real value and stores it in computer memory, the location of which is specified by the input statement. When output is desired, values stored in each memory cell involved are interpreted as real values (numbers) and placed in designated fields in an output medium. The F statement should also specify the length of the field and the number of decimal places required.

Thus, the F specification statement takes the general format:

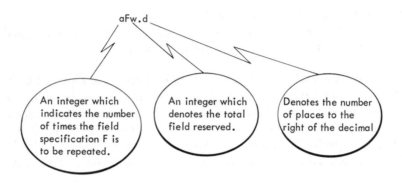

It should be noted that a period between the *w* and *d* in the F specification format is mandatory. When it comes to the input data, no decimal point is required, since its position is implied in the F format specifications. However, if it is present, it will override the decimal point in the F format specifications.

In determining the total field length for real values, character positions should be reserved for signs which precede the first significant digit in input and output data fields.

To further illustrate the F format specifications, assume the following input data are punched in Columns 1-15 as follows:

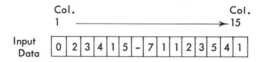

The input F specifications:

$$(2F2.2, \ 2F2.0, \ F3.2, \ F4.0) \ {}^{8}$$

[8] 2F2.2 means 2 fields, each consisting of two characters with two digits to the right of the decimal point.
2F2.0 means 2 fields, each consisting of two characters with no digits to the right of the decimal point.
F3.2 means 1 field consisting of three characters with two digits to the right of the decimal point.
F4.0 means 1 field consisting of four characters with no digit to the right of the decimal point.

show the values in six memory storage locations as follows:

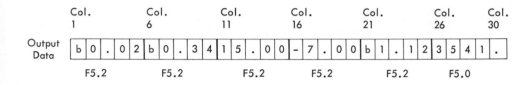

Given the output F specification, the output:

$$(5F5.2, F5.0)$$

would be punched in Columns 1-30 as follows:

Col. 1					Col. 6					Col. 11					Col. 16					Col. 21					Col. 26					Col. 30

Output Data: | b | 0 | . | 0 | 2 | b | 0 | . | 3 | 4 | 1 | 5 | . | 0 | 0 | - | 7 | . | 0 | 0 | b | 1 | . | 1 | 2 | 3 | 5 | 4 | 1 | . |

F5.2   F5.2   F5.2   F5.2   F5.2   F5.0

A Specifications. The A (meaning alphameric) specifications take alphabetic, numeric, and special characters in the form of input data and are stored in computer memory in the form of words. Each computer varies in the manner of representing data in its memory and in the number of characters per word of storage. The IBM 360 computer, for instance, stores up to four characters per word of storage. Generally, most currently used FORTRAN compilers execute programs written with six alphameric character words.

The A specification statement takes the form:

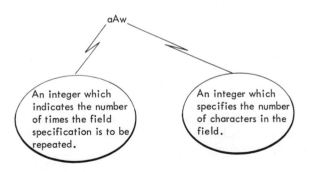

aAw

An integer which indicates the number of times the field specification is to be repeated.

An integer which specifies the number of characters in the field.

Thus, each w is read into one word of storage and left-justified. Any unused positions are interpreted as blanks. On input, if the characters read exceed the field length, all excess leading characters are left out. On output, any unfilled character positions of a given word of storage are filled with leading blanks.

Assuming the following alphameric data are punched in Columns 1-15:

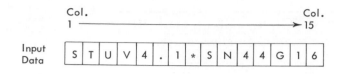

specifying six characters per word of storage, the input A specifications statement:

$$(3A2, \ 2A3, \ A3)$$

shows the values in six memory locations as follows:

Given the output A specifications:

$$(A6, \ 3A2, \ 2A4)$$

the output would be punched in Columns 1-20 as follows:

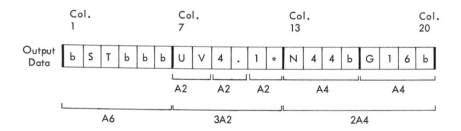

H Specifications. H (meaning Hollerith) specifications statement is used in cases where certain alphameric constants are desired in the data output. Any such constants are included in the statement. The general format statement takes the following form:

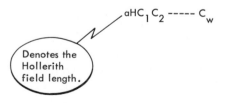

$aHC_1 C_2 ----- C_w$

Denotes the Hollerith field length.

The spacing of values within a given line is signified by X specifications. For example, the H specification statement:

$$(4X,14HRECTANGLEbBCD.)$$

results in eighteen consecutive card columns 1-18, as follows:

A carriage control character is a necessary part of the WRITE OUTPUT statement and is used to control the printer. The first character of an output line is interpreted as a carriage control character. The primary control characters are:

b (blank) single space before printing
0   double space before printing
1   skip to a new page
+   no paper motion

The carriage control character is most commonly provided by incorporating it in an H specification of the type 1Hx (where x is the carriage control character) as the first entry in the FORMAT list. For single spacing, the alternative 1X may be used. The following example illustrates the FORMAT statement in conjunction with a WRITE statement.

Assume the following requirements:

1. To print on the top of a new page the answers to three problems.
   The answer to problem one consists of three alphabetic characters. The answer to problem two consists of 5-digit integer numeric characters, and the answer to problem three consists of 9-digit real numeric characters (5 of the digits to follow the decimal point).
2. To print the statement "The Answers Are" followed by five blanks and the three answers, respectively.
3. Each of the three answers is to be separated by three blanks.

Given the digit six to denote the output device and variable names ALPHA, IANSR, and RANSB, we would have:

PRINT 10,   ALPHA, IANSR, RANSR

10   FORMAT(1H1, 14HTHEbANSWERSbARE, 5X, A3, 3X, I5, 3X, F10. 5)

Control Statements

FORTRAN statements are executed according to their sequence in the program deck, unless a control statement clearly interrupts sequential execution by transferring control to a statement elsewhere in the program. Transfers may be either conditional or unconditional, depending on the type of operation and evaluation desired.

The Unconditional GO TO Statement. The Unconditional GO TO Statement causes unconditional transfer of control. Its general form is GO TO w, where w specifies the statement number which will be executed next. For example:

Statement No.	Instruction
12	GO TO 20
6	X = 3. *Y
20	Y = 4. *B
	STOP

The GO TO statement above tells the computer to alter the next two sequential instructions and to execute the STOP statement, causing termination of the program.

The Conditional GO TO Statement. This type of GO TO statement causes optional transfer of control to any of the series of statements (enclosed in parentheses), depending on the value of i in the general form:

$$\text{GO TO } (n_1, n_2, - - - -n_m), i$$

This means that if the value of i is 1, control is transferred to execute statement number n_1; i=2, n_2;- - -;if i=m, n_m. For example, in the statement:

$$\text{GO TO } (5, 6, 7, 9, 11), 4$$

the program transfers to the statement numbered 9 (fourth value between parentheses).

The Arithmetic IF Statement. The IF statement is a conditional transfer of the control statement, in that control is transferred to a given statement number only IF a particular condition is met. The general form is:

$$\text{IF (expression)} n_1, n_2, n_3$$

where n_1, n_2, n_3 are executable statement numbers.

The execution of the arithmetic IF statement follows three key rules:

1. If the expression is negative, control is transferred to n_1.
2. If the expression is zero, control is transferred to n_2.
3. If the expression is positive, control is transferred to n_3.

For example, in the following IF statement,

$$IF(A*3.0-40)1,2,3$$

if $A = 4$, control goes to statement 1, since the result is -28.

An IF statement is quite powerful in operations which require routine, repetitive computations. To further illustrate its use, assume a banking routine where 500 customer accounts must be updated on Monday of each week. The basic operation requires subtraction of payments from balance outstanding. After the subtraction is performed, the balance outstanding takes on the new value.

In preparing the partial program, we need to set up an index to count the number of accounts updated and, when it contains 500, to branch the program to a specific statement that would proceed in executing the remaining part(s) of the program.

Given an index K, PREB (for previous balance), and PAYM (for payments), the partial program would be as shown in Fig. 20-3.

FIG. 20-3 A partial program

Statement Number Cols. 1-5	Statement Cols. 7-72	Description
	⋮	Input and other necessary statements.
	K=0	Set index K to 0.
110	K=K+1	Add 1 to index K.
115	PREB(K)=PREB(K)-PAYM(K)	Subtract payment from balance outstanding and replace it by the new remainder.
120	IF(500-K)125, 125, 110	If the index is equal to or greater than 500, go to statement 125; otherwise go to statement 110 (in effect, update the next account).
125		The remaining part of the program.
	⋮	
200	STOP	

Logical IF Statements. A logical IF statement causes transfer of control based on whether a specific expression is *true* or *false*. If the expression is found to be true, control is transferred to the statement number following the parentheses in the IF statement. Otherwise, the next sequential statement is executed.

The general form of the logical IF statement is:

IF (expression) statement a

statement b

Relational IF Statements. Not only is an expression evaluated by logical operands, but also by relational operators. The operands may be expressions, variables, or constants. FORTRAN's six relational operators are:

Relational Operator	Description
.GE.	greater than or equal to
.GT.	greater than
.EQ.	equal to
.NE.	not equal to
.LE.	less than or equal to
.LT.	less than

Note that a period before and after each relational operator is mandatory.

Examples of relational expressions and their evaluation are:

Relational Expression	Evaluation
100.EQ.100	true
400.GE.399	true
941.LT.940	false

Thus, the expressions are logical as well as relational.

Relational expressions can be linked within a given logical IF statement by the logical operators .AND. and .OR.

The general form is:

$$n_1.AND.n_2 \qquad n_1.OR.n_2$$

Using the logical operator .AND., the relational expressions n_1 and n_2 are considered as true only when both of them are true. However, with the logical operator .OR. the relational expression is considered as true when either n_1 or n_2 or both are true. Some examples follow:

1. IF(X*4.1.LE.A)J=4
2. IF(X.EQ.10.0)GO TO 100

3. IF(X.LT.3.AND.A.GT.Y)J=10
4. IF(A.LE.0.4.OR.A.GE.6.0)K=40.0/A

It should be kept in mind that precedence of execution takes the following order of priority—arithmetic operators, relational operators, logical operators.

Imperative Statements

The DO Statement. The DO statement is basically a convenient method of repetitive looping through a series of FORTRAN statements. The general form is:

$$DO\ n\ i = m_1,\ m_2,\ m_3$$

where n is an executable statement number located at some later point in the program, i is an integer variable representing a counter to be incremented, and m_1, m_2, m_3 are unsigned integer constants such that m_1 designates the initial value of the counter, m_2 designates the final value of the counter, and m_3 designates the value by which the counter is to be incremented each time through the loop. If m_3 is not explicitly stated, it is assumed to be 1.

The function of the DO statement is to execute all of the statements immediately following it up to *and including* the statement with the number n. It will perform the designated series of statements as many times as necessary to increment the counter from its initial value to its final value. For example, if $m_1 = 1$, $m_2 = 5$, and $m_3 = 1$; then the DO loop will be executed five times, each time by an increment of 1. In practice, the counter is initialized and the series of statements is performed. Then control is returned to the DO statement which increments the counter by the appropriate value and determines if the counter has *exceeded* the final value specified (m_2). If the value of the counter *exceeds* m_2 control is transferred out of the loop. Otherwise the sequence is repeated. Exit from the loop will occur automatically when the counter exceeds the value of m_2.

It is also possible to exit from the DO loop before the completion of the loop by using a conditional transfer of control statement within the range of the DO statement. However, it is not valid to transfer control into the range of a DO statement from an outside point.

Several rules must be observed in constructing a DO statement.

1. The last statement in the range of a DO statement must be an executable statement. It *cannot be:*
   (a) any type of transfer of control statement;
   (b) another DO statement; or
   (c) a logical IF statement.

2. The parameters i, m_1, m_2, and m_3 *cannot* be changed by any other statement within the range of a DO statement. They may be changed outside the loop if transfer is not later made back into the loop.

3. A complete DO loop may be contained within another DO loop. This is commonly referred to as *nested* DO loops. There is no restriction on the extent of nesting that may be done. However, there is a restriction on transfer of control between nested DO loops. While control may be transferred from an inner DO loop into an outer DO loop without restriction, control must never be transferred from an outer loop into an inner loop.

To illustrate nested DO loops, assume the need to perform a given major operation ten times and for each occurrence we wish to perform a minor operation twenty times. Given that the minor operation increments the counter in steps of 2, the DO statements required would look as follows (Fig. 20-4).

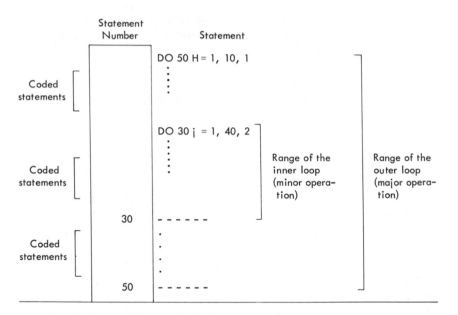

FIG. 20-4 Nested loops—an example

The CONTINUE Statement. This is a dummy executable statement which can be placed anywhere in a program. While it is executable, it does not perform any logical functions and does not change the sequence of instruction operation. It exists primarily to facilitate termination of a DO loop which would otherwise terminate on a prohibited statement. For example:

$$DO\ 10\ I=1,\ 15,\ 2$$
$$IF\ (A(I).EQ.0.0)A(I) = -A(I)$$
$$10\quad CONTINUE$$

STOP and END Statements. The STOP statement is executable. It terminates execution of the object program. The END statement is required and is the last statement in a FORTRAN program. It is nonexecutable and serves to terminate the compiling routine.

The statements described above are by no means a complete description of the FORTRAN language. They are, however, the most commonly used subset and are sufficient for a large proportion of applications. If a more extensive understanding of FORTRAN is desired, a text on FORTRAN or manuals provided by those offering FORTRAN compilers should be consulted. As a method of relating the above statements to their practical use, the solution of a problem using FORTRAN and the statements discussed previously will be presented on page 330. A flow chart of the sample problem (see Fig. 20-5, below) and a completed program (see Fig. 20-6, pages 328-329) are also presented by way of illustration.

FIG. 20-5 Flow chart for a sample FORTRAN program

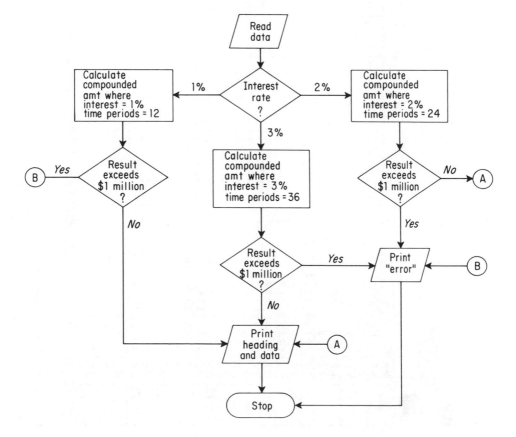

FORTRAN Coding Form

IBM

PROGRAM: SAMPLE PROGRAM
PROGRAMMER: JOHN GUERRA
DATE: DEC. 14, 1970

GRAPHIC / PUNCH
PUNCHING INSTRUCTIONS
PAGE ___ OF ___
CARD ELECTRO NUMBER*

FORTRAN STATEMENT

```
      M=10
      MAX=1000000.00
      READ(5,10)PRINC,I
   10 FORMAT(F6.2,I1)
      RESLT=PRINC
      XI=I/M
      GO TO(20,30,40),I
   20 DO 25 J=1,12,1
      XINT=RESLT*XI
      RESLT=RESLT+XINT
      IF(MAX-RESLT)100,25,25
   25 CONTINUE
      GO TO 50
   30 DO 35 K=1,24,1
      XINT=RESLT*XI
      RESLT=RESLT+XINT
      IF(MAX-RESLT)100,35,35
   35 CONTINUE
      GO TO 50
   40 DO 45 L=1,36,1
      XINT=RESLT*XI
      RESLT=RESLT+XINT
      IF(MAX-RESLT)100,45,45
   45 CONTINUE
```

FIG. 20-6 Completed FORTRAN program

IBM FORTRAN Coding Form

X25-7327-5
Printed in U.S.A.

PROGRAM SAMPLE PROGRAM

PROGRAMMER JOHN GUERRA DATE DEC. 14, 1970

PUNCHING INSTRUCTIONS | GRAPHIC | PUNCH | PAGE OF | CARD ELECTRO NUMBER*

STATEMENT NUMBER	CONT.	FORTRAN STATEMENT	IDENTIFICATION SEQUENCE
50		WRITE(6,60)	
60		FORMAT(1H1,45X,29HCOMPOUNDED AMOUNT CALCULATION,45X)	
		WRITE(6,70)PRINC,I,RESLT	
70		FORMAT(1H0,10HPRINCIPAL=,2X,F6·2,5X,9HINTEREST=,2X,I1,5X,7HRESULT=	
	1	,2X,F10·2)	
		GO TO 110	
100		WRITE(6,80)	
80		FORMAT(1H1,57X,5HERROR)	
110		STOP	
		END	

*A standard card form, IBM electro 888157, is available for punching statements from this form

FIG. 20-6 *(Continued)*

SAMPLE FORTRAN PROGRAM

To illustrate the FORTRAN coding of a problem solution the following sample program executes the routines for compounding a simple sum. Performing the calculations in a stepwise fashion, the basic procedure is: old amount (at beginning of time period) + (old amount x interest rate) = new amount (at end of time period). This new amount becomes the old amount for the next consecutive time period. The assumptions are:

1. The principal and interest rate will be constrained variables, their value to be read as input from input device number 5.
2. The allowable interest rates are 1 percent for twelve time periods, 2 percent for twenty-four time periods, and 3 percent for thirty-six time periods.
3. The maximum allowable principal is $999.99.
4. If the compounded amount exceeds $1,000,000.00, the program should immediately print "ERROR" and terminate execution.
5. Output to be printed on device 6 (assume 120 print positions). An appropriate heading is required; and the sequence of the output data to be: principal, interest rate, and compounded amount.
6. Name assignments: I = interest rate; PRINC = principal; RESLT = compounded amount; and MAX = maximum allowable compounded amount.

Glossary of Terms

ARRAY VARIABLE: A dimensioned variable which represents one or more memory cells specified in a dimensioned statement.

CONSTANT: Any specific value (a number) that does not change during program execution.

CONTROL STATEMENT: Serves to interrupt sequential execution of instructions by transferring control to a statement elewhere in the program.

FORMAT STATEMENT: A nonexecutable statement which serves input/output statements to specify the arrangement of data in an external medium such as a punched card, a magnetic tape, or on printed paper.

FORTRAN: *Formula Translater*, it is a data processing language which closely resembles mathematical language. It is a programming system (a language and a compiler) which allows the program to be written in a mathematical-type language. The program is later translated by the computer into machine language.

FORTRAN IV: Initially designed for scientific application, it is a problem-oriented language which allows the programmer to think in terms of the problem rather than the computer used in solving it. The language is quite convenient for many business applications.

IMPERATIVE STATEMENT: Commands the computer's immediate execution of specific sequential statements following it. Imperative statements include the DO statement, CONTINUE statement, and the STOP and END statements.

INTEGER VARIABLE: A series of alphameric characters with the first letter being I, J, K, L, M, or N.

REAL CONSTANT: A number written with a decimal point.

REAL VARIABLE: A series of alphameric characters with the first letter being any letter other than I, J, K, L, M, and N.

Questions for Review

1. What type of information is punched in Columns 1-6 of a FORTRAN card?
2. List and briefly explain the primary elements of FORTRAN.
3. What is the difference between an integer and/or real constant?
   An integer and real variable?
   Give an example of each.
4. Give an example of a 3x4 matrix.
5. When is a dimension statement used?
6. Explain the order of priority of evaluating an arithmetic statement.
7. Give the format of the following statements:
   a. arithmetic assignment statement
   b. input/output statement
   c. FORMAT statement
   d. logical IF statement
8. Explain briefly the function of the following specifications:
   a. F-Specifications
   b. A-Specifications
   c. H-Specifications
9. Distinguish the difference between a conditional and an unconditional statement. Give an example of each.
10. Distinguish the difference between a logical and a relational IF statement. Give an example of each.
11. Explain the function of the DO statement.
12. Write the following expressions and statements in FORTRAN notation. Use capital letters for identifiers.

    a. $x + y + c$
    b. $ax + by + cz$
    c. $x = y + z + 2a$

    d. $\dfrac{x}{a} + \dfrac{y}{b}$
    e. $a = int$
    f. $a + b = c - d$

13. Given J=3, K=4, L=6, and M=5, what is the value stored in I after the formula I=(J*K) + (L—M) is executed?
14. Flow chart and code a program to compute net pay.

    input data

G	(gross pay)
W	(federal withholding tax)
O	(other deductions)
formula:	N = G—(W+O)

    input format: (3F9.2)
    input device number: 1
    input FORMAT statement number: 40

    output data
    N,G,W,O
    output format: (4F9.2)
    output device number: 3
    output FORMAT statement number: 50

15. Which of the following are valid names for integer variables? real variables? Why?
    NADER, FAY, ZONA, L678P2, MONEY, COUNTER, TI, IT
16. Which of the following are valid names for integer constants? real constants? Why?
    4567, .456, —4567, —.04567, 100, 0, +210., 01247, 3.4E-10
17. Given J=15, K=4, L=9, M=19, determine the truth value of the following expressions:
    a. J.LT.L.OR.K.GE.M-J
    b. J.GT.L.OR.K.LT.M-J

COBOL CONCEPTS

THE PREVIOUS CHAPTER EXAMINED FORTRAN—a "high-level" programming language oriented to the solution of mathematical problems. This chapter presents an overview of COBOL—a "high-level" programming language oriented to the business problem.

COBOL is the acronym for *COmmon Business Oriented Language*—a procedure-oriented language designed to simplify the coding of computer applications in a business environment. It is based on the English language and allows program instructions to be constructed in paragraph- and sentence-like form, using words commonly encountered in business situations.

Like other languages, COBOL is comprised of a set of elements, rules, definitions and constraints. The appropriate manipulation of these various subsets produces a source program acceptable to a particular COBOL compiler. While various COBOL compilers in use today have their own peculiarities and limitations, the basic capabilities of the main subset of any COBOL language compiler is the same.

BASIC CONCEPTS

The basic structure of a COBOL program is a hierarchy consisting of the following (high to low) levels:

Division
Section
Paragraph
Sentence, Statement, or Independent Clause
Elements
Character Set

Certain level(s) *may be omitted* at the discretion of the programmer; some levels *must be omitted;* other levels *must be included* as a requirement of the language.

By definition, divisions, sections, and paragraphs must be preceded either by a *header* or a paragraph *name*, depending upon the situation. A *header* is a single reserved word,[1] a combination of reserved words and/or user-defined words that have a definite meaning in the context of COBOL. A *name* is a single user-defined word which identifies user-created paragraphs. All headers and paragraph names must terminate with a period. Division and section headers must appear on a line of their own.

COBOL FORMAT (CODING SHEET)

The COBOL coding sheet contains 25 lines and provides for 80 columns of information to correspond to the 80-column punched card.

Columns 1-3 are reserved for a 3-digit page number; page 1 is numbered 001; page 2, 002, etc.

Columns 4-6 are reserved for the line number. The first line number is 010; the second line, 020, etc. Thus, using the first 6 columns, 001110 means page 1 and line 11.

Column 7 is used for indicating the continuation of a statement into succeeding line(s). When a given statement requires more than one line, a dash is placed in column 7 of the next and other succeeding lines related to the statement (Fig. 21-1).

Column 8 is the beginning of margin A; it is where the names of divisions, paragraphs, and sections start. Other items start at margin B (column 12). A COBOL paragraph or sentence starts at column 12 and ends at column 72.

Columns 73-80 are reserved for program identification.

COBOL'S FOUR DIVISIONS

The COBOL language contains *four* divisions. They must be present in every COBOL program in the following sequence:

> IDENTIFICATION DIVISION.
> ENVIRONMENT DIVISION.
> DATA DIVISION.
> PROCEDURE DIVISION.

The Identification Division

The identification division serves the function of identifying the name of the programmer, the title of the COBOL program, and the compiler listing asso-

---

[1] A reserved word is a defined character string which has a particular meaning to the COBOL compiler and *must not be duplicated* in any user-defined name.

Page	Line		7	8 9 10 11 12 13 14 15 16 17 18 19 20 ...
0 0 1	0 1 0			ADD FOUR HUNDRED TO WORKING AREA. WRITE RESULT-RECORD FROM
	0 2 0		–	OLD FILE.
	0 3 0			
	0 4 0			
	0 5 0			
	0 6 0			
	0 7 0			
	0 8 0			
	0 9 0			
	1 0 0			
	1 1 0			
	1 2 0			
	1 3 0			
	1 4 0			
	1 5 0			
	1 6 0			
	1 7 0			
	1 8 0			
	1 9 0			
	2 0 0			

FIG. 21-1 COBOL coding sheet—an example

ciated with it. Its structure is composed of *one required paragraph* and up to *six optional paragraphs*. Each of the paragraphs (required and optional) is identified by a paragraph header. The required paragraph header, PROGRAM-ID, is the first entry on the line following the division header and the programmer-defined name of the program. For example, if the program name is PAYROLL-CALC, the identification division would be coded as shown in Fig. 21-2 below.

FORMAT

```
         SEQUENCE            A        B
        (PAGE) (SERIAL)              12    16    20    24    28    32    36    40
          3  4   6 7 8
Required → 0 1 0        IDENTIFICATION DIVISION.
           0 2 0        PROGRAM ID.    ((program name here))
           0 3 0        AUTHOR.        ((author's name here))
Optional   0 4 0        INSTALLATION.  ((any sentence(s)))
           0 5 0        DATE-WRITTEN.  ((any sentence(s)))
           0 6 0        DATE-COMPILED.
           0 7 0        REMARKS.       ((any sentence(s)))
```

EXAMPLE

```
         SEQUENCE            A        B
        (PAGE) (SERIAL)              12    16    20    24    28    32    36    40
          3  4   6 7 8
          0 1 0        IDENTIFICATION DIVISION.
          0 2 0        PROGRAM ID.    PAYROLL-CALC.²
          0 3 0        AUTHOR.        JOHN GUERRI.
          0 4 0        INSTALLATION.  IBM 360.
          0 5 0        DATE-WRITTEN.  DEC 28, 70.
          0 6 0        DATE-COMPILED.
          0 7 0        REMARKS.
          0 8 0                       INPUT FROM TIME CARD RUN
          0 9 0                       AND MERGE WITH NAME FILE.
```

FIG. 21-2

The Environment Division

The environment division describes the physical characteristics of the equipment being used and the aspects of the problem that are dependent upon that equipment. Various *special-names* are assigned to specific units of equipment for later reference. The environment division consists of two sections: the configuration section and the input/output section.

The Configuration Section. The Configuration Section deals with the characteristics of the source computer (the computer in which the program is compiled) and the object computer (the computer in which the compiled pro-

---

² All division, section, and paragraph headers and names must begin in Column 8 of the coding line. All other coding must begin in Column 12.

gram will be executed). Normally, the source and object computers are the same machine. Thus, in the configuration section, the two required paragraph headers are:

SOURCE-COMPUTER.
OBJECT-COMPUTER.

Each paragraph header is followed by the name of the appropriate computer (generally defined by the manufacturer of the equipment).

The Input/Output Section. The Input/Output Section deals with the information necessary to control the transfer and handling of data between input/output units and the object program. In addition to the required paragraph, FILE-CONTROL, every data file used by the COBOL program must be indicated by the following statement:

SELECT file-name ASSIGN TO device-name.

File-name is a programmer-defined name used to reference that file in the program.[3] The device-names are fixed names and are specified by the computer manufacturer.

Using the IBM 360 computer system as a reference, let us assume we have files named CARD-RCDS and PRINT-OUT, and that we wish to assign them to devices SYSRDR and SYSPTR, respectively. The input/output section would appear as follows:

INPUT-OUTPUT SECTION.
FILE-CONTROL. SELECT CARD-RCDS ASSIGN TO SYSRDR.
SELECT PRINT-OUT ASSIGN TO SYSPTR.

Combining the configuration section (described previously) and the above input/output section, we would have the environment division in Fig. 21-3, page 338.

The Data Division

The data division is the area of a COBOL program that holds in defined form all the data required for the execution of the program. It includes the data accepted as input, the data manipulated in the program, and the data produced as output. The data division contains three optional sections which (when present) are written as a part of the format in Fig. 21-4, page 338.

The File Section. The file section defines the contents of data stored in an external medium. The definition is a two-level affair composed of a de-

---

[3] The file is defined in the section explaining the data division on this page.

[4] Discussion of the report section is omitted, since it is similar to the other sections and is infrequently used.

FORMAT

```
SEQUENCE  |C|
(PAGE)(SERIAL)|O| A | B
 1   3 4  6 7|N|8  |12    16    20    24    28    32    36    40    44    48    52
            |T|

                ENVIRONMENT DIVISION.
                CONFIGURATION SECTION.
                SOURCE-COMPUTER.              (computer's name)
                OBJECT-COMPUTER.
                SPECIAL-NAMES.

                INPUT-OUTPUT SECTION.
                FILE-CONTROL.    SELECT(file(s) name)

                I-O-CONTROL.  APPLY(different I/O techniques)
```

Required Paragraphs

EXAMPLE

```
SEQUENCE  |C|
(PAGE)(SERIAL)|O| A | B
 1   3 4  6 7|N|8  |12    16    20    24    28    32    36    40    44    48    52    56
            |T|

 120            ENVIRONMENT DIVISION.
 130            CONFIGURATION SECTION.
 140            SOURCE-COMPUTER.      IBM 360.
 150            OBJECT-COMPUTER.      IBM 360.
 160            SPECIAL-NAMES.
 170                 XXX;   XXXX.
 180            INPUT-OUTPUT SECTION.
 190            FILE-CONTROL.    SELECT CARD-RCDS ASSIGN TO SYSRDR.
 200                 SELECT PRINT-OUT ASSIGN TO SYSPTR.
 210            I-O-CONTROL.  APPLY FILE-CONTROL ON TIME.
```

FIG. 21-3

```
SEQUENCE  |C|
(PAGE)(SERIAL)|O| A | B
 1   3 4  6 7|N|8  |12    16    20    24    28    32    36    40    44    48    52    56    60
            |T|

                DATA DIVISION.
                FILE SECTION.
                FD  XXXXX.
                01  XXXX.         (item name)
                    02 XX;  XXXX.        (series of independent clauses)
                       03  XXXX;  XXX.
                WORKING-STORAGE SECTION.
                77  XXX.
                01  XXX;  XXX.
                REPORT SECTION.⁴
```

FIG. 21-4

scription of the file, followed by one or more record descriptions. The file description consists of a level indicator (beginning in Column 8) FD which identifies the beginning of the file description. The FD is followed by a programmer-defined file name (beginning in Column 12), a required clause, and several optional clauses. The required clause (used for sequential access files) pertains to the type of labels present on the file for identification purposes. It takes the general form:

$$\text{LABEL} \left\{ \begin{array}{c} \text{RECORD IS} \\ \text{(or)} \\ \text{RECORDS ARE} \end{array} \right\} \left\{ \left\{ \begin{array}{c} \text{STANDARD} \\ \text{(or)} \\ \text{OMITTED} \end{array} \right. \right. \left\{ \begin{array}{l} \text{(Brackets indicate a} \\ \text{choice is to be made)} \end{array} \right.$$

To illustrate the data division format, suppose we have an inventory record in a master file. The record consists of a stock number, the unit of issue (each and dozen), quantity on hand, cost, and three areas of use (Area 1, Area 2 and Area 3).

The various levels are presented as follows shown in Fig. 21-5.

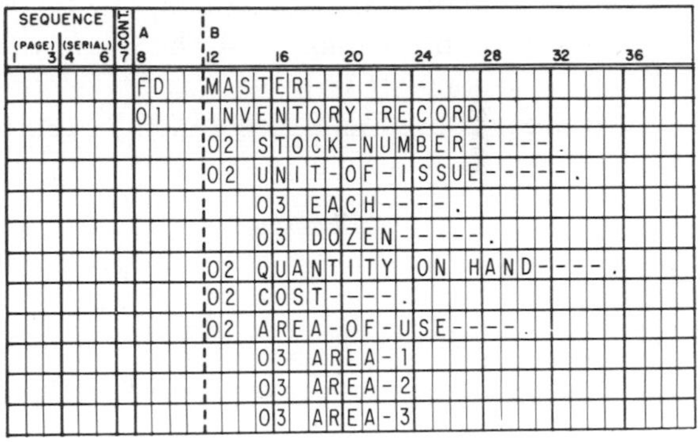

FIG. 21-5

In order to further define the composition of the file, several optional clauses are used. For example:

BLOCK CONTAINS (Integer) RECORD(S)   (Integer must be positive.)
and

or

RECORD CONTAINS (Integer) CHARACTER(S)

The BLOCK clause, while technically classified as optional, is required in the majority of cases. The RECORD clause is never required since the size of the record is completely defined in the record description entry. An example of a RECORD clause is:

RECORD CONTAINS 15 TO 70 CHARACTERS

To illustrate the use of BLOCK and RECORD clauses, suppose we need to describe a TRANSACTION file consisting of fixed 7-record blocks; and each record contains 185 characters. The required sentences are as shown in Fig. 21-6 at the top of page 340.

The record description entry describes in detail the contents of a particular record. That is, it specifies each data field in the record (either by assign-

```
SEQUENCE        A      B
(PAGE) (SERIAL)  8     12    16    20    24    28    32    36    40    44
   3    4   6 7
             D A T A   D I V I S I O N .
             F I L E   S E C T I O N .
             F D   T R A N S A C T I O N .
                   B L O C K   C O N T A I N S   7   R E C O R D S .
                   R E C O R D   C O N T A I N S   1 8 5   C H A R A C T E R S .
```

FIG. 21-6

ing it a name and describing its attributes) or as FILLER (ignoring the data in the positions it represents). Record description entries consist of various levels, where each level is comprised of a level number, a data-name,[5] and independent clauses describing attributes. To illustrate, the PICTURE clause describes the format and the permissible contents of a record field in a general form. It is written as PICTURE IS {Character-string}. Some of the characters used and their functions are given below:

Character	Function
A	Represents a character position which contains either an alphabetic character or a space.
B	Represents the position into which the space character will be inserted.
S	Indicates the presence of an operational sign ($+$ or $-$) and must be the leftmost character in the string.
V	Indicates the location of the assumed decimal point. It may appear only once in a character string.
X	Represents a position which can contain any allowable character from the *computer* character set.
Z	Represents leftmost positions which are to be "zero suppressed," i.e., zeroes replaced by spaces.
9	Represents a position which contains numeric (0–9) characters only.

Examples of PICTURE Clauses are:

PICTURE IS AAAAA	Indicates a 5 position alphabetic field.
PICTURE IS S999V99	Indicates a signed 5 position numeric field with two positions to the right of the decimal point.

[5] The word FILLER is used instead of a data-name if the item described has no assigned name. For example, 04 FILLER SIZE IS 7 would give the 7 desired blank positions in the record.

PICTURE IS ZZZ999   Indicates an unsigned 6 position
                      field, the first three of which are
                      to be "zero suppressed."

Other examples are presented in Fig. 21-7 which follows.

	Picture Is	Characters of the Item	Intepretation	Type	Picture Size	Item Size
1	XXX	BD21	BD21	alphanumeric	4	4
2	99V99	5678	56.78	numeric	5	4
3	S99V99	5678	+56.78	numeric	6	4
4	99999	56789	56789	numeric	5	5
5	A(4)X(5)	INVENTORY	INVENTORY	alphanumeric	10	9

FIG. 21-7

Let's take an illustrative file and construct the associated file section entries. Assume the availability of a file of customer invoice summary records, called INV-SUMMARY. The file is divided into a series of 5-record blocks with 100 characters per record. Assume further the use of standard labels and emphasis upon the first four fields of the record (called INV-SUMMARY-RCD). The fields are:

1. Customer Number—5 positions, one leading alphabetic and 4 numeric characters.
2. Customer Name—20 positions, all alphabetic. Last name—19, Initial—1.
3. Invoice Number—4 positions, all numeric.
4. Amount Field—7 positions, unsigned numeric with a decimal point preceding the rightmost two positions.

They are called, respectively, as follows:

1. CUSTOMER—NBR.
2. CUSTOMER—NAME (LAST NAME—INITIAL).
3. INVOICE—NBR.
4. SUMMARY—INVOICE—AMT.

The file section would appear as follows:

    FILE SECTION.
    FD INV—SUMMARY BLOCK CONTAINS 5 RECORDS
                  LABEL RECORD IS STANDARD.

```
01 INV–SUMMARY–RCD.
    02 CUSTOMER–NBR          PICTURE IS A9999.
    02 CUSTOMER–NAME
        03 LAST NAME         PICTURE IS A(19).
        03 INITIAL           PICTURE IS A.
    02 INVOICE–NBR           PICTURE IS 9999.
    02 SUMMARY–INVOICE–AMT   PICTURE IS 99999V99.
```

The Working-Storage Section.   The working-storage section describes logical records and/or independent data items that are developed and manipulated completely internally. It also describes data items with values assigned in the source program and remains constant throughout the execution of the object program. The two types of data items used are independent and grouped data items.

Independent data items are not members of a larger group and are not further subdivided. Each independent data item is defined in a separate data description entry requiring a level-number of 77.[6] *Grouped* data items maintain a hierarchical relationship to one another. They may have level-numbers from 01 to 10, with the highest level being the 01 level. The data description entries are constructed in the same manner as those for the record description entry in the file section.[7] An example of a group item is:

```
01 HEADER.
    02 FILLER SIZE 14.
    02 STK–NO PICTURE X (13).
    02 FILLER SIZE IS 11.
    02 NAME PICTURE A (14).
    02 FILLER SIZE IS 10.
    02 ADDR PICTURE X (11).
```

Blanks	Stock No.	Blanks	Name	Blanks	Address
(14)	13 alpha–numeric characters	(11)	20 alphanumeric characters	(10)	11 alpha–numeric characters

FIG. 21-8

[6] The 77 begins in Column 8 of the COBOL coding line; the data-name following begins in Column 12. An example of an independent item is: 77 WORK AREA-2. CLASS IS NUMERIC SIZE IS 210.
A 210-character area is set up in storage for processing data or for temporary storage.
[7] The 01 level-number begins in Column 8. The data-name following begins in Column 12. All other level-numbers begin either in Column 12 or may be further indented with each indentation beginning *four* columns in from the previous one.

The defined structure of the working storage section requires that all independent data item descriptions precede the first grouped data item description. A data description entry has the following format:

Level Number 77 (data-name) CLASS
or
PICTURE

In addition to the PICTURE clause, the VALUE clause (which has the general form VALUE IS *literal*) is used in the working-storage section to specify the *initial* value of a data item. The literal value is formed in the following ways:

(a) *Non-numeric Literal:* A string of characters enclosed by quotation marks. The characters may be any one of the *computer's* character set except the quotation mark.

(b) *Numeric Literal:* A string of numeric characters (0–9). The string may contain either a decimal point, a sign, or both, and *is not* enclosed in quotation marks.

Examples of the VALUE clause:

VALUE IS 'YES'	It uses a non-numeric literal with the initial value being Y, E, and S.
VALUE IS + 735.68	It uses a numeric literal with the initial value being the seven positions containing the characters indicated.

A Sample Working-Storage Section

Using as a reference the inventory summary file described in the file section example, suppose we need (1) to accumulate the total of the summary invoice amounts, and (2) accumulate the sum of the invoice numbers as a control total, and place each invoice summary record in a work area so that its contents can be manipulated without destroying the original record. The working-storage section would appear as follows:

```
WORKING–STORAGE SECTION.
77  TOTAL–SUMMARY–INVOICE–AMT        PICTURE IS 999999V99.
    (This is the description of the data item where the sum of the amounts
     will be placed.)
77  CONTROL–TOTAL           PICTURE IS 99999 VALUE IS 00000.
    (This is the field where the sum of invoice numbers will be accumulated.
     Note that it has been initialized to zeroes.)
01  INV–SUMMARY–WORK–RCD.
    02  WORK–CUSTOMER–NBR            PICTURE IS A 9999.
```

02	WORK–CUSTOMER–NAME	
	03 WORK–LAST–NAME	PICTURE IS A (19).
	03 WORK–INITIAL	PICTURE IS A.
02	WORK–INVOICE–NBR	PICTURE IS 9999.
02	WORK–SUMMARY–INVOICE–AMT	PICTURE IS 99999V99.

The Procedure Division

Completely programmer-defined, the procedure division defines the operations which perform the necessary processing of data. Its structure may include sections and paragraphs as well as the necessary sentences and statements. There are three classes of sentences/statements:

1. *Compiler-directing:* causes the compiler to take a specific action during compilation.
2. *Imperative:* initiates the specified action. It gives the computer no alternative course of action. For example:
   a. ADD A TO B.   (ADD is called the *Verb* and A and B are called the *operands*)
   b. SUBTRACT B FROM C.
   c. GO TO END-OF-JOB.
3. *Conditional:* initiates specified action every time a defined condition is met.

The primary components of sentences and statements are COBOL verbs (reserved words which specify action to be taken) and operands. Let's look at representative types of sentences/statements in each class.

The Compiler-Directing Sentence. The compiler-directing sentence with which we are concerned here is the NOTE sentence.[8] It permits the programmer to include commentary in his program coding that will be produced on the compiler listing, but will not be included in the object program. The general form of the sentence is:

NOTE   character string   (NOTE is a COBOL verb)

The character string may be any combination of the computer's character set. If the NOTE sentence is the first sentence of a paragraph, the entire paragraph is considered part of the character string. If it is other than the first, the character string terminates with the first occurrence of a period followed by a space. (A period followed by a space is the method of terminating *any* sentence.) For example:

[8] The ENTER verb is employed to allow various other languages to be used in the COBOL program. The EXIT verb is used to provide a common ending to a PERFORM statement (employed to loop the program), and returns the program to the next sequential sentence after the original PERFORM statement.

NOTE THIS COMMENT WILL APPEAR ONLY ON THE OUTPUT LISTING.

The Imperative Sentences. The imperative sentences and statements considered in this section are represented by the following verbs:

MOVE

DISPLAY

OPEN

CLOSE

GO TO

PERFORM

EXIT

STOP

The MOVE statement transfers data from one defined storage location to another. The storage locations are referenced by the data-names assigned in the data division. The form of the statement is: MOVE data-name TO data-name. An alphabetic data item must not be moved to a numeric data item (as described in the PICTURE clause), or vice versa. Examples are as follows:

MOVE CUSTOMER-NAME TO WORK-CUSTOMER NAME.

MOVE INVOICE-NBR TO SAVE-INVOICE-NBR.

The DISPLAY statement causes low volume data to be transferred to the standard display device used in the computer configuration (usually the console printer). The amount of data moved is limited to the capacity of the display device. The general form is:

$$\text{DISPLAY} \begin{Bmatrix} \text{non-numeric literal} \\ \text{(or)} \\ \text{data-name} \end{Bmatrix}$$

In the case of the non-numeric literal, the character string, enclosed in quotation marks, will follow the DISPLAY verb. In the case of data-name, the contents of the storage location referenced by the data-name will be transferred.

Examples:

DISPLAY 'END OF PROGRAM'.

DISPLAY SUMMARY-INVOICE-AMT.

The OPEN statement conditions a file for processing. It performs checking and/or writing of labels and other necessary preparatory steps. A file may be opened for use as INPUT or as OUTPUT. The OPEN statement for a file must be executed before any READ or WRITE is issued. The general form is:

$$\text{OPEN} \left\{ \begin{array}{c} \text{INPUT} \\ \text{(or)} \\ \text{OUTPUT} \end{array} \right\} \quad \text{(file-name as defined in the file section)}$$

Examples:

OPEN INPUT INV-SUMMARY.
OPEN OUTPUT PRINT-FILE.

The CLOSE statement is used to terminate the processing of a file. The general form is: CLOSE file-name.

Examples:

CLOSE INV-SUMMARY.
CLOSE PRINT-FILE.

The GO TO statement is a transfer of control from one part of the procedure to another. If the GO TO statement appears in an imperative *sentence*, it must be the only statement or the *last* statement in a sequence of imperative statements. The general form is:

$$\text{GO TO} \left\{ \begin{array}{c} \text{paragraph-name} \\ \text{(or)} \\ \text{section-name} \end{array} \right\}$$

The paragraph and section names are programmer-defined and reference specific parts of the Procedure Division.

Examples:

GO TO PAYROLL SECTION.
GO TO CALCULATE-GROSS-PAY.

The PERFORM statement is used to vary the normal sequence of program execution in order to execute one or more paragraphs and/or sections and then return control to the normal sequence. Upon execution of the PERFORM statement control will be transferred to the first statement of the paragraph or section specified. After the last statement of the paragraph or section has been executed, control is transferred automatically to the statement immediately following the PERFORM statement. The general form is:

$$\text{PERFORM} \left\{ \begin{array}{c} \text{paragraph-name} \\ \text{(or)} \\ \text{section-name} \end{array} \right\}$$

Example:

PERFORM CALC-NET-PAY.
GO TO PRINT-CHECK.
CALC-NET-PAY.   Subtract statement.

After the PERFORM statement has been executed, the next statement to be executed is the "subtract statement." Since the subtract statement is the only statement in the paragraph named CALC-NET-PAY, control is returned to the statement GO TO PRINT-CHECK, after its execution.

The STOP statement causes either a temporary or permanent halt in the execution of the object program. The general form is:

$$\text{STOP} \left\{ \begin{array}{c} \text{literal} \\ \text{(or)} \\ \text{RUN} \end{array} \right\}$$

If the RUN option is used, execution of the program will be permanently halted. If the literal option is used, the literal will be communicated to the operator and a temporary halt will occur. Continuation begins with execution of the next sequential statement.

Examples:

> STOP RUN.
>
> STOP 'ERROR.'

Four arithmetic statements are also considered.

> ADD
> SUBTRACT
> MULTIPLY
> DIVIDE

They are self-explanatory, except for the two options: ROUNDED and ON SIZE ERROR. The ROUNDED option specifies that if the number of decimal places in the result of an arithmetic operation exceeds the number of places provided in the PICTURE, the excess characters are dropped and the remaining least significant digit is increased by one if the most significant digit of the excess is greater than or equal to five.

Examples:

> 57.2|67 rounded yields 57.3
>
> 57.2|44 rounded yields 57.2

The SIZE ERROR option specifies that if the value of a result exceeds the largest value in the related data item, the imperative statement associated with the SIZE ERROR will be executed. The general form is: ON SIZE ERROR imperative statement. For example: If a result field is defined as four positions and the actual result is five, a SIZE ERROR occurs and, if the option is included, the imperative statement will be executed. If the SIZE ERROR option is included in an arithmetic statement, it becomes a conditional statement. Otherwise, it is an imperative statement.

Arithmetic statements. The general forms of arithmetic statements are as follows:

$$\text{ADD} \begin{Bmatrix} \text{literal} \\ (\text{or}) \\ \text{data-name} \end{Bmatrix} \begin{Bmatrix} \text{literal} \\ (\text{or}) \\ \text{data-name} \end{Bmatrix} \text{GIVING data-name [ROUNDED]}$$

[ON SIZE ERROR imperative statement.]

$$\text{ADD} \begin{Bmatrix} \text{literal} \\ (\text{or}) \\ \text{data-name} \end{Bmatrix} \text{TO data-name [ROUNDED]}$$

[ON SIZE ERROR imperative statement.]

Examples: 1. ADD A TO B.
2. ADD AREA TO HOLD ROUNDED.
3. ADD AREA, HOLD, BOX GIVING TOTAL ROUNDED; ON SIZE ERROR GO TO ROUTINE-2.

$$\text{SUBTRACT} \begin{Bmatrix} \text{literal} \\ (\text{or}) \\ \text{data-name} \end{Bmatrix} \text{FROM} \begin{Bmatrix} \text{literal} \\ (\text{or}) \\ \text{data-name} \end{Bmatrix} \text{[ROUNDED]}$$

[ON SIZE ERROR imperative statement.]

Examples: 1. SUBTRACT A FROM B.
2. SUBTRACT A FROM B GIVING X ROUNDED.
3. SUBTRACT A FROM B GIVING X ROUNDED; [ON SIZE ERROR imperative statement.]

$$\text{MULTIPLY} \begin{Bmatrix} \text{literal} \\ (\text{or}) \\ \text{data-name} \end{Bmatrix} \text{BY} \begin{Bmatrix} \text{literal} \\ (\text{or}) \\ \text{data-name} \end{Bmatrix} \text{GIVING data-name [ROUNDED]}$$

[ON SIZE ERROR imperative statement.]

Examples: 1. MULTIPLY A BY B.
2. MULTIPLY A BY B GIVING D ROUNDED; ON SIZE ERROR imperative statement.

$$\text{DIVIDE} \begin{Bmatrix} \text{literal} \\ (\text{or}) \\ \text{data-name} \end{Bmatrix} \text{INTO} \begin{Bmatrix} \text{literal} \\ (\text{or}) \\ \text{data-name} \end{Bmatrix} \text{GIVING data-name [ROUNDED]}$$

[ON SIZE ERROR imperative statement.]

Examples: 1. DIVIDE A INTO B GIVING C ROUNDED.
2. DIVIDE A INTO B GIVING C ROUNDED; ON SIZE ERROR imperative statement.

$$\text{DIVIDE} \begin{Bmatrix} \text{literal} \\ (\text{or}) \\ \text{data-name} \end{Bmatrix} \text{BY} \begin{Bmatrix} \text{literal} \\ (\text{or}) \\ \text{data-name} \end{Bmatrix} \text{GIVING data-name [ROUNDED]}$$

[ON SIZE ERROR imperative statement.]

Other examples:

ADD NET-PAY DEDUCTIONS GIVING GROSS-PAY ROUNDED ON SIZE ERROR GO TO CALC-ERROR.
ADD 1 TO COUNT ROUNDED ON SIZE ERROR DISPLAY '99'.

SUBTRACT 155 FROM 273.

MULTIPLY GROSS-PAY BY FIT-PERCENT GIVING WITHHOLD-TAX ROUNDED.

DIVIDE 30.5 INTO SUM-VAL GIVING NEW-SUM ROUNDED ON SIZE ERROR GO TO END-PGM.

DIVIDE INIT-AMT BY FACTOR GIVING RESULT-AMT ON SIZE ERROR STOP RUN.

The Conditional Statement. There are two types of conditional statements:

Type 1. A conditional expression is evaluated. If it is found to be true, the next sequential conditional expression is executed. If it is found to be false, the next statement is bypassed and the computer executes the conditional expression following it. For example:

IF INVENTORY LEVEL IS LESS THAN 10 GO TO REORDER-RUN.

Type 2. It requires the use of OTHERWISE or ELSE condition. The words NEXT SENTENCE are also used if a specific condition requires the computer to go to the next sentence. For example:

IF X IS GREATER THAN 7 NEXT SENTENCE OTHERWISE GO TO RESUPPLY-ROUTINE.

The conditional statements to be examined are represented by the following verbs:

IF

READ

WRITE

The IF statement causes a condition to be evaluated and to initiate actions depending on whether the condition is true or false. The general form is:

IF data-name IS { NOT } $\left\{\begin{array}{l}\text{GREATER THAN} \\ \text{LESS THAN} \\ \text{EQUAL TO}\end{array}\right\}$ $\left\{\begin{array}{l}\text{literal} \\ \text{(or)} \\ \text{data-name}\end{array}\right\}$ imperative statement

The execution of the statement causes the contents of storage referenced by the first data-name to be compared to the literal or the contents of storage referenced by the second data-name. If the comparison indicates that the chosen option is true, the imperative statements will be executed. Otherwise, the next sequential sentence will be executed.

Examples:

1. Assume DATA-ONE contains 01 and DATA-TWO contains 01; and we have the following IF statement:

IF DATA-ONE IS EQUAL TO DATA-TWO GO TO END-PGM.

Since the contents of DATA-ONE and DATA-TWO are equal, the GO TO statement will be executed.

2. Assume DATA-ONE contains 01 and the following coding is present:

IF DATA-ONE IS NOT GREATER THAN 02 DISPLAY 'ERROR'. GO TO END-PGM.

Since DATA-ONE contains 01, it is not greater than the literal 02. Therefore, the DISPLAY statement will be executed followed by the execution of the GO TO sentence.

The READ statement makes available the next logical record from an input file and allows execution of a specified imperative statement when the end of the file is recognized. The general formats are:

1. READ (name of file) RECORD.
2. READ (name of file) RECORD INTO (name of area).
3. READ (name of file) RECORD AT END (any imperative statement).

Examples:

1. READ MASTER RECORD. (A record from the master file is read into the input record area.)
2. READ (name of file) RECORD INTO (name of area—must be working-storage area or output area).
3. READ CARD-REC AT END GO TO END-PGM.[9]
   END-PGM. CLOSE CARD-IN STOP RUN.

   (This sequence of coding means to read the next logical record [named CARD-REC] from the file CARD-IN and, when the end of the file is recognized, execute the CLOSE statement and terminate the program.)

The WRITE statement considered here transfers a logical record to the printer and also performs vertical positioning of the page. The basic format is:

WRITE (record name) FROM (name of area).

Example:

WRITE UP-DETAIL FROM WORK-AREA-4.

[9] In practice, format statement number 3 is used.

When on-line printing is desired, an ADVANCING option is used to allow positioning of the printer tape and skipping between lines. The general format is:

$$\text{WRITE record-name} \left\{ \begin{array}{c} \text{BEFORE} \\ \text{(or)} \\ \text{AFTER} \end{array} \right\} ^{10} \text{ADVANCING (integer or data-name) LINES.}$$

The ADVANCING option allows spacing the printer the desired number of lines (the value of "integer") either before or after the logical record has been printed.

Examples:

1. WRITE CARD-REC BEFORE ADVANCING 2 LINES.
   (In this case, the record named CARD-REC will be printed followed by spacing the printer two lines.)
2. WRITE CARD-REC AFTER ADVANCING 5 LINES.
   (In this case, the printer will be spaced five lines followed by printing the logical record.)

Glossary of Terms

COBOL: Common Business Oriented Language; a procedural language developed for business data processing. The language is intended as a means for direct presentation of a business program to a computer with a suitable compiler.

COBOL DATA DIVISION: Describes the data to be processed by the object program. It contains primarily a file section which describes the file(s) used and a working-storage section which reserves memory space for storage of results.

COBOL ENVIRONMENT DIVISION: Describes the physical characteristics of the equipment being used and the aspects of the problems which are dependent on the program. Its two main sections are the configuration and the input/output sections.

COBOL IDENTIFICATION DIVISION: Identifies the name of the programmer, the title of the COBOL program, and the compiler listing associated with it.

COBOL LANGUAGE: Is made up of English-language statements which provide a relatively machine-independent method of expressing a business-oriented problem to the computer.

COBOL PROCEDURE DIVISION: Programmer-defined, it defines the operations which perform the necessary processing of data. Its structure includes sections and paragraphs as well as conditional, imperative, and compiler-directing classes of sentences/statements.

COBOL WORD: Also called "reserve word," it holds a preassigned meaning in COBOL to be used in its prescribed context.

Questions for Review

1. List in sequential order the four divisions of COBOL.
2. What are the primary sections of the environment division?
3. Write a valid expression to check if the data in AREA-4 is negative and to go to a SPECIAL-ROUTINE if it is positive.

[10] The choice depends on the requirements of the computer system in use.

4. Flow chart and code a program to compare X to Y. If X is greater than Y, the program is to go to ROUTINE-6. Otherwise, it should go to ROUTINE-4.

5. Flow chart and code a program to do the following:

IF	THEN
A is greater than B and A is greater than C	Add B to C and go to sub-routine-7
B is greater than A and B is gerater than C	Add A to C and go to sub-routine-2
B is greater than A but less than C	Subtract A from B and go to subroutine-1

6. Simplify the following statement:

   IF A>10 and if A<14, subtract A-X. If A<10 and if A>14, go to WORK-ROUTINE.

7. Write a valid COBOL sentence to solve the formula AREA $= \dfrac{A+B}{2}$.

   Assume that A, B, and AREA are predefined and are 4 characters each.

8. What is the meaning of the following PICTURE characters?

   X, V, 9, S, A

PL/1 CONCEPTS

The STOP Statement

PUT SKIP LIST Statement

The GET LIST Statement

The GO TO Statement

The DO and END Statements

PICTURE Specification

354

The preceding two chapters introduced a programming language designed to simplify the preparation of mathematically-oriented problems (FORTRAN) and a programming language designed to simplify the preparation of business-oriented problems (COBOL). This chapter presents the overview of a general purpose Programming Language/1 or PL/1.

As the name implies, PL/1 was developed as a general purpose programming language applicable to mathematical, commercial, real-time, and other common types of applications. It combines the desirable features of specialized languages (essentially, FORTRAN and COBOL) with extended capabilities. It has yet to be determined, however, whether PL/1 will receive widespread acceptance, since it is still subject to modifications. The speculation by some authorities of PL/1 becoming "the language of the future" justifies a brief presentation of its concepts.

BASIC CONCEPTS AND STRUCTURE OF THE PL/1 LANGUAGE

PL/1 is basically a highly permissive programming language, offering the programmer many options and freedom in constructing a PL/1 program. The language itself is statement-structured. Much like COBOL, a PL/1 *statement* is comparable to an English language sentence. Every PL/1 instruction falls into one of the following eight general classes of statements:

Assignment. Statements which are the most basic. They perform arithmetic calculations, logical operations, and assign values to the appropriate identifier(s). For example:

VALUE = UNITS * PRICE
identifiers

Control. Statements which control either the conditional execution or alter the normal execution of statements.

Data Declaration. Statements which specify the kind of value representation of a given variable.

Error Control and Debugging. Statements which direct the handling of, initiate, or simulate interrupt conditions.

Input/Output. Statements which request the data transfer between the computer and input/output devices.

Program Structure. Statements which specify the relationship among multiple program segments.

Storage Allocation. Statements which facilitate the efficient use of primary storage.

Asynchronous Operations Control. Statements which provide control for parallel processing and real-time applications.

COMPONENTS OF A PL/1 STATEMENT

The PL/1 statement is constructed by combining *identifiers, constants,* and *delimiters.* Identifiers and constants may be intermediately grouped into *expressions.*

An *identifier* is a string of alphanumeric and break characters (the break character is represented by the underscore symbol and is equivalent to the hyphen in COBOL). It must begin with a letter;[1] it cannot contain blanks, and must not exceed 31 characters.

There are two types of identifiers:

(a) *Programmer-defined identifiers* are words or letters arbitrarily chosen by the programmer to represent quantities. For example: A, JOHN, BOY 4, $ MONEY, B707.

(b) *PL/1 defined keywords* are those which have a fixed meaning in the language. The concept is similar to that of "reserved words" in COBOL, except that in PL/1 the keywords are not reserved. Keywords are recognizable by their string of characters *and* their position in a statement. Since it is permissible for a programmer-defined identifier to duplicate a keyword, the keyword is recognized by its position. PL/1 keywords are listed in Fig. 22-1.

A *constant* is a self-defining name. That is, the name of the data item is also its value. It may also be called a literal.

A *delimiter* specifies an elementary action, such as an arithmetic operation and/or provides punctuation. PL/1 delimiters are listed in Fig. 22-2.

The expression is a sequence of constants and identifiers, separated by operators and parentheses, which describe a rule for calculating a value.

---

[1] $, @, and # are recognized as letters in PL/1.

FIG. 22-1

PL/Keywords

(Permissible abbreviations are in Parentheses)

Statement Identifiers

ALLOCATE	DO	IF	REVERT
BEGIN	END	LOCATE	REWRITE
CALL	ENTRY	ON	SIGNAL
CLOSE	EXIT	OPEN	STOP
DECLARE (DCL)	FORMAT	PROCEDURE (PROC)	UNLOCK
DELAY	FREE	PUT	WRITE
DELETE	GET	READ	
DISPLAY	GO TO	RETURN	

General Statement Options

Statement type		Options
DO	ON	MAIN, OPTIONS, RECURSIVE
Assignment	ON and PROCEDURE	PRIORITY
IF	CALL	REPLY
CALL, DISPLAY, and I/O	BY, TO, WHILE	SNAP
ALLOCATE and I/O	BY NAME	SYSTEM
PROCEDURE	ELSE, THEN	TASK
CALL and I/O	EVENT	
DISPLAY	IN, SET	

I/O Statement Options

COLUMN	FROM	KEYFROM	NO LOCK	TITLE
COPY	IDENT	KEY TO	PAGE	
DATA	IGNORE	LINE	PAGESIZE	
EDIT	INTO	LINESIZE	SKIP	
FILE	KEY	LIST	STRING	

Data-type Attributes

AREA	COMPLEX (CPLX)	FIXED	REAL
BINARY (BIN)	DECIMAL (DEC)	FLOAT	TASK
BIT	ENTRY	LABEL	
CELL	EVENT	PICTURE (PIC)	
CHARACTER (CHAR)	FILE	POINTER (PTR)	

Secondary Attributes

ABNORMAL (ABNL)	ENVIRONMENT (ENV)	NORMAL	SET
ALIGNED	EXCLUSIVE	OUTPUT	STATIC
AUTOMATIC (AUTO)	EXTERNAL (EXT)	PACKED	STREAM
BACKWARDS	GENERIC	POSITION (POS)	UPDATE
BUFFERED	INITIAL (INIT)	PRINT	USES
BUILTIN	INPUT	RECORD	VARYING (VAR)
CONTROLLED (CTL)	INTERNAL (INT)	RETURNS	
DEFINED (DEF)	KEYED	SECONDARY	
DIRECT	LIKE	SEQUENTIAL	

Condition Keywords

AREA	FINISH	SIZE
CHECK	FIXEDOVERFLOW (FOFL)	TRANSMIT
CONDITION	KEY	UNDEFINEDFILE (UNDF)
CONVERSION (CONV)	NAME	UNDERFLOW (UFL)
ENDFILE	OVERFLOW (OFL)	ZERODIVIDE (ZDIV)
ENDPAGE	RECORD	
ERROR	SUBSCRIPTRANGE (SUBRG)	

Symbol	Definition
Arithmetic Operators	
+	addition, plus prefix
-	subtraction, minus prefix
*	multiplication
/	division
Comparison operators	
>	greater than
> =	greater than or equal to
=	equal to
| =	not equal to
< =	less than or equal to
<	less than
String Operators	
||	concatenation
|	negation
&	and
|	or
Separators and Other delimiters	
,	separates elements of a list
;	terminates statements
=	assignment symbol
:	terminates labels and condition prefixes
blank (b)	general separator
' (or")	encloses a string constants
.	separates items in qualified names
->	separates a pointer variable from the name so qualified
/*	indicates beginning of a comment
*/	indicates end of a comment
Grouping Characters	
,	comma
'	apostrophe
:	colon
;	semicolon
( )	parenthesis
Alphabetic Characters	
Capital letters of the alphabet (A-Z)	
Special Characters	
%	per cent
#	number
$	dollar
@	at cost
?	question
_	break

FIG. 22-2

BASIC CONCEPTS AND STRUCTURE OF A PL/1 PROGRAM

The coding of a PL/1 program is essentially a free-form affair. That is, the language demands very little in the way of structure. The only requirement is that PL/1 statements be grouped into blocks. Thus, a program may consist of one or more blocks at the discretion of the programmer.

Expressions in PL/1 are formed in a manner almost identical to those of FORTRAN. The basic arithmetic operators for addition, subtraction, multiplication, division, and exponentiation have the same symbols and priority of execution. Briefly, operations in a PL/1 language involve scanning each expression from left to right and performing them in the following order of priority.

1. All exponentiations.
2. All multiplications and/or divisions.
3. All additions and/or subtractions.

For example, in the expression:

$$X + Y + A ** 1 + C * 2$$

the two quantities involved in the first operation are A and 1.

In grouping quantities, parentheses are used and the computation of the values they contain are performed before any other operation in the expression. Furthermore, within the parenthesis, the same order of priorities of operating applies.

Assignment Statement

The assignment statement of PL/1 is also quite similar to the FORTRAN assignment statement. The expression on the right of the equal sign is evaluated and assigned to the variable on the left. However, where FORTRAN limits the left side of the statement to a single variable, PL/1 allows multiple variable names, separated by commas. The result of such a statement is that each of the left side variables is assigned the value of expression on the right side. For example: Assume an assignment statement as follows:

$$A, B, C = X + Y * Z,$$

where $X = 2$, $Y = 3$, and $Z = 4$. Evaluation of the expression would yield $2 + (3*4)$ or 14. In PL/1, then, A, B, and C would each be assigned the value 14.

The PROCEDURE Block

The required block, called the *external procedure-block*, provides the link which allows the operating system to initiate execution of the object program. The PROCEDURE block is headed by an identifier, a colon, and the capitalized word PROCEDURE, followed by the words OPTIONS and (MAIN), in parentheses. The PROCEDURE block is terminated by the word END and the same identifier that heads the block. Each statement must be terminated by a semicolon(;). For example:

VALUE: PROCEDURE OPTIONS (MAIN);

END VALUE;

Within the external procedure, two types of optional blocks may be included.

Internal Procedure Blocks. Similar to the External Procedure, they begin with a PROCEDURE statement and terminate with an END statement. An Internal Procedure is executed only when control is explicitly transferred to it by another statement. Otherwise (i.e., in the sequential flow of the program), all Internal Procedures are bypassed.

Begin Blocks. They begin with a BEGIN statement and terminate with an END statement. A Begin Block is executed as a part of the normal flow of the program, and need not be specifically entered from another statement.

The DECLARE Statement

In PL/1 programming, the DECLARE statement is used in deciding on the form of treating numeric quantities. One form of a DECLARE statement is:

DECLARE (identifier, – – – – –, identifier) FLOAT;

Relating to the example used in the PROCEDURE statement, we have:

DECLARE (UNITS, PRICE) FLOAT;

Note that all identifiers should be parenthesized after the word DECLARE and followed by the word FLOAT. The word FLOAT indicates the manner in which the identifiers will be used. Combining the statements presented thus far, the program consists of the following:

VALUE : PROCEDURE OPTIONS (MAIN);
DECLARE (UNITS, PRICE) FLOAT;

VALUE = UNITS ° PRICE;

END VALUE;

Like any other program, the computer must be instructed to stop the program upon the execution of all its instructions. The PL/1 STOP statement takes the form:

STOP;

indicating the last instruction to be executed by the computer. The STOP statement is placed preceding the END statement.

PUT SKIP LIST Statement

Each program must have an output statement to printout results of any computations requested in the program. One form of output statement is the PUT SKIP LIST statement which permits a printout of all the values of the identifiers listed in the PUT SKIP LIST statement. For example:

PUT SKIP LIST (UNITS, PRICE, VALUE);

Here, three values are printed. The value of the UNITS identifier appears first on the printed page, followed by the value of the PRICE identifier, and finally by the value of the VALUE identifier. When the values of UNITS and PRICE are given, two assignment statements are added. For example:

$$UNITS = 17$$
$$PRICE = 5$$

The program thus far would look as follows:

```
VALUE: PROCEDURE OPTIONS (MAIN);
DECLARE (UNITS, PRICE) FLOAT;
UNITS = 17;
PRICE = 5;
VALUE = UNITS * PRICE;
PUT SKIP LIST (UNITS, PRICE, VALUE);
STOP;
END VALUE;
```

The GET LIST Statement

While this program is considered complete (in so far as calculating the value of the units sold), a more effective way of providing data values to the computer is made through the use of the input statement GET LIST (list);

The GET LIST statement consists of a number of identifiers, the values of which are read from a data list (into the computer) every time the statement is executed. The amounts making up the data list are separated by commas. In our example, we have a data list consisting of:

UNITS = 17   and   PRICE = 5

Rather than inserting these assignment statements into the program, we substitute the GET LIST statement as follows:

GET LIST (UNITS, PRICE);

The program would be as follows:

```
VALUE: PROCEDURE OPTIONS (MAIN);
DECLARE (UNITS, PRICE) FLOAT;
GET LIST (UNITS, PRICE);
VALUE = UNITS * PRICE;
PUT SKIP LIST (UNITS, PRICE, VALUE);
STOP;
END VALUE;
```

The flow chart for the program (usually done before coding), is shown in Fig. 22-3.

The GO TO Statement

Most programs include instructions which allow flexibility and versatility. The preceding program is limited, in that it inputs, processes, and outputs only one data item. Flexibility can be made possible by using a branching instruction to handle many data items consecutively or to alter the program flow so that certain out-of-sequence segments of the program can be separately or repeatedly executed.

    The GO TO statement (a control statement) is an unconditional branching statement which consists of the words GO TO, followed by a label. For example:

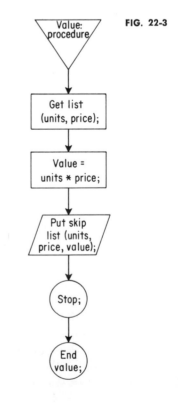

FIG. 22-3

GO TO START;   (a label)

This statement tells the computer to go to the first statement with the label START. For example:

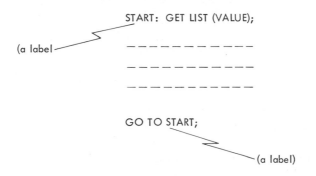

After executing the GO TO START; statement, the computer goes to the statement GET LIST (VALUE).

Thus, a statement label is an identifier (followed by a colon) written as a prefix to a statement for reference purposes. Any word can be used as a label, but no two statements may have the same label.

If we wish to input, process, and output many data items, we add an arbitrary label START to the input statement GET LIST (UNITS, PRICE); and the GO TO START; statement (inserted preceding the STOP; statement). The program becomes:

```
VALUE: PROCEDURE OPTIONS (MAIN);
DECLARE (UNITS, PRICE) FLOAT;
START: GET LIST (UNITS, PRICE);
VALUE = UNITS * PRICE;
PUT SKIP LIST (UNITS, PRICE, VALUE);
GO TO START;
STOP;
END VALUE;
```

It can be observed that the program, when executed, will go into a continuous loop without termination. To solve this problem, conditional branching statements called IF THEN and ELSE statements are used.

The computer can be instructed to choose between two alternative courses of action by the use of the THEN and ELSE statements. The word IF denotes that the statement involves a decision to be made. The word THEN tells the computer to execute the statement following, if the condition is true. The word ELSE tells the computer to execute the statement following, if the condition is false. For example:

Decision element	Condition 1 is true	A decision to execute	Statement

| IF | The Units exceed 100 | THEN | stop operation; |

	Otherwise execute		Statement

| | ELSE | | compute value; |

In other words, the computer is asked to test the condition following the word IF and, if the units exceed 100, execute the statement "stop operation." However, if the condition following the word IF (units exceed 100) is false, execute the statement following ELSE.

Using the IF THEN and ELSE statements in our program, it becomes:

```
VALUE: PROCEDURE OPTIONS (MAIN);
DECLARE (UNITS, PRICE) FLOAT;
START: GET LIST (UNITS, PRICE);
IF UNITS > 100
THEN STOP;
ELSE VALUE = UNITS * PRICE;
PUT SKIP LIST (UNITS, PRICE, VALUE);
GO TO START;
STOP;
END VALUE;
```

The DO and END Statements

In the PL/1 language, the programmer is permitted to group several statements for control purposes by using the DO and END statements. They take the form of:

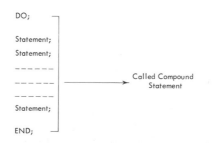

It is common for the programmer to use the DO and END compound statement to replace the IF THEN and ELSE statements in either their true or false branching. For example, see the format, top left of next page.

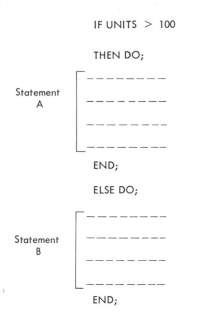

```
        IF UNITS > 100

            THEN DO;
                ┌─ ─ ─ ─ ─ ─ ─
Statement       │ ─ ─ ─ ─ ─ ─ ─
    A           │ ─ ─ ─ ─ ─ ─ ─
                └─ ─ ─ ─ ─ ─ ─
            END;

            ELSE DO;
                ┌─ ─ ─ ─ ─ ─ ─
Statement       │ ─ ─ ─ ─ ─ ─ ─
    B           │ ─ ─ ─ ─ ─ ─ ─
                └─ ─ ─ ─ ─ ─ ─
            END;
```

Based on this format, if the units exceeded 100, then the THEN DO set of statements will be executed. Otherwise, the computer executes the ELSE DO set of statements. The computer, in this case, treats the DO and END statements in either A or B group as a single statement.

PICTURE Specification

PICTURE Specification is a statement borrowed from COBOL, but not extensively used in PL/1. The general form is: PICTURE 'specification'; having a function similar to that in COBOL.

The PL/1 language is considerably more extensive and provides more inherent capabilities than either FORTRAN or COBOL, and includes many more options. Because of the extensive availability of options in statement construction, PL/1 is potentially much more powerful than FORTRAN or COBOL. However, the efficient use of the numerous options requires a skilled programmer.

Glossary of Terms

PL/1: Programming Language/1 is a new language with certain features similar to FORTRAN and some of the best features of other languages. It makes use of recent developments in computer technology and offers the programmer a relatively flexible problem-oriented language for programming problems which can best be worked out by using a combination of scientific and business compiling techniques.

PL/1 DECLARE STATEMENT: Is used in deciding on the form of treating numeric quantities.

PL/1 DELIMITER: Specifies an elementary action such as an arithmetic operation and/or provides punctuation.

PL/1 EXPRESSION: Is a sequence of constants and identifiers, separated by operators and parentheses, which describes a rule for calculating a value.

PL/1 GET LIST STATEMENT: Provides data values to the computer.

PL/1 GO TO STATEMENT: An unconditional branching statement which tells the computer to go directly to a statement with a specific label.

PL/1 IDENTIFIER: Is a string of alphanumeric and break characters. It begins with a letter, it cannot contain blanks, and must not exceed 31 characters.

PL/1 PROCEDURE BLOCK: Provides the link which allows the operating system to initiate execution of the object program. It begins with a PROCEDURE statement and terminates with an END statement.

PL/1 PUT SKIP LIST STATEMENT: Permits a printout of all the values of the identifiers in it.

Questions for Review

1. What are the primary features of the PL/1 language? How is it similar to FORTRAN and COBOL?
2. Explain the components of the PL/1 statement.
3. What is the difference between a programmer-defined identifier and a PL/1 defined keyword?
4. How are PL/1 expressions formed?
5. List the order of priority of executing a PL/1 expression.
6. What is an assignment statement? Give an example.
7. Explain the difference between an external and an internal procedure block.
8. For what purpose is a DECLARE statement used? Illustrate by giving an example.
9. Explain the PUT SKIP LIST and GET LIST statements. Give an example to illustrate their function.
10. Distinguish the difference between the GO TO and the IF THEN and ELSE statements.
11. When is a DO statement used? Give an example to illustrate its function.
12. Write the following statements in PL/1 notation. Use capital letters to represent identifiers:

    a. $x + y + z$ e. $X = a + b + c$
    b. $a + b + 4$ f. $a = int.$
    c. $a/X + B/y$ g. Value equals units times price.
    d. $X = 5y$ h. $xa + yb + zc$

13. Write the following statements in PL/1 notation:

    a. 3^2 d. 7^3
    b. 2^3 e. 3.2^3
    c. 2^2 f. 4.7^2

14. In each of the following statements, which quantities are handled in the first operation?

    a. $X+Y**4+Z*6+4$
    b. $X*Y+Z**6$

15. We wish to find the VALUE of a given item. Use the identifiers UNITS and PRICE in completing and coding the following flow chart. Assume that UNITS=41 and PRICE=10.

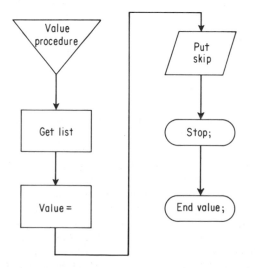

16. Correct the following statements:
    a. GO TO BED
    b. START:GET, LIST(COOKS)
    c. RETURN:
    d. X=(A+B) (C+D)
    e. I FX=10 THEN F=A:

17. Flowchart and code a program to convert bundles into dozens (10 dozens to a bundle) and units. Produce an output in 3 separate columns. Assume that the number of bundles to be converted ranges from 1 to 27.

chapter twenty-three

SYSTEMS ANALYSIS AND PROCEDURE

STEPS INVOLVED IN SOLVING A BUSINESS PROBLEM

The Manual System
The Punched Card Method
The Computer Method

THE ROLE OF MANAGEMENT SCIENCE
IN THE SYSTEMS FUNCTION

FOR A LONG TIME, LARGE COMPANIES HAVE EMPLOYED EXPERTS to study the efficiency of the methods and procedures used in their daily activities. You probably have heard of the efficiency expert, characteristically pictured with a stop watch in his hand. His primary duty is to measure the time required to perform given tasks, examine the flow of work from one employee to another, and analyze or evaluate the required number of finished items per day. His analysis and observations help him to devise a plan showing the number of employees required, their responsibilities, and the equipment they must have to meet the planned output.

Modern business organizations do not consider efficiency the only variable in analyzing or revising a system or a procedure. The interdependence of relationships among departments in most organizations makes it necessary to consider the effects of analysis of a given procedure on the various departments involved. Business organizations employ a systems analyst to undertake the task of analysis and design of systems. Historically, he treated the system or procedure in isolation and was concerned solely with maximizing the system's efficiency and economy of its operation. The steady increase of interdependence among departments expanded his scope and today it is critical that he handles a project with the *total systems concept* in mind.

Operationally, the term "systems" implies the logical overall approach or method that is used to carry out a program to its ultimate conclusion. In a more complex system, it often becomes necessary to break the system into segments for ease of handling, and also to outline and check each step so that all possible deviations may be recognized and evaluated for incorporation into the system.

The systems analyst (or systems engineer) is the focal point in the overall system concept. He is the one in charge of directing the "task force" designated to develop the necessary means for attaining a given end result.

He insures that his company's systems are kept at maximum efficiency through the employment of the latest management techniques and data processing equipment. Management techniques such as PERT (a specialized way of keeping management informed of the progress of large-scale projects) give information for making better decisions and allowing executives to offer better services at less cost. The systems analyst constantly must examine new techniques to see if, through their utilization, he can design a better system for his firm.

A systems analyst fills the gap between input and output and should be ready to optimize the system once the program is established and operates satisfactorily. Although complete knowledge of all the hardware is not necessary, he must be able to distinguish between the various types of requirements, and must know the capabilities of the equipment involved. He also must be prepared to evaluate cost differential and to assume responsibility for incorporating the system as an integral unit into the business. It is his business to make sure that the record keeping and paperwork of a business meet the desired specifications smoothly and efficiently.

Given his awareness of the total system, the systems analyst's continued job of attaining systems efficiency is important. The dynamic nature of a business firm requires periodic adjustment in the system. As a company grows, its needs and its structure change, often making current procedures inefficient and costly to operate. Suppose, for instance, Department A of a given firm forwards to Department B a complex weekly report which has taken forty hours to prepare. In the event the company later decides to shift certain functions from Department B to the main office, Department A's report may provide more details than necessary. If this has gone unnoticed, inefficiency results. The systems analyst occupies a helpful role by instituting new procedures, at the time of the change.

In the past, the systems analyst dealt with machine operators and their key-driven devices. He thought of reports and procedures passing from person-to-person and department-to-department. This thinking pattern has gradually changed to the present concept of evaluating the increasingly larger segments of the total business. In his attempt to integrate man's superior ability to reason with a machine's superior speed and accuracy, the analyst must justify the need for current reports, integrate individual steps into fewer ones, and relieve as many people as possible of routine duties so they can devote more time to creative work.

STEPS INVOLVED IN SOLVING A BUSINESS PROBLEM

The advent of data processing equipment shifted much of the routine work from the hands of people to the data processing machines. Beyond the basic decision making stage lies the field of operations research and scientific management. Computers today have taken over much of the work considered critical by executives. This work includes establishing safe stock levels, product mix for maximum profitability, and optimum shipping and distribution patterns. Computers also have proved an aid in displaying true operating conditions to management, improving the present business system in general, and guiding that business in a way approved by top management.

This evolution made it necessary to design new business systems with the idea of unifying all the factors involved for attaining the desired business goals set by management and for making use of the capabilities of the available data-processing equipment. In order to do this, a systems planner should take into account the three chief phases of *systems study and design, implementation,* and *operation.*

Before the analyst performs various primary tasks he checks on the fulfillment of certain preliminary steps.

1. Formal acceptance of a systems study by top management.
2. Determination of the needs, objectives, and goals of the systems function.
3. A preliminary study to determine the feasibility of the goals and objectives, followed by organization and staffing of a study team to pursue the project.

Study and design of a new system involves primarily a clear and thorough understanding of the present business system. In other words, information on what is being done can be used as a guide to a more realistic and accurate understanding of the business firm under study.

Once knowledge has been acquired regarding the present system, the next logical matter to be considered is determining the requirements of the system under study. This step actually is a transition between understanding the present system and designing a new one. Present facts about the existing system are used in conjunction with a projection of future needs of the business through a new system. The systems analyst defines the problem of future goals, makes necessary modifications on present functions, analyzes, and determines measures of effectiveness for each element involved.

The last stage of systems study and design involves a critical review of the alternative designs and equipment selection made earlier in the study, leading to the development of the design which would best serve the purpose. Once systems study and design is completed, the remaining phases (implementation and operation) follow. As soon as the new system has been determined and designed, implementation and operation of the new system are conducted to check and test the effectiveness of the new system. This involves implementation costs and economic analysis of the new system as compared with the present one. Other factors such as programming, physical planning, conversion and systems testing, and personnel responsibilities and relationships as a result of the new system are also considered. Related discussion on systems study and design, implementation, and operation is presented in the next chapter.

The Manual System

A business organization employing systems analysts would have a set of rules or a series of steps for preparing the flow of business applications. There must be a way of stating the procedure by which each department receives, processes, and distributes its paperwork.

In a *manual system,* a basic list of instructions will suffice. An insurance company might keep policyholder information in file drawers, arranged alphabetically by the policyholder's last name. Periodically, the folders are pulled from the files, perhaps to make a change or to process a claim. Whatever the case, a specific department may request a certain folder by sending a slip of paper containing the policyholder's name to the filing division. When a number of these requests has been received, a file clerk pulls the folders and sends them to the departments concerned. This is a relatively simple problem. A systems analyst might make out a list of instructions for the file clerk, so that when a new person is hired or temporary help is needed, the duties and procedures of the job will be readily apparent. The list might include:

1. All requests to be made on a special form containing policyholder's name and name of the requesting party. The form then is sent to the filing division to be placed on the clerk's desk.
2. The file clerk accumulates a minimum number of requests (for example, five).
3. When five or more requests have been accumulated, the clerk sorts them manually into alphabetical sequence.
4. The file clerk pulls the desired folders from the file.
5. The form requesting each policyholder folder is attached to the proper folder; the name of the requesting department is encircled; and the folder is placed in the "out" box for delivery. The clerk at this time maintains a record of each folder that leaves the file.
6. Folders in the "out" box should be picked up by a mail clerk once every hour. The clerk also brings back (to the box) any folders which have been used.
7. When at least five folders have been accumulated in the box, the file clerk places them in the file and removes the note indicating that the folder had been removed.

Instead of preparing a list of instructions, the analyst might produce a rather general chart, called a "systems-description" chart. For the operation just described, the chart would be similar to the one shown in Figs. 23-1 and 23-2. When the chart is being prepared, the systems analyst considers the waste in time if the file clerk has to seek a folder each time a request comes in, and decides it would be more efficient to have the job done whenever five or more requests have been accumulated. He knows that it will speed up the process by placing the requests in alphabetical sequence before the folders are pulled from the file. Knowledge about the frequency of intracompany mail pickup and delivery further helps to systematize this routine. These and other related points had to be thought out before an efficient and effective system could be devised.

The Punched Card Method

In a *punched card system*, the instructions normally are more complicated than in a manual method. The analyst lays out the process by developing a systems flow chart. Systems flow charts are maps that show the processing procedure. Special symbols represent machines and processes involved in a punched card installation (Fig. 23-3).

Assume that the insurance company mentioned earlier has its policyholder information on punched cards, rather than in folders. A systems flow chart would have to be drawn up to guide the tabulating (punched card) department to the cards in its files. The "file clerk" is a machine operator and the original cards in the file are not kept in the department. To send out the desired information, a report is prepared to show all the proper information. Since original data are kept in the tabulating department (on punched cards), there is no need to keep a record of the "out" folders.

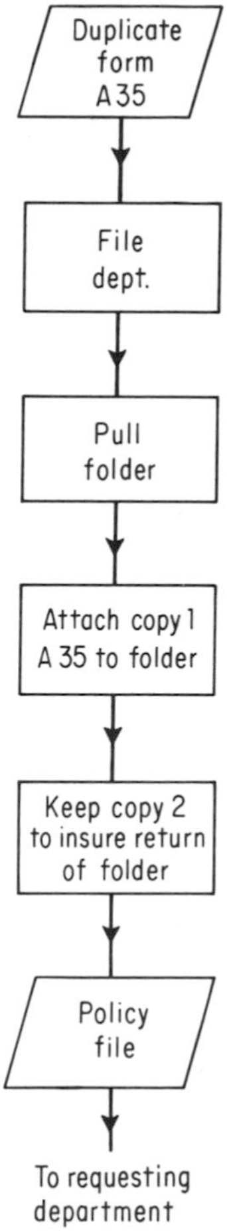

In a more complete routine, a special request form (punched card) can be prepared, whereby the requesting party fills in the policyholder's name, policy number, and other related information. When the form is received by the data processing department, it is keypunched and later used to extract the corresponding information from the policy file. The policy number is considered important because (1) it is easier to work with a short number, rather than a relatively long name; and (2) name similarities cease to be a problem; and (3) it is faster for a machine to manipulate numeric, rather than alphabetic, information. Under the manual system, if Department A had requested a particular policy also needed by Department B, B would have to wait until A was finished and had returned the folder to the filing department. With the punched-card system, Department B would wait only until the original

Flowchart (left):
Duplicate form A35 → File dept. → Pull folder → Attach copy 1 A35 to folder → Keep copy 2 to insure return of folder → Policy file → To requesting department

FIG. 23-1 System description—request for policyholder file

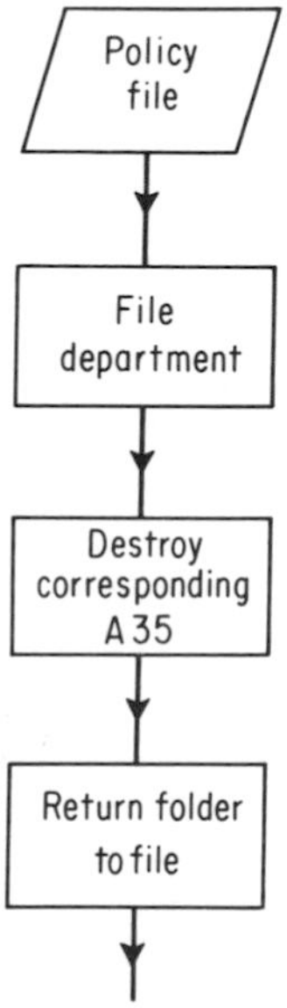

Flowchart (right):
Policy file → File department → Destroy corresponding A35 → Return folder to file

FIG. 23-2 System description — return of policyholder file

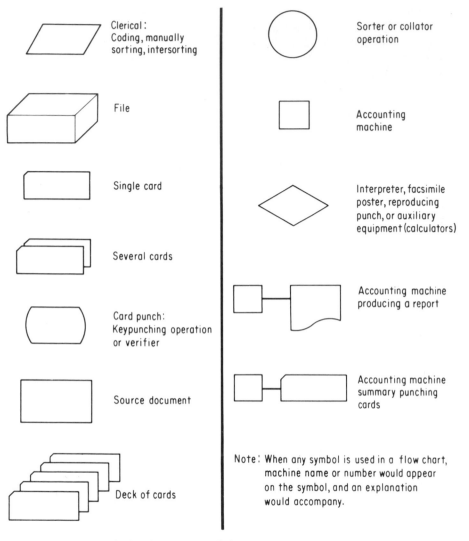

FIG. 23-3 Punched-card flow chart symbols

punched cards are returned to the file, at which time a report is prepared and promptly sent out (Fig. 23-4).

The Computer Method

As in the punched card system, the use of flow charts is equally desirable in a *computer system*. Two levels of flow charts are considered: (1) a systems flow chart, used to show the flow of paper (cards and reports) through the system. (2) A program flow chart, containing details of the central processor program (see Chapter 18 for pertinent description). The program flow chart

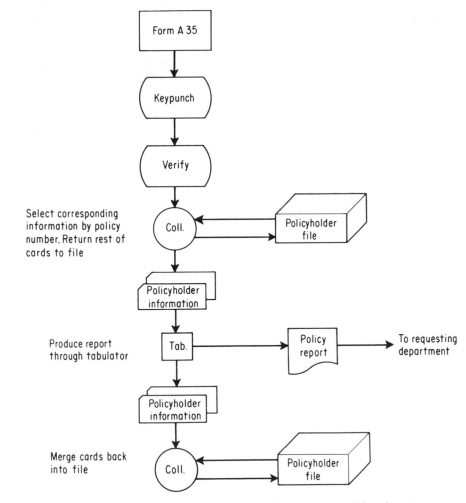

FIG. 23-4 Request for policyholder information

is used by the programmer to prepare the coding for the computer program. The symbols for both levels of flow-charting are shown in Fig. 23-5.

To illustrate the use of flow charts in a computer system, consider the same problem of requesting information about insurance policies. Assume that the company has grown considerably and that the main office (where all of the policy files are kept) is surrounded by several smaller offices. The offices demand immediate access to policy information whenever needed, so a computer system has been installed with a direct (random) access storage device and a data communications link between each small office and the main office.

Under this setup, all policy information is maintained on the direct-access device. When an office wishes to have information concerning a certain policy, an operator types the policy number, the policyholder's name, and the number of the requesting office into the Teletype. If the main office com-

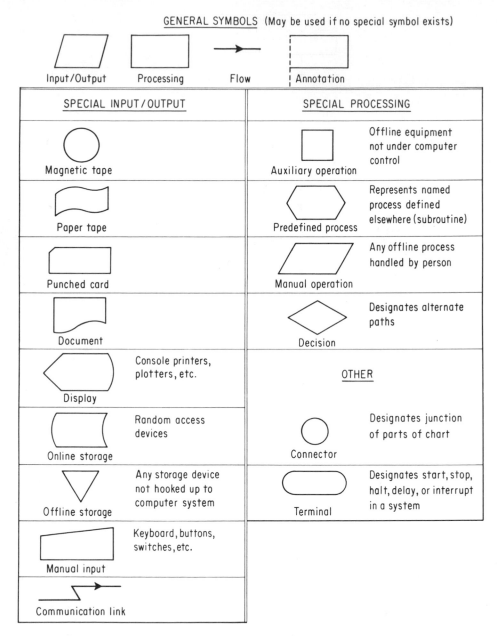

GENERAL SYMBOLS (May be used if no special symbol exists)

| Input/Output | Processing | Flow | Annotation |

SPECIAL INPUT/OUTPUT	SPECIAL PROCESSING
Magnetic tape	Auxiliary operation — Offline equipment not under computer control
Paper tape	Predefined process — Represents named process defined elsewhere (subroutine)
Punched card	Manual operation — Any offline process handled by person
Document	Decision — Designates alternate paths
Display — Console printers, plotters, etc.	OTHER
Online storage — Random access devices	Connector — Designates junction of parts of chart
Offline storage — Any storage device not hooked up to computer system	Terminal — Designates start, stop, halt, delay, or interrupt in a system
Manual input — Keyboard, buttons, switches, etc.	
Communication link	

FIG. 23-5 Standard flow chart symbols

puter is not answering another request, an immediate hookup will take place. The information is sent via telephone wires to the main office, where it is received by the computer. The policy number is searched on the direct-access device and the information is sent back to the requesting office via Teletype (Fig. 23-6). Original records on the direct-access equipment are never removed, not even for a short period. Requests do not have to be accumulated to attain maximum efficiency; to the contrary, such an accumulation of requests would slow down the operation. Requests are answered within minutes or a fraction thereof.

The foregoing method of direct access to original data is considered the most productive method. Its main disadvantage is cost, but such systems are becoming more economical. The systems detail chart presented in Fig. 23-6 is still fairly general. The box marked "look up policy information" doesn't adequately explain all of the processes which the computer system goes through. The program flow chart is used to "expand" this symbol into more meaningful computer steps as shown in Fig. 23-7. The chart is prepared either by a systems analyst or by a programmer.

In summary, it should be noted that while this chapter introduces basic and pertinent facts on systems analysis and design, it does not present the creative work often demanded of the systems analyst. The systems analyst should use available information only to the extent that it might assist him in organizing his facts. It is left for him to provide the creative work applicable to the specific system under study.

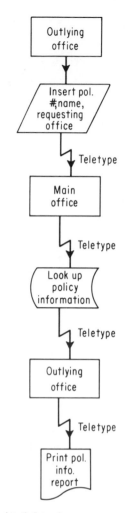

FIG. 23-6 System detail flow chart—request for policy information

THE ROLE OF MANAGEMENT SCIENCE IN THE SYSTEMS FUNCTION

The increasing use of computers, and their phenomenal calculating capability in business organizations has led the systems analyst into such fields as Operations Research (OR) and Management Science. A background in and use of probability and statistics, mathematical modeling and simulation, queuing theory, decision theory, game theory, and mathematical programming are common to the new breed of systems analysts. Probability and Statistics have been widely implemented in the current systems function. Their use has been most noticeable in the latest methods of forecasting, estimation, and predic-

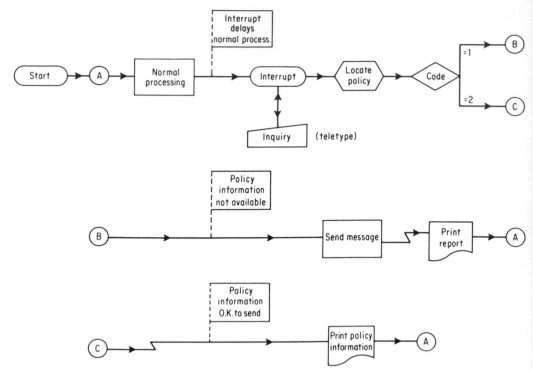

FIG. 23-7 Processing detail—inquiry for policy information

tion which, of necessity, must be based on sketchy data and historical documents. The application of the techniques of probability and statistics to such data is likely to result in more accurate forecasting, estimation, or prediction.

Mathematical Modeling and Simulation is moving to the forefront as a relatively inexpensive way of evaluating alternative physical systems. It is inexpensive in the sense that it allows various alternate constructions to be subjected to variations in condition without the need for physically building pilot models. Thus, the use of simulation results in greater saving in time and expense than pilot models. The need to construct pilot models makes many pilot models extremely time consuming and their cost prohibitive.

Mathematical programming is a general term encompassing several specific types of "programming" techniques. It includes linear programming, quadratic programming, nonlinear programming, and dynamic programming. While each of these techniques is used to solve sets of mathematical equations, linear programming is most widely used. Being well defined, it operates on sets of simultaneous linear equations in an attempt to arrive at the optimal feasible values for the variables in the problem within certain constraints. It has been commonly used in determining the optimal composition of chemical fertilizer and animal feeds, and optimal distribution routes between factories and warehouses, on one hand, and warehouses and retail outlets, on the other. Many other linear programming applications are currently being studied and tested. Several other techniques are currently available and more can be expected in the future, reflecting on the significance of the systems function in solving business problems through the aid of computers.

Glossary of Terms

PROGRAM FLOW CHART: A graphic representation of a computer problem using symbols to represent machine instructions or groups of instructions.

SYSTEM: (1) An organized collection of parts united by regulated interaction. (2) An organized collection of men, machines, and methods required to accomplish a specific objective.

SYSTEMS ANALYSIS: The examination of an activity, procedure, method, technique, or a business to determine what must be accomplished, and how the necessary operations may best be accomplished.

SYSTEMS ANALYST: A person skilled in the definition and development of techniques for the solving of a problem; especially those techniques for solutions on a computer.

SYSTEMS FLOW CHART: A graphic representation of the system in which data provided by a source document are converted to final documents.

SYSTEMS STUDY: The detailed process of determining a system or set of procedures for using a computer for definite functions or operations, and establishing specifications to be used as a base for the selection of equipment suitable to the specific needs.

SYSTEMS SYNTHESIS: To plan the procedures for solving a problem. This may involve among other things the analysis of the problem, preparation of a flow diagram, preparing details, testing, and developing subroutines, allocation of storage locations, specification of input and output formats, and the incorporation of a computer run into a complete data processing system.

Questions for Review

1. What are some of the functions and duties of a systems analyst? Explain.
2. List and discuss the primary phases considered important in designing new business systems.
3. Explain the primary stages of systems study for:
   (a) The manual method
   (b) The punched card method
   (c) The computer method
4. What is the role of management science in the systems function? Explain.

chapter twenty-four

DATA PROCESSING DOCUMENTATION

CONSIDERING WHAT WE HAVE DISCUSSED IN PREVIOUS CHAPTERS, it should be obvious that we now live in the computer age, where computer systems are becoming more the rule than the exception in most business organizations. The development of this new and dynamic technology over the past decade has generated thousands of jobs in an endeavor to improve the lot of mankind.

The nature and complexity of these specialized, highly skilled jobs brought forth the problems of standardizing information related to various projects and interpreting results received by users with different sets of backgrounds, orientation, and needs. Thus, in an effort to organize, standardize, and provide consistency in handling data processing details, the need for documentation becomes paramount.

WHAT IS DATA PROCESSING DOCUMENTATION?

Documentation is a method of communicating and refers to a written record of a phase(s) of a particular project. It describes a system at various steps and establishes design and performance criteria to be met at future stages of the project. Thus, better control of the project(s) becomes possible.

Of special significance, documentation serves the purposes of (1) minimizing distortion or ambiguity regarding the elements involved in various phases of an on-going project; (2) guarding against the loss of key information in the event that the staff member in charge of the project decided to leave the organization; (3) evaluating progress made on a project and allowing an opportunity to look into any inconsistencies between planned and actual target dates; a source of reference for modification of an organization system or using such historical data for developing a job(s) similar to the one already performed; (4) communicating between data processing specialists and nonspecialists such as the users. Often, the user needs to be instructed on proper application of his system. By doing so, good EDP-user relations are maintained; (5) thus, properly documented projects are essential for an efficient system to update and function as a vital source of reference for the development of future systems.

In discussing documentation techniques it should be noted that there are no uniform standards which are applicable to all computer systems. Although general documentation systems are adopted, each installation ultimately develops its own documentation routines, within given constraints. Some of these constraints include (1) management's attitude toward documentation, in general; (2) the number, complexity, and level of documentation; (3) the level of sophistication of the hardware and software systems; and (4) the structural makeup of the organization. Let us elaborate briefly on each of these factors.

When we speak of management, we mean to emphasize the person(s) in charge and in a position to command others to perform certain functions or to carry out certain instructions. Like any other selling technique, those in a managerial capacity must be sold on the need for good documentation within a reasonable cost range. Once convinced, management would be more willing to make a commitment to support and authorize the expenditure of adequate funds to initiate and implement a documentation system.

The degree of rigidity and complexity of documentation often depends on the type of project(s) involved, the amount of time it takes to develop it, the number of project members assigned to it, and the number of users affected. Given the use of documentation as a means to communicate information about a system, the larger the project team, the more desirable is the need for an effective documentation routine for improving communication flow. Thus, for maintaining adequate control, lengthy, complex projects requiring more project members demand more documentation than short straightforward projects. Furthermore, the greater the number of users having access to the system, the greater is the need for complete documentation.

Rigidity of documentation also has much to do with the frequency of use of a system. A "one-time" system, for example, which is intended for temporary use or is unlikely to be the basis for a long-term solution, would require less rigid documentation than a "many-time" system intended for permanent use and having a long life span.

In terms of volume of documentation, it is generally the case that larger computer installations (especially those with extensive transmission and peripheral links) demand more documentation than smaller computer installations. While the size of the hardware system is not, in itself, a mandatory criterion for documentation, it tends to generate over time the need for more and more (in terms of quantity rather than types of) documentation. Likewise, the software system influences, to some extent, the type of documentation required. Here, we find an inverse relationship between the level of software languages and the form of documentation required. High level languages, for example, require less rigorous technical documentation than low level languages.

Finally, the structural makeup of the organization is a contributing factor determining whether or not documentation is necessary. In a classical sense, a large organization with a rigid chain of command would normally require detailed and complete documentation of its operations, which, in turn, imposes the same requirements on its data processing documentation. The converse is the case in smaller, less rigidly structured organizations.

PRIMARY COMPONENTS OF DATA PROCESSING DOCUMENTATION

As mentioned earlier, each installation ultimately develops and implements its own documentation system to meet its needs within structural and other constraints. In developing such a system, however, there are primary components that serve as general guidelines. They consist of a project initiation phase, systems, program, and operations documentation. The last three phases are related to project development (Fig. 24-1).

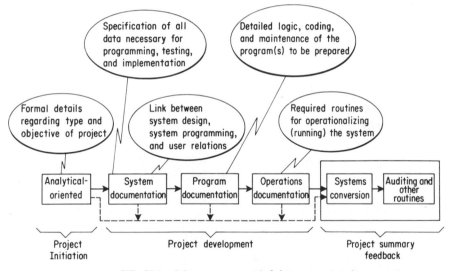

FIG. 24-1 Primary components of data processing documentation

In developing the details regarding each of the foregoing components, a series of steps (called documentation preparation steps) are followed. Figure 24-2, page 384, illustrates their sequence.

Project Initiation

The initial phase of a project encompasses the preparation of a formal, written statement of the nature, objectives, and analysis of the work requested by the

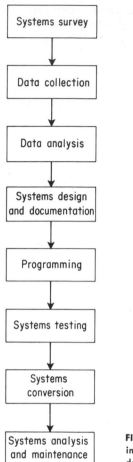

```
┌─────────────────┐
│ Systems survey  │
└─────────────────┘
         │
         ▼
┌─────────────────┐
│ Data collection │
└─────────────────┘
         │
         ▼
┌─────────────────┐
│  Data analysis  │
└─────────────────┘
         │
         ▼
┌─────────────────┐
│ Systems design  │
│and documentation│
└─────────────────┘
         │
         ▼
┌─────────────────┐
│   Programming   │
└─────────────────┘
         │
         ▼
┌─────────────────┐
│ Systems testing │
└─────────────────┘
         │
         ▼
┌─────────────────┐
│    Systems      │
│   conversion    │
└─────────────────┘
         │
         ▼
┌─────────────────┐
│Systems analysis │
│ and maintenance │
└─────────────────┘
```

FIG. 24-2 Basic steps in the preparation of documentation

user. The primary related documents in this phase are (1) the user request, (2) a feasibility study of the problem, (3) a detailed description of the proposed project, and (4) a detailed statement of the system's objectives (Fig. 24-3).

After an informal meeting with a data processing representative, the user initiates a new project by formally forwarding to the data processing department a written request for assistance. Given the formality of clearing this request through his line supervisor, the *user's request* defines in an outline form and briefly describes the nature of the problem. Generally, it provides such information as the name and official title of the user, a clear statement of what the project is expected to produce and whom it will accommodate, the source of input data, the desired output information, and the anticipated deadline. The degree of formality and demands regarding required details depend on the complexity of the organization structure and the familiarity of the system's staff with the overall operations of the particular user.

Once a user's request has been received, a systems analyst drafts a proposal describing the user's problem(s), the variables to be considered, and a tentative approach to its solution. In effect, such a system's proposal is analogous to a *feasibility study* which reviews present methods and requirements. The two steps (user request and feasibility study), in essence, establish a rapport between the user, on one hand, and the data processing staff, on the other, for a communication flow as the project is formally adopted and is on the way into the development phase.

The document representing a detailed description of the proposed project is analytic in orientation and can be used either as a supplement to or a substitute for a feasibility study. It clearly states functions, areas of responsibilities, project scheduling, and determining resource requirements. When tagged to the user's report, this document (depending on the requirements of the project) often portrays adequate details of the project initiation phase.

Finally, the detailed description of the system's objectives (an aspect of system design) specifies the anticipated results of the project. The weaker the user's request, the greater is the need for this document.

FIG. 24-3 Project initiation
—a schematic diagram

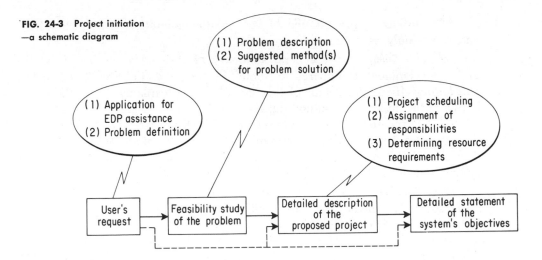

(1) Problem description
(2) Suggested method(s) for problem solution

(1) Application for EDP assistance
(2) Problem definition

(1) Project scheduling
(2) Assignment of responsibilities
(3) Determining resource requirements

User's request → Feasibility study of the problem → Detailed description of the proposed project → Detailed statement of the system's objectives

Project Development—System Documentation

System documentation generates key information for programming, testing, and project implementation in the form of a report, called *system specification.* Once completed, it indicates the fulfillment of the system analysis and design functions and serves as a communication link between the user, the programmer, and systems designer for later project development work.

While the complexity and size of the system specification is a function of the demands of the project under consideration, it is generally an involved and a lengthy form of documentation, requiring much care and detailed planning. Thus, it contains several "subdocumentations" (Fig. 24-4).

FIG. 24-4 A schematic system documentation diagram

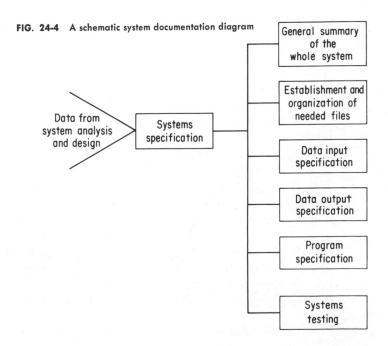

Data from system analysis and design → Systems specification

General summary of the whole system

Establishment and organization of needed files

Data input specification

Data output specification

Program specification

Systems testing

The following presentation of key subdocumentation is not exhaustive and serves only as a guideline.

General Summary. A general summary of the whole proposed system under development is prepared to orient the user and line executives on the nature, objectives, and details of the project. It also explains the relationships between the input and output data and their sources, the files containing related data records, and the required steps which are later taken for processing purposes. In illustrating a part or parts of these relationships, a systems flow chart is often prepared in order to show the logic pattern of the overall system and to pinpoint each operational step to be taken.

Establishment and Organization of Needed Files. All *files* related to data sources, storage media, etc., are *identified* and *coded*. Descriptions of the format and content (including name, type, length and sequence) of each file record are also made. Thus, in establishing and organizing such files, programmers and systems staff members can at any time refer to them for future modification or for updating the system. The user also finds it a useful source of information whenever a review of the system becomes necessary.

Data Input Specification. A key aspect of systems specification is the preparation and description of all data inputs related to the proposed system. Thus, a document, referred to as *data input specification* is prepared. It describes in proper order the required data inputs in a computer-acceptable form. Specifically, it begins with the identification of the system and the systems designer in charge of its preparation, summarizes the features and acceptable values of the input data and the media on which they are recorded, indicates the files involved in or those which are affected by the input data, the volume and frequency of entry of input data, and its originating source. Special forms are used to describe these details.

Data Output Specification. Similar to data input specifications in format, *data output specification* describes in detail the proposed system's output. It identifies the expected output in a predetermined sequence, and the person in charge of its preparation; summarizes the features, purpose, and content of the data output; specifies the media on which they will be recorded; and defines the volume, format, and number of copies needed and their destination. Special preprinted forms are also used to describe the details entailed in this phase.

Program Specifications. One of the functions of the systems designer is to help the programmer develop program logic for the proposed system. In order to formalize this phase, he prepares a *program specifications* document which lists the information requirements of the system with emphasis on the input and output specifications, existing files, and the processing details. The program specifications document includes the following information: (1) input and output information; (2) the rules, logic, and regulation to be followed in the process; (3) specific ways of handling, modifying, or evaluating such key information as inputs in the program; (4) clarifying the primary functions performed; (5) establishing a linkage between the proposed program and other available programs for ascertaining maximum results; (6) deciding on particular routines to be followed in handling exceptions or in correcting errors; and (7) providing whatever charts, formulae, or tables are required to carry out the processing details.

System Testing. A final stage in system documentation results in the preparation of a *system testing* document which determines the required steps that would operationalize the system. It specifies the purpose and lays out the procedure to be followed in testing the system, and defines the inputs involved and the expected outputs.

In determining the preoperationalization routines, the system testing document also includes details with regards to the person(s) responsible for carrying out the system's tests and those who would synchronize the required elements prior to testing. Furthermore, a "quality control" approach is emphasized throughout. Procedures related to the handling of errors, exceptions, and space constraints are carefully shown.

Once the foregoing stages have been laid out, the system testing document indicates the sequence in which the proposed system can be completely tested. Each operation is numbered and sequenced. Input information and files are referenced by names or numbers.

Project Development—Program Documentation

The preceding material introduced the project initiation phase and system documentation as a key component in the development of a proposed system. In elaborating on program documentation, emphasis is placed upon routines which would apply to a "many-time" business data processing system involving more than one programmer.

Unlike project initiation or system documentation, the clearly defined functions of the programming phase explain the relatively straightforward routine in the preparation of program documentation. Designing, coding, and testing a program generally follow the availability of system specification. These substeps lead to the preparation of a program document which makes up a program manual, and to final implementation.

Like other documentation components, business data processing program documentation carries with it certain required functions. Given the type and level of documentation, the primary programming functions are analysis of program logic, coding, checking out the data involved, program assembly and compilation, final documentation, and operationalization.

The foregoing tasks, while open for modification and overlapping, require documentation so as to allow (1) effective program modification, if necessary; (2) minimum delay resulting from possible reassignment of programming personnel; and (3) direct and immediate access to the details by management. Thus, both technical and nontechnical personnel (programmers and users, respectively) are likely to find use for the availability of program documentation.

The Program Manual

For several years, program documentation has been presented in a manual which basically (1) describes the functions and procedures of a given program, (2) indicates the input and output data and files involved, (3) presents the flow diagrams which show the sequential steps taken by the program, and (4) specifies coding and testing details as well as operating and other instructions.

A program manual is typically identified with a particular system (by name and/or by a special number) and indicates the serial number of the program, the programmer who developed it, and his title. It begins with the program specifications (described earlier) and a narrative prepared by the programmer regarding the programming logic he followed, formulae or other special-purpose routines, and any other data which is related to the overall program (Fig. 24-5).

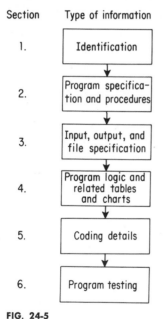

Section	Type of information
1.	Identification
2.	Program specifica-tion and procedures
3.	Input, output, and file specification
4.	Program logic and related tables and charts
5.	Coding details
6.	Program testing

FIG. 24-5

The basic components of a program manual

In addition to the foregoing information, a program manual also includes a copy of the input, output, and file specifications (described earlier) and illustrative details. This section is followed by a subsection consisting of tables and charts (optional) which are related to the program logic used in the project. Depending on their nature and complexity, it is common that some description is made of items such as complex tables and special search techniques.

The final sequential section of the program manual lays out the coding details of the program, followed by a carefully worked out plan for its testing. In preparing the program for testing, the programmer normally checks on the correctness of clerical and logical errors. Once checked out, artificial test data is used to test the various aspects of the program and the overall logic. It is assumed that the artificial data is valid and reliable. Testing can be extended to handle more complex artificial data until such a point is reached when the obtained results are comparable to what is expected in a "live data" program run. The methods followed and a list of the artificial data used in testing the program must be documented and incorporated in the program manual for reference.

Once the computer program becomes available for actual production run, formal documentation is prepared for instructing the operator how to run a program test, and a properly sequenced list of processing steps specifying the necessary operating requirements. Thus, in operation documentation, emphasis points to the need for developing (1) instructions for program testing, and (2) a processing routine for operating the system.

While the instructions for program testing are normally prepared by the programmer in charge of the system, the instructions for operating the system are prepared jointly by the programmer running the system and the systems staff. In terms of contents, however, it is not uncommon for the user, for example, to provide instructions related to ways of preparing and collecting the source data and the handling of input and output, while the data processing staff provides instructions and/or details related to job assembly (data and program availability requirements) and the overall work flow of the proposed system. In any case, it is expected that the user provides the required source data on schedule and in a usable form, while the data processing staff assumes the responsibility of handling all matters regarding processing details.

Development of instructions for operating the system are commonly made in a descriptive manner. However, a more formal, structural approach is used for greater effect. Many installations use various, special-purpose, preprinted forms. Among others are (1) forms for data preparation (in the case of keypunching—details regarding format, codes, destination, etc.), (2) computer operating instructions (supported by the program manual), and (3) a process flow chart related to each operating instruction form.

Project Summary and Feedback

The purpose of this final phase is to analyze and decide on the appropriateness of current documentation for system conversion. Actual results from a major test run are compared with a predetermined result. Discrepancies are detected and modification of the documentation involved is made to produce a workable, accurate, and completely debugged system.

The foregoing remarks point out the need for some form of control of the proposed system at various stages. Upon the termination of each stage in the project, key checkpoints are established when the rate of progress of the system is monitored and the quality of the documentation is evaluated. Thus, during the project initiation phase, a check is made (against prescribed standards) regarding (1) the clarity of the user's definition of the project and its objectives, (2) the assignment and availability of the needed staff, and (3) the amount of time allotted to the project. This last step is necessary for arriving at an estimation of the cost of the project.

During the project development phase, a check is made on the workability, accuracy and completeness of the system study and analysis, their pertinent documentation, the system summary, coding details, logic flow, and program testing.

In the project initiation phase (discussed earlier), it was mentioned that a proposed system is initiated when the user formally requests the assistance of the data processing department. It was assumed throughout this discussion that the user's request was made with management's approval and support. In developing and implementing a system, it is necessary not only to carry out the details which lead to an operational program but also to inform and instruct both the user and management in a nontechnical manner on the capabilities and limitations of the system. Thus, formal documents are prepared to both parties for that purpose.

User-oriented documentation (procedure manual) serves the purpose of allowing the user to understand and participate in running the system. Once implemented, he ultimately takes charge of its routine operation. The user's understanding of the system is vital in that it makes him more cognizant of its components and how well it satisfies his needs. It also helps him to better prepare the source data and interpret the output information he receives.

Management-oriented documentation (economic analysis) is designed to help management evaluate the impact of the system on the project involved and justify the investment committed towards its development. One of the documents they receive is a nontechnical summary of the current application or system in their division or area of responsibility. Other documents include reference manuals, which vary depending on the type and the function they perform. Written in simple language, each manual begins with a section indicating its title, purpose, function, and how it should be used and updated.

Some of the reference manuals available to users and management are (1) coding manuals illustrating the contents and sequence of the codes used in the project implementation phase, and (2) instructional manuals aimed at educating the system user. They explain the system and provide related background information for user participation. Each of these types of manuals can be supplemented by a system conversion guide, which presents detailed conversion steps from a manual to a computer system.

Glossary of Terms

DOCUMENTATION: A means to communicate, it refers to a written record of a phase(s) of a specific project and establishes design and performance criteria for various phases of the project.

FEASIBILITY STUDY: A phase of project initiation, it is a proposal which describes the user's problem(s), the variables involved, and a tentative approach to its solution.

OPERATIONS DOCUMENTATIONS: Related to project development, it emphasizes the need for developing instructions for program testing and a processing routine for operating the system.

PROGRAM SPECIFICATIONS: Related to systems specifications, it lists the information requirements of the system with emphasis upon the input and output specifications, existing files, and the processing details.

SYSTEM SPECIFICATIONS: A report which provides key information for programming, testing, and project implementation. It serves as a communication link between the user, the programmer, and the systems designer for later development work.

USER'S REQUEST: A phase of project initiation, it is a statement of what a proposed system is expected to produce and whom it will accommodate, source of data input, desired output information, and anticipated deadline.

Questions for Review

1. List and briefly explain the reasons why documentation is developed.
2. For what reason do we find lack of uniform documentation standards? Explain.
3. What steps are followed in documentation preparation?
4. Explain briefly the primary components of data processing documentation.
5. Describe the sequence of steps followed in project initiation.
6. What is meant by system documentation? Describe briefly its primary subdocumentations.
7. Distinguish the difference between program and system specifications.
8. What is the difference between system and program documentation?
9. What purpose does a program manual serve? What information does it contain?
10. Distinguish the difference between program and operations documentation.
11. Explain briefly the uses of nondata processing personnel aids.

chapter twenty-five

BASIC PROCESSING METHODS— BATCH PROCESSING

MAGNETIC TAPE PROCESSING

Tape Labels
Tape File Handling
Tape Sorting
Tape Timing
Stringing
Merging

BUSINESS ACTIVITY GROWS with the steady increase of population and its demand for more and better products and services. Accelerated growth induces small firms to expand or to merge with other firms so that the skills of the craftsmen, the salesmen, the rank-and-file workers, and the financial administrators can be organized to best serve the needs of the consumer—the user of the finished product.

To operate a large and complex organization involves obtaining executive and managerial talent and securing the necessary capital to finance its projects. Direction requires the coordination of the various elements of the organization and the supply of vital information. This requires an information system which has the ability to collect and maintain up-to-date files of descriptive and quantitative data, reorganize them, and present them in a readable summary manner that can be used for decision making.

The method chosen for file maintenance is dependent on the requirements of the system, cost of equipment, and related side benefits. The terms used to describe the two basic methods of approaching a file maintenance application are *batch processing* and *real-time processing*.

Historically, the processing of business data originated as a "real-time" operation. That is, transactions were handled in their entirety as they occurred. In the direct-barter system, data processing began and ended when the bartered material changed hands. Before there was a credit system, currency was immediately exchanged for goods, creating an immediate data processing cycle. As more formal business-accounting systems developed, transactions were recorded by posting them in a ledger each time a transaction occurred. If a bootmaker sold a pair of shoes, for example, he immediately reduced the inventory account and increased his cash account or his receivable account. Thus, he posted two accounts. If his next transaction happened to be the receipt of a cash payment for a previous sale, he would post the amount to his cash and receivable accounts.

Although this system of accounting was relatively slow and subject to many clerical errors, it had the distinct advantage of being constantly in balance. Since it offered immediate access to ledger accounts, transactions could be recorded as they occurred in random order.

With the steady increase in the number of transactions and ledgers that businesses have had to maintain, this manual approach made it impossible to handle the volume and keep the records up to date. Even when additional clerks were hired, it was difficult to post the ledgers soon after the transactions occurred. An apparent solution was to batch transactions by type, so that selected clerks could handle each type with greater efficiency. Even this system had its limitations, however. Ledger posting often was delayed, with the result that accounts were not current.

The mechanization of business data processing appeared to offer a solution. The concept of batching—that is, accumulating transactions which require the same data processing steps—became an inherent characteristic of mechanization.

The development of punched card (unit-record) data processing is an excellent example of employing the same batching principles that are so successful in the mass production of manufactured goods. Following the tradition of mass production technology, an array of single purpose machines was built to perform a series of simple repetitive operations as batches of cards passed through each of them in turn.

Naturally, the time necessary to accumulate an economically efficient batch before processing creates delays, but that time has been generally accepted as a small loss in view of the large amount of overall time and money saved through mechanization.

Commonly then, the techniques of automatic processing of business data are (1) to collect data in "batches"; (2) sort it into the sequence of the master file, which is on tape or cards; and (3) "update" this master file at a specific time.

MAGNETIC TAPE PROCESSING

In magnetic tape systems, input data are usually punched into cards, the cards converted to tape, sorted, and then run against the master tape to create a new master. This necessarily means delay, especially since it is uneconomical to run a few input cards (say on a daily basis) against a comparatively large master file. In a discussion of magnetic tape data processing techniques, stress is placed on the proper ways of handling magnetic tape and the sorting of the information it contains into desired sequences.

There are several ways of setting up tape files. In each particular installation, some standards should be followed. Since reels of tape contain invisible characters, there is nothing to distinguish one reel from another. The plastic case (and in most cases, the tape reel) carries a label identifying the information it contains as to application, date last used, etc. However, this does not guarantee that the operator will select the right tape for use in running a program.

Tape Labels

When a new application is set up and the initial records for that application are copied onto the magnetic tape (for example, from punched cards), a special record, called a *tape label,* is written as the first block of the tape. Like other data on the tape, the label is readable only to the read-write head of the unit. The tape label usually has a standard size (length) and contains such data as the name of the application, date of tape creation, record length of data within the file, reel number, etc.

Once all records have been placed in the file, an ending tape label is necessary. Like the beginning tape label, the ending tape label is of a specific length. It indicates whether it is the last label (last reel of tape in the file) or whether there are other reels to be used. Further, it contains the number of records stored on the tape. This particular information is useful when the reel is used for updating purposes, since the number of records is always counted by the program and checked against the number stored in the ending tape label. There are a beginning and an ending tape label on each reel, even if the records extend to more than one reel.

A programmer not only is responsible for writing the tape labels as new files are created, but he also is in charge of checking them in any program he writes. A program involving magnetic tape input reads the beginning tape label and checks to make sure it is the proper reel to be processed. If the operator fails to place the right reel on the tape unit, the program detects the error, notifies the operator by printing out an indication of what is wrong, and then halts the system.

Tape File Handling

Certain operations are common to most magnetic tape file processing applications. The most important of these are:

1. At some time during or after the transfer of the input transactions onto magnetic tape (usually from punched cards), the data must be edited. Input editing consists of reviewing data in an effort to insure accuracy. This might be a programmed operation involving the checking of data between limits, checking batches of data to control totals, checking data for improbable combinations of factors, double punches and blank columns.

2. Before updating on tape, input transactions must be sorted into the same sequence as that of the tape file.

3. During the updating routine, the following steps (called the "copy technique") take place: (a) The tape label from the input tape is read and the tape itself is checked to make sure it is the right one. Thus, the tape label is copied onto the blank tape to create a new label showing the correct date.

(b) An input transaction is read, followed by the reading of a tape record and adding "one" to the record count. When the two types of data become available, the identification of the input transaction is matched against the tape-record identification number [1] to see if they are the same. If they are not the same, the tape record is written on the output tape and another tape record is read and compared. These two steps are repeated until a match is detected, in which case the tape record is updated in memory and finally is written on the output tape (Fig. 25-1). (c) The program reverts to reading another input transaction, going through the same procedure until the last one has been processed. (d) The last step involves writing onto an output tape any tape records remaining in the input file. When the ending tape label from this input file is read, the record count accumulated during the processing is checked against the ending label count. If the two counts are the same, the new ending label is written onto the output tape.

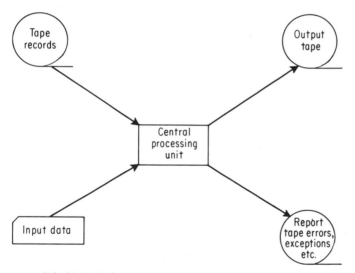

FIG. 25-1   Updating tape—basic routine

4. When a new file has been created through an updating procedure, it becomes input for the next processing run. The former (older) tape is stored for safety's sake until the next processing occurs, at which time the tape from the output run becomes the "safety" tape and another becomes the most current. This routine is called *cycling tape*. After two updating runs have been made, there will be three tapes: the new updated tape, called the "son" tape;

---

[1] Data records are identified by individual identification numbers (ID), which may be numeric or alphanumeric. The (ID) numbers in a customer file might be the account numbers, the customer numbers, or even the customer names and/or addresses. Each data record is stored in a definite position within the storage unit and each such place has a numeric address.

the tape used as input to this most recent processing, called the "father" tape; and the tape used to create the input tape, called the "grandfather" tape (Fig. 25-2). This technique establishes backup reference in case any failure occurs along the way. Usually, by the time the third tape is built, the validity of the grandfather tape has been established, and it can be put back into the computer system as a "free" or "scratch" tape.

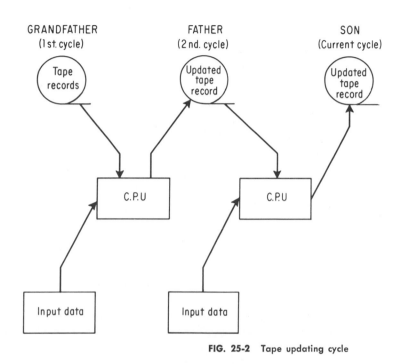

FIG. 25-2 Tape updating cycle

5. A report tape is created which lists information pertinent to management reports, exceptions, errors, or documents. This tape must be run through other programs later to pull off the appropriate information and list it on the printer. During these runs, output editing takes place, which includes the insertion of punctuation and special characters, the elimination of lead zeros from numeric fields, etc. Special instructions are available in most computer languages to provide this type of editing automatically.

Some people wonder why a complete file is always copied, even though only a few records may require updating. To update records without recopying the tape would involve backspacing the tape, to reposition it after reading so that the same record may be rewritten in the same area.

There are several obstacles inherent in such an updating system:

1. It is impractical, considering the possibility of failure in the event the tape is backspaced too far, thus causing it to write over the wrong record.

2. There is the possibility that the tape mechanism will not write exactly at the beginning of a given record, but in such a place as to absorb the interrecord gap.
3. If the input transactions are incorrect and the record is updated incorrectly, there is no convenient way of tracing the original record. Auditing the information from files being updated in this manner can be a painstaking and futile task. Discovery of the error might come too late and the entire record would need to be removed and recreated from the beginning.

Tape Sorting

Sorting is basic to batch processing, whether by card or tape. However, the fact that a reel of tape represents a great many records, all strung together, with no way to break them apart physically, creates a vastly different sorting problem from that of dealing with a deck of cards. A card deck can always be broken apart and resorted into any desired sequence. In an inventory application, for example, each card could represent an item taken from stock, and could be arranged in part-number sequence. For use in billing the customer, they could be resorted into customer-number sequence (customer number was added to the card when the item was removed from stock). But what about magnetic tape? Must the tape be converted to punched cards before resorting? No, magnetic tape can be sorted, but the sorting is done on the computer.

Generally speaking, to sort a tape, the records are read into the memory of the computer, rearranged into a different sequence, and written onto an output tape. The program (or sort routine) which performs this function is a fairly complicated one. Regardless of the specific sort routine used, the job is basically the same: to sort an input file into a different sequence and write out a new tape file. Depending on the size of the system (the memory size, the number of tape units on the system, the speed of the instructions, etc.), tape sorting varies in method and in total sorting time.

Tape Timing. Tape timing (the time it takes to read and write information) is based on two factors: (1) the start-stop time, and (2) the transfer rate of the data. Start time is the time it takes the tape unit to overcome its inertia and bring the tape to the speed at which reading or writing is done. This wastes tape, which is a portion of the interrecord gap. Stop time is the time it takes the unit to come to a stop after the record has been written. In a sort run, the computer "loafs" during acceleration or deceleration of tape. Not until actual data have been transferred to memory does it really operate efficiently.

Stringing. A stringing phase refers to a stage in which the input file is read completely (the first pass). The number of records (the length of the string) is determined by the amount of memory available in the system.

Initially, a specific number of records from the input file is read into memory. The string in memory is rearranged into the desired sequence. When the string has been sorted, it is written onto the first reel of output tape (Fig. 25-3).

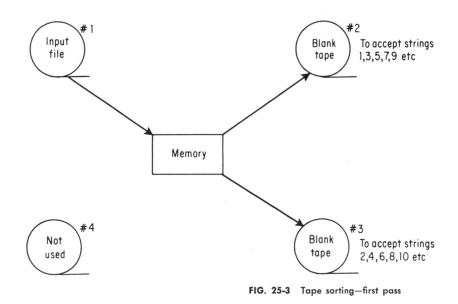

FIG. 25-3 Tape sorting—first pass

Next, another string is read in, sorted, and this time, written onto the second reel of tape. This "ping-pong" effect continues—one string to the first output tape, the next to the second tape—until the input file is finished. At that time, the input tape is dismounted to be replaced by a free tape.

Merging. The next pass takes the two output tapes and merges one string from the first unit with one string from the second unit. This is much like the work done by a punched card collator, in which cards from the secondary hopper are merged with those from the primary hopper. The two strings are combined into a longer string (twice the length of the initial string size) and in the proper sequence (Fig. 25-4).

The merge routine involves comparing the first record from the first string with the first record from the second string. The lower record of the two will be written onto the third tape unit (formerly the input unit, but now containing a free tape) and another record is compared. The two strings are intermixed until the merge is finished. When this takes place, two more strings are read into memory—one from each of the two units now being treated as the input file. This string goes to the fourth tape unit (Fig. 25-5). Merging continues until all the strings from the two units are completed. Each time a merge pass takes place, the size of the strings doubles and the number of the strings is cut in half. The result is two reels of tape (in strings) representing the entire file. In the last pass, these two strings are merged, and the final string (the

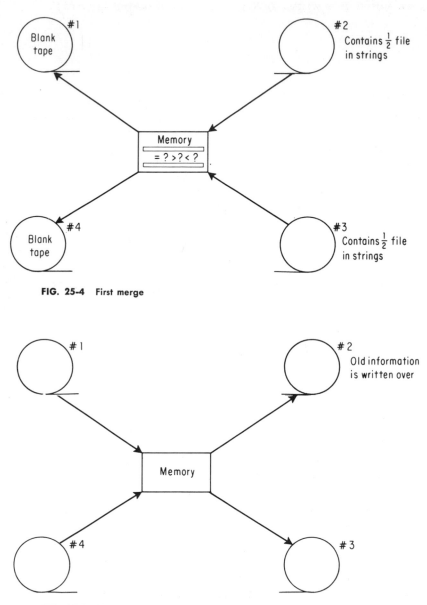

#1
Blank
tape

#2
Contains $\frac{1}{2}$ file
in strings

Memory
= ? > ? < ?

#4
Blank
tape

#3
Contains $\frac{1}{2}$ file
in strings

FIG. 25-4 First merge

#1

#2
Old information
is written over

Memory

#4

#3

FIG. 25-5 Merging continues

entire sorted file) is written onto one output tape. We now have a completely resorted tape.

Timing of a tape sort is based primarily on how many times the file must be reshuffled from tape to tape, consisting of the reading and writing of the first pass, plus all the subsequent merges. The number of merges depends upon the number of strings created on the first pass (the fewer the strings, the fewer the merges). The number of strings, on the other hand, depends upon the number of records in a string, which in turn depends upon how much memory space is available to build the string in the first place.

File time is the time it takes to transfer the required characters, plus start-stop time. Assuming a transfer rate of 50,000 characters per second and 10 million characters in the file (50,000 records of 200 characters each) read time is 200 seconds and write time is 200 seconds—a total of 6.7 minutes per read and write of the file. After allowing five milliseconds per record for start time and five milliseconds for stop time (a total of 8.4 minutes), it would take 15.1 minutes to completely read and write a file. With 12 merges, and one initial stringing phase, the total sort time would be 12 × 15.1 minutes or 3.02 hours.

To show the clear advantage of using magnetic tape, let us contrast it with a punched card installation, specifically a 1,000-card-per-minute sorter. Assuming the processing of 50,000 records (200 characters each), we would need three cards to store one record—150,000 cards in all. At a speed of 1,000 cards per minute, it would take 150 minutes to sort each column. For 50,000 records, there usually is at least a five-column identification field, which would increase the sorting time by a factor of five. Thus, it would take 12.5 hours of machine sorting, plus approximately 1.3 hours of handling time and full-time human supervision, or 13.8 hours, to handle this assignment.

Glossary of Terms

BATCH PROCESSING: A technique by which items to be processed are coded and collected into groups prior to processing.

CYCLING TAPE: Creating a new tape file through an updating procedure.

Questions for Review

1. What advantage does the batching process have over the manual method of business data processing?
2. What steps are involved in the automatic processing of business data?
3. Why is a tape label used? Where on tape is it located? Who is responsible for preparing it? Explain.
4. List and explain some of the main operations common to most magnetic tape file processing applications.
5. In an updating routine, a computer file is copied even though only a few records may require updating. What are some of the obstacles inherent in such a routine? Explain.
6. Explain how a tape is sorted, the factors which determine the methods used, and the overall sorting time.
7. What two factors determine tape timing? Explain each factor briefly.
8. What is meant by stringing? Give an example.
9. Explain the routine used in merging records on tape. Illustrate.
10. What is file time?

chapter twenty-six

BASIC PROCESSING METHODS— REAL-TIME PROCESSING

REAL-TIME PROCESSING VERSUS BATCHING

DIRECT-ACCESS STORAGE INQUIRY

DISK STORAGE AND LOW ACTIVITY DATA PROCESSING
High Activity Data Processing

RANDOM AND SEQUENTIAL DATA PROCESSING

DISK FILE ADDRESSING TECHNIQUES
Recorded Identification Number (Pseudo Direct)
Various Uses of Identification Number
Consecutive Multiple Segments for a Record
Trailer Record for File Density
Indexing
Randomizing

REAL-TIME PROCESSING VERSUS BATCHING

THE USE OF PUNCHED CARD AND MAGNETIC TAPE SYSTEMS implies that transactions would have to be batched for economical handling. That is, it would not be practical to process transactions as they occur, since so much time would be consumed in looking up items at random. Also, for tape systems, there is the cost of recopying the file on a new tape as a usual part of the updating procedure. However, there also are applications which, because of a time factor, require files to be updated as transactions occur.

Real-time processing means that data may be processed as they become available regardless of the order in which they arrive. It means that input data are not subjected to editing or sorting prior to entering the system, whether the input is for various transactions of a single application or for intermixed transactions of many applications (Fig. 26-1). This presents problems of accuracy control which are not typical of batch processing systems.

The ability to process transactions on-line, as they are received, has been of keen interest to computer manufacturers and users. Until the recent development of faster and less expensive direct-access devices it has rarely been practical for small- or medium-scale users. Today, devices are available which can store large amounts of data in directly addressable units and can obtain information quickly from each unit with equal ease and at reasonable cost. These devices were introduced in Chapter 13.

Further, the demand for real-time processing has increased because some jobs do not lend themselves to batch processing. The batching time is often longer than the actual process time. In many cases, a number of other batching problems have been apparent:

1. Certain data are out of date even before they are processed.
2. Reports are available infrequently and often too late to be used as a basis for management decision and action.

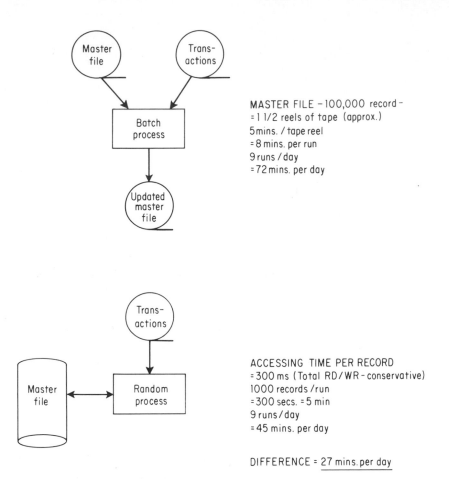

MASTER FILE – 100,000 record –
= 1 1/2 reels of tape (approx.)
5 mins. / tape reel
= 8 mins. per run
9 runs / day
= 72 mins. per day

ACCESSING TIME PER RECORD
= 300 ms (Total RD/WR – conservative)
1000 records /run
= 300 secs. = 5 min
9 runs /day
= 45 mins. per day

DIFFERENCE = 27 mins. per day

FIG. 26-1   **Example of sequential and random processing**

3. Requests for information, such as item status or account balance, are sometimes extremely difficult to answer. It often is impossible to locate data records during the processing cycle, and an inquiry may have to go unanswered
until the cycle is complete.

4. Since batch processing requires that input data and all files be maintained
sequentially, much money and time are spent in sorting data.

For applications that require information in large volumes and on short
notice, the disadvantages of the batch approach are even more obvious. The
real-time approach is becoming more vital every day. Some of the reasons are:

1. The computer can directly refer all the necessary data for processing a transaction. Data can be efficiently processed in any sequence as they become
available.

2. While removing the absolute requirement that file records and input transactions always be available in a fixed sequential order, new disk-storage units can make efficient use of sequential order to do high-speed batch processing for those applications which require it.

3. Jobs are more highly integrated, and manual intervention is less a factor in the processing of an application.

DIRECT-ACCESS STORAGE INQUIRY

Data processing installations have always found it necessary to obtain specific information from files during an operation. Prior to the development of direct-access mass storage, the ability to request information directly from temporary or permanent storage devices was relatively limited. Procedures were developed, but at best they resulted in time-consuming interruptions, and often the information was not completely up-to-date when received. The special ability of disk and other mass-storage systems to process input data of various types on-line and to update all affected records immediately makes it possible to request information directly from storage and receive an immediate reply. This is significant because information requests no longer disrupt normal processing, and there no longer is a need for delay between a request for information and a reply.

To illustrate, a major national airline operated a number of reservations offices throughout the country and attempted to maintain a record of all flights and passenger reservations on ledger-type cards in a central location. The records were updated and inquiries were made by telephone. Replies often were inaccurate and delayed. When a disk-storage system was installed, flight-passenger records were maintained there and communications were linked from the reservations desks to a computer, thus permitting all inquiries to be answered quickly, accurately, and automatically.

The need for immediate retrieval of business information is prevalent in industry. In demand-deposit accounting, for instance, one might ask: "What is the balance of account number 133420?" In inventory control: "How many units of part number 55632 are on order?" In manufacturing: "How many subassemblies of part number 16414 are on hand?" In payroll: "What are the year-to-date earnings of employee number 13862?" It is true that each of these questions could be answered eventually through other data processing means. However, unreasonable delay might make the resulting information out-of-date or insignificant.

The ability to request information directly from a computer and to receive an immediate response with a minimum of operational procedures is strong justification for the use of direct-access mass-storage devices for a growing number of applications. As costs for such devices are reduced they can be expected to play a leading role in data processing systems of the future.

Many applications call for the processing of a limited number of input transactions against very large master files. Although few master file records are altered or referenced by the input data during a particular run on magnetic tape, the entire master tape must be searched. Assume, for example, that a billing system maintains 100,000 customer master records, of which only 9,000 are referenced daily. One approach would be to collect and sort the 9,000 records into customer number sequence and then process them against the master file in a single daily run. If the billing operation requires that bills be completed throughout the day, however, the data would have to be batch-processed nine times a day, resulting in 1,000 input transactions being processed against the 100,000 master records on each run. Since there is no practical way to skip through a file, every record would have to be examined by the system in each of the nine runs.

An answer to the problem lies in the use of direct (random) access devices, which permit the retrieval of records without the examination of intervening records. Figure 26-2 illustrates the difference in the sequential and random processes.

High Activity Data Processing

Direct-access storage also is used in "high activity" applications where a comparatively small number of records is updated or referenced frequently. For example, assume a company has 10,000 employees and each works on 10 or more different jobs per day with a specific rate and guarantee for each job. In the processing of a piecework payroll such as this, each calculation would be based on the employee's unique work history. In this case, there is a need for continuous reference to a comparatively small number of rate tables.

Using the batch approach, job completion tickets would be batched *by employee* as they are received and a master file of employee rate tables would be searched in order to process each employee's job tickets. As an alternative, a separate edit run could be made to determine which rate tables would be required, but in either case, job-ticket data would be tagged with a rate table code; data would be sorted into rate-table sequence; and all reference to a particular rate table would be completed in sequence order. When all rate data are extracted, another run would be required to complete the calculations. Figure 26-2a shows how such an approach would be implemented.

By contrast, in a random-access approach, all rate tables would be accessible as they are required, without having to batch or search through the file for each one or to go through an involved procedure of repeated sorting and processing to complete the job. Figure 26-2b shows how this approach would work.

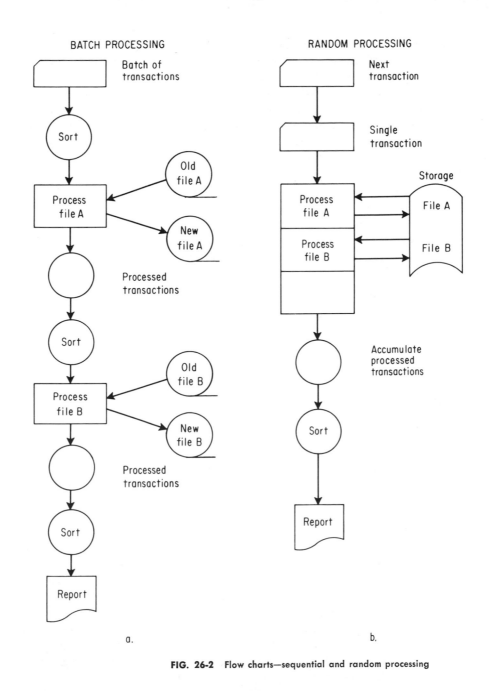

BATCH PROCESSING

Batch of transactions

Sort

Old file A

Process file A

New file A

Processed transactions

Sort

Old file B

Process file B

New file B

Processed transactions

Sort

Report

a.

RANDOM PROCESSING

Next transaction

Single transaction

Storage

Process file A

File A

Process file B

File B

Accumulate processed transactions

Sort

Report

b.

FIG. 26-2 Flow charts—sequential and random processing

RANDOM AND SEQUENTIAL DATA PROCESSING

It is important to distinguish between the organization of a master file and the order of the input detail records processed against it. When used with the term "processing," the terms "random" and "sequential" refer to the order of the input transaction records and to the order of reference to records in the master file, respectively. *Random processing* is the processing of detail transactions against a master file, regardless of the order in which they occur. In *sequential processing*, the input transactions are grouped and sorted into master file control-number sequence, after which the resulting batch is processed against the master file. When the master files are stored on tape or cards, sequential processing is the most efficient procedure.

Direct-access storage units are considered very efficient sequential processors as well as random processors. They make it possible to choose the best processing method to suit the application. Thus, some applications can be processed sequentially, while those in which sorting or batching is undesirable can be processed randomly. Either approach can be used, whether the master file is in random or in sequential order, illustrating the additional flexibility obtained by sorting a master file on direct-access storage units.

Real savings in overall job time often can be made by combining runs in which each input affects several master files. The details can be processed sequentially against a primary file and randomly against the secondary files, all in a single run. This is the basis of one-line processing.

DISK FILE ADDRESSING TECHNIQUES

When using mass-storage devices, a business firm will make efficient use of every character position possible. Only the amount of usable storage is ordered at a particular point in time since more storage can be added at a later date. Consequently, the firm must consider the matter of "packing" information onto the file, wasting a minimum amount of space, and keeping in mind the problem of cost.

In order to explain disk file addressing techniques, assume you have a typical disk file in which each disk is divided into segments of 200 alphanumeric character positions of storage. The two techniques used for locating information on a random-access file are *direct addressing* and *indirect addressing*. Generally, direct addressing is used whenever the input data record carries the absolute disk file address for those data. Indirect addressing, on the other hand, is used when the absolute address on the disk file is first found on a list that carries both the actual identification number and the location of the desired information.

In a direct-access application, an identification code in the input data must be used to locate the corresponding information in the file. This does not imply that the identification number of the input data must be identical to the addressing system of the direct-access device; it simply means that the identification must be used in one way or another to determine the location of the information on the file.

Direct and indirect addressing have their advantages and limitations. At times, a combination of the two techniques is the most efficient. The application under consideration is a major factor in determining which method is to be used.

When a new application is being transferred to an automatic system, it may be assigned the same numbers as the addresses on the disk file. For instance, in a disk file containing addresses which run from 000000 to 999999, a particular application may be assigned by any of these addresses, if all of its records are contained within this range. The advantage of this system is the speed at which information may be accessed; the absolute address is available immediately for access to the file. Its chief limitation is that once records become obsolete and are dropped from the file, they leave gaps which cannot be used to store other information. If the numbering system does not use all or at least most of the available numbers, much of the file will be left blank.

Recorded Identification Number (Pseudo Direct)

When an application is ready to be recorded on disk storage, an "open list" will be made available to the personnel working on the problem. This list carries all the addresses on the file which are not in use. All existing identification numbers for the particular application are typed up in a sequential list, and an open address from the disk file is placed next to each number. The address just assigned is then crossed off the open list. From that time on, all documents used as input to the computer system must carry both the actual identification of the input data and the assigned disk file address. If a card is keypunched for a particular item, the operator must look up the disk address from the prepared list so that it also can appear on the card.

The advantage of this system is that as numbers "die out," the disk addresses may be placed back on the open list. This way, the locations do not have to remain filled (as they do in a straight direct address) unless there is no possibility of the number recurring in the system. However, the chief disadvantage is that the maintenance of the dictionary list is very time-consuming, and it is possible that personnel might pick up an incorrect disk address. The latter possibility usually is discovered, however, since the information on the disk file also carries the actual identification number, which is compared to the input document by the program before any updating takes place.

Various Uses of Identification Number

Certain problems might occur in an installation where several applications lend themselves to the direct-addressing scheme. In a billing application, for instance, the account numbers of customers might have the same format as the employee numbers established for the firm's payroll. It would seem at first glance that a customer number and an employee number (both being the same), would have to have the same area assigned to them on the file. Naturally, this is not possible.

To see how a system with more than one file for each identification number works, consider an example in which both the employee numbers and the customer numbers run from 0000000 to 0009999. If we were to assign disk locations 0000000 through 0009999 to employee payroll information, the employee program would have to refer only to the actual employee number to find the proper data. In assigning locations for the billing application, a distinction can be made by assigning them to locations 0010000 to 0099999 (Fig. 26-3). These two areas on the file do not cause any conflict.

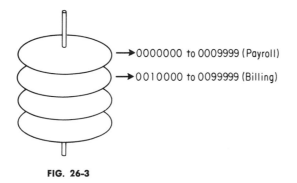
→ 0000000 to 0009999 (Payroll)
→ 0010000 to 0099999 (Billing)

FIG. 26-3

But how would anyone be able to find the proper billing location for account number 12685, for instance? First the transactions to be processed carry a specific code to distinguish the information they contain from that used in other applications. Payroll cards might carry a "1" code; billing cards might carry a "2" code. Whenever the payroll program is running, the program "knows" that the employee numbers represent the actual disk address. When the billing program runs, the program "knows" that the customer information is addressed by the customer number plus 10,000. The program then adds the account number (12685) to a program constant of 10,000 (which is carried in the program), and comes up with a disk file address of 0022685. The only apparent danger in this technique is the possibility that improper input data might be used (for example, payroll cards might be used as input to the billing run). However, the program can be instructed to check the application code carried on the input document to avoid any confusion.

Consecutive Multiple Segments for a Record

There are cases where the identification number can be used as a direct reference to a disk file address but the information required to be kept on the file exceeds the disk's segment size; that is, the data exceed the assumed segment storage of 200 characters. If, for instance, the record size for a particular application requires two segments (or 400 characters) the 0000000 identification number would occupy locations 0000000 and 0000001, causing identification number 0000001 to "lose a home." To rectify this, the identification number is multiplied by a factor of two, since two segments are used per identification number. To locate the address for a particular identification, the program would be set up to perform the multiplication of the ID by the desired factor. If the application needed three segments for a record (600 characters), the factor would be three; a four-segment requirement, four.

Trailer Record for File Density

A trailer record is used in cases involving identification numbers which match the disk file addresses and might or might not have more than 200 characters as a requirement for storage on the file. In a commercial bank that keeps records for Demand Deposit Accounting, for instance, certain basic information such as customer name, customer account number, home address, balance, and service charge is retained for every account held. Determining a standard record size in this type of work is difficult, since each customer writes a different number of checks each month. With the trailer method, each account has a basic record (the home record), containing a standard amount of information common to all accounts and kept at the address correspondent to the ID.

As the file is developed and an "open list" is kept, accounts expanding in information beyond one segment would cause the program to look at a computer table (open list), find a free segment, and assign it as the trailer record. The address of this trailer record then would be inserted into the main record (the last seven positions of the main segment) for reference. When that account comes up for processing, the main record is brought into memory and the last seven positions are examined. If they have a trailer address in them, that segment is sought and also read into memory, making all 400 positions available to the program when updating the account. If more than two segments are necessary, the first trailer will carry the address of the next trailer, and so on.

The advantage of this system is that it sets aside for storage only segments which actually are needed. This keeps the file densely packed. In the previous system (consecutive multiple segments for a record), an account that did not use all of the multiple segments which were set aside simply wasted them.

Indexing

Indexing is synonymous with the terms "Dictionary" and "Table Look-Up." It is similar to recorded ID Number (Pseudo Direct), described earlier, except that the computer program, rather than a person, looks up the actual address.

The most popular technique for practicing Table Look-Up on a computer is called a *binary search*. A list of numbers is set up in ascending sequence (for example, 64 numbers). Instead of writing a program to look at the first number, the program is set up to look at the middle number 32 and compare it to the one which is being searched. The number in the table will be too high, too low, or equal to the one being matched. If it is equal, the answer has been found. If it is too high, the program examines the 16th number and makes the same comparison. This process continues, taking half of what is left after the comparison, until the actual number is found. For a table of 64 numbers, the maximum number of comparisons would be five.

In indexing, where the range of ID numbers might run to as many as 10,000, it would be impossible to keep the entire dictionary in the memory of the computer. The entire table would require 70,000 positions for the account numbers and 70,000 more for the disk addresses—a total of 140,000 character positions, divided into two types: rough tables and fine tables. The *rough table* is kept in memory constantly and is set up in a practical size for the particular computer being used. *Fine tables,* on the other hand, are kept in an auxiliary storage device (for example, a disk file) in an area not used for normal accounting information, where they will be available to the program at any time they are needed.

Below is an example of a rough table for account numbers 029 through 899:

Account Number	Disk File Address
029	0000010
059	0000020
089	0000030
119	0000040
149	0000050
179	0000060
209	0000070
239	0000080
269	0000090
299	0000100
329	0000110
359	0000120
389	0000130
419	0000140
449	0000150
479	0000160
509	0000170
539	0000180
569	0000190
599	0000200
629	0000210
659	0000220
689	0000230
719	0000240
749	0000250
779	0000260
809	0000270
839	0000280
869	0000290
899	0000300

The first column of figures shows the account numbers in increments of 30, carrying only the highest number in each 30-number range. The second column represents the address on the disk file where the *fine table* is located (not the account information).

When a transaction is to be processed and an account number is received, it is compared to the first column of figures using the binary search principle. This determines the general range into which it falls. The number 345, for example, falls somewhere between the 11th and 12th entries in the table; in other words, it is greater than 329, but less than 359. The entry at the 12th position tells us that the fine table for the account numbers from 329 through 358 is found on the disk file at location 0000120.

The rough table is composed of the range of numbers, plus a disk-file address. It takes only 300 memory positions (30 numbers at three digits per number plus 30 addresses at seven digits per address).

As soon as the address for the next table is located (0000120), that table is read into memory. It is the fine table for the rough range 329 through 358, and might look like the following:

Fine Account No.	Disk File Address
329	0000400
330	0000401
331	0000402
332	0000403
333	0000404
334	0000405
335	0000406
336	0000407
337	0000408
338	0000409
339	0000410
340	0000411
341	0000412
342	0000413
343	0000414
344	0000415
345	0000416
346	0000417
347	0000418
348	0000419
349	0000420
350	0000421
351	0000422
352	0000423
353	0000424
354	0000425
355	0000426
356	0000427
357	0000428
358	0000429

Again, the account number would be brought into the table. This time the range has been established however, and the actual number will be found. Account number 345 will be found on the disk file at address 0000416.

The table also requires 300 positions of memory—a total of 600 positions for Table Look-Up. There would be 300 for the rough table (kept in memory at all times) and 300 for a fine table (brought into memory at any time). As different fine tables are used, they are written over the ones previously used.

Without this method, 9,000 positions of memory would be required to do the same job done here by 600. Indexing is fairly fast. Two references to the file usually are necessary: one to bring in the fine table, and another to read the actual information desired. The Table Look-Up process would not be possible where random alphabetic characters are part of the ID, as they often are with part numbers in an inventory application.

Randomizing

A firm may retain its present numbering system through randomizing. In this technique, the original ID has a specific type of formula applied to it for producing a generated number or numeric address and is within the range of the addressing system on the disk file. For example, the disk file address of the number 123456789 is obtained as follows:

(a) Add every other number (1, 3, 5, 7, 9 equal 25).
(b) Add the remaining numbers (2, 4, 6, 8 equal 20).
(c) Multiply the two low-order digits (8 × 9 equal 72).
(d) Providing a disk file address of 0252072.

To set up a randomized file, the following steps should be observed:

1. Use a mathematical formula on the ID and create a legitimate segment address.
2. Examine the contents of the segment address just created. If it is not filled, put the ID number and the information belonging to it in that address.
3. Continue seeking successive information until a disk file address is generated. It should be noted that as this process goes on, the program keeps track of addresses that are being filled, thus allowing the preparation of an "open list."
4. No matter how complicated the formula, duplicates are bound to occur. When a duplicate occurs, the data for that particular ID is punched out in cards, or set aside in some way for later handling.
5. When the rest of the file is finished, certain parts of it (duplicates) are found not copied onto the disk memory. They are processed again, and this time, when the duplicate number is calculated, that segment is read into memory; an address is selected from the open list; and the address is stored,

representing the last seven digits of the duplicate segment. Finally, the segment is rewritten on the file.

6. The duplicate information is stored at the selected open-list address, writing the information for that record as well as the original identification. The duplicate-address segment still contains the original information.

Let us see what happens when some information is to be processed for an ID which was a duplicate. The ID is used and the formula used to create the file is applied to it. This disk address reads in the appropriate segment, and the ID from the input transaction is compared to the ID from that segment. If they are not the same, the segment address in the last seven positions of the segment in memory is used to read in the next link of the chain, and the input ID is compared against the ID of that segment. This process continues until the record has been found. In addressing, no set rules can be laid down. Each mass storage installation has different problems, resulting in the need for a careful review of numbering systems so that the disk file can be used as efficiently as possible. Randomizing appears to be the most complicated, and therefore the least desirable. However, it is widely accepted because of its great flexibility.

Glossary of Terms

DIRECT-ACCESS STORAGE: (1) pertaining to the process of obtaining information from or placing information into storage where the time required for such access is independent of the location of the information most recently obtained or placed in storage; (2) pertaining to a device in which random access can be achieved without effective penalty in time.

DIRECT ADDRESS: An address that specifies the location of an operand. Synonymous with one level address.

INDEXED ADDRESS: An address that is to be modified, or has been modified, by an index register or similar device.

INDIRECT ADDRESS: An address that specifies a storage location that contains either a direct address or another indirect address. Synonymous with multilevel address.

ON-LINE PROCESSING: Descriptive of a system and of the peripheral equipment or devices in a system in which the operation of such equipment is under control of the central processing unit, and in which information reflecting current activity is introduced into the data processing system as soon as it occurs. Thus, directly in-line with the main flow of transaction processing.

SEQUENTIAL DATA PROCESSING: A technique by which items to be processed must be coded and collected into groups prior to processing.

TABLE LOOK-UP: A procedure for obtaining the function value corresponding to an argument from a table of function values.

Questions for Review

1. What is meant by on-line processing?
2. For what reasons has the on-line approach become vital? Explain.
3. Explain and illustrate the role of direct access storage systems in data acquisition.
4. What is the difference between low activity data processing and high activity data processing?
5. Distinguish the difference between random and sequential data processing. Give an example.
6. What is an "open list"? Discuss its advantages and limitations.
7. Describe the various uses of identification numbers. Give an example.
8. What is a trailer record? Explain its uses for file density.
9. What is meant by "binary search"? How is it used for practicing table look-up on a computer? Give an example.
10. Distinguish and explain the difference between a fine table and a rough table.
11. What is randomizing? What steps are usually taken to set up a randomized file?

chapter twenty-seven

FILE ORGANIZATION TECHNIQUES

FILE ORGANIZATION IS THE PROCESS of relating the ID number of a file record to the address of that record in the storage unit. The ID numbers used by the outside world must be related to the addressing scheme designed into the equipment. The primary objective of file organization is to retain data in storage systematically so as to retrieve them in the fastest way possible when needed. The method used for a particular file varies, and its final form is dependent on the requirements of the given application.

In setting up a file for a direct-access device, there are many questions to be considered. What addressing technique will be used? How frequently will the file be referred to? Are disk files only to be used, or will there be a combination of other gear, such as magnetic tapes? What are the inquiry requirements? What will be the predominant reporting sequence? In updating records, are all records and information for an application consolidated, or are they kept individually? Will there be random processing, batched sequential processing, or both? What are the file maintenance requirements?

Guidelines for answering the first question are outlined in Chapter 26. The frequency of reference to the file (question 2) can be determined by the past experience of the firm. In considering the use of a combination of magnetic tape and direct-access devices, some believe that at least one tape unit, and probably two, are necessary with a direct-access device. In mass-storage usage, certain errors are bound to crop up, or a malfunction of the hardware may occur. Because of this, the contents of the file often are copied (or "dumped") onto tape periodically.

Another good reason for having a combination of tape and direct-access storage is the cost factor. Mass storage is fairly expensive. A tape unit is expensive also, but the amount of information which can be kept on additional reels of tape is far greater than that by the mass-storage device. Sometimes, it may be feasible to keep only the information needed for inquiries on the disk file and to use magnetic tape to store data which are not referenced as often.

In file organization, reporting sequence is a considerable factor. In a large manufacturing firm where inventory is a major application, for example, it makes a lot more sense to have the disk file in part-number sequence than to have it in vendor sequence. All of this implies that a serious systems study should be made prior to setting up a file for a direct-access device.

In manual or even in tabulating operations, each application usually is handled separately. There might be a group of people who take care of accounts receivable, one for payables, one for payroll, another for stock or inventory control. A mass-storage file may be set up in the same way, part of the file allocated to information on accounts receivable, another section for payables, and so on.

Another, more concise method to set up a file for direct-access is to consolidate all pertinent processing. To illustrate, consider what happens when an order is received from a customer. First, the stock is checked to see if the full order can be filled or if a purchase order must be issued to get the desired parts. Once the order has been filled, the customer must be billed. Each of these steps involves a separate application. The receipt of the order precipitates the calculation of sales commission (payroll application) as well as a stock-room search for parts (inventory application). If parts have to be ordered, a vendor must be notified (order processing application) and he will send the firm a bill (accounts payable). When the customer's order is sent, he must be billed (accounts receivable). Rather than start documents going to many separate departments, it would be better to handle the entire job at one time (consolidate).

In a manual, semiautomatic, or automatic system not utilizing mass storage, the total system is impractical. With mass storage, however, the file can be set up so that the order starts a search within the device for individual parts records, which also can carry the percentage of commission to be used for the salesman's payroll records. The same records can carry the name of the vendor from whom parts must be ordered if the record shows an out-of-stock condition. An immediate purchase order can be issued by the system, to the proper vendor, after checking the stock records in the disk file. At the same time, the customer's bill can be made up and printed out, and the customer's records can be updated. Certainly, setting up the total system is more time-consuming, but it pays off in the elimination of duplication and saves time in taking care of the customer's and the firm's needs during day-to-day operations.

In setting up mass-storage files, systems people must make decisions on how they should be organized, basing their opinions on factors such as the account-numbering system, speed of access to a file, and so on. The file maintenance requirements also must be estimated. It is relatively easy to dump an entire file and reload it when an emergency occurs, but sometimes a firm might wish to copy the file onto magnetic tape for other reasons. In that case, perhaps the dump will take place according to the application; that is, all of the billing information copied onto one reel, the payroll information onto another, and so on. With a file that has these applications intermixed throughout, the dumping is a problem. If the applications are kept separate, such a dump is relatively simple.

FILE COMPOSITION—SEQUENTIAL, INDEX SEQUENTIAL, AND RANDOM

A file of records can be arranged within a storage unit in three major ways: *sequentially, index sequentially,* and *randomly.*

A sequential file is treated in the same way as a magnetic tape file. Records are sorted and stored in the disk-storage unit in control-number sequence so that records with successively higher ID numbers will have successively higher addresses. It is not necessary (or even usual) for the ID to be the same number as the file address; the only requirement is that the ID's be in sequence.

In an index sequential file, records are arranged in sequence by control number and grouped into blocks for storage. Then an index is created, containing two related entries: the highest control number within a given block and that block's storage address. The records now can be accessed sequentially by starting with the first block and proceeding with the operation in sequence. They can also be accessed more directly by scanning the index to locate the block that contains the desired record and then reading that block into primary storage. Once the block is in primary storage, each record it contains must be examined individually to find the desired one.

In a random file, each record is at an address computed by a *randomizing routine*—a program that calculates the address from the item's control number. The order of the records within the storage unit generally is not sequential. To find a record in such a file, its address is simply computed from the ID by the same formula used to put it there. The main reason for using the random approach is to eliminate index tables.

RANDOM ORDER TECHNIQUES

Activity Sequence

When identification numbers are randomized, duplicates or "synonyms" are created. In setting up a file based on activity sequence, it is desirable to put the most active information at the home location and the least active at the farthest location in the chain. In other words, the sequence of the file as it is first loaded onto the disks would not be in ID sequence, but in decreasing activity sequence. A great saving in time can be realized by placing the most active records in such a way that there will be only one access to the file. To maintain the file in the correct activity sequence, it is necessary during the accounting period to tally the number of references to each record. Periodically, based on this tally, the file is reorganized.

Correspondence Method

When applications are related to one another, it is simple to set up the first application to occupy just a part of the file. This can be done by altering the randomizing formula to generate addresses which are restricted to a single section. Then, when the next application is put on the file, the corresponding record will be stored in the next section of the file, and will be put at the location relative to the initial record. If the first address were 0000008, for example, and the section to which this application is restricted fills addresses 0000000 through 0000100, the first record of the next application would be stored at 0000108, an increment of 100 addresses away. When the time comes for updating the disk file, the first address would be generated through randomizing, and all other records which might be affected could be accessed easily by adding a factor to the address of the original record.

To see how this technique can save time, consider a record which is fourth in a chain. It would take four accesses to the file to reach that record. For any record which has a correspondence to it, other accesses would have to be made (recalculating or generating each of their individual addresses). With the correspondence method, the addresses for corresponding records are known immediately, even if the records are chained.

Associative Method

For somewhat the same purpose as that in the foregoing illustration, the original record filed by the associative method would carry the addresses of all associated records. To get an additional record, instead of *incrementing* as one does in the correspondence method, the addresses are kept in the main record.

Tree Method

In setting up chained records, the number of accesses to reach the records at the end of the chain can be reduced considerably by using the tree method. The first ID to create an address is stored in the same manner as the first pass of the example illustrating randomizing records. When a duplicate address appears, however, the original ID is tested to see whether it is even or odd. If it is even, an address from the open list will be selected and stored in the seven characters of the record just in front of the last seven. If the original ID is odd, the address from the open list is stored in the last seven characters of the original record. As more duplicates occur, the even or odd path is followed (Fig. 27-1).

Actually, there are two chains—one for all duplicate records with even IDs and one for all those with odd IDs. Notice that the address of these records can be any address, since it is only the ID which matters. This system cuts down the number of accesses required.

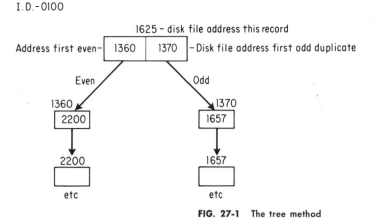

FIG. 27-1   The tree method

SEQUENTIAL ORDER TECHNIQUES

Assigned File Address

Using the direct-address and indexing techniques, the input file to be stored on the disks is sorted and read into memory, followed by the building of the fine tables. This implies that fine tables do not need to carry all possible IDs —only the ones that actually are going to be used. For a range of 100 numbers in the rough table, for instance, there may be only 30 in the fine table. As soon as a range has been read and the numbers listed, this list is stored on the disk as the fine table and the procedure continues until all addresses have been assigned.

Unassigned File Address

This method treats the disk file as if it were continuous reels of magnetic tape with all records in sequence. First, input transactions are presented in batched sequence. Next, as many segments as possible are read into the memory of the computer. One input transaction at a time is read and matched to a memory segment for updating purposes. When the appropriate segment is updated, that segment is rewritten on the disk file. To update an entire file, all segments must be read into memory, but only those segments which have input transactions matching them will be rewritten on the file.

Linkage

In automatic accounting systems of the past, application information was collected on what is called a "minor" level. In a sales organization, for instance, sales information might be collected by product throughout the country. When it is time to prepare reports, the information will be totaled by sorting the product information by salesman and taking salesman totals. Then it will be sorted in branch sequence and totaled by branch, followed by a final total to produce a national figure.

Using the linkage technique, the product record is updated on the disk when product information is received. At the same time, the salesman record is sought and updated, as well as the branch and countrywide records. When reports are needed, all accumulations are readily available, with neither sorting time nor accumulation necessary.

INDEX SEQUENTIAL VERSUS RANDOM FILE ORGANIZATION

Choosing between index sequential and random organizational techniques can be simple in some cases, difficult in others. Basically, it involves choosing either tables or direct computation as a means of finding an address. The following are some comparisons that can be made between the two techniques:

1. The index sequential (table) method allows denser packing and permits the use of a higher percentage of disk storage space.
2. The random method is faster for random processing.
3. The index sequential method is more efficient for generating reports that depend on a search of the file in control-number sequence. To accomplish the same thing with random organization, a finder file (a list of control numbers of all the records in the file) is needed.
4. The random method more readily handles addition to and deletions from the file. With an index sequential file, a large number of additions and deletions forces frequent reorganization.

Based upon the foregoing comparisons, the following generalizations can be made:

1. If storage capacity is very limited and files must be tightly packed, the index sequential method would be preferable.
2. If random throughput and job time are the main criteria, the random organization may give better performance.
3. If there are numerous additions to and deletions from the file, the random method may be a wiser choice.
4. If there are many reports to be run and the control numbers are long, the index sequential method may be the better choice.

Both sequential and random-file organization are valid techniques for doing a job and both should be explored thoroughly. Approaches to file organization may be combinations of the two techniques. After a thorough study, it may be found that some files in an application should be in random order, while others should be sequential.

Record Composition

When getting an overall view of a direct-access device, the composition of the record is as important as the makeup of the file. There are several ways in which information may be arranged within the record to save time or to make updating easier.

Abstracting

Whenever a firm decides that mass storage is justified on the basis of inquiry purposes, but cannot be justified in terms of size, an abstracting technique may be used to reduce the size and thus reduce the cost of the system. In abstracting, only essential record information is carried on the direct-access file. The rest of the information can be stored on reels of magnetic tape, which are processed together with the direct-access file at regular accounting periods.

Trailer Record

If reference time to the most pertinent data is of more consideration than size and cost, the same technique can apply, but this time the remaining information might appear elsewhere on the file.

Consolidated Files

Often, many firms wish to have different application information consolidated into one record. This is typical of an insurance company that carries Auto, Life, Homeowners, Accident and Health, and other lines of insurance. Rather than having separate files for each of these types, the company might prefer to keep the information by policyholder. Under this set-up, a customer who carries Homeowners, Auto, and Life insurance with the same company will not have his name, address, and other basic information duplicated three times in the file.

Consolidation does save storage space. A more important consideration to the insurance company, however, is customer service. All billing, customer inquiry, etc., can be handled by examining one record, rather than many records.

Multiple Records Per Segment

When the size of the segment is larger than the information to be stored (such as records which occupy only 100 out of the 200 available character positions of the segment), it would be desirable to pack more records into it. In a direct-addressing scheme where the IDs of two related application areas coincide, the first part of the record could be used for one application and the last part for the other. For example, payroll information for employee number 2345 would occupy the first 100 characters in the address position. The billing data for customer number 2345 would occupy the last 100 character positions of that same record. The computer payroll program would be instructed to be aware of the sequence of the applications.

Random-Access and On-Line Systems

"On-line" refers to the operation of input/output devices under direct control of the central processing unit. When this can be accomplished, it eliminates the need for human intervention between input origination and output destination within computer processing. "On-line" can be applied to the units near to and under direct control of the central processing unit (for example, an on-line printer), or for units which are not located near the central processing unit, but which require a communication link.

In an airline flight reservation application, the need for data inquiry is considered. The remoteness of the many reservations offices makes communication links necessary. Communication equipment and random-access storage are mutually supplemental. The maintenance of and access to flight records on a computer system would be extremely difficulty without disk storage. Without communications on-line equipment, changing records or making inquiries regarding information on those records would be difficult. The lack of either hardware would make a computerized reservations system impractical.

In batch-type installations, many operations are reserved for "off-line" handling. Typical of these are operations dealing with the transfer of data from cards to tape, tape to printer, etc. Since the card readers and line printers are relatively slow devices, it is less expensive to have them operate separately and not hold up the central processing unit. To do this, the information is written "on-line" on magnetic tape. This tape then is moved to a smaller system when the reports are run.

Mass (Direct Access) Storage and Responsive Systems

The ability to process input data on-line, regardless of the diversity of applications, and the ability to store both master records and programs make mass storage systems uniquely responsive. They can process data randomly, give an immediate response, or even more appropriately, give responses on a priority basis.

When a system is called upon to process many applications, and the input data are received randomly, it often becomes necessary to schedule the processing and establish a priority for processing. The use of mass storage gives unlimited flexibility to this work without creating an overpowering burden upon the operators of the system. For example, a general-file maintenance run can be interrupted to process an inquiry, then the machine can return to its file maintenance run. A payroll job-ticket calculation run can be interrupted to assemble a new program or even to test a new one.

In other words, a mass-storage system responds to changing priorities and requirements. Rather than processing data on a first-come, first-served basis, a mass-storage system can respond effectively on a controlled "first-things-first" priority. Thus, the capability of altering priority according to the immediate requirements of daily activity becomes a practical reality. Significant reduction is found in the tasks of program modification or the incorporation of new programs into an existing system, and both can be accomplished in a minimum time with a minimum of perplexity.

Selective Updating

Where records take up more than one consecutive segment, the most likely information to be updated (the "dynamic" information) is kept in one segment, and the least likely data to be updated (the "static" data) are kept in another segment. Thus, when the segments are read into memory, only one segment needs to be rewritten.

Glossary of Terms

TRAILER RECORD: A record which follows a group of records and contains pertinent data related to the group of records.

Questions for Review

1. Define file organization. What is the primary objective of its use?
2. What methods are used to set up a file for direct access? Illustrate.
3. Describe each of the following random-order techniques:
   a. correspondence method
   b. associative method
   c. tree method.
4. Discuss and compare the factors involved in choosing between random and sequential file organization.
5. What is abstracting? Explain briefly.
6. How do insurance companies apply consolidated files to improve customer service?
7. Explain how airlines make use of on-line systems for handling reservations.

chapter twenty-eight

PAYROLL— A COMPUTER APPROACH

PREPARATION OF INPUT DATA

The Master Payroll Card
The Bond Card
The Time Card
The Year-to-Date Card

SUPPLEMENTARY REPORTS

Payroll Register (Journal)
Other Registers
Government Reports

Gross Pay by Department
Miscellaneous Reports

THE COMPUTER PAYROLL RUN

PREPARATION OF THE PAYROLL REGISTER

PREPARATION OF THE BOND REGISTER

PREPARATION OF THE QUARTERLY EARNINGS REPORT

THE WITHHOLDING TAX STATEMENT

To ILLUSTRATE A PAYROLL APPLICATION USING A COMPUTER SYSTEM, assume there is an office staff of 300 to be paid on Monday of each week for the hours worked during the previous week. When a person is hired, he completes a form with information to be used in the master personnel record. In Fig. 28-1, the employee number, department, pay rate, and starting date are filled in by the personnel manager according to the form completed by the applicant. The last name is given first to facilitate alphabetic filing. Address and phone number are kept in case of an emergency. Sex and marital status are requested for general information. The Social Security number is important in that all Social Security withholdings must be reported periodically to the Social Security office by Social Security number.

There are ways for an employee to save part of his salary: (1) He might elect to have part of his pay go toward a retirement program. (2) He might have part of his pay go toward the purchase of U.S. Savings Bonds. (3) He might wish to save a portion of his pay in the company's credit union —an organization which invests employee savings and returns a certain amount of interest to the employee each year.

PREPARATION OF INPUT DATA

The Master Payroll Card

When this personnel form has been properly signed by the personnel manager, it is sent to the data-processing center, where the information is keypunched into a card, referred to as a *master payroll card*. The data fields on the

FIG. 28-1   Personnel form

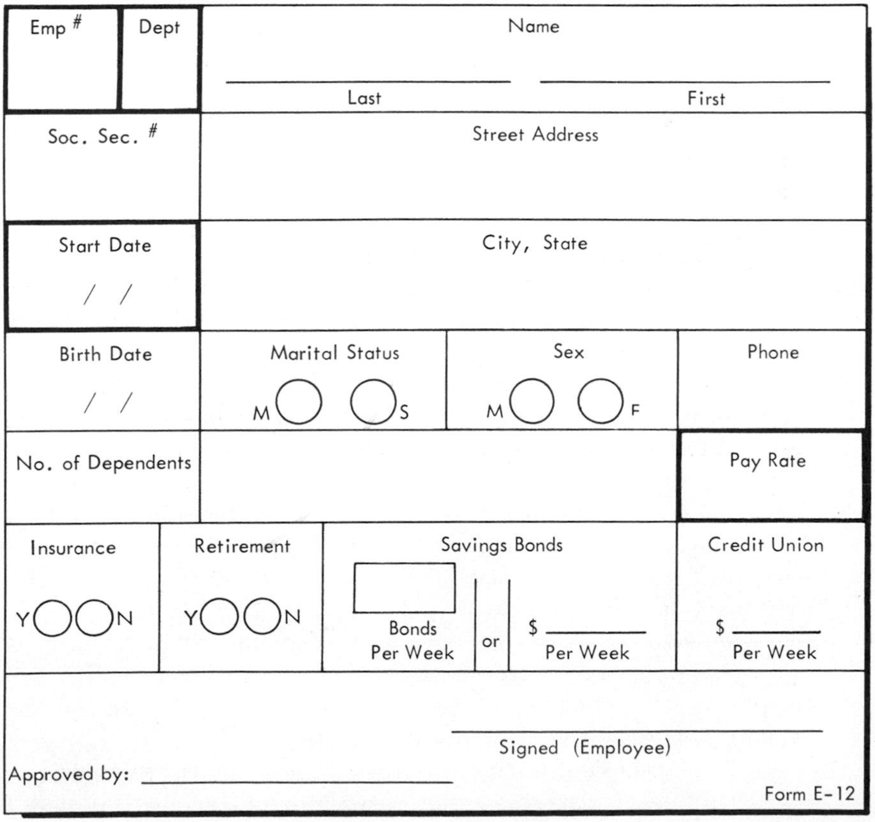

Emp #	Dept	Name
		Last First

Soc. Sec. #	Street Address

Start Date / /	City, State

Birth Date / /	Marital Status M ◯ ◯ S	Sex M ◯ ◯ F	Phone

No. of Dependents			Pay Rate

Insurance Y ◯◯ N	Retirement Y ◯◯ N	Savings Bonds Bonds Per Week or $ ____ Per Week	Credit Union $ ____ Per Week

Signed (Employee)

Approved by: _____

Form E-12

form have been set up in advance by a systems man, thus making the keypunching routine as convenient as possible. In Fig. 28-2, note that the areas on the personnel form correspond to the sequence in which they appear on the punched card to simplify the keypunching.

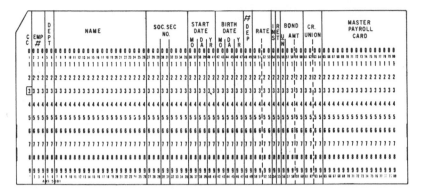

FIG. 28-2   Master payroll card—punched from personnel form

Column *1* on the master card is reserved for a "card code":

1. To distinguish it from another card and to make it easier to extract it from a mixed deck of cards. A master deck may be extracted from a mixed deck by sorting the merged deck on column *1*.
2. It is possible that the person running the payroll application might pick up the wrong deck of cards for processing. With a specific code punched into the card, the computer could be programmed to test for that code and halt processing if the wrong cards turn up. According to the code in Fig. 28-2, there always should be a "3" punched in column *1* of each master payroll card.

Note that the employee number precedes the name field on the master card. It is assumed that the personnel department keeps its personnel forms in sequence by name; however, computers lend themselves more easily to number sequences, so the master cards in the data processing department are kept in employee-number sequence. The employee number field is assigned three columns (columns *2–4*), since there are about 300 employees to be accounted for. If the firm increases its personnel to more than 999, the card will have to be redesigned to allow another column (column *5*) for proper coding.

Columns *5* and *6* are reserved for the department number to which each employee is assigned. All master cards are kept in employee-number sequence within their respective departments.

The name field has been allocated 20 columns (columns *7–26*). Over a period of years, data processing installations have learned that 20 columns usually are sufficient for this purpose. The last name usually can be punched in this amount of space, and the first initial can be used if there is too little room left for the entire first name.

Social Security numbers are allowed nine columns (columns 27–35), since they are nine figure numbers.

The starting date field is punched in six consecutive columns (columns 36–41): two for the month, punched in numeric form (01 through 12); two for the day; and two for the year (the prefix "19" is not necessary). Following the starting-date field is the birthdate field (columns 42–47). Note that all information to this point is of a fixed nature, except for the possibility of a name change due to marriage.

The field reflecting the number of dependents is given two columns (48–49). Rate of pay requires four columns (50–53). Note that the decimal point is not punched into the card; the dotted line in the face of the card denotes the location of the decimal point. A rate of 3.50, for example, would be punched as 0350; a rate of 4.00, as 0400. The pennies always are indicated in columns 52 and 53, which is called "right justifying" a field.

Column 54 is reserved for insurance. If the insurance box in the personnel card is checked "yes," a "1" is punched in column 54; otherwise, a zero is punched. The next column (column 55) is used for a retirement deduction and the same coding applies. Column 56 indicates the number of bonds to be purchased by the employee each week; if none, a "0" is punched. Columns 57–60 are reserved for the amount to be deducted from the employee's pay toward the purchase of bonds; if none, the field is punched with 0000. The last data field, Credit Union (columns 61–64) is punched with the amount to be deducted each week, if any, for investment purposes.

After the original document (personnel form) has been key-punched, the master payroll card is verified. Then the source document is returned to the personnel department for reference. Pertinent data from the master card are reproduced and sent to the payroll department. The two data cards are distinguished by using different colors (for example, blue for data processing and white for the payroll department). An X-punch also is made in column 1 of the payroll department's card. This step, as well as others mentioned to date, are shown in Fig. 28-3 on page 434.

The Bond Card

Before the master card is filed, it is used for creating another card, called the *bond card* (Fig. 28-4). This card is punched by reproducing columns 2–23 from the master, and gang punching a "9" in column 1 and a date in columns 24–26. Columns 27–30 are left blank. The flow chart for the preparation of a bond card is shown in Fig. 28-5.

In the bond card, the date consists of a week number (1–52) and the last digit of the year. Other details are presented later in this chapter.

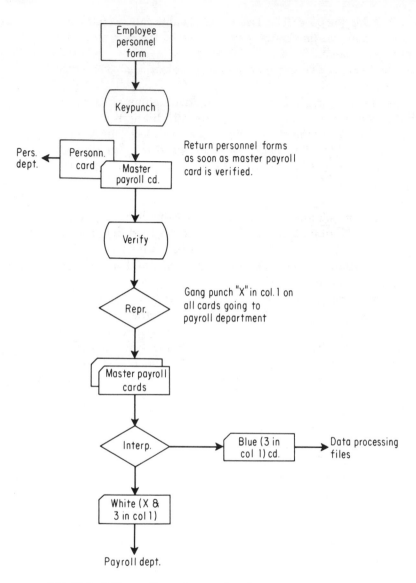

Return personnel forms
as soon as master payroll
card is verified.

Gang punch "X" in col. 1 on
all cards going to
payroll department

FIG. 28-3 Setting up the master payroll cards

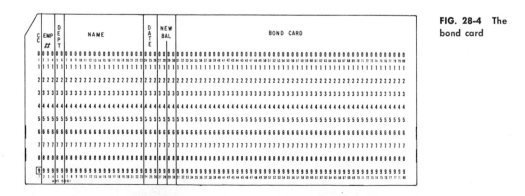

FIG. 28-4 The bond card

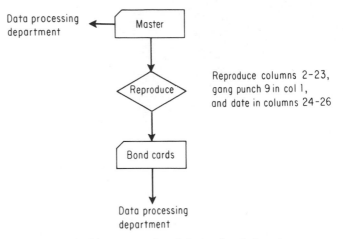

Data processing department

Master

Reproduce columns 2-23, gang punch 9 in col 1, and date in columns 24-26

Reproduce

Bond cards

Data processing department

FIG. 28-5 Preparation of the bond card—flow chart

The Time Card

Toward the end of each week, the data processing department must prepare individual time cards to be given to each employee for recording the hours he has worked. Employees, especially those who work over the weekend, must have the cards no later than Friday. Prepunched into the card are a card code (assume a "2"), department number, employee number, name, week, and year (Fig. 28-6). Any prepunched data are interpreted for readability before they are sent out to the employees. The system flow chart for this routine is shown in Fig. 28-7.

As the week progresses, each employee fills in the hours worked in the appropriate space on his card. On Friday, all cards are signed, collected by the department, and sent to the data processing center. There, the information concerning hours is punched, verified, and then sorted into employee sequence

FIG. 28-6 Weekly detail time cards

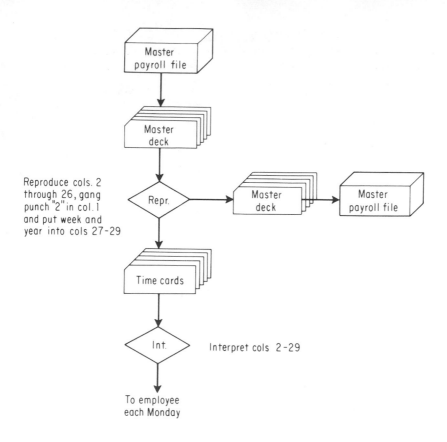

Reproduce cols. 2 through 26, gang punch "2" in col. 1 and put week and year into cols 27-29

Interpret cols 2-29

FIG. 28-7 Preparation of the weekly detail time card—flow chart

and department sequence, respectively. If the keypunch operator makes a mistake, one of two things can happen. Either a new card is prepared and the incorrect card kept aside until all payroll processing is complete (this is called preparing a substitute document), or a small piece of tape can be placed over the incorrect hole, thus preventing any equipment from reading the incorrect punch, and the correct punch can be made.

Since the master card contains certain information required in the processing of a paycheck (for example: deductions, exemptions, pay rate, etc.), it is merged on a collator with the detail card. It should be noted that the master file is sorted in the same sequence as the detail cards.

The Year-to-Date Card

Included in the processing of employee payroll is the preparation of required reports to be submitted periodically to the government. One of these reports is a quarterly statement showing the amount withheld for FICA (Social Security). A special file is provided for keeping a running total of year-to-date figures for each employee. The *year-to-date card* contains such identifying information as card code (7), department number, employee number, and name (Fig. 28-8). Other information also is included and is updated each week whenever a new card is produced.

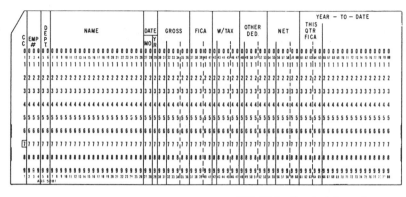

FIG. 28-8   Year-to-date card

Other than the date, all fields will contain year-to-date information (progressive totals) regarding gross pay (total money earned), FICA (Social Security withheld) to date and for the quarter, withholding tax (income tax withheld), total of all other deductions (insurance, retirement, bonds, credit union), and net pay (amount of check: gross, minus all taxes and deduction). At the end of the 13th, 26th, 39th, and 52nd weeks, the quarterly FICA figure is dropped, since it does not represent a year-to-date figure, but only an accumulated figure for the current quarter. The flow chart prepared by the systems analyst for this operation is presented in Fig. 28-9, page 438.

SUPPLEMENTARY REPORTS

It can be concluded from the foregoing discussion that although the prime objective of a payroll application is the production of a paycheck, the "side effects" take more time and consideration than the preparation of the check itself. These "offshoots" affect many areas of the company.

Payroll Register (Journal)

As each paycheck is produced, a listing of all transactions must be kept (Fig. 28-10). The listing is prepared from the information recorded on a check.

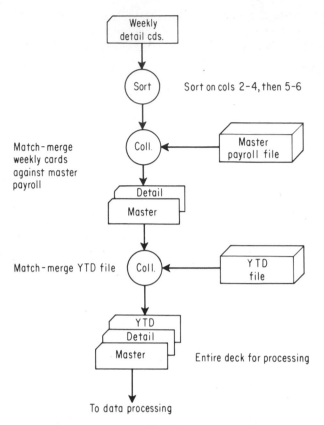

FIG. 28-9 Operations flow chart

Weekly
detail cds.

Sort — Sort on cols 2-4, then 5-6

Match-merge
weekly cards
against master
payroll

Coll. ← Master payroll file

Detail
Master

Match-merge YTD file — Coll. ← YTD file

YTD
Detail
Master — Entire deck for processing

To data processing

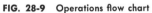

PAYROLL REGISTER

Date

Dept #	Emp #	Name	Reg. Hrs	O.T. Hrs	Reg. Pay	O.T. Pay	Tot. Gross	FICA	W/tax	Other	Ins.	Ret.	Bonds	Cr. Union	Check No.	Net Pay
(2)	(3)	(20)	(3)	(3)	(5)	(5)	(5)	(3)	(4)	(4)	(3)	(3)	(4)	(4)	(3)	(5)

Misc. Ded.

FIG. 28-10 Payroll register

Separate reports or registers must be kept of all of the deductions taken from employees' pay so that the proper departments and agencies can give credit. Credit union, insurance, and retirement information may be taken from the second, third, and fourth copies of the payroll register. The bond register is separate, however (Fig. 28-11).

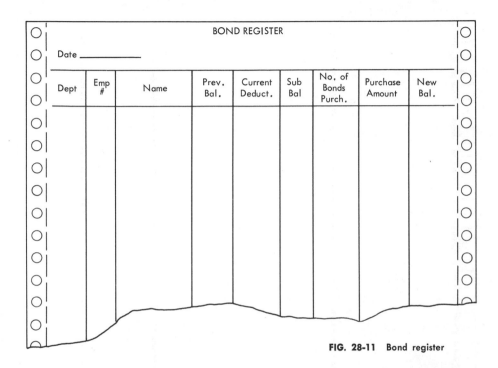

FIG. 28-11 Bond register

Government Reports

Information (FICA and withholding tax) must be collected in order to prepare quarterly reports to the government (Figs. 28-12 and 28-13).

Gross Pay by Department

In making business decisions, cost or overhead often is considered, especially in matters relating to budget appropriations on a departmental basis. The payroll register is set up to show totals in all fields by department. In manufacturing, management needs more data than department totals. Manufacturing employees often fill out a time card showing the amount of time worked to complete a specific job. Job-cost data are valuable to management in determining the cost to be charged to the customer. At the end of the week, the data

FORM 941a (Rev. Oct. 1964)
U.S. Treasury Department
Internal Revenue Service

CONTINUATION SHEET FOR SCHEDULE A OF FORMS 941, 941–M, 941SS, OR 943
REPORT OF WAGES TAXABLE UNDER THE FEDERAL INSURANCE CONTRIBUTIONS ACT

Type or print in this space employer's identification number, name, and address exactly as shown on the return.

Date Quarter Ended	Page Number

If this form is used as a continuation sheet for Form 943, Employer's Annual Tax Return for Agricultural Employees, please check here. ▶ ☐

READ INSTRUCTIONS CAREFULLY

Attach only original continuation sheets to your tax return. Do not send a carbon copy to the U.S. District Director of Internal Revenue.

EMPLOYEE'S SOCIAL SECURITY ACCOUNT NUMBER (If number is unknown, see Circular E) 000 00 0000	NAME OF EMPLOYEE (Please type or print)	TAXABLE F.I.C.A. WAGES Paid to employee in Quarter (Before deductions) Dollars Cents	SEE INSTRUCTIONS Item 20, Form 941

TOTALS FOR THIS PAGE—Taxable wages and number of employees . . $ ______ Number of employees ______

FIG. 28-12 Report of taxable wages

1

Type or print EMPLOYER'S identification number, name, and address above.

Copy A—For Internal Revenue Service

FEDERAL INCOME TAX INFORMATION			SOCIAL SECURITY INFORMATION		
Federal income tax withheld	Wages paid subject to withholding in 1969 ¹	Other compensation paid in 1969 ²	F.I.C.A. employee tax withheld ³	Total F.I.C.A. wages paid in 1969 ⁴	

EMPLOYEE'S social security number ▶

¹ Includes tips reported by employee. Amount is before payroll deductions or sick pay exclusion.

² Report salary or other employee compensation which was not subject to withholding. See Circular E. Farmers, see Circular A.

³ One-eighth of this amount was withheld to finance the cost of Hospital Insurance Benefits. The remainder is for old-age, survivors, and disability insurance.

⁴ Includes tips reported by employee.

Type or print EMPLOYEE'S name and address (including ZIP code) above.

Uncollected Employee Tax on Tips . . . . $

FORM **W-2** U.S. Treasury Department, Internal Revenue Service

16—80183-1

EMPLOYER: See instructions on back of copy D.

FIG. 28-13 Wage and tax statement—sample

processing department sorts out all time cards by job number and produces a report showing the payroll involved in each of the jobs in the factory. This is called a labor distribution report.

Miscellaneous Reports

The personnel department might wish to make morale surveys and needs information regarding absenteeism. A weekly report could be run by department, showing hours not worked and overtime hours worked (hours over 40 per week per employee). This report would give the personnel department an idea of how many people were late to work and how many had to work beyond the 40-hour limit to get the job done. It also might tell them if there are particular times of the year when absenteeism is at its height.

Other special management reports also might be presented upon request, covering such matters as the average pay per person, overall average pay increase or decrease over the last year, projected pay next year based on present increases in pay, percentage of employees enrolled in the retirement program versus the number of employees who are quitting, etc. When a manager wishes to have this information, he sends a request to the data processing manager and a programmer is assigned to write a program to obtain this special information.

THE COMPUTER PAYROLL RUN

To complete the payroll application, the processing is performed by the central processing unit. It is assumed that the computer system includes a central processing unit, a card reader, a card punch, a printer, and a console type-writer.

The most important aspect of the payroll job is the actual production of the paycheck, which is prepared before any other work is done. The steps involved in a paycheck processing run are shown in Fig. 28-14. The deck of cards for all employees (three cards per employee) is the input to the computer. The computer calculates the pay of each employee and prints the paychecks at the same time it punches out two cards: an employee's new year-to-date card and a journal card. As each employee's record is processed, any discrepancies are noted on the console printer. For instance, if the year-to-date card is missing, a note is printed. The record is not processed until the error is corrected. To complete the application, another computer run is made which includes all the employees who were not included on the original run (Fig. 28-14).

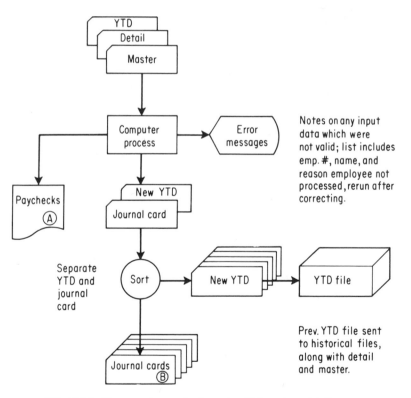

FIG. 28-14 The computer paycheck run (weekly)—systems detail

A paycheck is divided into two parts: the check and the stub. The former is the negotiable section and represents the employee's net pay. The blank checks come through the printer in a continuous sequence (Fig. 28-15). These "continuous forms" are fed into the printer by a sprocket wheel which engages the holes on the edges of the paper. The wheel turns as printing occurs, one line at a time, in a predetermined manner.

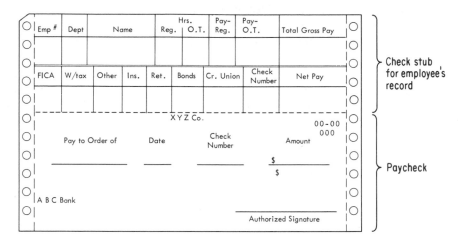

FIG. 28-15 The paycheck

The stub of the check is detachable by the employee and is prepared for the employee's own record. It contains all the information regarding payroll deductions. Total hours worked are recorded from the weekly detail card, and any hours over eight hours per day are considered overtime. During the computer run, a constant of eight is subtracted from each day's hours, and the total number of overtime hours is accumulated. Separating regular hours from overtime hours is necessary because regular hours are multiplied by the normal pay rate; overtime hours are paid at time and a half. Total gross pay is the sum of regular and overtime pay. Social Security (FICA) is a tax based upon a percentage of the gross pay. A maximum limit is set by the Social Security office regarding the amount of tax which can be deducted during the year. The FICA year-to-date figures are kept on the year-to-date card.

"W/tax" is the federal income tax. It is based on a percentage of gross pay, depending on the number of dependents claimed.

The next five fields are miscellaneous deductions. The field entitled "Other" represents such things as a salary advance made to the employee or a correction to his pay, perhaps from a mistake made the previous week.

Insurance is a fixed rate per week per employee and is maintained as a program constant by the computer. If the rate changes, a corrective instruction is made in the program.

Retirement is calculated as a percentage of gross pay. Bonds and credit union deductions are made based on instructions shown on the master card.

The check number is added by the computer. At the beginning of the run, the operator furnishes a starting number to the computer, after which it is incremented by one every time a check is printed.

Finally, net pay represents gross pay minus the sum of all taxes and miscellaneous deductions.

After all the employees' checks have been processed, the checks are separated from the continuous form into individual copies and are run through a machine which prints the authorized signature. This machine also imprints a special ink through the amount (light enough that it does not cover up the amount), so that no changes can be made.

The last step in the payroll run involves separating the journal cards and year-to-date cards by sorting them on column 1. The new year-to-date card is sent to a file to await other uses. The old file can be sent to the historical files. Just as in magnetic-tape processing, old files are retained until all processing has proved to be correct. Journal cards also will be used for other processes (Fig. 28-16).

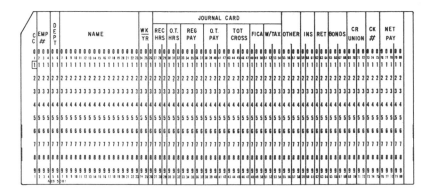

FIG. 28-16   A journal card

PREPARATION OF THE PAYROLL REGISTER

As soon as the paychecks have been processed and distributed, other details must be completed. The journal card is used to produce the *payroll register* (Fig. 28-17). Since all necessary calculations have been made, the use of a computer is not necessary for this run. Figure 24-10 shows a continuous-form payroll register for this application. The date printed on each page is controlled through the control panel of the accounting machine. Certain wires are changed each week so that a new date will be printed.

The payroll register includes headings and columns representing all the information used during payroll processing. The numbers in parentheses show the number of print positions set aside for each field. The continuous-form register can be run in several copies (with carbons between sheets). Many of the fields on the register are accumulated by department as they are printed on the tabulator. These data are valuable to the payroll department in determining the cost of the payroll for each department of the firm.

The *bond register* is prepared on a computer, since it is a little more complicated. Figure 28-18 shows a systems flow chart of this routine. Before the beginning of the computer run, the bond cards (with a zero new balance field for new employees) are match-merged against the journal cards. Not all employees are enrolled in the bond program; therefore, some journal cards fall in

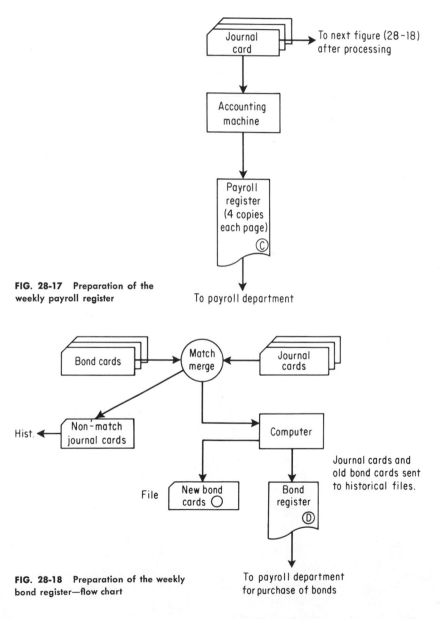

FIG. 28-17 Preparation of the weekly payroll register

FIG. 28-18 Preparation of the weekly bond register—flow chart

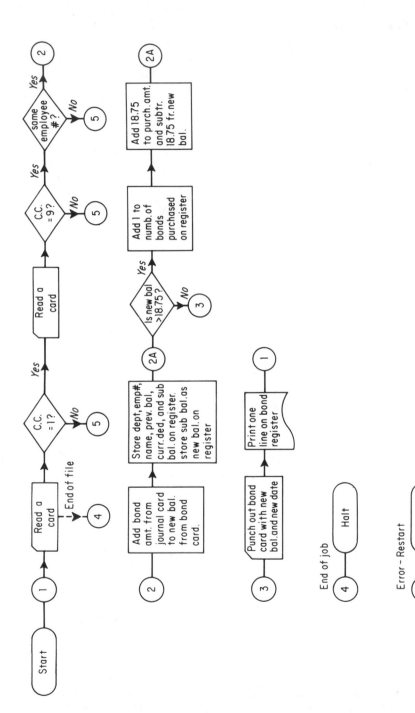

FIG. 28-19 Processing detail chart—weekly bond register preparation

the unmatched pocket of the collator and are sent to the historical file. The merged deck (bond cards and journal cards) can then be processed. The journal card shows the amount of the current week's bond deduction, previously calculated during the paycheck run. The result of the bond run produces a register and new bond cards; the input deck (old bond cards and matched journal cards) is sent to the historical files; and the new bond cards will be used to run the succeeding week's register (Fig. 28-19).

The main problem in processing the foregoing routine is that the total amount collected seldom equals the purchase price of a bond. Each week, the total dollars available for bond purchase are examined. If a total equals or exceeds the bond price (for example, $18.75), a bond is purchased. Any remaining amount is examined again to see if perhaps another bond may be purchased. If so, another $18.75 is subtracted from the accumulated funds. This process continues until no more bonds may be purchased for the week. The money left over is punched into the new bond card to carry over for the following week. The bond register (Fig. 28-11) shows this complete transaction, including the balance from the previous week's card (previous balance); the deduction made this week according to the journal card (current deduction); the sum of the two (subbalance); the number of bonds purchased and the value they represent; and finally, the new balance, which goes on the register as well as on the new bond card.

PREPARATION OF THE QUARTERLY EARNINGS REPORT

As we mentioned before, a report goes to the government each quarter (every 13 weeks) showing employee earnings. A copy of this report is shown in Fig. 28-12. The employee's account number is the Social Security number. The taxable-wages field is reserved for the quarter-to-date earnings that are taxable for FICA; for example, if an employee earned more than the allowable taxable income, only that taxable portion is shown—not the total gross earnings. Note that this report can be prepared on a general accounting machine from the current year-to-date file (Fig. 28-20).

THE WITHHOLDING TAX STATEMENT

At the end of the year, a report is needed for total earnings information, a copy of which is shown in Fig. 28-13. Note that there are four copies—one for the government, one for the employer, and two for the employee. The employee keeps one copy and submits the other with his income-tax report. The report may be prepared from the year-to-date cards at the end of the year (Fig. 28-21). As soon as all end-of-the-year reporting is finished, the year-to-date cards are run through a reproducer and all accumulated information is dropped. The old cards become part of the historical files, and the new blank cards are used to begin payroll processing for the new year (Fig. 28-22).

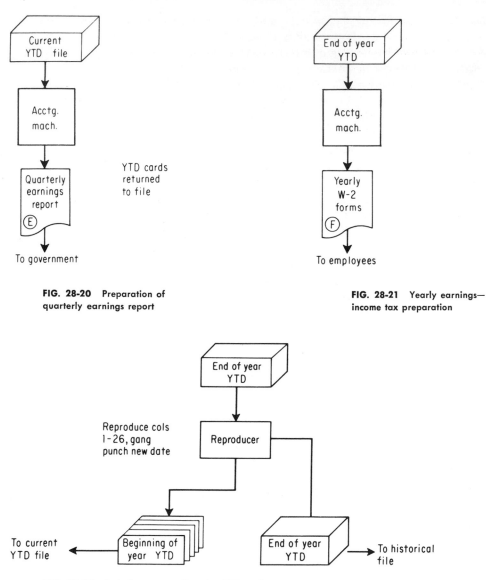

FIG. 28-20 Preparation of quarterly earnings report

FIG. 28-21 Yearly earnings—income tax preparation

FIG. 28-22 End of year—creating new YTD cards

Glossary of Terms

GROSS PAY: An employee's total pay with no deductions.
PAYROLL REGISTER: A record of employees to be paid with the amount due to each.
TIME CARD: A card used for showing the number of hours an employee has worked.

Questions for Review

1. Describe the steps involved in the preparation of payroll input data.
2. What is the difference between a bond card and a time card?
3. What is the main function of a year-to-date card? What information does it contain?
4. What types of reports and records are prepared as a part of a payroll application? Explain each briefly.
5. Explain the actual payroll routine performed by the central processing unit.
6. What type of information does a paycheck include?
7. Summarize briefly the computer routine involved in the preparation of the following reports:
   (a) Payroll register
   (b) Bond register
   (c) Quarterly earning report.

chapter twenty-nine

CAREER OPPORTUNITIES AND MANAGEMENT'S ROLE

DATA PROCESSING MANAGEMENT
The Data Processing Manager
Manager of Computer Operations

SYSTEMS ANALYSIS AND PROGRAMMING
The Systems Analyst
The Computer Programmer

DATA PROCESSING OPERATIONS
The Computer Operator
The Keypunch Operator

MANAGEMENT AND AUTOMATIC DATA PROCESSING
The Management Tool

THE TOPICS DISCUSSED IN THE TEXT THUS FAR HAVE STRESSED the need, the operations, and the manipulating aspects of data processing hardware with a brief coverage of computer programming techniques and methods. Behind all the equipment and the various components making up a computer installation are men and women whose jobs vary from keypunching the data in cards and preparing source data for input, to the task of programming, debugging, operating, and managing a computer system. In this chapter, emphasis will be placed upon career opportunities which have grown out of the increasing need for better electronic data processing systems.

Every year, more computers (in number and complexity) introduced on the market require more specialized and highly trained data processing personnel at all levels. The more an organization depends on a computer, the more it realizes the need for qualified people to plan, organize, direct, and control the many data processing tasks.

Not all computer systems have been successful. A major factor in a successful or unsuccessful computer system is the caliber of the people involved with, and responsible for, its operation. A successful installation is one run by competent data processing personnel and supported by key managers. The need for highly skilled data processors has created a new profession for thousands of men and women. Working efficiency in the EDP system has been shown to be based to a large degree on a new profession of specialists. The computer is a helpless tangle of wires until a "program" has been prepared to direct its action—and programs are prepared by human beings. A computer program may be the result of weeks or months of analysis to determine exactly how output information may be obtained from the input data available. This calls for the combined talents of (1) data processing managers, (2) systems analysts, and (3) programmers. Behind them a whole echelon of operations personnel must control the day-to-day "care and feeding" of the equipment itself.

DATA PROCESSING MANAGEMENT

The Data Processing Manager

A data processing department is organized on the same pattern as that of a formal organization. At the top is a *data processing manager* aided by one or more assistants who act in his behalf to carry out assigned duties. Below the top position are several subordinate employees responsible for producing predetermined results.

The data processing manager is reponsible for the planning, coordinating, and directing of data processing activities for the entire organization. He must supervise the work of others and should possess high managerial as well as technical skills. Many of those now occupying this position have moved up from within the department after acquiring the necessary background and experience. Persons seeking a career in computer management should, however, attempt to earn a college degree, since "outsiders" considered for a top position usually are expected to present a more attractive background than those from within the firm. In many cases a master's degree will be desired. The college course required will vary according to the type of installation. For example, a degree in business administration with some emphasis on data processing would be more suitable for work in a business-oriented computer installation than in a scientific-oriented one. The latter one would require, in most cases, a degree in mathematics, physics, statistics, or other related fields with a background in management and some practical experience in computer science.

It should be emphasized at this point that a data processing manager must possess, in addition to his technical and practical background, "know-how" to lead and get things done through people, since it is people who operate and produce the overall detailed activities of the department. A good manager will be instrumental in optimizing the output of the computer department.

A data processing manager's salary varies with different companies, geographic locations, and size of data processing installations. A recent survey [1] gave the salaries available in different metropolitan areas, and showed a national average of $303 per week. The salaries ranged widely, however, from a low of $100 to a high of $520 per week.

Manager of Computer Operations

The next management position in a data processing department is the direction of computer operations. The *manager of computer operations* directs the computer installation, plans the scheduling of computer time, allocates personnel, maintains the program library, and controls operations within the computer center.

---

[1] *Business Automation* (Business Press International, Inc., 288 Park Avenue West, Elmhurst, Illinois, June 1969).

The educational requirements for this position vary considerably, depending on the size and functions of the computer. Although many persons presently holding the position of computer operations manager do not have college degrees, the trend is to hire and promote operations managers who have completed degrees, or at least a significant amount of college work. The college course should include business subjects as well as mathematics, statistics, and computer science.

Like the data processing manager's salary, the salary of a computer operation's manager also differs depending on the size, type of firm, and the geographic location of the installation. The same survey mentioned earlier shows a national salary average of $211 per week.

SYSTEMS ANALYSIS AND PROGRAMMING

The Systems Analyst

As explained in a separate chapter, the *systems analyst* is responsible for creating an ordered system for data collection, processing, and the production of useful information. His objective is to improve control and decision making and at the same time to make the most efficient use of available data-processing equipment. The highly abstract nature of his work, like that of the computer programmer, requires strong logical and creative abilities.

On the basis of present practices for hiring systems analysts, a college graduate appears to have the best prospect for the job and advancement in this area. Again, the desired major field of college study depends on the type of installation and the specific projects to be worked on. Generally speaking, however, a balanced background in mathematics, computer science, and business management would be desirable.

Senior systems analysts are paid about $230 per week on the average; the manager of systems analysis is generally paid between $245 and $340 per week.

The Computer Programmer

The job of *programmer* is one of the newest in the country. Before 1950, this job classification did not exist; it was not until early 1951 that the first commercial computers were installed. In 1951, only one computer (UNIVAC) was installed; in 1952, there were 7 computers (4 UNIVACS, 3 NCRS); in 1955, 244 computers; in 1958, 3,638 computers; in 1960, 5,400 computers; in 1963, 17,840 computers; and today, there are about 60,000 computers installed, with a commulative net value of 26 billion dollars. With the steadily increasing demand for computers comes equal demand for programmers at all levels to "put the computer to work." It is estimated that as many as 200,000 computers and 500,000 programmers will be needed by 1975. In large computing systems, several programmers at different levels of responsibility work as a team on a given project, often a complex one. The highly experienced, or *senior*, programmer usually directs the work of junior and other programmers throughout the duration of the project. Each programmer is assigned a part of the system to program.

Except for sophisticated, highly specialized, or scientific engineering applications, programming does not necessarily require a college background. Still, college work is desirable since many employers use the degree as a screening device for applicants. Also, a background of general education helps programmers understand the basis for the company procedures and problems. Programming does require a logical mind, an attention to detail, and an ability to determine what steps are necessary to complete a task or solve a problem. Some of the best programmers in industry today have a college background in music, philosophy, and the liberal arts since data processing courses in college were not available. But new programs are being designed especially to train programmers in high schools and colleges. This should result in better prepared programmers for industry in the future.

Persons seeking an opportunity in a scientific-oriented computer installation (scientific programming) would find it helpful to have taken as many college courses in mathematics and computer science as possible. On the other hand, those interested in working in a business-oriented installation (business programming) would find a background that includes business subjects and some mathematics most valuable. For a top position in programming sophisticated projects, a bachelor's or master's degree in mathematics, computer science, or business administration is an important asset in the long run. Financial remuneration and working conditions for programmers are generally good. A beginning programmer should start at $7,000 to $8,000 per year depending on his academic background and work experience, and gradually move up to a senior programmer's level at about $12,000. Many senior programmers, however, with a college or a graduate degree in a specialized science area, earn well over $18,000 a year and some with management responsibility and extensive experience earn over $20,000.

How does one know whether he has the aptitude for programming? A number of computer users, manufacturers, and employment services offer various *programming aptitude tests;* most tests measure the following:

1. Attention to detail and facility with numbers.
2. Logical or reasoning ability.
3. Ability to grasp abstract representations.
4. Problem solving ability.

Some tests are more extensive. In addition to the above areas, they measure:

1. General intelligence.
2. Verbal ability.
3. Comprehension of written material.

Those interested might wish to inquire about these tests through their school guidance counselor, the State or Federal Employment Service, or by getting in touch with the educational center of a computer manufacturer.

DATA PROCESSING OPERATIONS

The Computer Operator

A *computer operator* is in direct command of the computer during a program run. He must load and unload programs, prepare input data for entry, and be on hand to monitor error messages and keep the machines operating smoothly. He should be intelligent, alert, and mindful of the expensive equipment he is operating.

At the present time most computer operators are high school graduates who were previously operators of unit record (tabulating or EAM) equipment. However, the more sophisticated computer systems being marketed today promise to place additional educational demands on operators.

Training for computer operating jobs is provided through private business and technical schools, junior colleges, and some high schools. Most operators have learned on the job and through schools conducted by the computer manufacturers for their customers' personnel. Most of those who train for computer operating jobs either have a high school diploma or are presently in high school and are preparing to enter the computer operation field after graduation. Persons planning to attend a private data processing training institution are advised to check first the reputation of the private school. The state departments of education and the local Better Business Bureaus may be of assistance in locating the best schools. Salaries for computer operators range from $119 per week for beginners to $160 per week for lead operators.

The Keypunch Operator

Keypunch operators transcribe input data from the original documents to punched cards, using keypunch equipment. Keypunch supervisors schedule activities in the keypunch section and instruct operators on procedures for keypunch applications. The educational background necessary is similar to that of tabulator operators: a high school diploma is desirable but not necessarily required. Salaries for keypunch operators average between $81 per week for trainees to $156 for supervisors. Some keypunch supervisors earn over $300 per week. Generally, entry-level jobs in computer or keypunch operations do not require the breadth of educational background or abstract logical ability necessary for systems and computer programming work. They do require, however, a high level of manual dexterity, alertness, and practical thinking.

There has been much misleading publicity about computers, but the less publicized fact is that before any machine can function, a human being first has to think through the problem, reduce it to its basic logic, and then prepare a machine program to follow that logic. Buried under the millions of published words about computers is the truly significant fact that we have at last begun to analyze problems in a disciplined and logical manner, reducing them to basics and assigning quantitative measures where only subjective analysis and emotion existed in the past. The desire to use this relatively new tool in solving our problems has forced us to become more scientific in our thinking about them.

This lesson has not been learned easily, as evidenced by the disappointments many companies have experienced in their early attempts to use computers for problem solving. The fault is not with the machines—the hardware technology is far ahead of the applications and is accelerating more rapidly. The problem is directly attributable to the scarcity of competent, experienced people and the traditional caution of many people in management positions. It is just as important for management to know the capabilities and limitations of the computer as it is for the shop foreman to know the capabilities of the machines in his shop.

The Management Tool

How does one learn about computers to be able to use them intelligently in a business situation? The problem is primarily one of attitude—of placing the use of the machine in its proper perspective. The manager must overcome the fear that the machine poses a threat to his ability to exercise full control over operations and realize that a computer, properly used, can increase his ability to exercise control by making more information available to him when he needs it. It is unimportant for him to know all about the machine itself as long as he realizes that:

1. The computer is only a tool, one component in a man-machine-information system.
2. Information coming out of the machine can be only a combination or permutation of the data which went into it. The machine cannot create information, nor can it extract information which is not inherent in the raw data going in.
3. Information coming out of the machine is useful only when it is interpreted in terms of the combined limits of error of the input data and the program which processed them.

To apply this knowledge, the manager must have considerable depth of understanding about each subsystem in which the computer is used. But in assessing and evaluating what comes out of the machine, he now must analyze what he knows about his operations more exactly than ever before. He must take the time to state his information requirements precisely, so that the people who are directing the machine will develop answers within the limits he sets forth.

In the rapidly changing environment of today's business, high speed data processing machines offer a means through which the manager of a business can respond dynamically to the challenge of making fast decisions correctly. That, for the manager, is the most significant "why" of automatic data processing.

chapter thirty

ORGANIZATION
AND GROWTH
OF THE COMPUTER INDUSTRY

THE COMPUTER INDUSTRY SEEMS DESTINED TO BECOME one of the largest industries in the world within the next ten to fifteen years. Its growth in the future promises to be even more dramatic than its impressive development to date.

CURRENT SIGNIFICANCE OF THE INDUSTRY [1]

The many current uses of electronic data processing equipment raise the question of whether the computer industry has not reached the limits of its potential. Many experts believe that this is not the case. Most mature current applications will require the use of more efficient computers in the years ahead. Numerous other uses for computers are in their infancy, and the development of entirely new applications is being made possible by the gradual removal of technological bottlenecks that have prevented their development to date.

The industry is now becoming increasingly active in the fields of education and medicine, where the market for electronic data processing equipment still seems to be largely untapped. By means of programmed techniques, the machine-aided student is able to advance at his own speed. As the learning process becomes better understood, the computer will no doubt be adapted to new methods of instruction. The teacher will then have more time to handle the problems of individual students. Equally intriguing are the possible medical uses of computers, which include the diagnosis of disease, the monitoring and testing of patients, and countless other applications involved in the overall operation of a large hospital.

[1] Adapted from the brochure, "Investing in the Computer Industry" and used by permission of Merrill Lynch, Pierce, Fenner & Smith, Inc.

TIME SHARING

Time sharing enables a number of users at remote locations to have simultaneous access to a single computer. The machine switches so rapidly from one user to another that each has the illusion of having exclusive use of the machine. Although time sharing has come into use more slowly than its proponents anticipated, its use is growing. In contrast, the present, generally used batch processing methods permit the computer to handle only one problem at a time. Despite this fact, however, batch processing is likely to remain important for some years to come until experience with time sharing shows whether it is practical for widespread use.

The immediate access offered by time sharing may also allow the user to solve by heuristic methods problems that cannot be solved easily by present computer procedures. Heuristic methods enable the user to solve problems by exploratory techniques whereby the solution is gradually developed as progress toward the final result is made. Thus, the successful development of time sharing will enable the user to tackle problems, such as the launching of a sales campaign for a new product or service, that have to be done now without the aid of a computer.

The growth of time sharing to date has been limited by difficulties surrounding the complexities of machine programming. Because data have to be transmitted over telephone lines, the cost is high when the distance between terminals is considerable. In addition, the question of protection of confidential information once it has left the physical control of the individual user presents another problem. Where problems such as these are solved satisfactorily, very likely time sharing will develop into a major business. How rapidly this part of the computer industry expands will depend upon the rapidity of technological advances, together with changes in acceptance by users.

COMPUTER INSTALLATIONS IN THE U.S.

Many observers predict that the industry can more than double in size in the next several years. The value of computer industry shipments, including peripheral equipment, software, and supplies, totaled $300-$400 million in 1955 and grew to more than $26 billion in 1970. In light of potential uses, such as those mentioned above, plus others as yet undiscovered, shipments could reach an annual rate of $30 billion by 1975.

The present computer industry consists of: (1) the manufacturers; (2) the firms supplying peripheral equipment; (3) the software and service firms; and (4) the firms whose sole activity is leasing equipment. Thus, the industry can expand and grow in four different directions, to say nothing of the possibilities of expansion into directions as yet undeveloped.

The process of bringing a new series of computers from the development stage through production to installation with satisfactory programming support is long, difficult, and costly. As the industry has developed technologically, however, the cost of executing one instruction or storing one bit of information has declined dramatically, providing the customer with more and more computing power per dollar. Many computers ·delivered today are of the "third-generation" variety. Beginning about 1964 several companies started introducing new lines incorporating microelectronic concepts and other improved features—hence, the third generation of computers. Second-generation machines, however, constitute a sizable portion of the total now in use; in many cases, this equipment can still fulfill the needs of its users and remains in demand.

Most companies introduce a new line with the hope that at least several years will pass before the line is superseded by a technologically more advanced line, since a company needs time enough to recover its high developmental costs and to attain a satisfactory level of profits. Industry experts, generally, believe that the third generation of computers will remain in the forefront for a number of years, or at least into the early 1970s. This expectation does not preclude the introduction of new computers each year, but does imply that an early shift to fourth-generation machines is unlikely. The situation, of course, could change as a result of some major technological advance or drastic shift in the competitive positions of various manufacturers.

Because a large part of shipments consists of leased equipment, manufacturers derive substantial rental revenues from this type of equipment. The figures in rentals include those received on previously installed equipment as well as that installed currently. Because of this, the total value of all electronic data processing equipment installed at the present time has to be estimated. Although official industry statistics are not available, people in the industry believe the total value of existing equipment is somewhere in the neighborhood of $30 billion. An estimated 86 percent of computers installed in 1970 for business data processing will be on a lease basis. Of computers installed for scientific uses, the percentage of machines leased is considerably smaller.

Leasing has important financial implications for the manufacturer. After large sums of money have been spent to develop, build, and install the equipment, the company begins to receive rent on a monthly basis. Under a lease, the manufacturer retains title to the equipment and depreciates its cost over the useful life of the machine. Companies that use conservative accounting methods depreciate their computers on a straight-line basis over a period of four or five years. Owing to the threat of a rapid change in technology, however, the highly conservative firms use accelerated depreciation methods, so that a large part of the cost of the machine is depreciated in the first year or two. This cost alone may offset income from rentals in the early stages of an installation, to say nothing of the company's other costs. Hence, from an accounting standpoint, initial installations may be unprofitable. If they are not made obsolete by new technological developments, however, they show an accounting profit, usually, in the years following.

As a lease installation reaches its third, fourth, or fifth year, it can become highly profitable if the equipment can still command its original rental, or a rental close to that figure. The industry has grown so fast that by the time installations are a few years old, they are far outnumbered by "unprofitable" new installations. In addition to using conservative depreciation methods, some firms defer or capitalize costs associated with obtaining leases. This can have an important effect on the amount reported as earnings by the company to its stockholders, present and prospective, in the stage of initial installation.

Thus, leasing has been a major influence in the relatively poor financial records of several computer manufacturers and places a strain on the firm's cash position, necessitating the raising of large sums of capital. Most leases are relatively short term, and after a year, can be cancelled by the user with one month's notice. The fact is, however, that users are likely to utilize the equipment for much longer periods, provided it is meeting their requirements satisfactorily.

A recent accounting change allows the manufacturer to treat long-term leases as outright sales. This change can be financially advantageous for manufacturers, if users agree to take longer-term leases. The growth in third-party leasing—to be discussed in a later section—increases the percentage of manufacturers' revenues from outright sales.

PERIPHERAL EQUIPMENT MANUFACTURERS

Official industry estimates indicate that the basic construction cost of the main frame portion of a computer in a typical configuration accounts for about 50 percent of its total cost, while necessary peripheral equipment accounts for the remainder. Trade sources, generally, believe that this relationship will change and that by 1975 some two thirds to three quarters of the total cost will involve peripheral units. Peripheral equipment is that used with the main frame as part of, or in close conjunction with, a computer.

The demand for peripheral equipment made by firms that supplement the work of the computer manufacturers proper is estimated at approximately $200 million annually. The total amount of peripheral equipment shipped annually is much larger, however, because much of it is manufactured by the computer manufacturers themselves. The latter have been making more of their own peripheral equipment and, in some cases they have been supplying other manufacturers as well. To keep abreast of a rapidly advancing technology, the purely peripheral equipment manufacturer incurs extra heavy costs periodically. Generally, he has a relatively small sales base consisting of one or two major products. As a result, several firms have shown mediocre or even negative results, although the overall trend of sales and earnings for the group has been upward.

Technicians point out that because arithmetic or logic units have already attained tremendous speeds, the greatest potential improvement lies in the devices used for the input or output of information. The market for input devices consists of items such as card punchers and readers, magnetic ink character readers, magnetic data recorders, tape drives, and optical character readers. In the process of development is more versatile optical-scanning equipment that can read varied type fonts and, within closely prescribed limits, handwritten numbers and letters. Information can also enter the computer from teletypewriters through terminals or can be transmitted as sound signals by telephone. Studies on the feasibility of translating human speech into patterns that can be recognized by a machine are also being made.

Devices such as disk files, disk packs, and core memories could also be considered peripheral equipment. Studies with lasers could eventually lead to computer memories that store data in optical rather than magnetic form.

The demand for peripheral equipment should grow rapidly. As in the case of all new products, however, it is likely to remain a highly competitive field. A premium is placed on technological advances, reliability of equipment, and competitive pricing. *The most successful peripheral firms will be those that can offer equipment with uniquely practical capabilities.*

SOFTWARE AND SERVICE COMPANIES

Software and services include programming, systems analysis, service bureau operations, programming schools, and training centers. In dollar volume, this segment of the computer industry is believed to be as large as, or larger than the hardware, or computer manufacturing, portion of the industry. Expenditures for software and services during the next several years are expected to grow at least as rapidly as those for hardware. Computer manufacturers often spend heavily for software, and the amount spent is indirectly reflected in the price of computer hardware. Computer users, including corporations, colleges, government, and nonprofit organizations, account for the largest portion of spending. The strictly software firms now account for only a moderate part of industry volume, but they are becoming increasingly important, as witnessed by the fact that the annual volume as a group amounts at present to hundreds of millions of dollars.

Programmers in this country today probably *number over 150,000*, but present needs alone demand a substantial increase in this number, as the perusal of the want ads of any newspaper will reveal. The training of new programmers is often done by computer manufacturers themselves, but more and more business schools are offering programming courses in their curriculums, and independent service firms are developing programming schools of their own.

Application programs for performing common tasks, such as the preparation of payrolls, have been fertile ground for the software firms, while the manufacturers have been busy meeting hardware needs and solving the problems of developing basic machine instructions. Experience in solving the particular problems of one user can greatly simplify the task of developing programs for other users wishing to do similar jobs. Some of the computer manufacturers have also called upon firms specializing strictly in software to help develop the basic instructions that control the organization and flow of work in the computer and to translate programming codes into numerical machine language. In some cases, an individual computer user may temporarily have heavy programming needs and thus may need to employ an outside firm during such a period. In other cases, organizations may wish to try out a new system and employ outside help until they determine whether the need is permanent.

PURCHASE OF COMPUTER TIME

The sale of computer time has received much attention and has developed very rapidly even though the complexity of programming machines has limited the speed with which time-sharing uses of computers have developed. As time sharing becomes commonplace, it should receive increasing attention. Computer time can be purchased from several sources: (1) manufacturers, (2) computer owners who are not fully utilizing their own equipment, and (3) independent firms specializing in the field. By means of typewriter consoles (terminals) or cathode-ray tube displays, which are tied to a central processing unit, the user may be provided with access to a remote computer. The sale of computer time has been likened to the use of electric power or an ordinary telephone, with the term *computer utility* evolving. For many users, having access to the capabilities of very powerful electronic data processing equipment, without the necessity of renting or buying smaller machines with lesser capabilities, has particular appeal. A number of users purchase computer time to supplement their own installations, or purchase time until they are convinced that their needs justify a computer installation of their own.

LEASING COMPANIES

A sizable majority of computers shipped today are leased to the user rather than sold outright. For the user, leasing may be more attractive than an outright purchase because it provides a flexible approach to equipment needs in a rapidly changing technological field. Computer leasing companies either purchase their machines from a manufacturer or a user who already owns a machine. They then lease the machine at rentals that are often 10 to 20 percent lower than those charged by the original manufacturer. Owing to the fact that they assume the risk of obsolescence, the manufacturers do not consider them to be competitors because of their lower charges.

Most leasing companies assume that: (1) the computers they are leasing today will have a long life; (2) present lease rates can be maintained for several years; and (3) even after new equipment is introduced, present computers will continue to have an important residual value as borne out by the experience with many of the older second-generation machines. The leasing companies, therefore, depreciate the computers they purchase over a much longer period than do the computer manufacturers. The principal risk involved is the possibility that presently owned equipment will become obsolete more rapidly than is assumed by the depreciation methods adopted. The risk of obsolescence also will probably tend to increase in future years, especially if the rapidity of change or innovation continues. Therefore, recovering the purchase price and realizing a profit on third-generation equipment, purchased at a time further removed from its introduction, will become more difficult. In other words, the older the equipment is when purchased, the greater the risk of obsolescence before recovery of cost or the earning of profit.

Since the leasing of electronic data processing equipment is a relatively easy industry to enter, competition is intense, and will probably become more so as time goes on. To date, perhaps 4 to 5 percent of the total computer installations have been accounted for by leasing firms. Expansion possibilities for the industry as a whole appear to be favorable for the foreseeable future. Several firms have indicated that lack of funds, and especially lack of trained personnel, rather than a shortage of customers, have limited the growth of the leasing industry.

Several leasing companies are broadening their operations to include software, services such as maintenance, and peripheral equipment. In offering users several services, these firms hope to be able to establish themselves as broadly based organizations. At present, for instance, most machine maintenance is done by the manufacturer rather than the leasing company.

If computer manufacturers should lower lease rates or raise purchase prices in relation to lease rates, leasing companies could have increasing difficulty buying equipment that can be offered for lease at rates below those of the manufacturers. Most observers, however, believe that such a change is unlikely to develop very soon. On the contrary, computer manufacturers have been using price incentives to encourage outright sales of computers as a means of easing their risks incident to obsolescence. To date, they have been aided by the leasing firms which have purchased, directly or indirectly, equipment that the manufacturer might otherwise be forced to retain and lease. If risks of obsolescence should ease, however, the manufacturers might seek more leasing business. Under such conditions, leasing companies would face stiff competition from them.

FUTURE CONSIDERATIONS—THE CHECKLESS SOCIETY AND OTHER APPLICATIONS

The growing volume of payments involved in the conduct of everyday life has caused much discussion about the possibility of a checkless society. Such a development still seems to be many years away, and initially may evolve on a selective basis. Some prognosticators see people paying for everything they buy by means of a credit card or other device. The store register would act as an input device to a computer, which would deduct the amount of the purchase directly from the customer's bank balance. If the customer prefers to pay later, he would be billed at home and would pay the amount due by means of his home computer. In addition to its financial duties, the home computer could control various mechanical and electrical functions in the home. Although such applications for computers may still be far in the future, they point up a potentially vast market for small electronic data processing devices. Perhaps closer at hand is the use of the home telephone to dial a computer and instruct it to perform a service or transaction. Still other industry followers see the development of computers that would be used in automobiles.

Further possibilities arise from the many applications in which electronic data processing equipment has been tried, but is not yet widely used. The simulation of management problems may help businessmen to make more accurate decisions on the courses their companies should take. In the hands of talented people, properly trained in its use, the computer may also attain a significant place in the arts. A common international language may become possible, which would make for better understanding between all peoples of the world.

Although these possibilities, and others, seem rather "out of the ordinary," the fact that they have been, and are being, experimented with indicates that growth possibilities in the computer industry are considered carefully from all possible vantage points. The present actual performance of the industry alone exhibits a high degree of optimism for future expansion and growth, while the "dreams" indicate that the key people in the industry are not afraid to "loosen their imagination" to carry it to greater heights of accomplishment. Such an attitude has always been essential in those industries that have succeeded in giving the people of the United States increasingly higher planes and standards of living. Thus, computer growth possibilities bode "good" rather than "ill" for the future progress of the computer industry.

PART

APPENDICES

5

APPENDIX A—DATA PROCESSING ASSOCIATIONS

American Federation of Information Processing Societies (AFIPS), 345 E. 47th Street, New York, New York, 10017.

Founded in May 1961, AFIPS represents an estimated 26,000 members of the information processing community. Its primary *purpose* is to advance the understanding and knowledge of the information processing sciences through active engagement in various scientific activities and cooperation with state, national and international (called IFPS) organizations on information processing.

The association's primary *activities* are the spring and fall joint computer conferences, traditionally held in the eastern and western parts of the country, respectively. *Proceedings* of each conference are published and made available to all members.

Association for Computing Machinery (ACM), 1130 Avenue of the Americas, New York, New York, 10036.

Founded in 1947, ACM has over 20,000 members in over 160 chapters. Its *function* is to advance the design, development, and application of information processing and interchange of such techniques between computer specialists and their users.

ACM's primary *activities* are chapter and regional meetings and an annual conference (usually held in August). It sponsors various seminars and special interest groups and *publishes Computing Reviews* (monthly), *Communications of the ACM* (monthly), and *Journal of the ACM* (quarterly).

Association for Educational Data Systems (AEDS), 1201 Sixteenth Street, N. W., Washington, D.C., 20036.

Founded in 1962 by professional educators, AEDS has approximately 1,600 members who are interested in sharing information related to the effect of data processing on the educational process. It acts as a clearinghouse of such information, recommends professional consultants, and organizes workshops and seminars on educational data processing. AEDS' major *periodicals* are *Monitor* (monthly) and *Journal of Educational Data Processing* (quarterly).

Association of Data Processing Service Organizations (ADAPSO), 947 Old York Road, Abington, Pennsylvania, 19001.

An association of commercial institutions, ADAPSO's members offer data processing services through systems they operate on their own premises. A *directory* is published annually.

Association for Systems Management (ASM), 24587 Bagley Road, Cleveland, Ohio, 44138.

Founded in 1944, SPA has approximately 7,000 members in 105 chapters in the United States, Mexico, Canada, Venezuela, and other foreign countries. Its *purpose* is to promote advanced management systems and procedures through seminars, professional education and research.

SPA's major *periodicals* are the monthly *Journal of Systems Management,* the *International Newsletter,* and the *Annual Ideas for Management.* Its other publications include *Total Systems, Profile of a Systems Man, An Annotated Bibliography for the Systems Professional,* and a *Guide to Office Clerical Standards.* In addition to chapter meetings, it also holds an annual international meeting in the United States.

Business Equipment Manufacturers Association (BEMA), 235 E. 42nd Street, New York, New York, 10017.

Founded in 1916, BEMA comprises the 55 companies which manufacture computing equipment and office machines. Its main *function* is to guide users in solving problems and applying information for general benefit. It sponsors the setting of standards for computers and information processing. It *publishes* a weekly *News Bulletin* and an *Annual Report.*

Data Processing Management Association (DPMA), 505 Busse Highway, Park Ridge, Illinois, 60068.

Founded in 1951 as the *National Machine Accountants Association* (name changed to DPMA in 1962), DPMA claims membership over 29,000 in the United States, Canada, and Japan.

The primary *purpose* of the DPMA is to develop and to promote business methods and education in data processing and data processing management. Through its chapters, it promotes a professional attitude among its members in understanding and applying data processing techniques.

The DPMA's major *periodicals* are the monthly *Journal of Data Management* and the *DPMA Quarterly*. It also publishes proceedings of its annual conference (usually held in June) and *Research and Career Information.*

Since 1962, the Certificate in Data Processing has been available to maintain professional standards in data processing (see Appendix C for details).

Other Associations, especially those with interest in data processing, include:

Administrative Management Society, Willow Grove, Pennsylvania, 19090.

American Documentation Institute, 2000 P Street, N. W., Washington, D.C., 20036.

American Management Association, 135 W. 50th Street, New York, New York, 10020.

American Records Management Association, 738 Builders Exchange, Minneapolis, Minnesota, 55402.

American Society for Information Science, 2000 P Street, N. W., Washington, D.C., 20036.

Digital Equipment Computer Users Society, Maynard, Massachusetts, 01754.

Federal Government Accountants Association, 1523 L Street, N. W., Washington, D.C., 20005.

Industrial Management Society, 330 S. Wells Street, Chicago, Illinois, 60606.

National Association of Accountants, 505 Park Avenue, New York, New York, 10022.

National Management Association, 333 W. First Street, Dayton, Ohio, 45402.

Society for Advancement of Management, 16 W. 40th Street, New York, New York, 10018.

Society for Information Display, 654 N. Sepulveda Boulevard, Suite 5, Los Angeles, California, 90040.

Special Library Association, 31 E. 10th Street, New York, New York, 10003.

APPENDIX B—PERIODICALS

Abstracts of Computer Literature, Burroughs Corporation Plant Library, 460 Sierra Madre Villa, Pasadena, California, 91109. Bimonthly, 36 page review of literature on various aspects of computing; free.

Automation-Data in State and Local Government, Michigan Department of Education,

Bureau of Educational Services, Library Division, 735 E. Michigan Avenue, Lansing, Michigan, 48913. Monthly, 4 page review of published EDP articles; free.

Business Automation, Business Press International, Inc., 288 Park Avenue, West Elmhurst, Illinois, 60126. Monthly, 85 page journal on various EDP subjects. Free to educators in data processing and to other qualified individuals.

Business Automation News Report, The Business Press, 288 Park Avenue, West Elmhurst, Illinois, 60126. Weekly, 8 page coverage of topics of general interest.

Communications of the ACM, Association for Computing Machinery (ACM), 1130 Avenue of the Americas, New York, New York, 10036. Monthly, 80 page journal covering technical articles and subjects of general interest.

Computer Characteristics Quarterly, Adams Associates, 128 The Great Road, Bedford, Massachusetts, 01730. A quarterly 250 page presentation of data on key characteristics of computers and peripheral devices.

Computer Design, Computer Design Publishing Company, P. O. Box A, Winchester, Massachusetts, 01890. A monthly 90 page coverage of subjects on circuitry. Free to qualified subscribers.

Computer Education, Data Processing Horizons, Inc., P. O. Box 99, South Pasadena, California, 91030. A monthly magazine covering latest developments in the teaching of data processing. It also covers such aspects of educational interest as computer characteristics, profiles on schools, book reviews, films, correspondence courses and seminars.

Computers and Automation, Berkeley Enterprises, Inc., 815 Washington Street, Newtonville, Massachusetts, 02160. A monthly 75 page journal covering topics of general interest.

Computers and the Humanities, Queens Colleges of the City University of New York, Flushing, New York, 11367. A 65 page journal published five times each year, covering topics related to the humanities.

Computerworld, Computerworld, Inc., 129 Mt. Auburn Street, Cambridge, Massachusetts, 02138. A weekly newspaper covering various aspects and developments in the electronic data processing field.

Computing Reviews, Association for Computing Machinery, 211 E. 43rd Street, New York, New York, 10017. A monthly 100 page journal presenting critical evaluation of books, articles and films on various aspects of computing.

Data Processing, North American Publishing Company, 134 N. 13th Street, Philadelphia, Pennsylvania, 19107. A monthly, 75 page magazine covering topics of general interest in data processing.

Data Processing Digest, Data Processing Digest, Inc., 1140 South Robertson Boulevard, Los Angeles, California, 90035. A monthly, 20 page coverage of general topics on data processing.

Data Processing for Education, American Data Processing, Inc., 4th floor, Book Building, Detroit, Michigan, 48226. A monthly, 12 page coverage of general data processing topics in education.

Datamation, F. D. Thompson Publications, Inc., 35 Mason Street, Greenwich, Connecticut, 06830. A monthly, 140 page magazine, covering current and prospective developments in the data processing field.

EDP Weekly, Industry Reports, Inc., 514 Tenth Street, N. W., Washington, D.C., 20004. A 15 page coverage of developments in data processing.

Information Processing Journal, Cambridge Communication Corporation, 1612 K Street, N. W., Washington, D.C., 20006. A quarterly, 215 page journal presenting critical evaluation of articles and books on various aspects of electronic data processing.

Journal of Data Management, Data Processing Management Association, 505 Busse Highway, Park Ridge, Illinois, 60068. A monthly, 68 page magazine covering business-oriented data processing topics. Free to members.

Journal of the Association for Computing Machinery, Association for Computing Machinery, 1130 Avenue of the Americas, New York, New York, 10036. A quarterly publication emphasizing technical papers. Free to members.

Software Age, Press-Tech, Inc., 1020 Church Street, Evanston, Illinois, 60201. A bimonthly, 50 page coverage of software and other related topics at a nontechnical level. Free to qualified subscribers.

Systems and Procedures Journal, Systems and Procedures Association, 24587 Bagley Road, Cleveland, Ohio, 44138. A bimonthly, 40 page journal covering various topics on analysis of information and management systems and procedures; free.

Other Periodicals of Interest

Data Processing for Management, American Data Processing, Inc., 22nd Floor, Book Tower, Detroit, Michigan, 48226.

Data Systems News, United Business Publications, P. O. Box 7387, Philadelphia, Pennsylvania, 19101.

Digital Computer Newsletter, Information Systems Branch, Office of Naval Research, Washington, D.C., 20360.

EDP Analyzer, EDP Analyzer, 134 Escondido Avenue, Vista, California, 92083.

Honeywell Computer Journal, Honeywell, Inc., Electronic Data Processing Division, Wellesley Hills, Massachusetts, 02181.

IBM Data Processor, International Business Machines Corporation, Data Processing Division, 112 E. Post Road, White Plains, New York, 10601.

IBM Systems Journal, International Business Machines Corporation, Armonk, New York, 10504.

Information Display, Information Display Publications, Inc., 647 N. Sepulveda Boulevard, Los Angeles, California, 90049.

Journal of Computer and System Sciences, Academic Press, Inc., 111 Fifth Avenue, New York, New York, 10003.

Scientific and Control Computer Reports, Auerbach Corporation, 121 N. Broad Street, Philadelphia, Pennsylvania, 19107.

APPENDIX C—GLOSSARY OF DATA PROCESSING TERMS

ABACUS: A manual calculating device that uses beads to represent decimal values.

ACCESS TIME: (1) The time interval between the instant at which data are called for from a storage device and the instant delivery is completed, i.e., the read time. (2) The time interval between the instant at which data are requested to be stored and the instant at which storage is completed, i.e., the write time.

ACCOUNTING MACHINE: (1) A keyboard actuated machine that prepares accounting records. (2) A machine that reads data from external storage media, such as cards or tapes, and automatically produces accounting records or tabulations, usually on continuous forms.

ACCUMULATOR: A register in which the result of an arithmetic or logic operation is formed.

ADDER: A device whose output is a representation of the sum of the quantities represented by its inputs.

ADDRESS: (1) An identification, as represented by a name, label, or number, for a register, location in storage, or any other data source or destination such as the location of a station in a communication network. (2) Loosely, any part of an instruction that specifies the location of an operand for the instruction.

ALGOL: *Algorithmic-oriented language;* an international procedure-oriented language.

ANALOG COMPUTER: A computer which represents variables by physical analogies. Thus, any computer which solves problems by translating physical conditions such as flow, temperature, pressure, angular position, or voltage into related mechanical or electrical quantities and uses mechanical or electrical equivalent circuits as an analog for the physical phenomenon being investigated. In general, it is a computer which uses an analog for each variable and produces analogs as output. Thus, an analog computer measures continuously whereas a digital computer counts discretely.

ARRAY VARIABLE: A dimensioned variable which represents one or more memory cells specified in a dimensioned statement.

ASSEMBLE: To prepare a machine language program from a symbolic language program by substituting absolute operation codes for symbolic operation codes and absolute relocatable addresses for symbolic addresses.

AUTOMATION: (1) The implementation of processes by automatic means. (2) The theory, art, or technique of making a process more automatic. (2) The investigation, design, development, and application of methods of rendering processes automatic, self-moving, or self-controlling.

AUXILIARY STORAGE: A storage that supplements another storage.

BAR PRINTER: A printing device that uses several type bars positioned side by side across the line. Printing data on a line involves activating specific bars to move vertically until the characters they contain are properly aligned. Then, the data are printed simultaneously.

BATCH PROCESSING: A technique by which items to be processed must be coded and collected into groups prior to processing.

BINARY: (1) Pertaining to a characteristic or property involving a selection, choice, or condition in which there are two possibilities. (2) Pertaining to the number representation system with a radix of two.

BINARY-CODED DECIMAL: Pertaining to a decimal notation in which the individual decimal digits are each represented by a group of binary digits, e.g., in the 8-4-2-1 binary-coded decimal notation, the number twenty-three is represented as 0010 0011 whereas in binary notation, twenty-three is represented as 10111.

BIT: (1) An abbreviation of *binary digit.* (2) A single character in a binary number. (3) A single pulse in a group of pulses. (4) A unit of information capacity of a storage device.

BLOCK: A set of things, such as words, characters, or digits, handled as a unit.

BRANCH: A set of instructions that is executed between two successive decision instructions.

BUFFER: A storage device used to compensate for a difference in rate of flow of data, or time of occurrence of events, when transmitting data from one device to another.

BUSINESS DATA PROCESSING: Data processing for business purposes, e.g., recording and summarizing the financial transactions of a business.

BUSINESS ORGANIZATION: A framework by means of which the activities of a business are tied together to provide for integrated performance. Also, a human relationship in group activity.

CALCULATING: Reconstructing or creating new data by compressing certain numeric facts.

CALCULATOR: (1) A device capable of performing arithmetic. (2) A calculator as in (1) that requires frequent manual intervention. (3) Generally and historically, a device for carrying out logic and arithmetic digital operations of any kind.

CARD STACKER: An output device that accumulates punched cards in a deck. Contrast with card hopper.

CASH DISCOUNT: A fixed amount or a percentage deducted by the seller from the price of an item for inducing cash payment by the buyer.

CHAIN PRINTER: A device which uses a chain of several links, each of which contains alphabetic and numeric characters. The chain rotates horizontally at constant speed. Hammers from the back of the paper are timed to fire against selected characters on the chain, causing the printing of a line.

CHARACTER: An elementary mark or event that is used to represent data. A character is often in the form of a graphic spatial arrangement of connected or adjacent strokes.

CLASSIFYING: Arranging data in a specific form, usually by sorting, grouping, or extracting.

COBOL: Common Business Oriented Language. It is a procedural language developed for business data processing. The language is intended as a means for direct presentation of a business program to a computer with a suitable compiler.

COBOL DATA DIVISION: Describes the data to be processed by the object program. It contains primarily a file section which describes the file(s) used and a working-storage section which reserves memory space for storage of results.

COBOL ENVIRONMENT DIVISION: Describes the physical characteristics of the equipment being used and the aspects of the problems which are dependent on the program. Its two main sections are the configuration and the input/output sections.

COBOL IDENTIFICATION DIVISION: Identifies the name of the programmer, the title of the COBOL program, and the compiler listing associated with it.

COBOL LANGUAGE: A computer language is made up of English-language statements which provide a relatively machine-independent method of expressing a business-oriented problem to the computer.

COBOL PROCEDURE DIVISION: Programmer-defined, it defines the operations which perform the necessary processing of data. Its structure includes sections and paragraphs as well as conditional, imperative, and compiler-directing classes of sentences/statements.

COBOL WORD: Also called "reserve word"; holds a preassigned meaning in COBOL to be used in its prescribed context.

CODING: The translation of flow diagrams into the language of the computer.

COLLATOR: A device to collate or merge sets of cards or other documents into a sequence.

COMB PRINTER: A device which consists of a set of characters mounted on a bar facing a paper form. As the bar passes over the paper (left to right), hammers strike the selected characters onto the form. When the bar reaches the right edge of the form, it returns to a home position to print another line.

COMPILE: To prepare a machine language program from a computer program written in another programming language by making use of the overall logic structure of the program, generating more than one machine instruction for each symbolic statement, or both, as well as performing the function of an assembler.

COMPOSITE CARD: A multipurpose data card, or a card that contains data needed in the processing of various applications.

COMPUTER: A calculating device which processes data represented by a combination of discrete (in digital computers) or continuous (descriptive of analog computers) data.

COMPUTER ASSISTED INSTRUCTION: A concept that applies computers and specialized input/output display terminals directly to individualized student instruction.

COMPUTER WORD: A sequence of bits or characters treated as a unit and capable of being stored in one computer location. Synonymous with *machine word*.

CONSOLE PRINTER: An auxiliary output printer used in several computer systems for relaying messages to the computer operator.

CONSTANT: Any specific value (a number) that does not change during program execution.

CONTROL: (1) The part of a digital computer or processor which determines the execution and interpretation of instructions in proper sequence, including the decoding of each instruction and the application of the proper signals to the arithmetic unit and other registers in accordance with the decoded information. (2) Frequently, it is one or more of the components in any mechanism responsible for interpreting and carrying out manually-initiated directions. Sometimes it is called manual control. (3) In some business applications, a mathematical check. (4) In programming, instructions which determine conditional jumps are often referred to as control instructions, and the time sequence of execution of instructions is called the flow of control.

CONTROL PANEL: (1) A part of a computer console that contains manual controls. (2) Same as *plugboard*.

CONTROL PUNCH: A specific code punched in a card to cause the machine to perform a specific operation.

CONTROL STATEMENT: Serves to interrupt sequential execution of instructions by transferring control to a statement elsewhere in the program.

COUNTER: A device such as a register or storage location used to represent the number of occurrences of an event.

CRAM: Card *Random-Access Memory*, a mass storage device that consists of a number of removable magnetic cards each of which is capable of storing magnetic bits of data.

CRYOGENICS: The study and use of devices utilizing properties of materials near absolute zero in temperature.

CYCLING TAPE: Creating a new tape file through an updating procedure.

DATA BASE: A single file containing information in a format applicable to any user's needs and available when needed.

DATA PROCESSING: Any operation or combination of operations on data.

DATA PROCESSING CYCLE: The sequence of steps involved in manipulating business information.

DATA WORD: A word which may be primarily regarded as part of the information manipulated by a given program. A data word may be used to modify a program instruction, or to be arithmetically combined with other data words.

DEBUG: To detect, locate, and remove mistakes from a routine or malfunctions from a computer. Synonymous with *troubleshoot*.

DECLARATIVE OPERATION: A coding sequence which involves writing symbolic labels and operation codes for data and constants. It is made up of a symbolic label, a declarative operation code, and an operand.

DETAIL PRINTING (LISTING): The printing of one line for each card read by the tabulator.

DIGIT-PUNCHING POSITION: The area on a punched card reserved to represent a decimal digit.

DIGITAL COMPUTER: A computer that operates on discrete data by performing arithmetic and logic processes on these data. Contrast with analog computer.

DIRECT-ACCESS STORAGE: (1) Pertaining to the process of obtaining information from or placing information into storage where the time required for such access is independent of the location of the information most recently obtained or placed in storage. (2) Pertaining to a device in which random access, is defined in (1), can be achieved without effective penalty in time.

DIRECT ADDRESS: An address that specifies the location of an operand. Synonymous with *one level address*.

DOCUMENT CARD: A special card form used in preparing a document such as a check, a purchase order, etc.

DOCUMENTATION: A means to communicate, it refers to a written record of a phase(s) of a specific project and establishes design and performance criteria for various phases of the project.

DRUM PRINTER: A printing device which uses a drum embossed with alphabetic and numeric characters. As the drum rotates, a hammer strikes the paper (from behind) at a time when the desired character(s) on the drum passes the line to be printed. To complete printing a given line, further rotation of the drum containing the remaining characters is necessary.

DUAL-GAP READ-WRITE HEAD: Used in magnetic tape data processing to insure the accuracy of recorded data on tape. A character written on tape is read immediately by a read head to verify its validity.

EDVAC: An electronic automatic computer which represents data in a binary form.

ELECTROSTATIC PRINTER: A device that prints an optical image on special paper. Spots of electricity are placed in matrix form on paper. When the paper is dusted with powdered ink material, the particles cling to the electrically charged characters. Later, they are moved to a high temperature zone where the ink is melted and is permanently fixed to the paper.

ENIAC: A high-speed electronic computer designed and built by Mauchly and Eckert at the University of Pennsylvania.

FEASIBILITY STUDY: A phase of project initiation, it is a proposal which describes the user's problem(s), the variables involved, and a tentative approach to its solution.

FEEDBACK: The part of a closed loop system which automatically brings back information about the condition under control.

FIELD: A specified area of a record used for a particular category of data, e.g., a group of card columns used to represent a wage rate or a set of bit locations in a computer word used to express the address of the operand.

FIXED WORD-LENGTH: Having the property that a machine word always contains the same number of characters or digits.

FLOATING-POINT: Usually a representation of numbers and a method of performing arithmetic. The point is at a location defined by the number itself.

FLOW CHART: A graphical representation for the definition, analysis, or solution of a problem in which symbols are used to represent operations, data, flow, and equipment.

FORMAT STATEMENT: A nonexecutable statement which serves input/output statements to specify the arrangement of data in an external medium such as a punched card, a magnetic tape, or on printed paper.

FORTRAN: *Formula translations;* any of several specific procedure-oriented programming languages.

FORTRAN IV: Initially designed for scientific application, it is a problem-oriented language which allows the programmer to think in terms of the problem rather than the computer used in solving it. The language is quite convenient for many business applications.

GANG PUNCH: To punch identical or constant information into all of a group of punch cards.

GENERAL PURPOSE COMPUTER: A computer that is designed to solve a wide class of problems.

GROSS PAY: An employee's total pay with no deductions.

GROUP PRINTING: A procedure whereby one line is printed for each group of cards having similar characteristics.

GROUPING: Arranging a mass of data into related groups, having common characteristics.

HARDWARE: Physical equipment, e.g., mechanical, magnetic, electrical, or electronic devices. Contrast with software.

HEXADECIMAL: A number representation system using base 16.

HOLLERITH: A widely used system of encoding alphanumeric information onto cards, hence Hollerith cards is synonymous with punch cards.

HOUSEKEEPING: For a computer program, housekeeping involves the setting up of constants and variables to be used in the program.

IMPERATIVE STATEMENT: Commands the computer's immediate execution of specific sequential statements following it. Imperative statements include the DO statement, CONTINUE statement, and the STOP and END statements.

INDIRECT ADDRESS: An address that specifies a storage location that contains either a direct address or another indirect address. Synonymous with *multilevel address.*

INFORMATION RETRIEVAL: A technique of classifying and indexing useful information in mass storage devices, in a format amenable to interaction with the user(s).

INPUT: (1) The data to be processed. (2) The state or sequence of states occurring on a specified input channel. (3) The device or collective set of devices used for bringing data into another device. (4) A channel for impressing a state on a device or logic element. (5) The processes of transferring data from an external storage to an internal storage. (6) See *Manual Input.*

INPUT DEVICE: The mechanical unit designed to bring data to be processed into a computer; e.g., a card reader, a tape reader, or a keyboard.

INSTRUCTION WORD: A computer word which contains an instruction.

INTEGER VARIABLE: A series of alphameric characters with the first letter being I, J, K, L, M, or N.

INTERPRETER: (1) A program that translates and executes each source language expression before translating and executing the next one. (2) A device that prints on a punched card the data already punched in the card.

INTERRECORD GAP: An interval of space or time deliberately left between recording portions of data or records. Such spacing is used to prevent errors through loss of data or overwriting and permits tape stop-start operations.

KEYBOARD: A group of marked levers operated manually for recording characters.

KEYPUNCH: A keyboard-operated device that punches holes in a card to represent data.

LABEL: One or more characters used to identify an item of data. Synonymous with *key*.

LIBRARY SUBROUTINE: A set of tested subroutines available on file for use when needed.

LINE-AT-A-TIME PRINTER: A device capable of printing one line of characters across a page; i.e., 100 or more characters simultaneously as continuous paper advances line-by-line in one direction past type bars or a type cylinder that contains all characters in all positions.

LOGIC: (1) The science dealing with the criteria or formal principles of reasoning and thought. (2) The systematic scheme which defines the interactions of signals in the design of an automatic data-processing system. (3) The basic principles and application of truth tables and interconnection between logical elements required for arithmetic computation in an automatic data-processing system.

LOOP: A sequence of instructions that is repeated until a terminal condition prevails.

MACRO INSTRUCTION: (1) An insruction consisting of a sequence of micro instructions which are inserted into the object routine for performing a specific operation. (2) The more powerful instructions which combine several operations in one instruction.

MAGNETIC CORE: A configuration of magnetic material that is, or is intended to be, placed in a spatial relationship to current-carrying conductors and whose magnetic properties are essential to its use. It may be used to concentrate an induced magnetic field as in a transformer, induction coil, or armature, to retain a magnetic polarization for the purpose of storing data, or for its nonlinear properties as in a logic element. It may be made of such material as iron, iron oxide, or ferrite, and in such shapes as wires and tapes.

MAGNETIC DRUM: A right circular cylinder with a magnetic surface on which data can be stored by selective magnetization of portions of the curved surface.

MANAGEMENT INFORMATION SYSTEM: An all-inclusive system designed to provide instant information to management for effective and efficient business operation.

MANIPULATION: The actual work performed on source data-processing.

MARK-SENSE CARD: A card designed to allow entering data on it with an electrographic pencil.

MASS-STORAGE FILE: A type of temporary secondary storage that supplies the computer with the necessary data for an immediate up-to-date report on a given account.

MATCHING: A data processing operation similar to a merge, except that instead of producing a sequence of items made up from the input, sequences are matched.

MATRIX PRINTER: Synonymous with *wire printer*. A high speed printer that prints character-like configurations of dots through the proper selection of wire-ends from a matrix of wire-ends, rather than conventional characters through the selection of type faces.

MEMORY: (1) Pertaining to a device into which data can be entered, in which it can be held, and from which it can be retrieved at a later time. (2) Loosely, any device that can store data.

MERGE: To combine two or more sets of data into one, usually in a specified sequence.

MICR: Magnetic-*I*nk Character Recognition, a technique involving the use of a device that senses and encodes into a machine language characters printed with an ink containing magnetized particles.

MICROSECOND: One millionth of a second.

MILLISECOND: One thousandth of a second.

NANOSECOND: One billionth of a second.

NAPIER'S BONES: A technique introduced by John Napier to aid multiplication through the use of data tables or rods.

9-EDGE: Denotes the bottom edge of a punched card.

NUMERALIZATION: Representation of alphabetic data through the use of digits; a desired step in automatic data processing.

OBJECT PROGRAM: The program which is the output of an automatic coding system. Often the object program is a machine language program ready for execution, but it may well be in an intermediate language.

OBJECT TIME: The time span during which a stored program is in active control of a specific application.

OCTAL: (1) Pertaining to a characteristic or property involving a selection, choice, or condition in which there are eight possibilities. (2) Pertaining to the number representation system with a radix of eight.

OFF-LINE: Pertaining to equipment or devices not under direct control of the central processing unit.

ON-LINE: Pertaining to peripheral equipment or devices in direct communication with the central processing unit.

ON-LINE INPUT: A system in which the input device transmits certain data directly to (and under control of) the control processing unit.

ON-LINE PROCESSING: Descriptive of a system and of the peripheral equipment or devices in a system in which the operation of such equipment is under control of the central processing unit, and in which information reflecting current activity is introduced into the data processing system as soon as it occurs. Thus, directly in-line with the main flow of transaction processing.

OPERAND: That which is operated upon. An operand is usually identified by an address part of an instruction.

OPERATION CODE: A code that represents specific operations. Synonymous with *instruction code*.

OPERATIONS DOCUMENTATONS: Related to project development, it emphasizes the need for developing instructions for program testing and a processing routine for operating the system.

OPTICAL SCANNING: Translation of printed or handwritten characters into machine language.

ORIGINATION: Determining the nature, type, and origin of some documents.

OUTPUT: (1) Data that has been processed. (2) The state or sequence of states occurring on a specified output channel. (3) The device or collective set of devices used for taking data out of a device. (4) A channel for expressing a state of a device or logic element. (5) The process of transferring data from an internal storage to an external storage.

OUTPUT DEVICE: That part of a machine which translates the electrical impulses representing data processed by the machine into permanent results such as printed forms, punched cards, and magnetic writing on tape.

PACKING DENSITY: The number of useful storage elements per unit of dimension, e.g., the number of bits per inch stored on a magnetic tape or drum track.

PARALLEL READING: Row-by-row reading of a data card.

PARAMETER: A variable that is given a constant value for a specific purpose or process.

PARITY CHECK: A check that tests whether the number of ones (or zeros) in an array of binary digits is odd or even. Synonymous with odd-even check.

PAYROLL REGISTER: A record of employees to be paid with the amount due to each.

PLOTTER: A visual display or board in which a dependent variable is graphed by an automatically controlled pen or pencil as a function of one or more variables.

PROCESS: A general term covering such terms as assemble, compile, generate, interpret, and compute.

PROCESSOR PROGRAM: A programming aid which prepares an object program first by reading symbolic instructions and then compares and converts them into a suitable computer language.

PROFIT AND LOSS STATEMENT: A financial statement showing the company's earning capability during a specific period of time.

PROGRAM: (1) A plan for solving a problem. (2) Loosely, a routine. (3) To devise a plan for solving a problem. (4) Loosely, to write a routine.

PROGRAM CARD: A coded card inserted in the program control unit of the keypunch to control operations such as skipping, duplicating, and shifting, automatically.

PROGRAM FLOW CHART: A graphic representation of a computer problem using symbols to represent machine instructions or groups of instructions.

PROGRAM SPECIFICATIONS: Related to systems specifications, it lists the information requirements of the system with emphasis upon the input and output specifications, existing files, and the processing details.

PL/1: Programming Language/1 is a new language with certain features similar to FORTRAN and some of the best features of other languages. It makes use of recent developments in computer technology and offers the programmer a relatively flexible problem-oriented language for programming problems which can best be worked out by using a combination of scientific and business compiling techniques.

PL/1 DECLARE STATEMENT: Is used in deciding on the form of treating numeric quantities.

PL/1 DELIMITER: Specifies an elementary action such as an arithmetic operation and/or provides punctuation.

PL/1 EXPRESSION: Is a sequence of constants and identifiers, separated by operators and parentheses, which describes a rule for calculating a value.

PL/1 GET LIST STATEMENT: Provides data values to the computer.

PL/1 GO TO STATEMENT: An unconditional branching statement which tells the computer to go directly to a statement with a specific label.

PL/1 IDENTIFIER: Is a string of alphanumeric and break characters. It begins with a letter, it cannot contain blanks, and must not exceed 31 characters.

PL/1 PROCEDURE BLOCK: Provides the link which allows the operating system to initiate execution of the object program. It begins with a PROCEDURE statement and terminates with an END statement.

PL/1 PUT SKIP LIST STATEMENT: Permits a printout of all the values of the identifiers it it.

PUNCHED CARD: (1) A card punched with a pattern of holes to represent data. (2) A card as in (1) before being punched.

PUNCHING STATION: The area on the keypunch where a card is aligned for the punching process.

PURCHASE ORDER: A requisition made by the purchasing department to a supplier for meeting the needs of a division or a department (for example, production department) of the firm.

RAMAC: *Random-Access Method of Accounting and Control,* a mass storage device that consists of a number of rotating disks stacked one on top of another to make up a data file.

READING STATION: The area on the keypunch where a data card is aligned for reading by a sensing mechanism to duplicate it automatically into another card located in the punching station.

REAL CONSTANT: A number written with a decimal point.

REAL VARIABLE: A series of alphameric characters with the first letter being any letter other than I, J, K, L, M, and N.

RECORD: A collection of related items of data, treated as a unit.

RECORDING: The process by which an input device facilitates the presentation of source data for processing.

REGISTER: A device capable of storing a specified amount of data, such as one word.

REPRODUCER: A machine that reproduces a punched card by duplicating another similar card.

SELECTING: Extracting certain cards from a deck for a specific purpose without disturbing the sequence in which they were originally filed.

SEQUENCE CHECK: A data processing operation designed to check the sequence of the items in a file assumed to be already in sequence.

SEQUENTIAL DATA PROCESSING: A technique by which items to be processed must be coded and collected into groups prior to processing.

SERIAL READING: Column-by-column reading of a data card.

SIMULATION: Symbolic representation (in terms of a model) of the essence of a system for testing an idea or a product before operationalizing its full-scale production.

SIMULTANEOUS-PUNCHING PRINCIPLE: Introduced by James Powers, whereby information to be punched is initially accumulated and then punched simultaneously in a card.

SOFTWARE: (1) The collection of programs and routines associated with a computer, e.g., compilers, library routines. (2) All the documents associated with a computer, e.g., manuals, circuit diagrams. (3) Contrasts with *hardware*.

SORTER: A machine capable of sorting punched cards either alphabetically or numerically.

SORTING: Arranging numeric or alphabetic data in a given sequence.

SOURCE DOCUMENT: A document from which basic data is extracted.

SOURCE PROGRAM: A program written in a source language. A language that is an input to a given translation process.

SPECIAL PURPOSE COMPUTER: A computer that is designed to solve a restricted class of problems.

STANDARDIZATION: Establishment of specific procedural requirements for the efficient production of a large volume of goods or for automatic processing of data.

STORAGE: The retention of data (source or finished) in memory until needed.

STORAGE MAP: A pictorial aid used by the programmer for estimating the proportion of storage capacity to be allocated to data.

STORED PROGRAM: A series of instructions in storage to direct the step-by-step operation of the machine.

STRINGING: The stage in which an input file is read completely.

STUB CARD: A card containing a detachable stub to serve as a receipt for future reference.

SUBROUTINE: A routine that can be part of another routine.

SUMMARIZING: Condensing a mass of data into a concise and meaningful form.

SUMMARY PUNCH: A card punch operating in conjunction with another machine, commonly a tabulator, to punch into cards data which have been summarized or calculated by the other machine.

SYSTEM: (1) An organized collection of parts united by regulated interaction. (2) An organized collection of men, machines, and methods required to accomplish a specific objective.

SYSTEMS ANALYSIS: The examination of an activity, procedure, method, technique, or a business to determine what must be accomplished, and how the necessary operations may best be accomplished.

SYSTEMS ANALYST: A person skilled in the definition and development of techniques for the solving of a problem; especially those techniques for solutions on a computer.

SYSTEMS FLOW CHART: A graphic representation of the system in which data provided by a source document are converted into final documents.

SYSTEMS STUDY: The detailed process of determining a system or set of procedures for using a computer for definite functions or operations, and establishing specifications to be used as a basis for the selection of equipment suitable to the specific needs.

SYSTEMS SYNTHESIS: The planning of the procedures for solving a problem. This may involve among other things the analysis of the problem, preparation of a flow diagram, preparing details, testing, and developing subroutines, allocation of storage locations, specification of input and output formats, and the incorporation of a computer run into a complete data processing system.

TABLE LOOK-UP: A procedure for obtaining the function value corresponding to an argument from a table of function values.

TELETYPE PRINTER: A device that presents type in a square block. The type square moves from left to right and positions one character at a time. When this happens, a hammer strikes the character from behind, depressing it against the inked ribbon that faces the paper form.

TIME CARD: A card used for showing the number of hours an employee has worked.

TOGGLE: (1) Same as flip-flop. (2) Pertaining to any device having two stable states.

TRAILER RECORD: A record which follows a group of records and contains pertinent data related to the group of records.

12-EDGE: A term used to designate the top edge of a punched card.

UNIT RECORD: (1) A separate record that is similar in form and content to other records; e.g., a summary of a particular employee's earnings to date. (2) Sometimes refers to a piece of nontape auxiliary equipment; e.g., card reader, printer, or console typewriter.

UNIVAC: An early automatic computer designed and manufactured by the Sperry Rand Corporation.

USER'S REQUEST: A phase of project initiation, it is a statement of what a proposed system is expected to produce and whom it will accommodate, source of data input, desired output information, and anticipated deadline.

VARIABLE WORD-LENGTH: Having the property that a machine word may have a variable number of characters. It may be applied either to a single entry whose information content may be changed from time to time, or to a group of functionally similar entries whose corresponding components are of different length.

VERIFIER: A device on which a record can be compared or tested for identity character-by-character with a retranscription or copy as it is being prepared.

WHEEL PRINTER: Similar in method of operation to the bar printer except that the type bars are replaced by wheels around which all the necessary characters are embossed.

WORD: An ordered set of characters which occupies one storage location and is treated by the computer circuits as a unit and transferred as such. Ordinarily a word is treated by the control unit as an instruction, and by the arithmetic unit as a quantity. Word lengths may be fixed or variable depending on the particular computer.

WORD LENGTH: The number of bits or other characters in a word.

X-PUNCH: A punch in the second row, one row above the zero row, on a Hollerith punched card.

ZONE PUNCH: A punch in the O, X, or Y row on a Hollerith punched card.

APPENDIX D—SELECTED BIBLIOGRAPHY

American Management Association, *Making the Computer Work for Management.* New York: American Management Association, 1967.

American Society for Information Science, *Annual Review of Information Science and Technology.* Washington, D.C.: American Society for Information Science, Vol. I, 1966; Vol. II, 1967.

Anderson, Decima M., *Computer Programming Fortran IV.* New York: Appleton, Century and Crofts, 1964.

Anton, Hector R., and Wayne S. Boutell, *Fortran and Business Data Processing.* New York: McGraw-Hill Book Co., 1968.

Arkadev, A. G., and E. M. Braverman (Translated from the Russian by J. D. Cowan and W. Turski), *Computers and Pattern Recognition.* Washington, D.C.: Thompson Book Company, 1967.

Arnold, Robert R., *Introduction to Data Processing.* New York: John Wiley and Sons, Inc., 1966.

Awad, Elias M., *Business Data Processing.* Englewood Cliffs, N.J.: Prentice-Hall, Inc., 1968.

————, *Problems and Exercises in Data Processing.* Englewood Cliffs, N.J.: Prentice-Hall, Inc., 1968.

Bank Administration Institute, *Data Transmission in Banking.* Park Ridge, Ill.: Bank Administration Institute, 1965.

Barnett, C. C., Jr., *The Future of the Computer Utility.* New York: The Macmillan Company, 1967.

Bartee, Thomas C., *Digital Computer Fundamentals,* 2nd ed. New York: McGraw-Hill Book Co., 1966.

Bates, Frank, *Programming Language/One.* Englewood Cliffs, N.J.: Prentice-Hall, Inc., 1967.

Bernard, S. M., *System/360 COBOL.* Englewood Cliffs, N.J.: Prentice-Hall, Inc., 1968.

Boore, William F., and Jerry R. Murphy, *The Computer Sampler: Management Perspectives on the Computer.* New York: McGraw-Hill Book Co., 1968.

Brightman, Richard W., Bernard J. Lusking, and Theodore Tilton, *Data Processing for Decision-Making.* New York: The Macmillan Company, 1968.

Brown, Harry L., *EDP for Auditors.* New York: John Wiley and Sons, Inc., 1968.

Burck, Gilbert, and the editors of *Fortune, The Computer Age.* Scranton, Pa.: Harper and Row Publishers, Inc., 1965.

Canning, Richard G., *The Management of Data Processing.* North Hollywood, Calif.: Western Periodicals, 1967.

Carter, Byron L., *Data Processing for the Small Business.* New York: Macfadden-Bartell Corp., 1966.

Carter, Norman H., *Introduction to Business Data Processing.* Belmont, Calif.: Wadsworth Publishing Co., 1968.

Cashman and Keys, *Basic Projects in Data Processing.* Anaheim, Calif.: Anaheim Publishing Co., 1967.

Chapin, Ned, *360 Programming in Assembly Language.* New York: McGraw-Hill Book Co., 1968.

Chorafas, Dimitris N., *Selecting the Computer System.* London: Gee and Co., Ltd., 1967.

Claffey, William J., *Principles of Data Processing.* Belmont, Calif.: Wadsworth Publishing Co., 1967.

Cole, Ralph I., *Data/Information Availability.* Washington, D.C.: Thompson Book Company (n. d.).

Computer Usage Company, *Programming the IBM System/360.* New York: John Wiley and Sons, Inc., 1966.

Crawford, F. R., *Introduction to Data Processing.* Englewood Cliffs, N.J.: Prentice-Hall, Inc., 1968.

Data Processing Horizons, Inc., *Computer Education Directory.* South Pasadena, Calif.: Data Processing Horizons, Inc., 1968.

Davis, Gordon B., *Computer Data Processing.* New York: McGraw-Hill Book Co., 1969.
————, *An Introduction to Electronic Computers.* New York: The Macmillan Company, 1966.

Dimitry, Donald L., *Introduction to FORTRAN IV Programming.* New York: Holt, Rinehart and Winston, Inc., 1966.

Elliott, C. Orville, and Robert S. Wasley, *Business Information Processing Systems.* Homewood, Ill.: Richard D. Irwin, Inc., 1965.

Farina, Mario V., *COBOL Simplified.* Englewood Cliffs, N.J.: Prentice-Hall, Inc., 1968.
————, *FORTRAN IV Self-Taught.* Englewood Cliffs, N.J.: Prentice-Hall, Inc., 1968.

Financial Executives, *Effect of Computers on Management Technology.* New York: Financial Executives, 1968.

Flores, Ivan, *Computer Design.* Englewood Cliffs, N.J.: Prentice-Hall, Inc. 1967.
————, *The Logic of Computer Arithmetic.* Englewood Cliffs, N.J.: Prentice-Hall, Inc., 1963.

Freeman, W. H., and Co., *Information.* San Francisco, Calif.: W. H. Freeman and Co., 1966.

Gentle, Edgar C., Jr. (ed.), *Data Communications in Business.* New York: American Telephone and Telegraph Co., 1966.

Germain, Clarence B., *Programming the IBM 360.* Englewood Cliffs, N.J.: Prentice-Hall, Inc., 1967.

Gibson, E. Dana, *An Introduction to Automated Data Processing*. Elmhurst, Ill.: Business Press.

Golden, James T., *FORTRAN IV: Programming and Computing*. Englewood Cliffs, N.J.: Prentice-Hall, Inc., 1965.

————, and R. Leichus, *IBM 360 Programming and Computing*. Englewood Cliffs, N.J.: Prentice-Hall, Inc., 1967.

Gruenberger, Fred, *Computers and Communication*. Englewood Cliffs, N.J.: Prentice-Hall, Inc. 1968.

Head, Robert V., *Real-Time Business Systems*. New York: Holt, Rinehart and Winston, Inc., 1964.

Healy, Jeremiah J., and Dalward J. DeBruzzi, *Basic FORTRAN IV Programming*. Reading, Mass.: Addison-Wesley Publishing Co., 1968.

Hellerman, Herbert, *Digital Computer System Principles*. New York: McGraw-Hill Book Co., 1967.

Hersee, E. H. W., *A Simple Approach to Electronic Computers*, 2nd ed. New York: Gordon and Breach, 1966.

Higman, Bryan, *A Comparative Study of Programming Languages*. New York: American Elsevier Publishing Co., 1967.

Jacobowitz, Henry, *Computer Arithmetic*. New York: Hayden Book Co. (n. d.).

Joslin, Edward O., *Computer Selection*. Reading, Mass.: Addison-Wesley Publishing Co., 1968.

Kanter, Jerome, *The Computer and the Executive*. Englewood Cliffs, N.J.: Prentice-Hall, Inc., 1967.

Karplus, Walter J., *On-Line Computing*. New York: McGraw-Hill Book Co., 1966.

Kintner, Paul M., *Electronic Digital Techniques*. New York: McGraw-Hill Book Co., 1967.

Kovalevsky, V. A., *Character Readers and Pattern Recognition*. New York: Spartan Books, 1968.

Langenbach, Robert G., *Introduction to Automated Data Processing*. Englewood Cliffs, N.J.: Prentice-Hall, Inc., 1968.

Lecht, Charles P., *The Programmer's PL/1: A Complete Reference*. New York: McGraw-Hill Book Co., 1968.

Ledley, Robert S., *FORTRAN IV Programming*. New York: McGraw-Hill Book Co., 1966.

Leeds, Herbert D., *Computer Programming, Fundamentals*, 2nd ed. New York: McGraw-Hill Book Co., 1966.

Levy, Joseph, *Punched Card Data Processing*. New York: McGraw-Hill Book Co., 1967.

Li, David H., *Accounting/Computers/Management Information Systems*. New York: McGraw-Hill Book Co., 1968.

Lott, Richard W., *Basic Data Processing*. Englewood Cliffs, N.J.: Prentice-Hall, Inc., 1967.

Malcolm, Robert E., and Malcolm H. Gotterer, *Computers in Business: A FORTRAN Introduction*. Scranton, Pa.: International Textbook Co., 1967.

Martin, E. W., J., *Electronic Data Processing, An Introduction*. Homewood, Ill.: Dow Jones-Irwin, Inc., 1965.

Martin, James, *Design of Real-Time Computer Systems*. Englewood Cliffs, N.J.: Prentice-Hall, Inc., 1967.

Martin, James T., *Programming Real-Time Computer Systems*. Englewood Cliffs, N.J.: Prentice-Hall, Inc., 1965.

McCameron, Fritz A., *COBOL Logic and Programming*. Homewood, Ill.: Dow Jones-Irwin, Inc., 1966.

McMillan, Claude, and Richard F. Gonzalez, *Systems Analysis: A Computer Approach to Decision Models.* Homewood, Ill.: Richard D. Irwin, Inc., 1965.

Meadow, Charles T., *The Analysis of Information Systems.* New York: John Wiley and Sons, Inc. 1967.

Mize, Joe H., and J. Grady Cox, *Essentials of Simulation.* Englewood Cliffs, N.J.: Prentice-Hall, Inc., 1967.

Mullish, Henry, *An Introduction to Computer Programming.* New York: Gordon and Breach, 1966.

Optner, Stanford L., *Systems Analysis for Business Management,* 2nd ed. Englewood Cliffs, N.J.: Prentice-Hall, Inc., 1968.

Organick, Elliot I., *A FORTRAN IV Primer.* Reading, Mass.: Addison-Wesley Publishing Co., 1966.

Parkhill, Douglas F., *The Challenge of the Computer Utility.* Reading, Mass.: Addison-Wesley Publishing Co., 1966.

Pollack, Seymour V., *A Guide to FORTRAN IV.* New York: Columbia, University Press, 1965

Popell, Steven D., et al., *Computer Time-Sharing: Dynamic Information Handling for Business.* Englewood Cliffs, N.J.: Prentice-Hall, Inc., 1966.

Porter, W. Thomas, *Auditing Electronic Systems.* Belmont, Calif.: Wadsworth Publishing Co., Inc., 1966.

Price, Wilson T., and Merlin Miller, *Elements of Data Processing Mathematics.* New York: Holt, Rinehart and Winston, Inc., 1967.

Richards, R. K., *Electronic Digital Systems.* North Hollywood, Calif.: Western Periodicals, 1966.

Rosen, Saul, *Programming Systems and Languages.* New York: McGraw-Hill Book Co., 1967.

Rosove, Perry E., *Developing a Computer-Based Information System.* North Hollywood, Calif.: Western Periodicals, 1967.

Sackham, H., *Computers, System Science and Evolving Society: The Challenge of Man-Machine Digital Systems.* North Hollywood, Calif.: Western Periodicals, 1967.

Salton, Gerald, *Automatic Information Organization and Retrieval.* New York: McGraw-Hill Book Co., 1968.

Sanders, Donald H., *Computers in Business: An Introduction.* New York: McGraw-Hill Co., 1968.

Saxon, James A., *Basic Principles of Data Processing.* Englewood Cliffs, N.J.: Prentice-Hall, Inc., 1967.

————, *COBOL: A Self-Instructional Programmed Manual.* Englewood Cliffs, N.J.: Prentice-Hall, Inc., 1963.

————, *System 360 Programming: A Self-Instructional Manual.* Englewood Cliffs, N.J.: Prentice-Hall, Inc., 1968.

Science Research Associates, Inc., *FORTRAN for IBM 360.* Chicago, Ill.: Science Research Associates, Inc., 1968.

Seligsohn, I. J., *Your Career in Computer Programming.* New York: Julian Messner, 1967.

Sippl, Charles J., *Computer Dictionary.* Indianapolis, Ind.: Howard W. Sams and Co., 1966.

Sisson, Roger L., *A Manager's Guide to Computer Processing.* New York: John Wiley and Sons, Inc., 1967.

Smith, Paul T., *How to Live with Your Computer*. New York: The Macmillan Company, 1965.

Solomon, Irving I., *Management Uses of the Computer*. New York: New American Library, Inc., 1968.

Spencer, D. D., *Game Playing with Computers*. New York: Spartan Books, 1968.

Stark, Peter A., *Digital Computer Programming*. New York: The Macmillan Company, 1967.

Stein, Marvin L., and William D. Munro, *A FORTRAN Introduction to Programming and Computers*. New York: Academic Press, Inc., 1966.

Swallow, Kenneth P., and Wilson T. Price, *Elements of Computer Programming*. New York: Holt, Rinehart and Winston, Inc., 1965.

Swanson, Robert W., *An Introduction to Business Data Processing and Computer Programming*. Belmont, Calif.: Wadsworth Publishing Co., 1967.

Thatcher, Charles M., and Anthony J. Capato, *Computer Programming: Logic and Language*. Reading, Mass.: Addison-Wesley Publishing Co., 1967.

The Third Generation Computer. New York: The Macmillan Company, 1966.

Training Systems, Inc., and Stanley L. Levine, *Computer Numbering Systems and Binary Arithmetic*. New York: Hayden Book Co. (n. d.).

USA Standard Flowchart Symbols and Their Usage in Information Processing (X 3. 5-1968). New York: United States of American Standards Institute, 1968.

Van Ness, Robert G., *Principles of Data Processing with Computers*. Elmhurst, Ill.: Business Press, 1967.

————, *Principles of Punched Card Data Processing*. Elmhurst, Ill.: Business Press, 1967.

Veldman, Donald J., *FORTRAN Programming for the Behavioral Sciences*. New York: Holt, Rinehart and Winston, 1967.

Walnut, Francis K., *Introduction to Computer Programming and Coding*. Englewood Cliffs, N.J.: Prentice-Hall, Inc., 1968.

Wegner, Peter, *Programming Languages Information Structures and Machine Organization*. New York: McGraw-Hill Book Co., 1968.

Weinberg, Gerald M., *PL/1 Programming Primer*. New York: McGraw-Hill Book Co., 1966.

Weinstein, Seymour M., *Fundamentals of Digital Computers*. New York: Holt, Rinehart and Winston, Inc., 1965.

Williams, William F., *Principles of Automated Information Retrieval*. Elmhurst, Ill.: Business Press, 1967.

Wilson, Ira G., and Marthann E. Wilson, *Information, Computers, and System Design*. New York: John Wiley and Sons, Inc., 1965.

Withington, Frederic G., *The Use of Computers in Business Organizations*. Reading, Mass.: Addison-Wesley Publishing Co., 1966.

Wofsey, Marvin M., *Management of Automatic Data Processing Systems*. Washington, D.C.: Thompson Book Co., 1968.

Ziegler, James R., *Time-Sharing Data Processing Systems*. Englewood Cliffs, N.J.: Prentice-Hall, Inc., 1967.

INDEX

M

Machine language coding, *see* Computer Language
Macro language, 296-98
Main line, 277
Magnetic character reader, 232
Magnetic cores as storage devices, 138-40
Magnetic disk devices, 200-202
  pack of, 200
  speed in use of, 202
  tracks on, 200
Magnetic drum storage, 202-203
Magnetic ink, 126
Magnetic-ink character recognition (MICR), 135, 210-13, 214
  advantages of, 211
  international use of, 211-12
Magnetic spots, 191-92
Magnetic tape, 191-98
  accuracy control of, 195-97
  description of, 191-98
  devices for
    terminal, 221
    UNIVAC 9200, 230
    UNIVAC 9400, 234-35
  errors on, 197
  MICR and, 212
  packing density of, 193
  programming symbol for, 275
  punched cards vs., 403
  storage on, 230
Magnetic tape processing, 394-401
  cycling in, 396
  files in, 394-401
    handling of, 395-98
    labels, 395
  files in:
    merging of, 399-400
    sorting of, 398-401
  punched card processing and, 401
Management Information System (MIS), 8
Manipulation, 59-62
Manual input, programming symbol for, 275
Manual operation, programming symbol for, 275
Manual systems, systems analysis of, 372-73
Mark sense reader, 214-15
Mark sensing, 97-98
Mass storage files, 203-204, 426-27
Master payroll card, 430, 434-35, 436
Master Unit Record card, 79-80
Matching, 113
Mathematical Modeling and Simulation, 378
Mathematical programming, 378
Matrix printer, 188
Medicine and computers, 10-11, 459
Memory in computers, 137-41
  character oriented, 138
  cryogenic, 141
  magnetic core, 138-40

Memory in computers (*Cont.*)
  photo-digital, 141
  thin film, 140-41
  word-oriented, 138
Memory map, 286
Merging, 111-13
MFCU, 232
MICR, 135, 210-13, 214
Microfilm (COM) system, 220
MIS, 8
Mixed-entry decision table, 284
Modulation, 216
Monolithic Systems Technology, 231
Multifunction card units (MFCU), 232
Multiple-use card, 80
Multiplication:
  binary, 170
  decimal, 170
  hexadecimal, 173-74
Multiprogramming, 303

N

Numeralization, 5
Numerical data representation, 145-58
  alphanumeric and, 154-58
American Standard Code for Information Interchange (ASCII), 157
  binary, 145-49
  Binary Coded Decimal (BCD), 154
  Extended Binary Coded Decimal Interchange Code (EBCDIC), 156-57
  hexadecimal, 151-53
  octal, 150-51
Numeric data recording, 73

O

Object program, 252, 254
OCR reader, 213-15
  handwriting and, 215
  problems of, 213
  types of, 214-15
Octal notation, 150-51
Odd parity, 196
Offline equipment, 136n, 212, 232
Offline storage, programming symbol for, 275
Online equipment, 136n, 212
Online storage, programming symbol for, 275
Online system, 426
Op-code, 175, 260, 292, 293
Open decision tables, 284-85
Operand, 175, 260, 292
Operation codes, 175, 260, 292, 293
Operations research, 370-72, 377-78
Operating systems, 303
Optical character recognition reader, 213-15
  handwriting and, 215